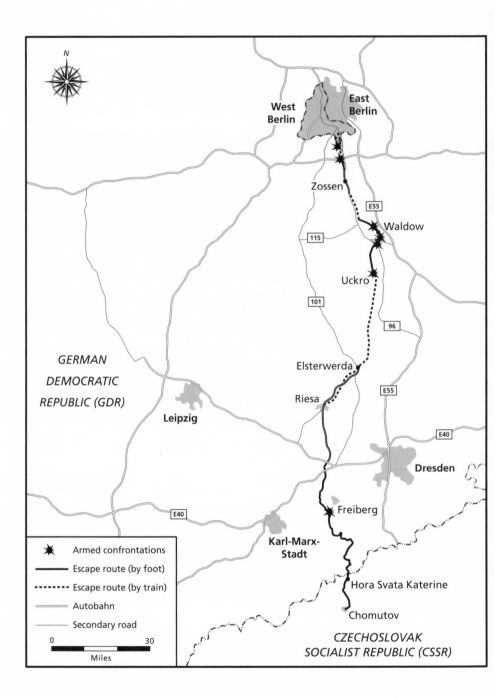

N

West Berlin

East Berlin

Zossen

E55

Waldow

115

Uckro

101

96

GERMAN
DEMOCRATIC
REPUBLIC (GDR)

Elsterwerda

Riesa

E55

Leipzig

E40

Dresden

E40

Freiberg

Karl-Marx-
Stadt

Hora Svata Katerine

Chomutov

CZECHOSLOVAK
SOCIALIST REPUBLIC (CSSR)

✳ Armed confrontations
—— Escape route (by foot)
------ Escape route (by train)
Autobahn
Secondary road

0   30
Miles

GA☭NTLET

Five Friends, 20,000 Enemy Troops, and the Secret
That Could Have Changed the Course of the Cold War

BARBARA MASIN

Naval Institute Press
Annapolis, Maryland

Naval Institute Press
291 Wood Road
Annapolis, MD 21402

Library of Congress Cataloging-in-Publication Data

Masin, Barbara, 1967–
  Gauntlet : five friends, twenty thousand enemy troops, and the secret that
could have changed the course of the Cold War / Barbara Masin.
    p. cm.
  Includes bibliographical references and index.
  ISBN 1-59114-515-5 (alk. paper)
  1. Anti-communist movements—Czechoslovakia. 2.
Czechoslovakia—History—1945–1992. I. Title.
  DB2217.M37 2006
  943.704'2—dc22

2006016647

Printed in the United States of America on acid-free paper ∞

13 12 11 10 09 08 07 06   9 8 7 6 5 4 3 2
First printing

All that is necessary for evil to succeed is for good men to do nothing.

—DAVID HUME

CONTENTS

Acknowledgments   ix

Prologue   1

Chapter 1   Birth of the Nation   8

Chapter 2   An Ally Betrayed   20

Chapter 3   Resistance   29

Chapter 4   The Home Front   41

Chapter 5   The Communists Seize Power   54

Chapter 6   Prophet of Liberation   63

Chapter 7   Joining the Battle   67

Chapter 8   In the Hands of the StB   84

Chapter 9   The Battle Continued   93

Chapter 10   The Class War Escalates   97

Chapter 11   Terra Incognita   115

Chapter 12   "Have the Wedding without Me"   118

Chapter 13   Across the Border and into the Unknown   126

Chapter 14   First Contact   138

Chapter 15   Trouble with Trains   158

Chapter 16   Gun Battle at Uckro   168

Chapter 17   Going to Ground   188

Chapter 18   The Hunt   196

Chapter 19   Which Way to Berlin?   200

Chapter 20   The Dragnet Snaps Shut   207

Chapter 21   Hot Pursuit   222

Chapter 22   Vasek's Road   231

Chapter 23   The Wait   235

Chapter 24   The Luckau War   237

Chapter 25   Lying Low   240

Chapter 26   Eternal Honor and Glory to Our Heroes!   247

Chapter 27   First-Class Accommodations   251

Chapter 28   East German Revolts   257

Chapter 29   Silent Heroes   262

Chapter 30   Potato Transport   271

Chapter 31   The Ring around Berlin   282

Chapter 32   Home Stretch Fiasco   289

Chapter 33   Berlin Safe House   302

Chapter 34   Red Revenge   306

Chapter 35   To Liberate Czechoslovakia   316

Epilogue   324

Appendix 1   343

Appendix 2   345

Abbreviations   349

Notes   351

Bibliography   361

Index   367

ACKNOWLEDGMENTS

One of my main goals in writing this book was to explore a gripping Cold War episode from the points of view of all the participants—the Czech resistance group members, the East German civilians, East German Vopos, Soviet authorities, and U.S. and British authorities. Many people generously contributed their time, their insights, and their recollections.

A number of area residents in the Uckro-Waldow areas were willing to tell about their personal impressions and experiences of those days in October 1953. Thank you to all of them. In particular my deepest thanks go to the Lühmann and Grunert families, who received us with unstinting hospitality and generously shared their memories. Without them, this story could never have been told, not least of all because I would not have been here to tell it.

Gerald Endres and Ute Bönnen were able to ferret out records on the interrogation of Zbyněk Janata and Václav Švéda and their extradition to Czechoslovakia through persistence and journalistic dedication; they obtained records that are ordinarily inaccessible, and they generously shared these with my family. I also made use of their interviews with Volkspolizei members who, understandably, would not have spoken as openly with the daughter of one of their antagonists.

Dr. Kurt Arlt of the Militärgeschichtliches Institut Potsdam explained to me the organization of the East German armed forces in the early 1950s and their relationship with the Soviet occupying forces. He also gave helpful tips regarding available archival resources. Dr. Christian Sachse spent an interesting and educational afternoon with me discussing the organization of the ZK, Politbüro, and party organs.

Numerous people helped me in my attempt to breach the wall of silence around the Soviet archives. Thank you to Dr. Vojtěch Mastný and to Hermine

Prügger in particular. Unfortunately, as I was to learn from personal experience, the brief window of relative openness that existed in the early 1990s has slammed shut under the present Russian administration, and so the one major gap in this narrative is the absence of the Soviet perspective.

My understanding of the current conflicted situation in the Czech Republic with respect to the process of Vergangenheitsbewältigung was deepened by conversations and correspondence with a number of individuals about their personal experiences and insights, most particularly Dr. Jiří Málek, formerly of the Ústav pro Dokumentování a Vyšetřování Zločinů Komunismu Ministerstva Vnitra (UDV), the late Mrs. Svatava Reichertova, Dr. Milan Hulík, and Dr. Lubomír Blažek. Mr. Zahrádek, docent at the Museum of the Third Resistance in Příbram, gave me an extremely informative guided tour of the museum, which documents the shocking human rights abuses that occurred under the Communist regime, and also pointed out a number of helpful archival resources.

Milan Paumer and Vladimir Hradec were wonderful travel companions on one of my most memorable road trips ever. Both of them generously shared their recollections and insights, and recalled for me a couple of key incidents that others had forgotten. Milan Paumer also generously shared many photographs showing himself, my father, my uncle, and their friends during their Podebrady years.

In the Czech Republic, Martin Vadas was a tireless guide through the city of Prague during a period when the city was undergoing an unprecedented natural disaster, helping me navigate a byzantine bureaucracy with an unfailing sixth sense for where to find allegedly missing documentation. Monika Elšiková and Vlasta Vadasová unstintingly extended their friendship and hospitality, graciously providing me with room and board during my stay in the city. Petr Majšajdr and Radek Schovánek of the UDV gave many helpful suggestions with respect to locating archival materials. I'd also like to thank Dr. Pavlík, Dr. Formánek, Jan Beneš, Pavel Pobříslo and Jiří Jožák for their suggestions and the documentation they provided from their personal files. Jaroslav Čvančara generously shared with me rare pictures of the three Kings, their collaborators, and their Gestapo opponents, which he has published, along with others, in his superb two-volume pictorial history *Někomu Život, Někomu Smrt*. Alena Šimánkova, PhD, and Alena Noková, PhD, of the Státního ústředuího archiv (SUA) generously assisted me in locating and accessing archival records essential to my project. During my visit to Prague Jarmila Bartůnková provided hospitality and put me in touch with a number of helpful contacts.

In the U.S. National Archives, John Taylor gave generously of his time and his encyclopedic knowledge of the archives and also provided valuable contacts. Thank you also to Rich Boylan, as well as John Clagett and Herb Rawlings-Milton for their assistance with FOIA queries.

Christian Ostermann, Director of the Cold War International History Project, shared his very extensive knowledge about sources and provided me with numerous contacts.

Lipiin Sung and Dan Mearns unstintingly extended their hospitality and helped to make my research trips to the Washington, D.C., area a pleasure; Gabi Becker and her enchanting daughter Lili shared the carnival spirit and graciously put me up during my stay in Berlin, even as they were in the middle of moving preparations.

Frau Risse, Frau Grüner, Frau Gräfe, and Frau Nestler of the Bundesarchiv Lichterfelde helped me locate invaluable resources and archival materials relating to the manhunt. Dieter Salomon managed to obtain an appointment for me at the Berlin archives at very short notice and miraculously succeeded in extracting my photocopied materials when it appeared they were gone, never to be seen again.

Leonard B. Jankowski shared with me his recollections about the Masin brothers' arrival in West Berlin. Duval Edwards, Conrad "Mac" McCormick, and Jerry Malme of the National Counter Intelligence Corps Association helped me in my search for CIC members with memories of those October days. Ozzie Kinat kindly put out the word about my search to fellow CIC alumni.

Bob Obdržálek obtained a copy of the SNB oath and Jan Beneš sent me a copy of the Communist Militiamen's oath. Skrivanek prekladatelske sluzby, s.r.o., provided translation services for this project.

Clare Macdonald, Zdeněk Procházka, Laddie Mencl, Bryan Davis, Bob Obdržálek, Jan Beneš, and Petr Koura read drafts of the manuscript and provided feedback that helped to make this a better book; Dean Garner patiently answered numerous questions on all things military.

Sandy Masin, my sister, stayed up for many hours late at night reading and rereading various drafts of this book and providing invaluable suggestions in her notes and our telephone conversations.

My friend Iris Chang first heard me tell this story over the kitchen table and told me there was a book in it. She inspired me to begin the daunting task of committing this story to paper and to do the archival research necessary for telling the whole story.

My aunt Zdena Mašínová shared valuable insights into the life of the family, the personalities of various actors in this story, and the way things were in times past. She also made available many of the family photographs in this book. My uncle Ray Masin had the foresight to write down the chronology of the escape in 1957, only four short years after it happened. This extensive monograph was invaluable in reconstructing the events of October 1953, as was his monograph on his experiences in Bartholomějská. In addition to preserving a level of authentic detail and intimate thought processes that are often lost to memory as time passes, his notes helped jolt memories and elicit valuable recollections in others.

Special thanks go especially to my parents, who provided moral support and encouragement during this three-year process and read numerous versions of this manuscript. My dad, Joseph Masin, patiently helped me translate particularly vexing sections of numerous Czech documents, newspaper articles, as well as sections of several monographs, and helped me penetrate the bureaucratically convoluted language of the official records. He and my uncle, Ray Masin, dug deeply to share their sometimes-painful personal memories, ransacking their minds for details and patiently answering my interminable questions.

A note on the dialogue: After fifty-odd years, my father's and uncle's memories of the Chlumec, Čelákovice, Hedvikov, and Uckro incidents were still completely fresh, up to and including verbatim dialogue, hand gestures, and facial expressions. Other dialogue was recreated with the help of my uncle's 1957 monograph, which outlined much dialogue and gave some verbatim excerpts, and the personal recollections of eyewitnesses and participants.

I am deeply grateful to Connie Buchanan, an extraordinarily talented editor who provided line-by-line scrutiny of my manuscript and whose insightful analysis helped me pull this book together, and to Mark Gatlin at the Naval Institute Press, who was instrumental in making this project a reality: I couldn't have been in better hands.

Some of the individuals who helped me have chosen to remain anonymous due to the current political situation in their countries, which leads them to fear reprisals. I am deeply grateful to all who helped me in my quest to tell this story. Of course, any errors or omissions in my narration of the events described in this book are my sole responsibility.

Note: The Czech words in the main text of this book have been rendered without diacritics. Appendix 2 shows each word with its correct Czech diacritical marks and a pronunciation guide.

PROLOGUE

The first snow of the season fell on 6 October 1953, and thereafter every night brought subzero temperatures. Now, two weeks later, another gray dawn pushed its chilly fingers over the horizon, touching fir trees and haystacks that glittered white with hoar frost. In the cold morning air sound carried far, and from their cramped hideout under a pile of dead branches they could hear the woods ringing with sharp bursts of automatic weapons fire.

The piled branches sat in a clearing beyond the trees, hulking like a large carbuncle in the brown, frost-burned grass. Three pairs of eyes stared out, apprehensively scanning the forest perimeter. They belonged to three young men—not much more than boys, really—gaunt, mud-caked, and unshaven, their thinly clad bodies numb from the frozen ground and the chill air flowing through the gaps in the branches that were the only thing that stood between them and death.

The gunfire ceased. At once the sound of hundreds of tromping feet filled the air.

Under the pile, the tension was palpable.

"I can't move my fingers!" one of the ragged figures croaked. "Flex your fingers or you won't be able to pull the trigger!"

And then a line of troops in black jackboots and uniforms burst into view, resuming their fire, spraying the bushes and stands of tall grass at the edge of the clearing with bullets.

A sharp command from one of the officers brought the line to a halt. "Check the treetops, comrades!" he shouted.

Another crisp command set the line in motion again and it rolled inexorably forward, toward the woodpile. There had to be at least a hundred men—and those were only the ones they could see! Again the shooting stopped as the pounding feet and clanking weapons drew steadily nearer.

It was a struggle to move in the cramped hideaway—the three fugitives were jammed together under the branches—but one of them fought to raise his pistol and take aim.

"Hold your fire, Radek!" Pepa hissed.

"I'm taking out a few more of those bastards before they get us!"

"Cut it out—you'll give us away!"

"They're hosing this pile down either way. At least make them pay!"

"Shut up, both of you!" Milan snapped.

They fell silent as the line of heavily booted feet approached and halted at the woodpile, no more than six feet from their heads. Pepa, Radek, and Milan were on their way to enlist in the U.S. Army—but they hadn't expected to fight their way through thousands of East German troops to get to the recruiter's office.

One of those three youths was my father, and the story of how he, his brother Radek, and their friend Milan ended up under a pile of People's timber deep in the East German provinces was a favorite bedtime story for me and my sister. "Don't, dear," my mother always admonished Dad. "If you tell them stories like that, they'll never be able to sleep." This was met with wails of protest from my sister, Sandy, and me, so loud that Dad relented and delivered another installment of the cliff-hanger. As we lay under our blankets in the dark, trembling with anticipation, he told of his daring escape from Communist Czechoslovakia by way of East Germany. Five had begun the journey: Dad, Uncle Radek, and their friends Milan, Vasek, and Zbynek. Over the course of a month they trekked two hundred miles, with twenty-four thousand Soviet and East German troops in hot pursuit. So many troops sent after just five young men! It seemed incredible that Dad had survived. Each time he came to the part in his story where a member of the band was caught or shot, we found ourselves blinking back tears. We hoped against hope that on this retelling the victim's fate might be different.

My father's narrative stopped when he and the other survivors reached Berlin. The story seemed to have a happy ending for the survivors. But Dad was silent about what came afterward. As soon as they reached Berlin, Dad, Uncle Radek, and Milan joined the U.S. Army and prepared to confront the Communist juggernaut again, this time for the final showdown. Earlier, from Western reports reaching Czechoslovakia by radio, they had been led to believe that the Americans were on the verge of invading their native land and wresting it from the hands of the Communists. Though he must have been gravely disappointed when the final showdown didn't come, Dad didn't tell us that. Nor did he tell us what fate befell the friends and family who didn't make it to Berlin. "Your grandmother died in a Communist prison," was all he would say when we pushed him, adding with controlled fury, "Those goddamn bastards murdered her!"

Nor did he say much about what came before the escape. Sometimes he spoke of his time in a Communist jail. He had thrilling stories about fooling the guards and tapping messages in Morse code on the walls of his cell. And he always said that in his whole life he never felt as free and at peace with himself as when he was locked up in that prison, where death might be just one interrogation away. But there was much that he wouldn't tell. It wasn't until I was in my early twenties that I learned—from my mother— that Uncle Radek had almost died from Hodgkin's disease in the 1960s, the bitter consequence of his enslavement in uranium mines, where he was forced to handle radioactive material with his bare hands. Of my Czech grandfather Dad said only, "Your grandfather was a hero of the resistance against the Nazis. He died fighting for freedom," adding emphatically, "You are Masins. Be proud of the Masin name. And always remember that the Masins fought for freedom."

Then, in 1985, our parents took Sandy and me to see the invasion beaches at Normandy. We walked through the wrecked bunkers and studied the concrete fortifications of the Axis defenders. Forty-one years after D-Day, the gun slits where cannons formerly spat death stared black and empty at the waves lapping the shore. Grass and shrubs pushed patient roots into the bomb craters that still peppered the landing areas. It was a picture of violent destruction, softened by the decay of passing years.

When we visited the provisional harbor at Arromanches with its listing, half-sunk barges, I imagined them floating again, whole and new, bustling with purposeful activity as troops and vehicles disembarked from ships. The invasion had been an awesome undertaking, audacious and vast in scope. In 1944 victory was not at all a foregone conclusion, but Americans, Britons, and Canadians, along with exiled French, Czechs, Poles, and peoples of many other nations, had stood shoulder to shoulder, committed to destroying the Nazi empire.

We also visited Allied cemeteries where row upon row of simple white crosses and Stars of David marched in precise military formation across manicured lawns. It was one of the most powerful, humbling experiences of my life. Tens of thousands of Allied soldiers, not much older than my sister and I, had died here. Just like us, they had harbored hopes and dreams—and they had paid the ultimate price for our freedom half a world away from home. As we walked up one row and down the next, we gazed at the names of all these young men, wondering who they had been and what their lives might have amounted to had they not been cut short that June in 1944.

Here and there, bouquets rested against grave markers, splashes of color in the great sea of green and white. Some were obviously expensive affairs, with gold-lettered ribbon and hothouse flowers. But there was one that in its artless simplicity drove home the enormous sacrifice those cemeteries represented. It was a small bunch of freshly picked garden blossoms with a handwritten note on plain white paper: "To the father I never knew." I looked over at my father, who was struggling with his emotions. He was too young to have fought this battle, but for him the visit represented a pilgrimage nonetheless. He too had lost a father, one he had barely known, in the fight against Nazi dictatorship. Normandy was the vindication of his own father's struggle and death, and of the terrible price his family had paid.

Walking through the cemeteries and across the cold, windswept beaches, Sandy and I reflected on the nature of this cataclysmic struggle and the price of victory. Normandy was about the promise of freedom for all peoples. One nation, America, had played the leading role in turning that promise into reality; Normandy was about America, my father's adopted homeland, coming to save Europe, the land of his birth, when Europe could no longer save itself.

For Dad it was all deeply personal. Watching him there in front of a Sherman tank, spontaneously flashing his fingers in a V for victory, his emotions surging just below a controlled surface, I began to understand something else. He had been driven by a powerful sense of duty. In his struggle against Communist dictatorship he felt compelled to live up to the standard set by his father and the other brave fighters of that earlier generation.

Dad had been tested in his own kind of Normandy. Like the boys on the invasion beaches, he participated in a struggle against a criminal regime without any assurance of final success. But there was a difference. Whereas in 1944 a consensus among democratic nations moved them to do everything in their power to end the Nazi regime, no such international consensus condemned the Soviet reign of terror. The poignant truth was that in 1985 there was no vindication for my father's struggle against Communism, no vindication for the bitter price he had paid. The Iron Curtain stood unbreached, carving Europe into two halves and locking away half its people in slavery.

These were only fragments of a bigger picture, and I spent my teenage years scouring bookstores and libraries to fill in the gaps. I didn't find much—precious little about Czech resisters in World War II and nothing at all about the October 1953 mobilization in East Germany. In college I came across a few books with passing references to General Josef Masin, my grandfather, and his comrades-in-arms Josef Balaban and Vaclav Moravek. At home we had a few yellowing books written in Czech, a difficult language I didn't understand. Leafing through the brittle pages I studied grainy photographs of the handsome, aristocratic-looking man in military uniform whom the captions identified as my grandfather. But when I asked Dad to translate the strange, consonant-laden text, he always begged off. He was too tired. Translating was too difficult.

I asked him to speak to Sandy and me in Czech, to teach us the language. He only shook his head. "We live in America," he told me. "You're much better off studying French and Spanish. Those are useful languages. Besides, it's silly for me to speak to you in Czech. You wouldn't understand a thing." Eventually I stopped asking—I sensed that he was trying to bury the past. But why?

And why *would* the Soviets and East Germans send twenty-four thousand troops against five young men? It seemed an extraordinarily excessive reaction. What had become of the people who had risked their lives to help my dad, his brother, and his friends in those dark days of totalitarian terror? What had motivated them? These were mysteries to which there were no ready answers.

Dad often said that he had one life before his great escape and another afterward, and that every day of this second life was a bonus, a gift. After his cliff-hanger escape from Communist Czechoslovakia, he didn't opt for a quiet life. Whereas his friend Milan, when last sighted, was a taxi driver, and Uncle Radek was content to run his automotive repair business and later start a company to sell his inventions, Dad seemed congenitally drawn to hair-raising adventure.

Ever since boyhood he had dreamed of flying. He wanted to join the Czech air force, but that proved impossible after the Communist coup. When he came to the United States he wanted to join the U.S. Air Force, but foreign-born men were barred. So after finishing his service in the U.S. Army, he returned to Germany to live, marry my mother, and eventually start an aviation consulting business, trading in airplanes and spare parts.

Finally he realized his dream of flying. He and his band of intrepid pilots ferried airplanes of every imaginable type and description from one continent to another. All of them were aviation enthusiasts—American and Canadian freelancers, former German air force pilots, and even some Germans who held day jobs as pharmacists or accountants and had obtained their pilot's licenses on their own time. At a call from my father they would drop everything and head off on another airplane-ferrying adventure.

Dad spent up to two hundred days a year in exotic locales ranging from India to Africa and South America and returned bearing tales about scorpions in hotel beds and the megalomaniacal fetishes of foreign heads of state. My mother often worried about him, and once she even had to contact the German embassy in some godforsaken third-world country to find out whether he was still alive. Dad was imperturbable and laughed it all off. When he was back from his travels he would usually spend a few days getting over some nameless exotic grippe. Then we would do all the things that normal families did: picnic along the bank of the Rhine River on Saturdays and take after-lunch walks on Sundays.

My father's was the quintessential American success story, but he never planned it that way. He set out for America with five dollars in his pocket, built his own business from scratch, and ultimately retired a millionaire several times over. Yet unlike so many other immigrants, his goal in coming to America wasn't to better himself economically. He was emphatic about that. His goal was to join the U.S. Army and topple the Communist regime that had enslaved his country.

When the Iron Curtain endured, Dad was compelled to build a new life for himself, a life radically different from the one he had envisioned. He was proud to be an American citizen and would remind my sister and me that we, too, were citizens of the nation that, during its finest hour, represented and fought for the principles of freedom and self-determination around the world. The United States, he told us, was a beacon of hope for all peoples oppressed by dictatorships. Yet for nearly twenty years, until he retired from his aviation business, he chose to live in Germany. I vaguely sensed that at some point after 1953 something had died for my father, and that this choice somehow reflected it.

Twelve years after graduating from college, I resolved to find answers to my questions and began by teaching myself rudimentary Czech. When business took me to Washington, D.C., Berlin, London, and Prague, I would stay a few extra days to do research in archives and libraries.

Dad was sixty-nine at the time and Uncle Radek seventy-one. Though neither had returned to the land of their birth and the events of the story lay almost fifty years behind them, my father had reached a stage in his life when he needed to take stock. He was finally ready to help me delve into the past. Also, after the Czech Communist regime fell in 1989, the Czech media revived the story of the Masins' daring escape. Each time Dad and Uncle Radek were approached by reporters and ordinary Czech citizens, they seemed more willing to speak about their experiences. Their newfound openness was, in part, an attempt to educate Czechs about the void in their national history. For decades the evils of the Communist legacy had been systematically whitewashed by the Communist leadership and their retainers, and these representations were accepted at face value by credulous audiences in the West. Dad and Uncle Radek believed that the time was ripe to bring the truth into the open so that justice and redemption could be achieved.

As I watched them tell of their flight to the West and answer the same uncomprehending questions over and over again, I sensed that the story was not just about a fascinating cliff-hanger escape. It was more complicated than that. I discovered that there was a great difference of opinion in Czechoslovakia about what my father and uncle had done and what they stood for. The Communist government had pursued them as enemies of the state. The postcommunist government of Vaclav Havel maintained studious silence about their legacy. On the other hand, a respected leader in the Catholic Church, Czech Abbot Anastaz Opasek, proclaimed their armed opposition to Communism worthy of honor. More than fifty years after the Masin story had played out, the subject was still a controversial one in post-Communist Czechoslovakia. And it had all begun with my mysterious grandfather.

Chapter 1

BIRTH OF THE NATION

My grandfather wouldn't have treated a dog the way the Hungarian officer treated him. When the officer struck him across the face with his riding crop, it was the last straw. He had had it with the Kaiser's army! That night he simply took his weapon and crept through the mud and barbed wire of no-man's-land to the Russian side. He never fired a single shot in battle for Emperor Franz Josef.

Josef Frantisek Masin was the son and only child of Bohemian landowners. The Masin family had owned and farmed a large property outside the town of Kolin for more than four hundred years. When Josef was born in 1896, Bohemia was still part of the Austro-Hungarian empire. He graduated from the Realgymnasium, the university-prep high school, and was promptly drafted at age eighteen and packed off the officer's academy, where he watched a succession of pompous Austrian officers strut about describing battle tactics that were state of the art during the Napoleonic wars a hundred years earlier. The year was 1914, and the Hapsburg Empire had just embarked on the four-year misadventure that would culminate in its dissolution—the conflict we know today as World War I.

The culmination of Josef's Austro-Hungarian army career was a class taught by a particularly obtuse officer, whose favorite expression was "Säbel hoch und hurrah!"—"Sabers up and hurrah!" One day when the officer called on Josef to answer a question on tactics, the young man cockily shot back "Säbel hoch und hurrah!" Within hours he found himself en route to the front as a lowly NCO, dismissed from the officers' academy in disgrace.[1]

When they arrived at the front in Bosnia after an arduous road march in army-issue boots, Josef and his fellow draftees were hobbling on painful, bloody feet. It was autumn 1915 and the Austrians were preparing a great offensive against the Russians in Bukovina. The commanding officer, expecting an attack at any moment, forbade the troops to take off their boots. Josef, in agony, disobeyed. That is when he had his run-in with the Hungarian officer. Soon afterward, his widowed mother received a dreaded pink letter from the military command. The Austrian army regretted to inform her that Josef Frantisek Masin had fallen on 2 September 1915, at Sinkova village, in the service of Kaiser and country. Marie Masinova was devastated.[2]

But Josef was very much alive. The Russians had shipped him to a POW camp at Dárnice, near Kiev, with other prisoners from the front.[3] As it turned out, Josef's defection didn't liberate him from the Austro-Hungarian caste system: the camp was full of German and Austrian soldiers and officers with an attitude of God-given superiority, who insisted upon, and got, preferential treatment—better food, better housing, more privileges. Conditions were harsh and many Czechs died of starvation and disease.

One day Josef heard that a force of Czech volunteers was forming to fight the Austrians and Germans for the Russian side. With their own fortunes in battle turning against them, the Russians were increasingly willing to try anything that might work. They started recruiting Czech POWs. Josef applied repeatedly before being accepted, at long last, on 15 May 1916.[4] Together with his fellow Czechs, both émigrés and POWs, he embarked on the quest to create an independent Czechoslovakia. These POWs believed that the Czech people were part of a larger Pan-Slavic brotherhood and that the Czech state could be reborn with the help of their Russian "big brothers." The Czechs in the Russian army were fighting not for the czar, but to gain their own country.

After signing up for the Czechoslovak Legion, Josef Frantisek became Vladimir. The name Josef Frantisek reminded him, he would later confirm laughingly, of the Austrian emperor Franz Josef.[5] In a mass baptism, he and thirteen hundred other Czechs had themselves inducted into the Russian Orthodox faith, selecting Slavic names to go with their conversion. Josef was never a religious man. His baptism was first and foremost a political statement, affirming his identity as a Slav and earning the trust of the still-leery Russian command.

Initially the Czechs were scattered about the front in small units, doing reconnaissance work behind enemy lines. Six months after his acceptance into the Legion, Josef was awarded his first medal, the Cross of St. George of the 4th degree, on 19 November 1916. The order doesn't state the deed for which it was awarded.[6] Four months later, on 22 March 1917, he received the Cross of St. George of the 3rd degree for his part in a combined Russian and Czech sally into the German trenches in the Nadvorana/Stanislavov sector, where fifteen Germans were captured. On 9 April 1917, he was selected for promotion and sent to a new school that had been established to train Czech officer candidates serving in the Russian army.[7] Two months later he graduated with good grades and the rank of second lieutenant.

By then the Czech troops were getting heartily sick of doing recon work. They longed for a big engagement, one in which they could fight together and prove their mettle as an army to the Russians and the western Allies. Finally, thanks to their sterling record of individual achievement in skirmishes and small engagements, and the able diplomacy of Czech nationalist Thomas Masaryk, the Russian command acquiesced. It was July 1917. With the German offensive grinding inexorably forward and the Russian front collapsing, the thirty-five-hundred-man Czech brigade was pulled together and assigned its own sector of the front in the western Ukraine, near the town of Zborov. The Russians planned a last-ditch offensive along the entire Galician sector.

As the so-called Kerensky Offensive began on 2 July, the Czechs charged out across the blasted, cratered no-man's-land. They rushed straight through the barbed wire and bomb craters while the opening artillery barrage was still under way, reaching the Austrian trenches with artillery shells exploding around them. Their opposite numbers in the Austrian trenches, mostly Czechs, were so dazed by the ferocious onslaught that they surrendered in droves. It was a battle pitting brother against brother. Although the all-Czech brigade was poorly equipped, inexperienced, and outnumbered nearly four to one, it had one overwhelming factor in its favor as it faced off against the 12,500 troops in the Austrian lines: absolute dedication to the cause. That day the Czech brigade took more than 1,200 prisoners, 62 of them officers, and captured twenty heavy guns.[8]

Josef never had much to say about his contributions to the victory at Zborov, but his friends Generals R. Mrázek and O. Pejsa wrote the following in a commemorative book issued on the twentieth anniversary of the engagement: "It isn't mere coincidence that we remember him [Masin] on precisely this day. It was he, who at the Battle of Zborov, with a handful of the most courageous men, broke through the three Austrian lines and had to retreat, since nobody else got as far. He returned back to his lines carrying a seriously wounded soldier on his back. If Zborov symbolizes the rebirth of our army, Masin is the personification of what we call Zborov. Brave, decisive, and loyal to the death."[9] The insubordinate Austro-Hungarian recruit had begun his ascent into the pantheon of Czechoslovak national heroes. Josef was determined to demonstrate to the Western democracies that the Czechs were worthy allies and valiant fighters deserving of their own state.

Along the rest of the front, the offensive quickly fizzled, and by 16 July the advantage passed to the Germans, who had arrived to shore up the crumbling Austro-Hungarian forces. Morale among the Russian troops was abysmal; many of them mutinied and refused to fight. While Russian troops were streaming toward the rear in total disorder, the Czechs fought on tenaciously to avoid being surrounded and captured. During these actions, Josef continued to fight with exemplary courage. He was promoted three times in quick succession: on 22 July, on 1 August, and again on 25 August. He received a second Cross of St. George of the 4th degree for the action at Zborov and another Cross of St. George of the 3rd degree on 21 September.[10]

Though the Battle of Zborov conferred no lasting strategic advantage upon the Russians, it proved to be a watershed for Czech and Slovak aspirations to nationhood. As a result of their successes, the Russian government permitted continued recruitment of POWs for the Czechoslovak Legion, which quickly expanded from a token force of a thousand to more than seventy thousand men.

Meanwhile, the military situation was deteriorating rapidly and Tomas Masaryk was frantically negotiating for an evacuation of his army without a country. The plan was to evacuate the Czechs and Slovaks at the Black Sea ports of Archangelsk and Murmansk, where ships of the French and British expeditionary forces would transport them to France for deployment. As a result of delays and foot-dragging on the part of the French and the Russian provisional government, only seventeen hundred men shipped out before this route was cut off.[11] The remainder of the Czechoslovak force was left stranded as Russia slid into anarchy and civil war.

The situation around Kiev, where the Czechoslovak Legion was deployed, was desperate. As the German army drove swiftly toward the city, the Russian army continued disintegrating in the face of the onslaught. Both the Ukrainians and the Bolsheviks, locked in mortal combat with each other, rushed to sign separate peace treaties with the Germans. The Czechs saw the writing on the wall: the Ukrainians and the Bolsheviks would turn them over to the tender mercies of the Austrians and Germans in a heartbeat.

The way to the West was closed.

The escape route via Archangelsk was out of the question.

There remained only one way out: a daunting twenty-thousand-mile odyssey via the Trans-Siberian Railroad, across the Urals and the whole of Asia to the port of Vladivostok on the distant shores of the Pacific Ocean, then onward, via Japan and the Panama Canal, back to Europe.

Out of options, short of materiel and food, the Czechs scoured the area for weapons and ammunition, requisitioning trains that had been abandoned by their Russian crews. Then they converged on Kiev, falling back across the Dnieper River with the Germans in hot pursuit. Already the Czech rear guard was skirmishing with advance detachments of the German troops.

As the last columns of Czech troops marched away over the long Dnieper bridge on 28 February 1918, a young soldier in a dust-covered Russian uniform stood to the side, watching. He was tall, 6'4", but other than that he looked indistinguishable from all the young Russian conscripts who had fled their units and were making their way home as best they could. The unit insignia had been torn off his uniform, and he stood with his worn, military-issue coat slung over one shoulder, clutching his wadded-up cap in the other hand. When the troops and most of the stragglers had gone, the rearguard of the Czech 2nd Regiment marched to the bridge and set up a barricade and machine gun nest to hold off the Germans.

The young soldier slowly turned his back on them and headed into the city. All day long he hung around the railway station, waiting. After nightfall, an armored train pulled in and a battalion of Germans disembarked. They were well equipped, disciplined, and in excellent physical condition. It was the first of many trains. Long, dusty columns of German troops marched past the station, headed east. Within twenty-four hours the Germans had seized control of Kiev.

The Germans wasted no time posting signs with assorted prohibitions and directives. They cleaned the grimy station until it was in tip-top condition and set up a canteen to provision the arriving troops. On the platform a smartly turned-out guard patrolled back and forth. Meanwhile the young Russian conscript still loitered. Sometimes he walked around on the platform, but mostly he lay on the ground and ate sunflower seeds, spitting out the husks the way Russian soldiers were wont to do when they waited for trains or were bored. He lay directly underneath two proclamations the

Germans had posted: "Aufenthalt auf dem Bahnsteig verboten" (Loitering on the platform forbidden) and "Der Bahnsteig darf nicht verunreinigt werden" (Littering prohibited on the platform). Before long, the German guard went into action.

"Du darfst hier nicht herumlungern! You can't loiter here. Can't you read the sign?" The Russian deserter looked up innocently and answered, "I don't understand German, tovarich." He showed the German a ticket that he had picked up from the ground the day before. The German jabbed a finger at the sign again and barked out some more German.

"I can't read, tovarich," the Russian soldier said and offered the guard some sunflower seeds, all the while popping them into his own mouth and calmly spitting out the husks on the just-cleaned platform.

"And no littering on the platform!" the exasperated guard bellowed.

Josef looked at him in bewildered incomprehension, even though he could speak German like a native. He let himself be thrown out and then crawled back in through a hole in the fence. He didn't resist when the Germans pushed him around with their rifle butts. For three days he hung around the German soldiers, waiting for a train that never came. But he learned everything he needed to know: How many German troops had arrived in the area. Which regiments. Their level of preparedness. Their armament. Their military objectives. Satisfied, Josef left the train station for the last time and walked toward the Dnieper bridge. The next step was to find his unit—wherever that might be.

He found the bridge impassable. Where the Czech rearguard had grimly held their ground several days ago, eight Germans were demanding ID papers stamped with the German *Kommandatura*'s authorization from all comers.

Only one week earlier the river had been covered by solid ice, and Josef could have easily walked across it. That was impossible now; the ice had broken up in the spring thaw. He decided to walk along the riverbank for thirty miles until he reached the next ford. Hours later, still trudging along the river, he spotted a horse-drawn farmer's cart approaching. In the back sat two German officers. Without hesitating Josef jumped aboard. The shocked officers shouted and swore at him, but Josef looked as if he understood nothing and spoke to them congenially in Russian. After some more swearing and screaming on the part of the Germans, Josef pulled some papers from his pocket and handed them over with the reverence due important documents. The Germans examined them: a shoe repair bill, a pawn note for a pocket watch on which there was still an old czarist stamp, and other useless papers. The officers guffawed and then laughed out loud at such incredible stupidity.

After Josef said "Tovarich Germanski" for about the fiftieth time, they started teaching him to say "Der Deutsche ist gut" (the German is good), which Josef, much to their amusement, could repeat pretty well on his second try and kept repeating again and again without interruption. And thus he rode onto the bridge with the officers amidst great hilarity, where the duty guards saluted them smartly. After crossing the Dnieper, Josef thanked the officers effusively and using gestures asked them for a cigarette for the road. They parted ways in the best of spirits, the Germans laughing about the stupid Russian and Josef heading off in search of the closest train station.

"This part of the Ukraine is supposed to be very beautiful," Josef recalled later to a fellow soldier who was a better diarist than he was. "I wouldn't know because I didn't look around. I just counted kilometers and railway cars filled with soldiers."

The regular trains were not running and Josef couldn't afford to wait, so he jumped onto the next German troop train and settled down on the running board. The Germans scolded him out the window and threw him off at the next railway platform. "It wasn't so bad," remembered Josef. "In this way I covered at least ten kilometers.* The next train had better Germans inside. I rode with them until that evening." At sunset they too pushed him off his perch on the running board. But now Bachmach, where the Czech troops were, was only thirty kilometers away.† As he fell asleep in an abandoned camp at the train station, he could hear the thundering of the artillery.

At around 4:00 AM, he spied an incoming train. It was moving so fast that he didn't even have time to properly look it over—he just jumped into a railway carriage. Only then did he notice it was a German armored train. Eight machine guns pointed out through narrow slits near the roof. Small slivers of sky were visible through the openings next to the weapons. Ten astonished soldiers stopped cleaning their weapons and turned to stare at him. Josef grinned back. "Aren't you surprised!" he thought to himself, and made his smile wider still. The Germans approached him menacingly. Josef kept smiling and heard them tell each other that they would throw him out of the speeding train. Josef had goose bumps on his back, as he tried to

---

*Roughly six miles
†Roughly nineteen miles

visualize how to take the fall so that he suffered the least amount of damage. He laughed at the Germans disarmingly. In the end, to his amazement, they let him be. He listened to them talking about how the Czechoslovak forces had fended off the German attacks, and how the Germans would heat them up with new forces that day. They passed two hospital trains heading west, full of German wounded.

When the train came to a stop, one of the Germans finally booted Josef out of the railway carriage. The track ahead was destroyed and the whole area was a hive of chaotic activity—heavy artillery was booming nearby and the rattling of small arms fire was clearly audible. Stretcher bearers hurried past, carrying wounded soldiers to a nearby field hospital. Reinforcements marched by in formation and couriers scurried back and forth. Unnoticed, Josef lay down near a fence with some displaced Russian villagers. "We didn't talk much," he remembered, "so I wouldn't betray myself by my accent." Making his way into the train station, he lingered near the command post of a German officer, listening surreptitiously to the orders the officer shouted into his telephone and making a mental note of the German gun emplacements.

That night, he evaded the German guards and made his way to the Czech lines. This was easily the most hazardous part of the whole mission. He was out of uniform and he didn't know the day's challenge and password. The natural reaction of troops on an active front is to shoot first and ask questions later, but he safely made his way to the division headquarters. After delivering a full reconnaissance report and announcing that two German brigades were on the way, he joined his brothers in battle.[12] The Battle of Bachmach was a bloody, six-day ordeal. In the end the Czechs only just managed to drive the Germans back.

On 3 March 1918, the Russian Bolshevik government capitulated to Germany and signed the Treaty of Brest-Litovsk. Russia was out of the war, but German forces continued to push deeper into Ukrainian territory, hot on the heels of the retreating Czechs. Knowing that capture by the Germans meant they would hang as deserters, the Czechs fought the Germans with an intensity born of desperation.

Theirs was an improvised army, cut off in the middle of a vast, hostile land. Because the Russian and, before that, Austro-Hungarian high command had filled all staff positions with fellow nationals, Czechs and Slovaks had not been able to rise in either military hierarchy. In 1918, young Czech and Slovak captains became generals virtually overnight.

Men in their thirties were running an army of seventy thousand strung out along thousands of versts of railroad, without formal supply lines, without reliable communications, and without the benefit of staff officers' training.[13] But they and their men were motivated—they were hell-bent on getting back home, and nothing was going to stop them.

It was in this army that Josef Masin came into his own. His strengths were charismatic leadership, courage, and the ability to improvise. He earned the undying loyalty of the men who served under him. To them he was the best. The best soldier. The best officer. Even after his death this admiration and undying respect shone through in the stilted, formal letters they addressed to Josef's first biographer, Jaroslav Prochazka. Captain Endt wrote, "Because of his courage, the most difficult assignments were assigned to him, which he joyfully took on. He is one of the best soldiers I have ever met."[14]

Major Alois Janotka recounted that whenever word came of danger ahead, Masin wouldn't wait around for orders. He simply said "Nazdar" (See you later) and disappeared with a few equally courageous associates. After his return he would laconically announce that everything was okay, without dwelling on details.[15]

Fellow veteran Karel Fibich agreed. "Masin was a rare personality and a hero in every respect. He had a very good name in the whole first regiment. He was a very good scout and all the most difficult tasks were entrusted to him."[16]

Josef would never ask his men to do anything he wasn't willing to do himself. He led by example and shared the hardships of the enlisted man, claiming no privileges of rank for himself. He had little to say about his own exploits and achievements, but his men knew they could count on him to look after them, even putting himself in the line of fire to protect them. Vojta Holecek related how the unit once came under heavy fire and, weighed down by his equipment, he sank deep into the mud without anybody noticing. Once the unit had moved out of danger, somebody called out that Holecek was missing. Josef immediately turned back to look for him. As grenades exploded around him, he found Holecek and dragged him to safety. Holecek was convinced that Masin's split-second decision making and levelheadedness under fire saved his life.[17]

Josef's men, in turn, came through for him. When he was shot in the stomach near Sheberta, they hauled him through thirty kilometers of primeval forest on a farmer's handcart, able to give him only the crudest of care.

Despite their heroic efforts, by the time they finally got him to a hospital train and into the hands of medical professionals, the wound had turned gangrenous. He wasted away until the doctors feared he would die. In the end he pulled through, thanks to a good constitution. According to his service record, he was discharged from the hospital after one month and twelve days, on 7 August 1918. The very next day he was back with his men.[18]

The Czechoslovak Legion was the largest cohesive fighting force in Russia, and the Bolsheviks, still struggling to secure their hold on power, rightly feared it. They demanded that the Czechs surrender their weapons. Leery of the Communists' promise of safe passage, the Czechs refused and seized control of the Trans-Siberian railroad to secure passage to the Pacific Ocean.

Again and again the Czechs clashed with the Reds. As the highly motivated legionnaires emerged victorious more often than not, the British, French, and American governments sensed an opportunity to topple the Bolshevik regime. The heads of the French military mission at Ufa urged the Czechs to stay in Russia and become the core of an anti-Bolshevik expeditionary army. The Czech military leadership agreed, but after initial brilliant successes, the supplies and reinforcements promised by the French and British didn't materialize. The Czech initiative faltered.

In any case the Czech rank and file were in no mood to fight other people's wars. After the armistice of 28 October 1918, the Czech legionnaires had achieved their objective: Czechoslovakia was an independent state. Now the men only wanted to go home. Mutinies forced the young Czech generals to yield to their men's wishes.

The focus of the Czechoslovak Legion turned to the push along the Trans-Siberian railroad, into Asia and toward the Pacific Ocean. By the time the legionnaires had fought their way to Vladivostok, their presence in Siberia had become an inconvenient anachronism to the allies that had initially supported them. Since the Czechs depended upon allied shipping to get them home, it was many more months before Josef Masin and his fellow legionnaires returned to their native villages and towns in Central Europe via Japan and the Panama Canal.

In 1920, two years after the guns on Europe's battlefields had fallen silent, Josef finally came home. He had left his home in the Austro-Hungarian empire an inexperienced youth of eighteen and returned six years later to the new nation of Czechoslovakia, a man who had traveled the world—a battle-hardened, much-decorated officer.

Nationalism had proved itself a force of unprecedented power. It completely reshaped the face of Europe. Over a space of four years, three polyglot, multinational empires cobbled together by dynastic marriages and conquest had crumbled, and independent nation-states had arisen to take their place. Captain Josef Masin played his part in the process, and, in turn, it shaped his outlook and convictions for the rest of his life.

Once he got back to Czechoslovakia, Josef resigned his captain's commission and left the service to farm his family's estate in Losany. But a brief stint running the farm convinced him that the military was his true calling and he quickly rejoined.

When Josef found the woman he wanted to marry, he went after his objective with his characteristic single-mindedness. He first laid eyes on the charming young Zdena Novakova at a large party in the provincial city of Olomouc, and he was instantly smitten. Eleven years his junior, Zdena had a round, china-doll face and fine features. More importantly, she was the first woman graduate of the prestigious Charles University civil engineering faculty. Her ambitious mother had been grooming Zdena to take over her father's business, the largest civil engineering firm in Moravia, but Zdena's true love was music. She was an accomplished pianist and, given a choice, she would have preferred pursuing a career as a pianist.

Zdena's would-be suitors faced some daunting obstacles. Her watchful mother chaperoned her everywhere and wouldn't let her out of her sight. She had even left her husband and son to shift for themselves when Zdena was accepted to university, moving to Prague with her daughter to oversee the girl's studies and chase away male admirers. And if that wasn't enough, Josef's fellow officers told him that the girl's father, a leading citizen in town, adamantly opposed a military marriage.

Zdena and Josef met only a few times at large social gatherings before Josef was transferred out of town. By the time of his next posting in Olomouc, they hadn't corresponded, but Josef had made up his mind—he would marry Zdena. The courtship was conducted in record time. On 30 March 1929, he asked her for a rendezvous. Two days later the couple announced their engagement.

The news shocked both families, but the dashing young officer, hero of the Great War, quickly found favor in the eyes of authoritarian Emma Novakova, Zdena's mother, and her nationalistic father, Leopold. Nevertheless, Emma had a serious talk with her future son-in-law before she consented to the match. She had watched her own mother wear herself out bearing and raising sixteen children, struggling to run the household on her husband's paltry income as a minor official in the royal customs service. "My daughter is an educated woman and an artist," she told Josef. "She does not know how to cook and I did not raise her to scrub floors and wash diapers. Promise me that you will always see to it that she has help in the household." Josef promised. He was true to his word until the day he died.

For Zdena, it was a love match. She idolized her husband. The couple had three children. Ctirad ("Radek"), the eldest, was born on 11 August 1930. My father, Josef Vladimir ("Pepa"), was born on 8 March 1932, and little Zdena ("Nenda") was born on 7 November 1933. Zdena was born severely handicapped, without properly functioning joints in her arms and legs. An undemonstrative man, Josef never spoke of his feelings, yet he deeply loved his wife and children. By all accounts, he was happy to be a father.

Josef Masin was a soldier's soldier, promoted rapidly and showered with medals for his exploits on the battlefield. But his career stagnated in the peacetime army. He wouldn't engage in the politicking, back-scratching, horse-trading, and tactful minuets essential to peacetime career advancement. His peers and subordinates were promoted past him, many becoming general officers while his career stalled at the rank of lieutenant colonel. In 1938 he became executive officer of the 1st Artillery Regiment, and in the spring of that year his promotion to full colonel was administratively approved. Yet the gathering firestorm that would soon engulf Europe prevented conferment.

Chapter 2

AN ALLY BETRAYED

For Czechoslovakia, World War II began and ended with abandonment by the West. In 1938 the country was an industrialized democracy with a large middle class. Although the global depression had damaged its export-driven economy, exacerbating ethnic tensions among the Germans and Czechs within its borders, the nation was still prosperous compared to many of its neighbors. It was the only functioning democracy among all the new states created by the Versailles Treaty. Well-armed with modern guns, tanks, and aircraft, it had constructed a line of formidable fortifications along the German border modeled on France's Maginot Line. Czechoslovakia, which had defensive treaties with both Britain and France, was the "aircraft carrier in Germany's rear," a serious threat should Germany launch an attack on Britain and France in the West, as Hitler's officer corps never tired of pointing out.[1]

But when Hitler announced his intention to annex the Sudetenland, the ethnic German border territories of Czechoslovakia, the British government under Prime Minister Neville Chamberlain was not prepared to go to war to defend Czechoslovakia. Chamberlain's trusted advisor Sir Horace Wilson reasoned, "It was not a real country at all. It was created out of the necessities of Versailles. It didn't really mean a thing."[2] As for the French government, it succumbed to panic, believing that Germany had overwhelming resources on its side. Foreign Minister Georges Bonnet assured British Ambassador Sir Eric Phipps that the French would force the stubborn Czechs to agree to Germany's terms.[3] The U.S. ambassador to Britain, Joseph P. Kennedy, told German ambassador Herbert von Dirksen that he would "do his utmost" to keep the United States out of any European war.[4] The most important thing, in the minds of these men, was to preserve peace. And that meant accommodating the Germans and seeing that they got the Sudetenland.

Neville Chamberlain readily agreed to Hitler's demand for the Sudetenland. Apprised of the deal by the British, the French in turn pushed the Czechs to accept Hitler's terms. The Czechs refused, and war seemed imminent.

On 20 September, Josef Masin's Artillery Regiment, ordinarily garrisoned near Prague, had been deployed to Jihlava to defend the border. He wrote a farewell letter to his wife.

Beloved Zdena,

I am writing this letter to you with the expectation that we will not see each other again in life. Should war break out (may God preserve us) it would be a terrible trial for our republic and nation. We must however, all of us, defend the freedom of our nation firmly and decisively and fight to the last breath, sacrificing our lives without hesitation. . . . I know that you, too, honor these principles above everything, and that you shall do everything in your power toward those ends. Be strong and be a mother to the Jugovic.* Your task is to raise our children so that they become honest, proud, and tough Czechs who know how to defend their own nation manfully, and that they will give their own lives to that end. Engrave it into their souls that an honest death is better than life as a slave.

Teach them an implacable hatred against our eternal enemies, the detestable liars and cynical barbarians.† . . . I would very much have loved to see my darling children one more time and press them against my breast. Please do it for me. Kiss my Radek, Pepa, and Nenda and don't let them forget me ever. I also leave you my dear old mother. Do not abandon her. . . . She is already old and she will probably not be here much longer, and she should have quiet last moments in her life. And you, my dear Zdena, forgive me should I ever have hurt you and don't think of me in anger.

With a heartfelt embrace and kiss,
your Pepa

---

*See Němeček, Jan, *Mašínové, zpráva o dvou generacích*, Torst, Prague, 1998. Němeček points out that Croat author Ivo Vojnovič wrote five dramas, which were published in Czech translation in 1938. The titles: *Equinox, Dobrovnic trilogy, Death of the Mother of the Jugovic, Resurrection of Lazarus, Imperatrice.* They were based on the Kosovo legend, an epic cycle in which the Mother loses her husband and nine sons (the Jugovič, literally "sons of Jug") in the decisive battle against the Turks on Kosovo field in 1389 without shedding a single tear.

†Mašín is referring to the Germans.

The Czechoslovak army, one of the most modern in Europe, was ready to fight.[5] But assertive Czechoslovak resistance was not at all what the British and French wanted. Sir Basil Newton and Victor de Lacroix paid Czechoslovak President Eduard Benes a visit expressly to threaten him that he would "bear the responsibility for the war." The British would declare themselves neutral in the coming conflict, and when "war starts, France will not take part, i.e., she will not fulfill her treaty obligations."[6]

While enormous crowds demonstrated in the streets of Prague, denouncing France and Britain and calling for the government to defend the nation, Benes caved in. He informed Lacroix and Newton that he accepted the terms and agreed to the dismembering of his country. Chamberlain, enormously pleased with himself, reported back to Hitler that the Czechs would yield the Sudetenland without a fight. But Hitler, seeing the ease of his victory, upped the ante. He informed the stunned Chamberlain that the Czechoslovak concessions were "no longer enough"[7] and demanded that all Czechs evacuate the Sudetenland, leaving their entire property behind: furniture, livestock, and arms.[8] What is more, they would have to be out before 1 October—only nine days away.[9]

Ordinary Czech citizens, politicians, and military men bitterly resented Benes's capitulation. Within hours of his announcement, the Cabinet unanimously resigned. Benes felt compelled to reverse himself. He appointed the World War I hero General Jan Syrovy Premier and War Minister,[10] and Syrovy ordered the army to mobilize.

The crisis was peaking. Smelling blood, the Hungarian and Polish governments dispatched ultimata of their own to Prague, demanding chunks of Czechoslovak territory. To back up their threats, they mobilized their own armies.[11]

On 29 September, Germany, Italy, England, and France convened in Munich to resolve "the Czech problem." The Czechs were not invited. When Benes belatedly learned of the meeting and rushed a delegation to Munich, the Czechs were told to wait outside while the fate of their country was determined behind closed doors. Eight hours later they were presented with a done deal: Germany would take over the Sudetenland and Hungary and Poland would each get a chunk of Czechoslovak territory. Betrayed by all its allies, the Czechoslovak government decided to accept the outcome. Hitler had won.

In Czechoslovakia the mood was one of stunned disbelief. Crowds wandered the streets of Prague crying and singing the Czechoslovak national anthem, "Where Is My Homeland?" Benes, broken and defeated, told his cabinet: "It was difficult to decide whether to accept the conditions [of Munich] and save the nation or to fight and let ourselves be murdered. . . . History will judge what was correct."[12] Under government orders the undefeated Czechoslovak army abandoned its border fortifications and top-of-the-line armaments and retreated without having fired a shot in the nation's defense. In the pouring rain, columns of demoralized troops trudged east into the heartland. Unable to come to grips with this national catastrophe, numerous officers committed suicide.

But suicide was not for Josef Masin. Wracked by fury and despair, Masin poured out his heart to his wife in a letter dated 1 October 1938.

> My Dear Zdena,
>
> I am writing to you in a shattered state . . . the vile so-called leaders of the nation accepted conditions that the people wouldn't have accepted had it been apprised of them. The nation, that is the common people, would have, I believe, at least found enough courage to defend their honor. It would be better if half of our nation had died, because then the other half would have lived, as it would have felt morally obligated to avenge the dead. They [the leaders] believed that they were "saving the nation" by their actions, however, the nation will perish thereof. . . . Woe unto our nation!"

Munich was a tragedy of the first order to Josef. His anger was directed not so much at Hitler—after all, German aggression was to be expected*— but at the Czechoslovak leadership that had failed to defend the nation. At Zborov, he had seen men outnumbered by a factor of four to one prevail because they were motivated by the justness of their cause. He had nothing but contempt for those who forsook their duty and didn't live by a code of honor.

Near panic seized the Czechs living in the Sudetenland. Masses of the dispossessed thronged the roads, trudging east and north toward the rump state of Czechoslovakia. According to the terms of the Munich Agreement, they were not allowed to take their livestock or household goods. SS men at checkpoints allowed nothing larger than a watch to pass.[13]

---

*See his earlier letter dated 20 September, where he refers to the Germans as "our eternal enemies, the detestable liars and cynical barbarians."

The German army swept through the abandoned Czech defenses into the Sudetenland. As the SS *Einsatzkommandos* went to work arresting and murdering, Benes presided over the capitulation, resigned from the presidency, and headed into exile on 5 October.

Flush from the success of his latest bluff, Hitler immediately set about erasing the rest of Czechoslovakia from the map. Beginning in late February, Czechoslovak army intelligence obtained a stream of information showing that a German invasion was imminent. Its head, Lieutenant Colonel Frantisek Moravec, repeatedly briefed the leadership, but the government dismissed Moravec's predictions as "impossible."[14]

By 14 March, twenty-four hours before the predicted invasion, the Czechoslovak General Staff still had not issued orders of any kind.* It clung to the delusion that the Germans wouldn't invade. Lieutenant Colonel Masin, still second in command of the 1st Artillery Regiment, was frustrated by his superiors' paralysis. Aware that time was running out, he drove to General Staff headquarters, determined to prod it into action. Walking through the halls and offices, he witnessed scenes of unbridled helplessness and panic. In the office of Colonel Frantisek Havel, the second-in-command at the Second (Intelligence) Directorate, Josef cut to the chase:

"So what will we do?"

"Nothing," rejoined Havel.

Josef and Havel went to see Officer Ptak in the Third Directorate.

"What are you doing here?" Ptak demanded of Josef, surprised that he had left his post at Ruzyne. When Josef repeated his question, Ptak replied, "We can't do anything about it."

"Let's go see Syrovy,"† Josef urged. He was not about to give up.

"He's probably gluing stamps," Havel said acidly.‡ Syrovy and his aides were meeting behind closed doors and were not seeing anyone. But neither were they issuing any orders.

"We should summon the nation to the defense by radio broadcast!" said Josef.

"The government won't allow us to speak by radio," Ptak said, squelching the idea.

---

*The account is based on an undated, typewritten report by Josef Masin. Personal papers of Zdena Mašínová.

†General Jan Syrový was the Minister of Defense.

‡A sarcastic reference to Syrovy's hobby: he was a stamp collector. Although he was a hero of World War I during the Czechoslovak Legion's odyssey in Russia, after 1938 many officers felt that he was no longer at the height of his powers.

"I will do it by force! We can take care of it with one hundred men!" countered Josef. It was a dramatic step of insubordination. Josef was a military professional, and to a military man insubordination is a heinous offense, almost unthinkable. But in the country's greatest hour of need, its government had failed it and the General Staff was incapable of action.

Josef spoke passionately. He was the only one with a plan, and he soon persuaded the others. Josef would return to Prague with the troops. Before leaving he told Ptak, "In the meantime, write up the appeal."

With that, Josef drove back to his artillery regiment. At Ruzyne he briefed his commanding officer, Colonel Albin Holoubek, on the state of total panic and confusion at the General Staff headquarters and on the plan to broadcast an appeal directly to the people.

"All I ask is that you not prevent me from assembling a company of soldiers," Josef said.

Holoubek was totally opposed. "You do that," he threatened, "and I will issue an order confining everybody to barracks. Come with me, we're going to see Ptak."

Back at the General Staff headquarters, Josef used all his powers of persuasion to marshal support for independent action by the field commanders. The meeting was tumultuous. Josef urged that the commanders of regiments stationed near the capital prepare for the capital's defense without orders from Syrovy. Though his fellow officers finally agreed to summon the garrison commanders for a meeting, only a couple showed up and in the end none could bring themselves to act without orders from Syrovy.

"At least the weapons and supplies should be destroyed! They must not fall into the enemy's hands," Josef urged.

The others wouldn't agree to this either.

When it was clear that none of the General Staff officers or regimental commanders would act, Josef left the meeting, furious and bitterly disappointed. Determined not to surrender without a fight, he decided to act on his own. This time he wouldn't consult Holoubek. Back at Ruzyne barracks, he ordered all the officers and NCOs of the 1st Artillery Regiment into the officers' mess and explained the calamitous situation. The mood was somber. Josef led them in a solemn oath to execute the defense at all costs and organized a combined action.* At 9:00 AM everything was ready. Josef returned to see Colonel Havel at the General Staff headquarters.

---

*The "combined action" of infantry and artillery was probably intended to deny access to the road to Prague to the invading German troops.

To Josef's frustration and amazement, nobody believed that an occupation was imminent. "Hácha,"* the General Staff officers said, "has taken care of everything in the meantime." Josef told Havel what he was doing on his own authority at Ruzyne and requested that Havel telephone him in the event the Germans invaded. Then he returned to Ruzyne.

The call from Havel never came. When Josef found out for himself that German forces had crossed the border some hours previously and informed Colonel Holoubek, the regimental commander collapsed. Outraged at the incompetence of his superiors, who had just squandered the last opportunity to mount a defense of the nation, Josef informed the distraught Holoubek that the 1st Artillery Regiment would defend itself. Then he dispatched the unhinged commander to the General Staff, ostensibly to advise it of the regiment's course of action.

With Holoubek out of the way, Josef was everywhere, finalizing arrangements to blow up the weapons stores and the supplies, seeing to it that the soldiers in the store distributed the equipment and telling them to take home with them whatever they wanted to take. Josef was already shipping quantities of ammunition and small arms to hiding places of his own, outside the regimental barracks. As quantities of pistols and other equipment disappeared, Josef returned to the regimental headquarters and locked himself in the office. He placed telephone calls, trying to get through to Holoubek or Havel, but not reaching either of them. And then an excited adjutant gave him the grim news: the Germans were already in Prague.

As Josef stepped out of his office to execute his plan,† he heard someone in the CO's office calling his name. The doors opened and out walked General Vaclav Sara, commander of the 1st Artillery Corps, accompanied by some other officers.

"Pepa, I heard about the foolish thing you want to do. Such a rash deed would have nefarious consequences for the nation. You do not have the right to act this way! I understand you, but our time will come later. And for that, determined people will be necessary. Since Holoubek has just

---

*Emil Hácha, JUDr., succeeded Beneš after the latter resigned. At this point Hácha was in Berlin, pleading with Hitler to call off the imminent invasion.

†Just what Josef's plan was at this point is ambiguous. In his typewritten record he uses the wording "execute my intention." He doesn't explicitly say whether the intention was armed defense or, at this point, only the destruction of the equipment. Sára's tone seems to indicate that Josef insisted on independent military action as opposed to simply blowing up the regimental munitions dump.

had a nervous collapse, you're being promoted to Regimental Commander. Congratulations, my friend!"

Masin was having none of it. Unswayed by the proffered bribe, he insisted on executing his plan. A shouting match ensued.

"I only want to do my duty!" Josef thundered. "Today, however, nobody is issuing any order to me. I am master of my conscience and I am responsible for my deeds and I will execute my own plan!"

When Sara saw that the field promotion within an army that would cease to exist within a few hours hadn't appeased Josef, Sara relieved Josef of his command, effective immediately. Then he and the other officers barred Josef's path. Telling Sara exactly what he thought of him in the most unflattering terms, Josef reached for the pistol in his pocket. Sara and another officer threw themselves on him and, after a violent physical struggle in which Josef was disarmed, led him off to his apartment. And so the only fighting that took place on 15 March was in the regimental headquarters of the 1st Artillery Regiment. Czechoslovakia surrendered to the German Wehrmacht, and once again, its army had not fired a shot in the nation's defense.

Josef Masin, the decorated war hero, was cashiered from the army in disgrace. When put to the test, Josef pulled his gun on a senior officer and old friend rather than violate his duty to defend his country. As the eminent British jurist Hartley Shawcross put it, "There comes a point, when a man must refuse to answer to his leader if he is also to answer to his conscience."* For Josef that time came on 15 March 1939. His actions that day were consistent with his track record during World War I. But this time they came in a radically different context. In Russia in 1914–16, they had led to a rapid succession of field promotions and a remarkable number of medals for extraordinary valor. In Czechoslovakia in 1939, they led to his disgrace and dismissal from the army.

What had changed? The Czechoslovak Legion in World War I was under the leadership of a young, dynamic officer corps and the visionary nation-builder Tomas Masaryk. After Masaryk was dead, his erstwhile junior partner Benes assumed the presidency. But Benes was no Masaryk. Threatened with violence, Benes caved in. As a result of this fateful decision, when the nation's second existential crisis struck in 1939, both the civilian and the military leadership were demoralized and already resigned to defeat.

---

*Shawcross was the chief British judge at the Nüremberg trials, and this comment was made during his opening address during those proceedings.

The Munich frontiers had endured less than five months. Once again France and Britain broke their promises to Czechoslovakia and stood by passively as Hitler's Wehrmacht swept into Prague. By the stunning ease of his victory Hitler silenced German opposition to war. With one bold stroke he seized the massive Skoda arms production complex at Plzen and the entire arsenal of the Czechoslovak air force and army, including six hundred state-of-the-art tanks and one thousand aircraft, as well as the nation's stockpiles of raw materials. In a final blow, the British authorized the transfer of all of Czechoslovakia's gold reserves to Hitler. Hitler wasted no time deploying Czechoslovak tanks, guns, and treasure against Poland, which fell in less than a month. Next, in a stroke of irony, he turned those resources against the French.

In his London exile ex-President Benes was forced to recognize that his meek compliance with the demands of Britain and France had not earned him anyone's respect or appreciation, nor had it preserved his people from bloodshed. Britain, France, and the United States stood by inactively as the Nazis rapidly launched a rigorous campaign of ethnic cleansing and political repression in the rump state of Czechia, which they renamed the Protectorate of Bohemia and Moravia. Hundreds of people were killed. Thousands were abducted and sent as forced labor to farms and factories of the Reich, untold others disappeared into concentration camps.

Britain and France refused to recognize Benes's government-in-exile, and even the United States government, which had hosted him in Washington in June 1939, wouldn't extend recognition. With no assurance that British, American, or French support would ever be forthcoming and the Czechoslovak government-in-exile in no position to provide financial or material sustenance, Josef Masin began his own war against the Nazis. He had two close associates in this effort: Lieutenant Colonel Josef Balaban and Captain Vaclav Moravek. They would go down in history as the *Tri Kralové*, the Three Kings. By the time the Czechoslovak government-in-exile finally got around to declaring war on Germany on 16 December 1941, the Three Kings had been fighting the Germans for more than two difficult and dangerous years.

Chapter 3

RESISTANCE

When Josef returned home to Dolni Liboc on 15 March 1939, his wife was shocked at his appearance. The insignia, shoulder boards, and medals had been torn off his uniform. Bruises, scrapes, and cuts covered his face and hands. He was inconsolable. While the citizens of Prague lined the streets watching the triumphant arrival of the Wehrmacht in stunned, sorrowful silence, Josef locked himself into the living room to wrestle with his conscience. He had a momentous decision to make: should he act against his superiors' orders once more, or should he abandon his duty to his nation? When he reemerged, he told Zdena, "Until now I obeyed orders, but from now on I am going to act on my own." From that day on, Josef dedicated himself completely to his resistance work. Whenever anybody asked him what his profession was, he would answer, tongue in cheek, "I'm self-employed."

Josef didn't work alone for long. His friend Lieutenant Colonel Josef Balaban worked for a time in the military liquidation office, but as a dedicated Czech nationalist and military man, Balaban found this job repugnant. He soon got in touch with Josef and joined the underground organization. When his elderly mother, fearing for her son's life, begged him to go abroad, Balaban replied, "What about Masin? He has three children and he does such dangerous deeds. I would be ashamed of myself to abandon him in his work." To Balaban there was no question of giving up the fight.

The third member of the trio was Captain Vaclav Moravek, a God-fearing Protestant and a devout reader of the Bible from the town of Kolin, near Losany. He was introduced to Josef by a fellow resistance member and soon became a trusted collaborator. Like Josef and Balaban, he was an accomplished horseman and marksman. Moravek's unique brand of humor would become the group's hallmark.

In those first days after Czechoslovakia's capitulation, with the situation on the ground still fluid, Josef and his associates contravened their superiors' orders by returning repeatedly to the Ruzyne barracks and smuggling light weapons out of the regimental arms room to prepare for the upcoming resistance. By the time the Germans moved in and took possession, Josef and his associates had removed 18 machine guns and 300 rifles with seventy thousand rounds of ammunition and 580 army pistols with twelve thousand rounds of ammunition, which they stashed in quarries, private gardens, and basements around Bohemia.

Chief Warrant Officer Josef Palat, who hid some of Josef's weapons in his apartment, recalled that Josef once arrived with a carload full of guns. "Where did you get so many weapons?" Palat asked him in amazement. Josf replied: "I drove into Vrchovicke barracks. I loaded them up, and you should have seen how quickly the German soldier opened the gate for me so I could drive out." The next time he brought new submachine guns, he told Palat: "I took them out of the Germans' car on the street."[1]

Josef repeatedly infiltrated Gestapo headquarters at the Petschkov Palace after obtaining German ID documents and military insignia. One Mr. Cabicar, a tailor by trade, carefully maintained the Three Kings' various disguises, ranging from railway men's uniforms, to workmen's overalls, to a green loden coat with a swastika badge on the lapel. Wearing this Nazi outfit, Josef repeatedly bluffed his way into Gestapo headquarters and reconned it with impunity.

Over a period of several months, Josef developed a network comprising dozens of dedicated collaborators across all strata of Czechoslovak society. They included well-known personalities from political and military circles, rank-and-file military men, simple tradesmen, government functionaries, and even a cemetery watchman. Many were contacts Josef had made through Sokol, a patriotic gymnastics organization to which he belonged.[2]

Despite Josef's vow to take no more orders, he and his associates were soon coordinating closely with the exiled Czechoslovak military leadership in London. As in World War I, the Czechs would have to prove themselves. Only if the British, French, and Americans found them worthwhile allies would they have any hope of winning back their own state.

The Three Kings and their collaborators ran an underground railroad, smuggling people who wanted to join Allied armies out of Axis territory. Their organization printed fliers and illegal newspapers. It obtained valuable intelligence on new German weapons systems. Through contacts in the Plzen Skoda works, the massive complex of armaments factories that produced tanks, armored troop carriers, and guns of all kinds, they obtained blueprints for a new German twin-barrel machine gun and smuggled them to London. They also managed to assemble a complete set of blueprints of the formidable new Tiger tank and dispatch them to London via Romania.[3]

Just months after the fall of Czechoslovakia, the Germans steamrolled through Poland. Within four weeks, the country ceased to exist. France fell in just under six weeks, and by 1941 Britain was fighting for its life. The German war machine seemed unstoppable, and American reporters in Berlin were grimly witnessing bets on the number of weeks until the swastika flew over London.[4] Air Minister Hermann Goering's boast that German cities would never feel the scourge of Allied bombs seemed to have the force of inevitability on its side. It was during these darkest hours of the war that the Three Kings brought the war into the heart of the Reich—right to Hitler's doorstep.

They orchestrated a sabotage campaign that resulted in the destruction of telephone lines, railway lines, bridges, and fuel depots. Dr. Felix Man, another collaborator of Josef's who was employed at the Semtin works, which manufactured explosives, smuggled hundreds of pounds of dynamite and several boxes of blasting caps out of the heavily guarded plant. Associates who repaired Gestapo vehicles at their shop audaciously ferried these explosives and other weapons to Prague right under the Gestapo's nose, in the Gestapo's very own automobiles, which they took out for extended "test drives."[5] Master tinsmith Josef Likar, his wife Marie, and her brothers Vaclav and Frantisek Rehak turned their Prague-area workshop into a clandestine armaments factory. Using the materials from Semtin, they manufactured over two thousand bombs to Josef Masin's design. Disguised as coal briquettes, they were hidden in coal shipments destined for factories in the Reich and planted in wagons of hay and straw.[6]

The Three Kings also went after high-profile targets right in the center of Berlin. Major Ctibor Novak, Zdena Masinova's brother, had found a new job as a Wehrmacht translator in Berlin. On 15 September 1939, he planted bombs from the Likar family's workshop at the Reich Luftfahrtsministerium (Aviation Ministry) and the Reich Police Directorate.* Novak got as far as

---

*News of these spectacular explosions was broadcast by the BBC. William Shirer mentions these explosions in his "Berlin Diary," 218. He points out that no German newspaper or radio program carried reports on these attacks. See also Procházka, *Sestupme ke kořením*, 109.

the Austro-Yugoslav border, where he was shot in the leg during a gun battle and taken prisoner.[7] But though the Germans managed to arrest him, they never figured out that he was the man who had bombed the government offices in Berlin:[8] Novak didn't crack under brutal Gestapo interrogations and he named no names. He disappeared into Gestapo jails, and his family had no further word of him.[9]

The Three Kings organization also made an unsuccessful attempt on Heinrich Himmler's life,* exploding a bomb in the Anhalt Railway Station in Berlin in February 1941. Two train conductors who had secretly transported the explosives to Berlin and deposited them in a luggage storage office at the Anhalt station were later arrested and executed.[10]

Most valuable to the war effort and to the government-in-exile's struggle to win recognition from Britain and the United States was the Three Kings' contact with "René." "René," aka "Franta," aka "Eva," aka "A-54," was actually Paul Thümmel—a high-ranking Nazi party member and personal friend of Heinrich Himmler. The quality of the information he delivered was peerless. Indeed, the Allies had no other agent within the Nazi power structure with his unparalleled access to such a vast range of highly privileged information. A trusted employee of the Abwehr, Germany's powerful counterintelligence apparatus, he sat at the confluence point of all German intelligence and military planning. René provided London, through his contacts with the Three Kings, with accurate and detailed information about Hitler's military strategy for the invasion of Poland; about Operation Sealion, the planned invasion of Britain; and about Operation Barbarossa, the German invasion of the Soviet Union. The Three Kings forwarded this information to Britain by means of their secret transmitter, code-named Sparta II.

During this time the Gestapo did not sit idle. It infiltrated noncommunist resistance groups in the Bohemian protectorate. A wave of arrests rolled outward from the group operating Sparta I, the other secret transmitter in the Bohemian protectorate. Through these captives, and through agents infiltrated into the resistance, the Gestapo learned the identities of the Three Kings, their major nemesis, and the existence of their transmitter, Sparta II. From then on Masin, Balaban, and Moravek were on the run. One after another, their apartments and safe houses were compromised. They hauled

---

*Himmler was the second most powerful individual in the Nazi state after Hitler. He created the SS, eventually building it into an empire within the Third Reich. He was also the architect of the vast system of concentration camps, and controlled the Gestapo and the entire German police system.

their bulky transmitters from one safe house to another as the noose around them drew steadily tighter.

The Gestapo's first direct move against the Three Kings was a raid on their flat in Perstejn. It housed Moravek's card file on informers, forged police forms with the appropriate stamps, and other essential materials. Moravek, forewarned of the raid by René and his counterintelligence connections, was able to evacuate the materials in time. Even in the face of adversity, Moravek couldn't resist baiting the Gestapo. Before locking up the apartment he left a note on the table, written first in German, then in Czech, exactly as the regulations of the Protectorate dictated:

Leck' mich am arsch
Polibte mi prdel!
(Kiss my ass!)[11]

The battle of wits and words between the Three Kings and Oskar Fleischer, the head of the Gestapo's Counterintelligence Department, continued. When the Three Kings had to evacuate yet another apartment, the only thing they left behind for the Gestapo was Moravek's overcoat. Not long afterward Fleischer got a postcard from Yugoslavia in German:

Lieber Oskar,

You scoundrel! I have to inform you that I have had to move to a warmer clime since you stole my overcoat, you villain! I no longer feel safe under the protection of your Great German Reich. . . .

Fleischer was convinced now that the Three Kings had fled abroad.[12] One evening as he was relaxing at the Prikopy bar, smoking a cigar and enjoying a drink, a German fellow with a swastika on his lapel approached and politely requested a light for his cigarette. Fleischer obligingly held out his cigar, the Nazi lit his cigarette and thanked him. A few days later the head of the Prague Gestapo called Fleischer into his office and asked him how things were going with those Three Kings.* Fleischer explained to him that they were abroad. Geschke handed him a sealed envelope addressed to

---

*On Epiphany, the Day of the Three Kings, young Catholics walk from house to house singing and writing the letters C + M + B (for Caspar, Melchior, and Balthasar) over the front doors. The moniker "Three Kings," by which the Gestapo designated Balabán, Morávek, and Mašín, was derived from their signature B + M + M.

the head of the Gestapo, with a respectful request to pass it on to Commissar Fleischer. Inside was a letter:

> Oskar you scoundrel!
>
> I had a bet with Masin and Balaban that I could light my cigarette from your cigar. I bet them one thousand crowns and I am hereby informing you that I won the bet on Tuesday. Stop tormenting the Czech people or you will pay dearly. We know all about you and you won't escape our revenge. Don't forget it.
>
> B + M + M

Fleischer was furious. Everyone was laughing at his expense and people stopped him in the halls to ask for a light.[13]

The Three Kings published an underground newspaper called "*V Boj*" (To Arms). A new issue was printed every Thursday, using equipment at an industrial print works. The Three Kings saw to it that the Gestapo got a complimentary copy with the following note:

> If you wish to know the truth, the editorial team is sending you a copy of this magazine free of charge, so that you do not have to go to the trouble of finding it yourselves. Furthermore, we pledge to send you a single copy of each subsequent edition.
>
> Yours sincerely. Death to the occupiers.
>
> B + M + M[14]

In May 1940 the Gestapo arrested Dr. Felix Man, the Three Kings' contact at the Semtin works, as well as two other underground associates. In April 1942 all three were executed in Berlin.[15] The Nazi authorities ratcheted up their hunt for the Three Kings. In addition to the Gestapo, the Czech police were mobilized, and it became increasingly difficult for the Three Kings to recruit collaborators and groom successors to take over in the event they were captured or killed.

Hell-bent on catching Josef and his collaborators, Gestapo Commissar Fleischer ordered the Masin family's apartment raided once a week, sometimes even more often.

Late one night a loud ring startled nine-year-old Radek, eight-year-old Pepa, and their little sister Nenda out of their sleep. It was the doorbell. The three children lay in their beds wide awake, straining to hear what was happening outside. Manya,* the family's maid, padded over to the door, the sound of her steps muffled by the hall rug. Then the bolt rattled and the door swung open. A man said something loudly in German.

"You have no business bothering the family so late at night!" Manya declared indignantly in broken Czech. Her German accent was strong.

"Schämen Sie sich nicht? Aren't you ashamed of yourself?" the men scolded. "How dare you work for that Czech scum! Where's your loyalty to your Führer and the fatherland?"

"I'm a Czech!" Manya's voice rose. "And I'm proud of it!"

"You're a traitor to your nation!" They shoved past her into the apartment.

Seconds later the door to the children's room flew open and the light came on. A couple of Gestapo men wearing leather coats strode inside while the children lay in their beds screwing their eyes shut, pretending to sleep. The strangers yanked open drawers and closets, dumping the contents out onto the floor and speaking to each other in harsh, guttural tones that the frightened children couldn't understand.

"Los, raus aus den Betten! Get out of bed!" the men ordered.

"Leave the little ones alone!" Manya cried as she hurried in. "They're only children!"

The men pushed her aside. They looked under the beds and tossed aside down comforters. Quickly Radek and Pepa scooted past them to Manya. She was blonde and petite, and the menacing strangers towered over her, but where the children and the welfare of their mother were concerned, she was fearless. She pushed the two boys behind her and stood facing the intruders like a protective mother hen. Nenda, her legs and arms immobilized in metal braces, lay in bed unable to move. She trembled in fear as the Gestapo men ripped the blanket off her.

Next door other Gestapo men were shouting at Zdena. The children could hear their mother's strained voice responding. "No, no. I don't know anything. He's in Yugoslavia! I told you, I haven't heard from him in months."

"Where is your father?" The men grabbed Radek and Pepa.

One of them turned to five-year-old Nenda, "I have a suitcase full of money for your daddy, if you tell me where he is! When is he coming home?"

Nenda stared at him with large, frightened eyes.

"If you lie to us you will go to hell!" the stranger threatened her.

---

*Maria Neubauer. The children called her Manya.

But all their threats and inducements were useless; it was the spring of 1940, and the children hadn't seen their father for more than a year.

One morning in March 1940, the Masins' doorbell rang. Manya looked down through the bedroom window. Two black Mercedes were parked in front of the house. When she opened the door, Gestapo men in civilian clothes burst in. The children saw them hustle their mother into her bedroom. They heard the men shout at her, cross-examining her in loud voices. Then they ordered her to take her clothes off and strip-searched her. "If your husband doesn't report to the Gestapo within three days," they said, "we'll arrest you, your maid, and your mother-in-law!" They left with a parting threat: "We'll be back this afternoon!" Peering through the bedroom curtains, Manya and Zdena watched them get into the cars and drive off. Once they were sure the coast was clear, the two women hurried downstairs to the family's basement storage room, keeping an eye out for any guards the Gestapo might have left. Hastily they dumped a mixture of water and sand into a barrel of gasoline that Josef had stored there. Then they shoved a box of sugar and a box of soap into the neighbor's storage room.

When the doorbell rang again, a green prisoners' van, a couple of military command cars and a black Mercedes had pulled up outside the house. Uniformed SS men were blocking off all the downstairs doors. Manya opened the door. Again a squad of Gestapo men burst into the apartment. Again they confined Zdena to her bedroom. Then the SS moved in and systematically began emptying drawers and closets, hauling the family's possessions downstairs and loading them into the waiting van. Manya gathered the kids together and told them to stay out of the way. She followed the Germans around the apartment while little Pepa, Nenda, and Radek watched from their corner in silence.

The Germans took linens, dishes, silverware, Zdena's personal effects, the sewing machine, the children's toys, even the family's food supply. One of the SS men left to requisition the family's nearly new Skoda Rapid car. When they rolled the barrel of gasoline out onto the street, the youngsters fiercely cherished the small revenge Zdena and Manya had taken. At least briefly, a few Gestapo cars would be put out of commission. When the Gestapo drove off with the last load, the family was left with Zdena's baby grand piano, which was too heavy to move, one box of soap, one box of sugar, and little else. In 1940, food rationing was strictly enforced in the Bohemian

Protectorate. The Gestapo's confiscation of the family's food stash was a major disaster.

Days later the Gestapo turned the family out of their empty apartment, confiscated all the money in the their bank accounts and stopped Josef's income from his investments. The Masins were homeless now and absolutely penniless. Fearing arrest, Zdena faked a nervous breakdown. A physician friend of the family checked her into his sanatorium and hid her from the Gestapo for almost three months. After she was discharged from the clinic at the end of June, Zdena joined her family in the Bohemian spa town of Podebrady where, she let it be known, she was continuing her cure. Meanwhile, Zdena's mother Emma had come to the rescue with emergency funds. She rented a house along with some odds and ends of furniture.

Zdena hoped for some respite in Podebrady. Before the war, the fashionable little spa town had been a favorite destination for civil servants, military officers and their wives. The pace of life was leisurely. There was a manicured park and a tree-shaded promenade lined with comfortable hotels. But in Zdena's eyes the best thing about the place was its location. Podebrady lay fifty kilometers outside Prague, far enough to deter the Prague Gestapo from conducting regular house searches.

Though less frequent, the Gestapo raids continued. When the Gestapo believed Masin might contact his family, agents shadowed all members of the household, even the children, around the clock, to no avail. The children's father did not turn up. That is, until one night in March 1941.

Radek woke up to see his father standing in the room, looking down at him. When Josef saw that he was awake, he ducked behind the sofa, but Radek, overcome with joy, leapt out of bed and ran over to him. Josef sat him on his knee and told him in a grave tone, "Radousku, don't tell anyone that you saw me. All right?"

Radek gave his solemn promise.

Josef gripped his son's shoulders and looked him in the eye. "In the end," he said, "the victory against the Germans will be ours. A death sentence has been passed on the Germans. They think they have overcome us and hold us in their hand. Look!" He closed his hand to make a fist. "They think they must only close their hand, but I will escape." He pointed to the small opening between his thumb and index finger, and Radek laughed with him.

It was the last time Radek saw his father. Pepa slept soundly through it all, but the next morning little Nenda happily called out: "I saw my daddy!"

It took a lot of persuasion from the adults and from Radek to convince her that she had only been dreaming.

The pressure on the Three Kings was relentless. Money was always in short supply. It was needed to support the members of the resistance, to buy equipment and supplies, and to sustain the families of resistance members who were arrested. There was never enough, and Josef often used his personal resources to make ends meet. Balaban was arrested on 22 April 1941. Josef and Moravek were shattered by the loss of their best friend and comrade-in-arms. "They've caught Balaban," Josef transmitted to London. "Everything is burning; it's getting so that we no longer know where to lay our tired limbs."[16] But they carried on.

The next blow came on 13 May 1941. At their rendezvous that afternoon, René had told Josef that the physical description of the Three Kings' last remaining safe house had been beaten out of one of Josef's contacts in the Gestapo jails and it was only a question of time until the Gestapo identified the location. At that same meeting René gave Josef another packet of intelligence materials.* Josef and Moravek agreed the information was hot. It had to be transmitted without delay, in spite of the risk.

The Gestapo had no idea what a great prize they would find in Pod Terebkou Street, an unremarkable suburban cul-de-sac lined with apartment buildings. Josef arrived first, shortly before 7:00 PM. His friends and family wouldn't have recognized him: normally clean-shaven, he now sported slicked-back hair, a trim little Hitler-style mustache and glasses with clear window-glass inserts. He had become a retiring, bookish type with a shy, self-effacing air. Moravek, also in disguise, showed up shortly afterward and greeted Josef inside the entryway with a slight nod.

"All clear, let's go."

The two men climbed the stairs to the fourth floor, their footsteps echoing off the bare walls in the stairwell. Frantisek Peltán, their radioman, cracked the door to his apartment and quickly admitted them. Inside the cramped space, the three men quickly set up the bulky wireless set with a smooth routine born of practice and started transmitting. A dog barked somewhere in the building. They disregarded it. Suddenly, the doorbell

---

*The materials may have related to Operation Barbarossa, the German attack on the Soviet Union, which was slated to begin on 22 June 1941.

shrilled three times, two long rings followed by a short one. Morse code for the letter G, the Gestapo's calling card.

"They're here!" Josef said.

The room erupted into a frenzy of activity. Moravek and Peltán rushed to destroy the transmitter and the documents. Josef strode over to the door. He cocked his pistol, opened the door, and shot the closest Gestapo agent. Another Gestapo man fired back. Josef returned fire. The remaining agents flung themselves on Josef and tried to disarm him. He was worth more to them alive than dead. The struggling knot of men tumbled out into the stairwell and Josef shouted for help. Behind him, the apartment door slammed shut and locked. Josef's foot caught in the iron bars of the banister. As he fell to the ground his leg broke at the shin, but he continued to fight furiously, repeatedly firing at the Gestapo agents, who returned fire at point-blank range. Two shots hit him, first his stomach, then his right wrist. Only then did the Gestapo men succeed in wresting the gun from his grasp.

Moravek and Peltán, trapped in the apartment, hurriedly improvised an exit. Tying a thin steel radio aerial to the leg of a sofa, they clambered out the window and slid down, free-falling most of the fifty feet to the courtyard below. In the process, Moravek nearly sliced off one of his fingers; it dangled from his hand by a piece of skin and he was losing a lot of blood. The two men hit the ground just as the Gestapo agents broke down the door and stormed the apartment. Peltán seriously injured both legs as he landed. He and Moravek barely escaped with their lives.

With Josef's capture, two of the Three Kings were in the hands of the Gestapo. The last transmitter and safe house were gone.[17]

When the Czech ambulance personnel arrived at the scene, they found Josef lying on the landing with his arms flung apart, a Gestapo man standing on each arm. He was unconscious and seriously wounded, yet they were instructed to treat and transport the Gestapo men first. Only then did they take Josef to an SS hospital for surgery.

Four days later, on 17 May 1941, the Gestapo ran ads in all the Prague daily papers. They screened appeals to the public before every movie shown in Prague theaters. Above a photo of the bespectacled man with the trim little moustache a headline shouted, "Who knows this man?" The ads called on the public to help identify the mysterious stranger who, they announced, had died after being found in the street, unconscious and gravely injured.[18]

Gestapo Commissar Fleischer went through the unknown man's pockets. The identity papers turned out to be false, and, although he found no corroboration, Fleischer was fairly sure that this man was one of the Three Kings, the trio of Czech ex-military men whose effective resistance group was a major thorn in the Germans' side.

When Josef regained consciousness, he attempted to escape from the hospital by hitting the guard over the head with his urine bottle and wresting away his weapon. But Josef was still weak. The blow failed to knock the Gestapo man out and he called for backup. Josef, quickly overpowered, was promptly shipped off to the Pankrac prison hospital.

Chapter 4

THE HOME FRONT

Zdena had maintained tenuous contact with her husband throughout his two long, difficult years in the underground. When the days stretched into weeks without word from him, she began to fear the worst. She kept her thoughts to herself, but in the evenings, after the children were put to bed, she was alone with the growing realization that she might have lost her husband. The children were too young—she couldn't talk with them. Her mother, Emma, lived several hundred kilometers away. Even though the two women never spoke about the emotional turmoil that Zdena was going through, Manya understood intuitively what was happening.

On 6 January 1942, the second blow fell. Hearing an automobile pull up in front of the house, nine-year-old Pepa ran to look. In those days, there were very few cars in Podebrady and any car in the street was an unusual event. From the living room window he saw four men in civilian clothes get out of a big black Mercedes. The driver remained by the car; the other three ran up the steps to the house and rang the bell. When Manya opened the door, their leader, a man in his 50s with a hard, meaty-looking face, announced himself. It was Gestapo Commissar Fleischer. He had come for Zdena. Manya tried to stop him, but he pushed her aside and told her to stay out of it. Zdena appeared at the door looking silent and pale.

"Get out into the car," Fleischer ordered.

"But the children . . ." Zdena protested.

Pepa was watching in silence. He could see that his mother was worried.

"Never mind the kids!" Fleischer said. And he told Manya, who was still protesting: "Shut up, woman, or we'll arrest you too! She'll be back shortly."

The other Gestapo men did a quick sweep of the house and then marched Zdena out to the car. She only had time for one backward glance before the doors slammed shut and the car roared off. Zdena was gone. Pepa stood beside Manya in the doorway. While Manya wept and prayed, imploring Jesus and Mary to save the children's mother, the little boy next to her stood dry-eyed and outwardly impassive. Pepa hated the Germans with a cold, deadly intensity. The fact that he was only a small boy made this hate even more intense, for it was suffused with a sense of impotence. They had taken everything from him. Even his mother.

Faithful Manya stayed on in the little house in Na Chmelnici Street to care for her three babies. She had come to the family just after Pepa's birth, and she loved these children like her very own. Money was short. Food in the shops was only available on ration cards, and the rations for non-Aryans weren't sufficient to nourish growing children, so Manya had to scrounge up supplementary food from farmers in the surrounding villages.

Then word reached her of a new calamity. The Nazi authorities had slated the two boys, who were healthy, blue-eyed, and blond, for aryanization. They were to be taken away, adopted by childless SS couples, and raised as members of the "master race." But a different fate awaited little Nenda. In the Nazi scheme of things handicapped children were considered unworthy of life. They were killed by lethal injection or gassed in one of the infamous death camps. Manya immediately alerted Grandmother Emma, who hurried to Podebrady. With her usual determination, she launched a frontal assault on Nazi officialdom. Emma Novakova was, as it happened, of German descent, and she impressed upon the official responsible, in flawless German, that these children were going to be raised as true Germans. She would see to it personally. The Nazi official was apparently convinced, because the aryanization order was rescinded and Emma stayed in the house on Na Chmelnici Street.

After several months, in May of 1942, Zdena returned home to Podebrady. She looked haggard and drawn, but for the sake of her children she put on a brave face and said little of her experiences in prison. The family's joy was of short duration. She was arrested again a mere six days later. No reason was given for her release or rearrest. In August Zdena Masinova returned home from the Theresienstadt concentration camp, exhausted, pale, and bone thin. She was diagnosed with a heart ailment.

By late 1944 the war had turned against the Germans. Vast formations of American bombers passed over Podebrady virtually unopposed, destined

for targets in Bohemia and southern Germany. As the high-flying formations droned overhead, streaking the sky with ribbons of white, the ground
shook and windows rattled. Thirteen-year-old Radek, eleven-year-old Pepa
and their friends watched in awed excitement. They idolized the American
pilots and fantasized about flying machines like these. Pepa made up his
mind: he would be a pilot when he grew up. One day the boys watched an
American P-51 Mustang chase and shoot down a slower German JU-88.
Pepa, Radek, and their friends cheered the American pilot and eagerly ran to
pick up the spent cartridges, which were still warm to the touch. But the airplanes and the war they represented remained always out of reach, always
over the horizon. The boys were too young to take part in the battles that
were shaping their destiny.

Nevertheless, Pepa and Radek were determined to do their part in the
war effort. At night they went to the railway line. When the semaphore
switched to red, they jumped aboard eastbound trains hauling tanks, airplanes, and guns. With their hammers they smashed the airplane hydraulic
lines, instrumentation, every component that would break.

In the fall of 1944, the Germans began bringing work gangs of pinched
and starving Russian POWs through Podebrady. Pepa furtively urged two
Russian officers to run away, telling them to meet him that night. When they
showed up at the appointed spot, he led them home. Sheltering one Russian
(the other man soon took off on his own) was an extremely hazardous proposition, since the family was already in the crosshairs of the Gestapo, under
constant surveillance, and subject to surprise house searches. Pepa and Radek
prepared a hiding place for the Russian by breaking a hole in the bathroom
ventilation shaft, but a determined search by the Gestapo was always a risk.
What was more, the family had to stretch their rations to feed an additional
mouth. They knew that they would suffer serious consequences if caught,
but that didn't deter them. They were committed to fighting the Germans.

During the last months of the war, trains from the extermination camps in
Poland began rolling through Bohemia toward the west. They hauled open
railroad cars packed with inmates. In the bitter cold, the emaciated prisoners succumbed in droves and the survivors stripped the dead naked and
threw them overboard. Local people scavenging for coal would find twisted,
skeletal corpses lying along the railroad tracks. In this terrible human detri-
tus, residents of nearby villages discovered three Jews who still showed signs
of life. The survivors ultimately ended up in the care of Josef Masin's friend

Colonel Frantisek Vanek, who hid them in the forest near the village of Kouty. Some time before, Pepa, Radek and their friends had found a collection of sand banks there that were home to a large rabbit colony and had enlarged some of the bigger rabbit holes with the idea of turning them into a secret clubhouse. Pepa and Radek showed Vanek the rabbit warren when he told them about the Jews. It ultimately accommodated the Russian, the three Jews, and two other Russians who had escaped and made contact with Colonel Vanek's network. Until the fugitives could be sent to join the partisans in Slovakia, the Masins helped feed them from their already meager rations and the food they scrounged up in the villages.

The terrible fate of the Jews also drew Podebrady families into its vortex. There was a family of Jewish evacuees in Podebrady, with whom Zdena and her sons were acquainted. They had two children. In 1941, they got an order to show up at the train station the next day, with a limited luggage allowance. "That's going to end badly," Zdena told Pepa. "We must get them out of here." She tried to talk them into fleeing, explaining that she would help them escape via Switzerland. Zdena urged them to meet her at the church by the museum in Podebrady on the night before the transport. But, though Zdena and Pepa waited as promised, the Jewish family didn't show up. "Oh no," they had assured Zdena. "The Germans said they only want to resettle us somewhere in Poland." They were resettled in Poland; in Auschwitz. They never returned.

By early 1945 the Soviet army was hurtling westward toward the Bohemian Protectorate. The German Wehrmacht was fleeing head-over-heels. German soldiers threw away their weapons and ran, stealing bicycles and baby carriages, anything with wheels, to get themselves and their wounded comrades away from the Soviets. They limped, shuffled, and cycled westward toward the Americans and safety, mingling with the endless treks of German civilians from Silesia and East Prussia, who were fleeing from the Soviet army with all their worldly goods piled high on horse-drawn wagons and handcarts. "It was totally chaotic," Pepa later remembered. "Panicked people pushing baby carriages filled with household goods. Oxcarts with bedsteads and old people in them." The streets of Podebrady were packed with the slow-moving refugee columns heading for the American lines. Hundreds of tanks, cars, and trucks stood abandoned along the roads where they had run out of gas. The only cars still moving were jury-rigged with wood-burning gas generators. The collapse of the Thousand-Year Reich was total.

American forces reached Czech lands before the Soviets. But when Patton's forces rolled into the city of Plzen, ninety miles west of Podebrady, Roosevelt stopped the American advance. At dawn on 6 May, General Eisenhower ordered Patton to reject the pleas of Czech democrats to take Prague. The United States would honor the Yalta agreement, which officially consigned Czechoslovakia to the Soviet sphere of influence.

The Yalta pact of February 1945 reflected a continuation of longstanding U.S. policy. "Do not rely too much on any considerable American participation in the postwar reorganization of Europe," John Foster Dulles had told Eduard Benes in July 1942. "In America there is very little idealism, and the United States will stand firm only where it has its own direct interests."[1] On 8 May 1945, Germany surrendered and the United States proceeded to disengage from Europe as rapidly as possible to concentrate on the war in the Pacific. The following day Soviet forces marched into Prague and Czechoslovakia was effectively under the Soviet yoke.

The day of the German surrender, a couple of strange-looking personnel carriers appeared in Podebrady, weaving their way among the masses of fleeing Germans. Then more showed up in clusters, and by afternoon there was a steady stream of trucks and jeeps. All Podebrady turned out to greet the arriving Red Army forces. People lined the roads cheering and laughing, waving flags and throwing flowers at them.

Within twenty-four hours, the Russians had rounded up more than ten thousand German soldiers in a field outside Podebrady and strung a barbed-wire fence around them, setting up a makeshift POW cage. Though Pepa, Radek, and their friends had no idea what happened to the POWs when they were finally taken away, one of the German soldiers in that field would later touch their lives in a surprising way. In any event, no one gave them much thought. The entire country surged with euphoria at being liberated, and along with that euphoria came a wave of Pan-Slavic fervor. Czechs were uncritically enthusiastic about everything having to do with the Russians. People joined the Communist Party in droves.

The young boys of Podebrady bitterly regretted being too young to fight the Germans. Pepa, Radek, and their friends were eleven, twelve, and thirteen years old. Descriptions of soldiers and their heroic deeds in battle were everywhere, and, more than anything, the boys wanted to emulate them and fight in the war. Discarded weapons and abandoned vehicles of the fleeing

Wehrmacht were scattered across the whole country. Antiaircraft projectiles lay in the fields and along the roads. In the train station, 30-mm antiaircraft guns and quantities of munitions stood where the Germans had left them. Eagerly the boys scavenged through the abandoned armaments and appropriated the best pieces for themselves. Junior Podebrady society became a gun culture. After the end of the war through 1947, almost every Boy Scout had at least one gun.

The children's uncle Ctibor Novak miraculously reemerged out of the chaos of the German collapse. He arrived in style, smartly attired and driving a luxurious Mercedes 540K Cab A, which he had received as a gift from the Americans, along with a generous quantity of gasoline canisters. After his arrest in September 1939, he had spent the duration of the war in Gestapo jails and upon his return he was so swept up in the Pan-Slavic euphoria that he immediately joined the Communist Party.

One by one, Josef's friends who had served in the allied forces in exile returned home to Czechoslovakia. One of these returnees was General Jan Studlar, who drove to Podebrady as soon as he returned from the Eastern Front, where he had been commanding a Czechoslovak unit attached to the Red Army. It was an emotional reunion. His staff car pulled up in front of the Masins' house unannounced. When the uniformed general got out, Pepa recognized him immediately, although he had not seen him for six years. The Studlars and the Masins had spent many country weekends together before the war. Jan Studlar and his wife were childless, and they had a special place in their heart for Josef and Zdena's children. Studlar looked at the three children through his glasses, spread his arms and gathered them in, with tears in his eyes. "If your father is still alive somewhere," he assured them, "he will come home. It won't be long." Yet he, too, feared the worst. He knew from communications with England during the war that Josef had been captured by the Gestapo, but he didn't have the heart to destroy Zdena's last hopes.

Now only Josef was still missing. Somewhere, somehow, in the devastation and ruin that followed the collapse of the Third Reich, Zdena hoped that he had managed to survive. Rumors periodically surfaced that he was with the Slovak partisans, then that he was in prison about to be released. Refusing to give up hope, Zdena made numerous radio appeals begging anyone with information about her husband to come forward. She chased down every rumor—to no avail. Josef had vanished.

Meanwhile, in 1945, Manya married and moved away. A new girl was hired to help in the household, but she didn't work out and before long the ailing Zdena found herself handling the household alone. Nenda's special needs and two rambunctious boys were more than she could handle. Once again Grandmother Emma returned to help, but Zdena's relaxed approach to housekeeping drove the highly organized, controlling Emma to distraction. Zdena's childrearing philosophy was another source of friction.

"My children are my friends," Zdena would say.

"Children cannot be friends," Emma replied. "That is impossible—they must be disciplined," to which Zdena retorted, "I don't want to be a police-man!" And Emma would scold her.

Josef, who had enjoyed the respect and boundless admiration of his iron-willed mother-in-law, had mediated conflicts between the two women in the past, but he wasn't around anymore to intercede. After a few months of argument with her daughter, Emma left. She took Nenda with her and went to keep house for her son Ctibor, or Borek, as the family knew him, who received an army posting in the Sudetenland. Zdena enrolled Pepa and Radek as boarding students in the brand-new King George College in Podebrady. Everyone believed the split-up of the family was temporary. When Josef returned, they would be reunited.

King George College was housed in Podebrady castle, a medieval pile with a moat and plumbing fixtures that hadn't been updated since the middle of the nineteenth century. The boarding school was the brainchild of one Dr. Jahoda, an educator who dreamt of building a top-flight academic institution in Czechoslovakia. He modeled his school on the great English public schools, Eton and Harrow, and recruited a team of dedicated teachers who shared his vision. When it became apparent that the new school would be offering an education second to none, high-ranking politicians and well-situated industrialists flocked to enroll their progeny. Ironically, top Communist apparatchiks had no qualms about sending their sons to this bastion of elitism. Other pupils included Milos Forman, who later became an Academy Award–winning film director; Ivan Passer and Jerzy Skolimovsky, who became acclaimed film directors in their own right; and Vaclav Havel, the future president of the Czech Republic.

While Radek was generally a model student, with flawless classroom comportment and a high grade point average, Pepa's favorite place in the classroom was the back row. Securely ensconced in the rear of the room, he kept up a steady flow of diversions that drove his teachers to distraction. Much to his teachers' despair, his quick mind and considerable inventiveness were firmly focused on keeping himself and his fellow backbenchers entertained.

For a while, life settled down again to a routine of sorts. The boys' lives revolved around the Sokol sports league and the Czech Boy Scouts, which were revived along with other civic organizations outlawed by the Nazis. Zdena tried to make her sons appreciate the finer things in life. She enrolled Pepa in violin lessons, which he attended with his friend Milan Paumer, and Radek in piano lessons. The boys, however, were more interested in weapons and cars. After school, when they weren't kicking soccer balls or attending scout meetings, the boys in Podebrady continued to go out to play with rocket launchers and submachine guns. Pepa did find a use for his violin case—minus the violin. He used it to carry his submachine gun to target practice. He never did acquire the taste for classical music that his mother wanted to impart to him.

In late 1945, through the good offices of Colonel Vanek, Radek joined the Czechoslovak irregulars who reoccupied the Sudetenland. The skinny fourteen-year-old, whose mother had returned from Theresienstadt concentration camp an ailing, broken woman, whose uncle had been tortured in Gestapo jails, whose father had been hunted down by the Gestapo, and who had seen the corpses and walking skeletons of Auschwitz and Birkenau with his own eyes, marched off into the Sudetenland to exact retribution. It was the fall of 1945, and he stood proudly to have his picture taken in uniform, a tall, gangly teenager in an ill-fitting uniform. Pepa was disappointed and terribly envious of his older brother: at age thirteen he was still too young to be a soldier. In 1945 and 1946 two and a half million ethnic Germans were forcibly evicted from the Sudetenland.

Hints of Josef Masin's fate began to reach the family, and they were not good. Shortly after the war, a Mrs. Vrnatova had gotten in touch with Zdena. She explained that her husband Vojtech had been incarcerated at Pankrac, the notorious Gestapo-run prison. Unlike Zdena, she'd had visitation rights, and her husband told her that Josef Masin was his cellmate. Vojtech himself was executed and the woman could tell Zdena nothing of Josef's fate, but Pankrac was known to be a way station to the concentration camps in the east and to the executioner's scaffold.

Sometime after this first meeting with Zdena, Mrs. Vrnatova looked through the letters her husband had written and secretly passed to her during their meetings. In one of them, she read that Josef Masin had hidden a letter in a crack in the wall of their prison cell. She reported her discovery.

On a sweltering July afternoon in 1946, a Czech Pankrac prison official placed a piece of folded toilet tissue into Zdena's hands.

When she returned to their home in Na Chmelnici Street, fifteen-year-old Radek, fourteen-year-old Pepa, and twelve-year-old Nenda followed her into the family's tiny living-dining room and took seats around the black lacquered table. They waited quietly, anxiously, while their mother carefully smoothed out the fragile paper. The door to the terrace was closed. Through the open windows no sound could be heard. Not even the crickets were chirping.

Zdena cleared her throat and began reading aloud, struggling to decipher the smudged letters on the fragile tissue. Tears ran down her cheeks. Her voice was thick with emotion.

My dear children!

I send you this last letter before my departure into eternity. My last thought is of you and I am especially sad that you are still small and in need of my greatest care. Unfortunately I must leave you.

Today you will not yet comprehend everything, but when you are older I am sure you will understand me. I fought for our dear homeland and nation against our eternal foes, the Germans, who have enslaved our nation and wish to destroy it. I do not wish for you to live as slaves in the future, rather, you should live as liberated and free citizens. Remember that the first obligation of every conscious Czech is to defend the freedom of the nation. You too must in the future proceed in this way. In this fight I was vanquished. I believe however that our sacred cause will prevail. You remain here now with your mother. You must obey her so that you lighten her heavy lot and lighten her tasks and her cares in you. You, Radek, are the oldest. I know that you are a responsible and serious boy. Be a support and advisor to Pepa and Nenda. You must stand in for me and I rely on you. You, Pepicku, must help your mommy and Radek. Care for Nenuska and never leave her. She, poor child, will need your care always. You should love each other and do not abandon each other. Help each other through

love and reason. Learn diligently so that you will be educated and successful people. Always be conscientious and honest and now you too, my dear
Nenuska, my sweet girl. Be happy and do not forget your daddy who loved
you so. I know that you have a good little heart and that you love your
mommy and your brothers. . . . Boys, I have one more wish. One of you
should take over the family farm. It is however no obligation. Should you
not wish it, you don't have to. With this I finish, my dear children. I kiss
you in my spirit and your mommy too. Be happy.

Your loving father

Zdena was weeping openly now. After months of searching and hoping,
after the countless radio appeals, after tirelessly chasing down every lead,
however tenuous, it was all over. The children sat in silence. They knew that
their father wouldn't be coming home.

Suddenly, there was a loud bang on the patio door. It sounded like a
heavy, booted foot.

"Who's there?" shouted Radek. "Who kicked the door?"

Pepa and Radek jumped up and ran outside, but there wasn't a soul in
sight. Everything was completely still, as before.

Radek knew that his father had given them a sign. His spirit was taking
leave from the family.

Although the two boys never discussed the letter after that reading,
it became the single most powerful influence in their lives. Their father
had dedicated his life to fighting for freedom. He believed that a man was
defined by his character. To the bitter end he had refused to compromise
his principles. It was this patriotism and sense of duty and honor that he
bequeathed his sons.

Gradually, over the following months and years, the family pieced together
the story of Josef's final months.

As soon as Josef arrived in the Pankrac prison, the director of the prison,
an infamous SS sadist named Soppa,* thrashed him with a whip so brutally
that the Czech prison personnel feared he would die. After that he was put
in solitary confinement and left without any medical care.[2] Josef had still
not recovered from his wounds when the Gestapo started its regimen of torture and intensive interrogation. But he continued to resist, and no Gestapo

---

*Soppa fled to Germany in 1945 and was returned to Czechoslovakia by the Allies. There he
was tried, found guilty of numerous atrocities, and executed.

man was willing to enter his cell alone. A note was posted on the door warning that the individual inside was dangerous.

Eyewitnesses saw the Gestapo transport him to night interrogations strapped into a straightjacket, through which blood flowed from open wounds. Josef lost all his hair, the skin on his head turned gray, and his body was covered with purulent scabs. Delirious and starved to a skeleton, Josef attempted suicide several times so as not to endanger his friends by forced testimony: once by hanging himself, once by cutting his veins, and once by dashing his head into a radiator. The third suicide attempt was observed by a Czech guard at Pankrac, Frantisek Kadlec. In the morning hours of 1 October 1941, upon leaving his office, Kadlec saw prison director Soppa with two Gestapo officials in the hospital garden. They were holding a man up by his chained hands and beating him against a concrete pillar. The man's face and hair were a bloody mess. He was barefoot and naked, wearing only his underwear, which was completely torn. Kadlec recognized this bloody wreck as Josef. When Soppa and the Gestapo men were done, Josef practically couldn't walk, so they dragged him off to the isolation cell. Josef tried to kill himself by running into the radiator. The attending doctor determined that he had a split skull.[3]

Josef spent thirteen months in captivity. Twice Moravek planned daring rescue attempts to free his friend, but both times his plans were thwarted by Josef's sudden removal to a different location.[4] Moravek also transmitted a message to London requesting that the Czechoslovak government-in-exile do everything in its power to save Josef, recommending an exchange for German POW officers. Though Moravek sent his message and its receipt was confirmed, London did nothing.[5]

Nevertheless, Moravek continued the contact with René, and whenever opportunity allowed would relay his valuable information to London. In March 1942, the Gestapo arrested René* and was lying in wait for Moravek at the next rendezvous. Moravek could have fled when he saw the Gestapo ambushing Vaclav Rehak, "Feshak," who was there to cover him, but abandoning his associate was not Moravek's way. He sprang to Rehak's defense. In the ensuing gun battle, Rehak was seized and Moravek was surrounded and hopelessly outgunned. With bullets in his torso and calves, he fired at

---

*Thümmel was incarcerated in Theresienstadt under a false name and killed only twelve days before the war's end, on 27 April 1945.

his pursuers a few more times. Then he put the gun to his head and pulled the trigger. Captain Vaclav Moravek died on 21 March 1942.[6]

Josef's principled resistance during the thirteen months of his captivity earned him the grudging respect of his Gestapo adversaries. In interrogations after the war, Gestapo personnel testified that he had not betrayed a single person. Soppa, during his frequent bouts of drunkenness, would marvel aloud to Czech prison employees about the extent of the torture Josef withstood: "If all the prisoners were that way," he would exclaim in a boozy haze, "we'd only have half as many prisoners here."[7]

Josef's fighting spirit was unbroken to the end. "I am no hero," he told his interrogators. "I am an officer of the Czechoslovak army and it is my sacred duty to fight for the liberation of the Czechoslovak state."[8] He was executed on 30 June 1942. As the firing squad loosed its shots at him, he cried out, "Long live the Czechoslovak Republic!"*

In 1946, President Benes personally decorated Radek and Pepa with the Czechoslovak Medal of Valor for their fight against the Nazis. It was awarded to soldiers for bravery on the battlefield and, at ages 15 and 14, the two brothers were the youngest recipients ever. They were enormously proud of this distinction. General Jan Studlar, who with Frantisek Vanek had informally assumed the role of guardian to the Masin children, saw in both boys a promise of great things to come:

6 November 1946
Dear Pepa,

Your aunt and I are proud of you and Radek. And why not? How many soldiers or officers can boast of receiving our highest honor, and the only one given for valor?

Your aunt and I congratulate you both on your high distinction. I have no doubt that in the event of war, both your chests will be decorated with

---

*Eyewitness testimony of Kripo officer Scharf as quoted in Procházka, *Sestupme ke kořenům*, 148. As is so often the case, history was written by those who survived to tell it. Others were quick to claim credit for the heroic actions of the Three Kings. Unfortunately, some of Mašín's erstwhile fellow officers, particularly those who had comfortably weathered the Nazi scourge in London exile, were irked by his scorn at their vacillation in 1938 and 1939. It took concerted action by his widow and a dedicated group of his friends in military and political circles for Josef to posthumously receive the promotion to colonel that was sidetracked by the German invasion in 1939. Subsequently, after some bureaucratic pontificating about the impossibility of a dual promotion for a dead man, he was posthumously promoted to brigadier general.

many more medals, because you are both Masins. You have in your blood all the essential characteristics of good soldiers and patriots. That is the most beautiful inheritance your famous father has left you, and you should defend it jealously. It is a command of your golden father, who loved you more than his own life, and it is his wish. Remember him often, and you will see that you will find strength in your memories. . . . I repeat, you are obligated by his memory and must fulfill his wish to become a whole man, who can make his contribution to the nation when called upon to do so. . . .

I salute you and sincerely press your right hand.

Your uncle*

Pepa and Radek saw their futures clearly: they would follow in their father's footsteps and join the Czechoslovak military. They, too, would defend their country. Eagerly they read everything about their father that they could get their hands on. They had been young children when their father disappeared from their lives forever, and now the two teenagers tried to reconcile fragmentary memories of him at home in Dolni Liboc with the towering legend described in the books and newspaper articles. "It was at that time," Radek recalled, "that we came to the decision which was to influence all of our later lives, never to surrender to anybody, to decisively resist evil and injustice, and to never let anybody or anything stop us."

---

*Personal papers of Zdena Mašínova. Studlar was not related to the Mašíns; "uncle" is used as a term of endearment.

Chapter 5

THE COMMUNISTS
SEIZE POWER

Stalin could easily have imposed a Communist government on Czechoslovakia at the end of the war. But he chose to wait, hoping that the
powerful and popular Czechoslovak Communist Party could seize power
by parliamentary means. The West viewed Czechoslovakia as a test case
of Soviet intentions, and Stalin hoped to gain the cooperation of hesitant
Western socialist parties and labor unions by showing a Communist Party
winning power by legitimate means. So, in 1947, Czechoslovakia was once
again a parliamentary democracy and life in Podebrady was peaceful.

Young high school students cruised Podebrady's promenade on foot.
Groups of girls and boys eyed each other. Those who worked up enough
courage might actually talk to a member of the opposite sex, but mostly the
young people walked and looked, and talked and laughed. On weekend evenings, everyone went dancing at the Tlapak café. While Radek and his set
came in through the front door, sometimes Pepa or one of his friends paid
the admission fee and let the rest of the gang in through the bathroom window, just to see if they could get away with it. Pepa prided himself on being
a sharp dresser and loved to dance—the girls told him he was a good dancer.
On one or two occasions, one of the rival sets needed sorting out, and the
fists would fly in Podebrady's main square under the impassive gaze of King
George on his bronze charger.

Although Pepa and Radek were close in age and shared a physical resemblance, their personalities were quite different. Where Pepa was carefree,
always up for a prank or a joke, Radek was a serious boy and mature beyond

his years. As the oldest son, with his father gone, he took his role as the man of the house seriously. He was focused on his goals, studied hard, got good grades and was interested in all things technical. Pepa, on the other hand, couldn't be bothered with schoolwork. The two brothers were intense rivals about girls, about who was right, but they always held together as brothers. Against outside threats they presented a united front.

Both Pepa and Radek were very protective of their sister. Because of her underdeveloped knee and elbow joints, Nenda suffered through an endless series of painful corrective surgeries, therapeutic baths, and agonizing exercise regimens. But in spite of it all, she was a fun-loving girl with a sunny disposition. When they were small, the boys would take her out in a little handcart, which they pulled along after them. Radek carried her on his back to and from school. When other children called her names and made fun of her handicaps, they would spring to her defense and thrash the offenders. In winter they would take her on hair-raising toboggan rides that drove their mother to distraction but thrilled the plucky little girl to no end. When Pepa came back home after an outing, Nenda, who couldn't join in the forays through the fields and woods, begged him to tell of his adventures outdoors and at school. This he did gladly and with lots of juicy detail. Pepa, closer to his sister in age and disposition than Radek, was her special protector and friend.

Both Nenda and Pepa were always up for a good joke or just plain silliness. For instance, Grandma Emma had strict rules about table manners: knives and forks had to be held just so, no drinking while eating, no laughing at the table. No silliness was allowed. In the middle of one of these solemn repasts Nenda would let herself fall down under the table, for no reason. Taking her cue, Pepa would fall down, too. Then the two of them would sit under the table and laugh. Then Pepa would tickle Nenda so she laughed harder still. Though Grandma Emma furiously scolded the two of them from above, her efforts were to no avail.

The country's peaceful idyll shattered suddenly. In February 1948 thousands of armed Communist militiamen* paraded menacingly through the streets of Prague, while frightened citizens locked themselves up at home and drew their curtains. Neither the military nor the police raised a finger against the militias. A few scattered student protests were quickly suppressed.

---

*An unconstitutional, paramilitary force created by the Communist Party as enforcers to intimidate the population.

Czechoslovak democracy died with hardly a whimper. As with the Nazis in 1938, the Communists' initial power grab was bloodless. Few people saw the putsch coming, and most had no idea that the Communists were training fighters and collecting weapons.

When martial law was declared it came as a total shock to most Podebrady residents. One morning in February, when Pepa and his brother set out for school, Communist militiamen stood everywhere. They were armed, and they were watching. The post office was occupied. The train station was occupied. The police station and the glass factory were occupied. Militiamen had taken over city hall. In each place the militia had posted five or six armed men. On every street groups of four or five men stood armed with submachine guns or rifles. A wave of arrests targeted political leaders and anybody in a position of authority who had expressed opposition to the Communists.

How could it happen? There had been signs that the Communists were prepared to resort to violence months, if not years, in advance, but either people missed them or refused to recognize them for what they were. As early as 1929, in a parliamentary speech, Klement Gottwald had threatened his bourgeois colleagues: "You are saying that we are under Moscow's command and that we go there to learn. Yes, our highest revolutionary staff is in Moscow and we do go to Moscow to learn. And do you know what? We go to Moscow to learn from the Russian Bolsheviks how to break your necks, you patriots."[1] They should have taken him at his word.

Klement Gottwald and his Communist Party rode the postwar wave of Pan-Slavic, pro-Soviet euphoria to victory in the national elections of 1946. The Communist Party won 38 percent of the vote. With the votes of the Social Democratic Party, headed by Zdenek Fierlinger, the Communists secured the 51 percent majority they needed to control the government. They wasted no time consolidating their power, systematically purging noncommunists from the national police force (SNB) and replacing them with trusted Party members. The Interior Ministry put top noncommunist politicians under surveillance. Then the Communist-controlled SNB began arresting prodemocracy public figures without explanation.[2] The Communists also set up extralegal paramilitary organizations in factories and larger business enterprises—the so-called factory militias—allegedly for the "protection of production units." They began training members of the working class in insurgency and guerrilla warfare methods. Beginning in 1947, vetted individuals could sign up for courses organized by the Military League and the Czechoslovak Youth League for practical training in "military prepared-ness." The course textbook was a slim volume entitled *Kill or Be Killed*. The lesson plan included step-by-step instruction on such useful skills as how to build explosives, attack trains, sabotage railway tracks, and slit a man's throat or strangle him with a wire noose. Other lessons included how to throw an opponent on the ground, stamp his face with the sole of one's boot, and kill him with a well-placed kick to the temple.

Unlike the majority of their compatriots, the Masin children were aware that a serious menace was looming. The family was well connected and in a position to know what was happening. As the storm clouds gathered, General Studlar told Zdena Masinova that he was not yet sure whether he would stay in the country or go into exile once again, but he reassured her, "If I leave, I will take the two boys with me."

Although the general population didn't know the full extent of the purges in the military and the police, which were underreported in the press, the popularity of the Communists was plummeting. The economy was stuck in the doldrums and the methods the Communists employed to consolidate their power alienated many members of the country's large middle class. A poll taken in 1948 by the Communist-controlled Ministry of Information showed that public support for the Communists had dropped to 28 percent.[3] Under pressure from Moscow, Communist Party leader Klement Gottwald made sure that the next election would never take place.

When the Interior Minister fired eight noncommunist Prague police commanders on 18 February 1948 and replaced them with Party members, all twelve noncommunist ministers resigned in protest. The next day, seven thousand Communist militia took to the streets of Prague, each one armed with a gun and two hundred rounds of live ammunition. Armed Communist militia cells in factories and farms mobilized and seized control of their production units. Town and village militia paraded themselves in a blatant show of force, guns in hand. All top-level anticommunist officers in the Defense Ministry were confined to quarters.

The democratic elements of society looked to President Benes to hold the line. After all, Benes had been the junior partner of Tomas Masaryk at the hour of the nation's birth, and after Masaryk's death he was the country's democratic *éminence grise*. Once again Benes proved he lacked Masaryk's mettle. With the police effectively under Communist control because of the purges, he talked of appealing to the people, the Sokol, the Legionnaires, and the elements of the military who were loyal to the government.[4] Then

Klement Gottwald paid him a visit, threatening violence in the streets if he
didn't approve the Communists' slate of ministers. Benes's resolve quickly
crumbled in the face of this blackmail, and he reluctantly did Gottwald's
bidding. The Communists had won. As in 1938, Benes resigned and left it to
his nation to suffer the consequences of his capitulation.

Within days of the putsch, Jan Studlar and other high-ranking generals
suddenly disappeared without a trace. The Communists had rounded them
up and locked them into a small house in the Prague castle compound, without food or water, subjecting them to brutal torture. Some never reemerged.
Studlar and a few others were ultimately released, but they didn't wait
around for the inevitable rearrest. Studlar and his wife hurriedly packed up
and fled to the United States without informing Zdena Masinova.

The wave of arrests continued. In September 1949, Zdena learned from the
newspapers that her friend Milada Horakova had been arrested. Horakova
was a member of parliament and leader of the Czechoslovak women's movement. She was one of more than six hundred men and women, mainly members of the Socialist, Catholic, and Social Democratic parties, arraigned for
a monster trial.

The Masins watched as the Communist-controlled press vilified
Horakova and proclaimed her guilty even before she was convicted. In
the local cinema, Radek and Pepa saw newsreel footage of the show trial.
This was like no trial under the democratic government. The judges, the
prosecution, even the defendants' attorneys and the witnesses were hand-
picked party toadies. All of them joined together in hurling accusations and
abuse at the defendants. The "progressive workers" in the invitation-only
audience carried signs calling for Horakova's death and screamed for the
defendants' blood. Mailbags full of "spontaneous" letters, sixty-three hundred petitions, inundated the court. Entire factory shifts and union locals
demanded that the judges liquidate these "enemies of the people."[5] Entire
classes of seven-year-old schoolchildren wrote letters calling for Horakova's
death in wobbly block letters. Though Dr. Horakova stood her ground with
exemplary courage, she was executed on fabricated charges of high treason and acts of terrorism plotted in collusion with Czech exile politicians
and the West. Her real "crime" was that she had courageously and publicly
objected to the Communist power grab.

Pepa, Radek, and their friends watched the Communist Party faithful
hang red posters and banners throughout town, declaring the dictatorship

of the proletariat and the launch of class war. The Party began an all-out assault on the lives, livelihood, and property of so-called class enemies. It confiscated businesses, property, and family heirlooms. The father of Pepa's friend Milan worked in the agricultural cooperative and witnessed the government's assault on independent farmers firsthand. Party members walked onto the farms and told the owners to pack their bags and get out. They impounded farmers' tractors and equipment, and when the farmers couldn't meet their production quotas, they sentenced them to hard time in the labor camps, sometimes without a trial.

The nation's two security forces, the SNB and StB,* arrested tens of thousands of men and women and threw them into forced-labor camps, often without a trial. Hundreds of these camps sprouted up around the country like toadstools after rain, the most notorious of which were the camp complexes around the uranium mines at Pribram and Jachymov. The Central Secretariat of the Communist Party of Czechoslovakia even fixed secret quotas: every month, three thousand class enemies were to be rounded up for shipment to slave labor camps.[6] Their only offense was that they were architects, lawyers, professional people, small business owners, or farm owners, or that they had said something critical about the Party. The stated Communist objective was to wipe out the middle class.

Instead of standard military service, the Communist authorities routinely drafted the sons of middle-class families into the notorious Pomocné Technické Prapory (PTP), the so-called Black Barons, where they had to do hard labor in the mines and elsewhere for up to ten years. In the early 1950s some 10 percent of the youths reaching draft age met this fate.[†]

The precise number of victims of the Czechoslovak Communist regime is unknowable. It is estimated that between 200,000 and 250,000 people were purged in the Czechoslovak version of the Cultural Revolution.[7] Thousands of others died in prisons and forced labor camps. For those who had lived through the Nazi occupation, it was déjà vu—only worse.

Immediately after the Communist coup in February 1948, Radek, Pepa, and their friends Milan Paumer and Zbynek Janata began engaging in small acts

---

*The SNB was the regular police and the StB was the state security service, equivalent to the Soviet KGB.

†*The Czechoslovak Political Trials 1950–54*, preface and postscript by Jiří Pelikán, 53. The term "Black Barons" came from the black shoulder patches that identified members of this unit.

of protest and sabotage against targets of opportunity. Initially there was no strategy. They broke the glass on the Party's public bulletin boards in town, where official announcements were posted. They scattered tacks and nails on the May 1st parade route and watched the self-proclaimed "fighting vanguard of the proletariat" grind to an unscheduled halt. They threw rocks at windows of officious Party members who displayed Comrade Stalin's picture on his birthday.

It was obvious to everyone that writing letters of protest to the editor, even if one could find a paper that would print them, was futile. In the Stalinist–Leninist state, there was no room for opinions other than those expressed by the Party. Those who objected or engaged in acts of peaceful noncompliance simply disappeared. Radek and Pepa were in no doubt that the time had come for them to fulfill their father's mandate.

At first they planned to attack the system from within. But their dream of attending the officers' academy and pursuing careers in the military was dashed—they didn't have the correct class profile. After his graduation from King George College in 1949, Radek's application to the officers' academy was rejected, in spite of his medal for valor and recommendations from a number of general officers. As the Communist class struggle sharpened, he considered himself lucky to be admitted to the mechanical engineering faculty of Charles University. Other classmates, such as Vladimir Hradec, were not so fortunate. Despite his top grades and high class rank, Vladimir was blacklisted by the Party for his bourgeois background and sent to work in a factory for a year.

Men came to install loudspeakers all along Podebrady's main streets and squares downtown and in the surrounding villages. "Volunteers are needed for a special weekend labor detail!" the PA system blared out during the day. "Buses will be ready Saturday at seven in the morning in front of the park." These labor details were unpaid; people were expected to participate out of sheer socialist enthusiasm. Pepa's entire class showed up, along with students from other grades and area schools. Everyone knew better than to skip this "opportunity" to help build socialism. Grumbling about the loss of a perfectly good Saturday, they filed onto the bus, accepting the flyers distributed by a Communist Party member who belted out a crisp "Honor to labor!" to each passing "volunteer." A second Party member officiously noted down who had reported for duty. Everyone knew they were being watched and that there would be consequences for those who didn't show up. An insufficient level of political consciousness meant that a student was not college material, or that his father did not get his promotion at work.

The flyer showed a large, angry-looking beetle with stripes on it. The text below it announced that these were capitalist potato bugs* sent by the American Counter Intelligence Corps[†] (CIC) in bundles of five attached to helium balloons, to sabotage the achievements of the Czech proletariat. The flyer pointed out that proof of the capitalist plot was that the potato bugs even had stripes on their wings, just like the American flag![8] For someone growing up in the United States, it is impossible to imagine the mass hysteria that existed at the time in the Eastern bloc. There were no potatoes, no fruit, no vegetables in the shops, while the harvest was rotting in the fields. The Party's paranoia would have been funny, except that the consequences were deadly serious.

Every day the newspapers spewed venom at America and the West. Hysterical exposés revealed plots by CIC agents to overthrow the Communist government. CIC agents were hiding everywhere, the newspapers warned, and it was each person's socialist responsibility to be vigilant and report them. People did. A rivalry about a girl, a spat between neighbors, an everyday dispute was quickly resolved in the complainant's favor if he went and denounced his opponent to the secret police. A web of fear and denunciation enveloped the country.

Pepa, Radek, and their friends were infuriated when the Communists disbanded the Sokol and Boy Scouts. The YMCA, the YWCA, Rotary, and all other noncommunist organizations were shut down, too. The only youth organization left was the Communist Youth League, which automatically absorbed the membership of the outlawed groups. The boys and their friends saw the offerings of Podebrady's news stands drastically diminish, as the Communists shut down noncommunist publications and banned Western media. Those papers that remained all hewed strictly to the Party line.

Every day there were new horror stories coursing through town, relayed in shocked whispers behind upheld hands, of noncommunist officials sacked from their posts, raids on the headquarters of other political parties, and people disappearing without a trace. Vladimir Hradec's father, the local head of the People's Party, was arrested. His uncle, a judge, was arrested because he refused to rubber-stamp the sentences fixed by the Party bosses

---

*Leptinotarsa decemlineata

[†]The Counter Intelligence Corps, or CIC, was the U.S. Army's intelligence gathering organ.

prior to trials. One of Milan's relatives disappeared, a tailor with several employees who never hesitated to speak his mind and complain about the Communists to anyone who would listen. Once, the police detained Radek himself. Radek was visiting a town near Podebrady, where he asked a man for directions. It turned out he had unluckily approached a police agent. Just asking for directions made him a suspect. The police agent made Radek walk in front of him all the way to the police station. They stripped Radek naked and interrogated him for more than an hour. Radek was lucky. After checking his bonafides with the Podebrady police, they let him go.

No one dared to publicly challenge the Party or its armed enforcers, the SNB, the StB, the factory militias, and the auxiliary militias. People did not even dare to talk about those the Party took away. If you asked about the people who disappeared, their relatives wouldn't answer, and you would know what had happened to them.

In this atmosphere of fear and terror, the United States was a beacon of hope. Everybody believed that the Americans were coming. The United States had saved the Czechs two times before. It was only a question of time until the invasion began.

Chapter 6

PROPHET OF LIBERATION

Were the Americans really coming to save the Czechs? The Communist putsch in Czechoslovakia sent shock waves through the western political establishment. In several Western European countries the Communist Party was becoming extremely powerful. Communists sat in the cabinet in Italy and France. If election results did not go their way, they might simply resort to force, just as they had in Czechoslovakia. A Soviet-supported Communist insurgency was underway in Greece. Communists had already seized power in Poland, Hungary, Romania, and Bulgaria using brute force. One nation after another appeared to be falling to Communism. Even the United States itself appeared to be under attack. The media was full of reports that Communist moles had infiltrated the U.S. government.

Every day in occupied Berlin, the Allies faced signs of Soviet aggression. Britain and France, exhausted by the war and facing restive populations at home, were in no position to counter it. It was beginning to dawn on Americans that if anyone was going to stop the Soviets, it would have to be them.

On 26 June 1948, Stalin stepped over the brink. Seemingly prepared to stop at nothing to get the Americans, British, and French out of Berlin, he closed all land routes to the city's western sector. War appeared imminent. The United States countered by launching a round-the-clock airlift to ferry food and fuel into the beleaguered sector. After a fifteen-month stand-off, Stalin finally backed down and reopened the land routes.

Meanwhile, hundreds of thousands of refugees were streaming into West Germany and Austria from Eastern Europe. They told heartbreaking stories of oppression and wholesale terror behind the Iron Curtain. These were people who reminded Americans of themselves. Many Americans had parents or grandparents of Eastern European origin and the "captive nations" quickly excited widespread popular sympathy. Millions of ordinary citizens donated money to the Crusade for Freedom (CFE), which organized a campaign to support the liberation of Eastern Europe. CFE forged a liberty bell modeled on America's own liberty bell in Philadelphia and published a "Liberty Oath" modeled on the Declaration of Independence, proclaiming the right of the people to "take a stand against tyranny and attacks on freedom."[1]

The CFE funneled donations to its sister organization, the National Committee for a Free Europe (NCFE) which supported émigré politicians and anticommunist journalists from Eastern Europe. On 4 July 1950, it launched Radio Free Europe (RFE) to take the message of liberation behind the Iron Curtain. The new radio launched with a thirty-minute broadcast into Czechoslovakia. Broadcasts to Poland, Hungary, and Romania soon followed.

While American money and equipment kept RFE on the air, Eastern European exiles staffing the radios determined the content. Passionately opposed to the Communist regimes in their native countries, these broadcasters developed their programming in an official policy vacuum, with little or no oversight from Washington.[2] This arrangement existed by design. As a private organization, the NCFE could operate without the constraints of U.S. government oversight. The State Department had recognized the Eastern European puppet regimes and had to maintain diplomatic relations with them.[3] When RFE programming provoked protests from the Eastern European Communist governments, the State Department could point out that the U.S. government was not involved—private individuals were exercising their freedom of speech and expressing popular grievances.[4] In fact, the divide was not quite so clear-cut. The CFE and NCFE supported U.S. government policy and received CIA funding.[5]

RFE broadcasters took their cues from the increasingly combative rhetoric coming out of Washington. On 25 July 1951 Wisconsin congressman Charles J. Kersten announced that the United States should "let the people behind the Iron Curtain know that we will do everything we can to work for their eventual liberation," and that "when the time is opportune we should actually assist the people behind the Iron Curtain to liberate themselves." He proposed granting asylum to all refugees from Eastern Europe and incorporating the men into a European Army.[6] The "Kersten Amendment" passed on 10 October, allocating $100 million to create an exile fighting force.[7] RFE duly broadcast Kersten's speech and the creation of this new fighting force into Eastern Europe.

Twenty-three transmitters beamed thousands of hours of encouragement from Frankfurt, Munich, and Lisbon, constantly reassuring the desperate people behind the Iron Curtain that the West had not forgotten them. The broadcasts spoke to Eastern Europeans of the "struggle for national honor," of "roll-back," and of "liberation."* RFE's programming was aggressive and messianic in tone. Every day Eastern Europeans heard on Voice of America (VOA) and RFE that the United States was finally making preparations to confront the Soviet Union, and they eagerly read between the lines for news that the conflict would begin.[†]

CIA director Allen Dulles, though he praised the anticommunist impact of RFE on many occasions, warned a congressional committee in closed session that outside efforts to stir up resistance movements behind the Iron Curtain "would need outside military support, which the U.S. government was not ready or able to provide."[8]

America's West European allies also opposed an armed confrontation with the Soviets. The risk that such a war might boil over into their own lands was too great.[9] But unlike the Western Europeans, the captive peoples behind the Iron Curtain looked forward to war—in spite of the pain and suffering it was bound to bring—because it meant liberation.[‡]

---

*U.S. News & World Report, 10 July 1953, 36. James Michener, The Bridge at Andau, New York, 1957, 250–53. Siegfried Kracauer and Paul L. Berkman interviewed several hundred East European refugees in 1955–56. Typical responses were: "News of possible liberation is the only reason for preferring to listen to the Voice of America," (170); "The VOA slogans like 'within a short time something decisive will happen' or 'the decisive hour is approaching' encouraged the hope for a change," (178–180); "VOA broadcasts openly that Communism will be done away with," and "VOA always promised the coming liberation and embellished its new services with political mottos" (181). "All these remarks calling on us to be persistent because we would be liberated sounded so that we believed that we would have to listen to the radio only two or three more times in the evening and then the American troops would be there." Siegfried Kracauer and Paul L. Berkman, Satellite Mentality: Political Attitudes and Propaganda Susceptibilities of Non-Communists in Hungary, Poland and Czechoslovakia, (New York: Frederick A. Praeger Publishers, 1956), 183.

†Though NCFE ran RFE, this legal nicety was completely lost on the Czech audience, who believed that RFE was an official voice of the U.S. government.

‡Kovrig, The Myth of Liberation, 93. Also Kracauer and Berkman, Satellite Mentality: Political Attitudes and Propaganda Susceptibilities of Non-Communists in Hungary, Poland and Czechoslovakia, 153. The opinion of one young Hungarian surveyed by Kracauer and Berkman is typical: "Everyone wants war. . . . It doesn't pay to live like this anyway, being afraid all the time of what would happen the next night."

In late 1951, border crossers from Czechoslovakia reported that Czech anti-communists were ready to mount an internal uprising whenever the United States wanted—an offer Washington rejected as too ambitious even for its policy of rollback. Testifying in closed session, Deputy Director of the CIA Allen Dulles admitted to the House Foreign Affairs Committee, "There are times when I feel we have almost stirred up Czechoslovakia too much, without the military ability to do something."[10]

The Masin brothers and their friends knew nothing of Allen Dulles's second thoughts. They only knew that the Americans would soon come to free Czechoslovakia. They believed American promises. And they acted on that belief.

Chapter 7

JOINING THE BATTLE

R adek, Pepa, and their friends decided to turn the tables on the Communists. They would strike at the grassroots level, using the Communists' own methods. But there was an important difference between the Masin group and the followers of Marx and Lenin. The Masins and their friends understood instinctively that if you are fighting for individual human life and dignity, you must do so with as much concern for innocent lives as humanly possible. While the government waged a broad-based campaign of terror against the civilian population, the Masins' terror would be reserved for the enforcers of the regime, the StB, the SNB, the militias and paramilitaries—those authorized to bear arms and enforce the regime's dictates.

Radek finagled his way into an intensive fourteen-day course in "military preparedness" and found himself the only junior college graduate among twenty or so specially selected members of the proletariat. The course instructor was a rabid Communist. A diligent student, Radek graduated with flying colors, then became an instructor in turn. Several times a week, Radek, Pepa, and their friends Zbynek Janata and Milan Paumer went into the woods and practiced take-downs, disarmament of armed opponents, and hand-to-hand combat until they could have done them in their sleep. They knew they had to perfect every move until they could execute automatically and without a moment's hesitation. It was the only way of ensuring that they would be capable of performing the act in combat. They practiced night navigation and long-distance runs. They moved their weapons practice from the Scout house to Vladimir Hradec's basement, where they trained with pistols and submachine guns using live ammunition. At the end of the day, every move had to be automatic and executed flawlessly. They knew that the price of a single hesitation or slip-up in combat was death.

From the beginning, Radek and Pepa operated on a need-to-know basis. Only a few trusted individuals learned of the group's existence. Many longtime friends were surprised to learn, years later, that there had even been a resistance group. Even the group members themselves knew only the minimum necessary to do their part in a given action. Radek, Pepa, Milan, Zbynek, and Vladimir formed the core. They had all grown up together. They knew each other as well as any boys could know each other, and they trusted each other completely.

Milan was the quiet one in the group. He was virtually the first boy Pepa and Radek had met upon their move to Podebrady in 1941, when he showed up on their doorstep struggling under an enormous sack of potatoes—an off-the-books delivery from his father, who ran the local agricultural sales cooperative. Milan lived with his little brother, his mother, and his father in an apartment three streets over from the Masins' house. A year older than Pepa, dark-haired and dark-eyed Milan was the retiring sort—the opposite of the gregarious Pepa—but the two boys were loyal friends. They had suffered through the shared ordeal of violin lessons, and now they were united by an interest in girls and cars. Milan was also a drummer in Vladimir Hradec's big band, and occasionally filled in with the trio that played at the Tlapak Hotel. When the trio's regular drummer got drunk, something that happened regularly after midnight, young Milan made sure he was around and happily filled in for him. While Pepa and Milan were tight friends, Milan admired the intense and self-assured Radek, who ran with a slightly older crowd, from a bit of a distance.

Zbynek was a dark-haired, good-looking youth, a rebel without a cause, and Pepa immediately recognized a kindred spirit. When they were younger, Zbynek was always game for a session of pick-up soccer or cherry pilfering in the neighbors' gardens. He was a gifted athlete and he had a sort of reckless courage that impressed Pepa. Zbynek's dad was the principal of the local elementary school, and, like Milan's father, a Sokol elder. The elder Janata believed in Discipline with a capital D, and in the power of the whip and the belt to train good citizens. Zbynek's mother had died when he was only two. Principal Janata soon married a teacher at his school who was half his age, and the stepmother very obviously favored her own children. Whenever push came to shove, Zbynek's dad sided with his wife. Zbynek didn't talk much about his home life, but it was obvious to his friends that he preferred to stay out of the reach of his stepmother's sharp tongue and his father's whip. Zbynek had a rebellious streak and sometimes could be argumentative and hotheaded, but Pepa knew that his heart was in the right place and found him a loyal, dependable friend.

Vladimir Hradec, Radek's best friend in high school, organized his own fifteen-man big band, which played gigs at the Savoy Hotel some Saturday nights. Headlining as "Kikina and His Band," it featured saxophones, trumpets, and a clarinet section, with Milan on the drums and Vladimir himself conducting and playing the piano. The band played regular gigs at several of the clubs around town. When another boy joined up who was a better pianist, Vladimir simply took up the saxophone instead.

Vladimir was a quiet, retiring boy with a dry sense of humor. Although he had known Radek for several years, the two boys only became close after they ended up classmates at King George College. Vladimir's father was a former Legionnaire, like General Masin, and the local head of the Lidová Strana, one of the country's largest pro-democracy political parties. Vladimir shared Radek's passion for weapons and all things military. They studied technical manuals for German, Czech, and Russian armaments until they had memorized them, and spent hours assembling and disassembling the guns and projectiles they had picked up along the roads and in the fields after the Germans fled.

Among the group members there was never any long-winded discussion of ideology and objectives. It was implicitly understood that everyone opposed the Communists and their methods. The objective was as simple as it was ambitious: to overthrow the dictatorship. But they had a major problem. Without weapons and money you cannot run a resistance organization. General Masin had had a whole regimental arms room at his disposal, an independent income from his farm, and RAF fliers from Britain dropping supplies in the dead of night. Even so, he had always struggled to make ends meet and continue the fight. Now his sons were starting from scratch, or close to it. They still had their collection of wartime finds—some German pistols, an MG-42 machine gun, a machine gun salvaged from a plane wreck, several MP40 Schmeisser submachine guns, and a few Czech-made handguns from 1938 that had been hidden by General Masin at the beginning of World War II. They had at best a few thousand rounds of ammunition for these weapons. But where could they get more arms?

German and Russian World War II–era submachine guns were on display at Podebrady's municipal museum. One day Radek went there during visiting hours, paid the price of admission and opened one of the windows a crack before leaving. That night he returned with Pepa and Milan. They broke the thick glass on the display cases and, toting all the guns they could carry, waded into the Elbe River. About a mile upstream, soaked to the bone and flush with success, they stopped to inspect their haul. Elation swung into disappointment: the guns had no firing pins. They threw the useless weapons into the river.

Next, Pepa, Radek, and Milan cased an apartment building whose ground floor housed the local Communist militia cell's arms room. After carefully preparing the operation, they broke in and took as many rifles as they could carry. The operation was a success, but once more the weapons were a disappointment. Cheap German models made at the end of the war for the Volkssturm,* they were poorly maintained and rusted.

Having completed two risky operations with still nothing to show for it, the group took stock. Their arsenal consisted of odds and ends. If they were going to launch a full-scale campaign, they would have to standardize and simplify their arsenal. They needed functional, modern armaments and an adequate supply of ammunition. There was one logical source: the SNB police stations.

Chlumec nad Cidlinou was a sleepy provincial town nestled in the woods about twenty kilometers east of Podebrady. Radek and Pepa traveled there by train to case the police station, which for Pepa meant taking time off work and making up excuses for his absences on several occasions. Radek, who was studying mechanical engineering at the university, didn't have to account for his absences.

Radek obtained chloroform from Vladimir Hradec, who was studying chemistry at Prague University. He and Pepa also got hold of parachute cord. These unusual items were part of their plan to send the authorities on a wild goose chase. But first they had to deal with another problem: transportation.

On 13 September 1951 in the early morning, Milan and Radek took the train from Podebrady to Prague. Then they flagged down a taxi. The driver, a man in his late fifties, hesitated when they named their destination a couple of towns over. But the two young men pleaded and begged so touchingly that he relented. He motioned them into the vehicle. After all, they had the full fare, looked clean-cut, and had nice manners.

---

*Last-ditch national defense units established by the Germans in World War II, consisting of overage men and amputees

The taxi merged into traffic and they were off, wending their way through the suburbs. Moving beyond the semi-detached villas with their little gardens, they gathered speed as they headed into the countryside. Milan and Radek sat quietly in the back seat.

Not far from Kersko, the road passed through some woods. Milan leaned forward.

"Can you please pull over?" he asked politely. "I have to relieve myself."

The driver agreed.

As the car rolled to a stop, Radek and Milan pointed their guns at him. The taxi driver looked at them, an expression of shock and incomprehension on his face.

"Get out of the car!" Radek commanded.

Clumsily the driver clambered out of the taxi. Radek and Milan marched him into the woods, where Pepa was already waiting with the parachute cord and chloroform. They tied him to a tree. By the time Pepa got out the chloroform and handkerchief, the man was clearly in a state.

"Please no chloroform!" he pleaded. "I've got a bad heart." His face was in fact a pasty white, his breath rapid and shallow.

Pepa, Radek, and Milan exchanged looks. Now what? Should they give him the chloroform and possibly have him meet his Maker? He didn't seem to be a bad fellow and they didn't want to hurt him; they just needed his car. They hesitated.

"Let it go," they agreed.

Pepa put away the chloroform.

They left the taxi driver tied to the tree, his arms loosely restrained behind his back, so his circulation wouldn't be cut off.

"This is for your own protection," Pepa told him.

"Don't try to untie yourself or you'll get in trouble with the StB!" Radek warned.

The three youths returned to the vehicle. Milan, their most experienced driver, took the wheel. Pepa and Radek sat in the back seat, checking their gear and checking it again. All the way to Chlumec they ran the plan through their heads, making sure they had every move down pat.

Milan pulled up at Chlumec railway station, idling the engine as Pepa and Radek crossed the street to the police station. Radek rang the doorbell. It sounded loud inside the building.

Silence.

Pepa thought he heard footsteps coming down some stairs. The door opened a crack, the safety chain still in place. An eye looked out.

"We've come to report a stolen motorcycle at the train station," Radek explained. "We'd like you to come inspect the scene and make a report."

The door opened.

"Fine," the policeman grunted sleepily. "Wait here, guys. I have to go collect a few items." He tugged at his slightly dissheveled uniform jacket to straighten it. Pepa and Radek noticed the pistol in his belt holster.

The brothers stepped into the small hallway. Behind it was the duty room and a flight of stairs, probably leading to a common room of some sort upstairs. As Pepa closed the door to the street, Radek pulled out an iron bar he had hidden in his sleeve and slammed it down on the back of the man's head. But to Radek's shock the man didn't go down. He took a staggering step, turned and clumsily fumbled for his pistol. As the policeman drew the gun from its holster, Pepa's right hand flew to his breast pocket and closed around the pistol grip. His training mode kicked in. He took aim, grasping the gun firmly with both hands, and pulled the trigger two times. Twice the gun recoiled sharply in his hands. As the spent casings pinged off the wall, the policeman tumbled to the ground.

They were compromised. Any other policemen in the building were double-timing it downstairs by now. The brothers dashed outside, closed the door and sprinted to the taxi.

"What happened?" Milan asked anxiously. He had heard the loud crack of shots clear across the street.

"Go! Get out of here!" Pepa and Radek hissed as they leaped into the car.

Milan floored the accelerator and the taxi shot away. As they raced out of town, Pepa felt a mix of pumping adrenaline and disappointment. The mission was a bust. Once again they had come away with no weapons, only this time the police would be out in force.

"Look!" Milan suddenly cried out. He pointed excitedly. "That idiot has untied himself and now he's trying to stop us!" As the taxi hurtled past, they caught sight of the taxi driver standing by the side of the road, frantically flapping his arms at them. Milan accelerated, pushing the taxi to even higher speeds. They were barreling down the road, tires squealing around the bends. Nearing the capital, Milan was forced to slow down to blend with traffic. Then, in one awful moment, a police car was behind them. Milan watched it in the rearview mirror and all of them waited, adrenaline pounding, for the SNB's next move. To their relief, the car turned off and they made it into Prague unimpeded. Abandoning the taxi in an inconspicuous place, the three young men split up and traveled home separately by train or bus.

On the bus back to Podebrady, Pepa suddenly noticed two plainclothes policemen moving down the aisle, checking passengers' papers. Was it a routine patrol? Or were they out looking for the Chlumec perpetrators?

"And where might you be going?" one of them asked.

"I'm on the way to Podebrady," Pepa said, his demeanor calm.

"What's your business in Podebrady?"

"I live there. I was visiting my brother in Prague and now I'm going home."

"Haven't you heard what happened tonight in Chlumec?" one asked sharply.

"No. What happened?"

"We are from the StB and we're on our way to Chlumec to investigate an attack on the police station."

Pepa gave them a look of wide-eyed astonishment.

"What's your name?" the StB man was saying.

"Josef Masin."

"The son of the general?" Both were looking at him now, surprised and somewhat awed. Despite having been officially declared a class enemy, Josef Masin's reputation lingered on, even among some police.

"Yes."

That seemed to satisfy them, and they moved on to the next passenger.

The attack on the Chlumec police station was never written up in any newspaper or reported on the radio. But the story spread like wildfire throughout the region, growing with every telling, so that eventually half a dozen policemen had been killed and the station building had been totally annihilated. The police treated the taxi driver, Eduard Sulc, as a suspect and accomplice, refusing to believe his protestations of innocence. To them it was a clear case: Sulc was at liberty and neither he nor the taxi had been harmed in any way. He would spend close to a year in jail before the police finally released him.

Pepa had to return to work. He had finished King George College the previous year but was barred from both the officers' academy and university studies because his father was now officially designated a class enemy. He had finally managed to land a job in Jesenik, near the Polish border, driving a logging truck, thanks to Uncle Borek's military connections.

But that didn't stop Radek, who was driven by a sense of urgency. They needed weapons. Now. Milan suggested they try the police station in Celakovice, another provincial town about twenty-eight kilometers from Podebrady, just off the main road to Prague. With Pepa gone, Radek tapped Zbynek to be his backup.

Once again Radek, Zbyna, and Milan cased their target in advance. Once again they made excuses to get off work or ditch classes to travel to Celakovice by train. And once again they wrestled with their eternal problem—transportation. Since the police would be keeping a close watch on taxis now, they had to find an alternative.

On 28 September, two weeks after the Chlumec raid, the trio rode the night train into Prague. They took the number five tram to the last stop. At midnight Radek telephoned the emergency dispatcher.

"There's a man with a broken leg here," he reported. "We need an ambulance. Quickly!"

It didn't take long for the ambulance to show up in the quiet, dark neighborhood. Radek hopped inside and directed the driver to the ditch where Milan sat, with Zbynek tending to his "injury." As the driver and paramedic got out and headed toward the invalid, Radek trailed slightly behind. On his cue, all three youths drew their guns.

"Hands up!"

The two men, looking bewildered, then fearful, complied. Radek, Milan, and Zbynek marched them back to the ambulance, where Milan took the wheel while Zbynek and Radek got in the back with the two captives, covering them with their pistols.

No one said anything during the drive to Celakovice. Milan stopped the ambulance in the woods near town and the three youths disembarked the captives. This time they didn't heed the men's protestations. They tied them firmly to a tree and began administering the chloroform. After a few breaths the paramedic began singing a weird, tuneless song, but a little more chloroform silenced him. Both men were fast asleep. Radek and his partners double-timed it back to the ambulance.

The Celakovice police station was a small, single-story affair at the edge of town. When Milan stopped the ambulance and killed the lights, it was completely black outside. Massive tree canopies cast deep shadows onto the street. Radek and Zbynek could hardly see their way over to the station building.

Radek rang the doorbell. For a long time nothing happened. Then the door opened a crack. Again the safety chain was in place.

"What do you want?" asked the policeman.

"There's been an accident nearby," Radek replied. "Two cars crashed. One of the drivers seems to be drunk and now he's trying to get away!"

The policeman nodded. "Go back and wait for me. I'll be along shortly on my bicycle."

Radek gave him directions and left. When the officer pedaled up, Radek and Zbynek had only just arrived themselves. They jumped the man with a gun, wrestled him to the ground, disarmed him, tied his hands and bundled him into the ambulance. Radek threw the bike into the ditch. Then he jumped into the vehicle, slamming the door as Milan accelerated away.

"Give me the keys!" Radek commanded.

"No!" replied the policeman.

Radek pointed the gun at him.

"Give me the keys!"

His eyes fixed on the gun, the policeman slowly pulled a key chain out of his pocket and handed it over.

Milan had pulled up at the station. Zbynek and Radek marched the policeman to the station door, unlocked it, and marched him into the duty room.

"Where are the weapons?" Radek demanded.

The policeman said nothing. He was unabashedly studying their faces in the light. He was experienced and made no bones about taking his time to commit their features to memory. When he was finished, he motioned his head toward a cabinet. It was fitted with a massive metal latch and outsize padlock.

"Give me the key!" Radek said.

"Only the the station commander has a key."

They didn't bother checking to see if he was lying. Striding over to the wooden cabinet, they pushed it away from the wall and threw it onto the ground. It landed with a resounding crash, the contents clattering heavily inside. The back panel was only a thin board, and they easily kicked a hole into it. Among the wooden debris lay a motley jumble of pistols, obviously old junk that had been confiscated. But that was not all. There were also five brand-new submachine guns, a number of magazines, and several new service pistols. At last, after three failed attempts and against tremendous odds, they had succeeded.

While Zbynek was hauling the weapons out to the ambulance, Radek turned to the policeman. The man was glaring at him defiantly.

"Comrade," Radek said, "we have to put you to sleep so that you don't do anything stupid before we disappear."

There was no question in his mind. This policeman knew their faces and would submit detailed descriptions of them. Radek couldn't let that happen. But he also had to avoid a repeat of the Chlumec fiasco: there could be no gunfire. He laid the policeman on the bunk, pressed a handkerchief doused with chloroform over his nose and mouth, and waited until the man was out cold. Then he pulled his scout's knife from its sheath on his belt and slit the man's throat—exactly as his instructor had showed him.

Radek closed the station door and hurried after Zbynek. As the ambulance door slammed shut, Milan floored the accelerator. The vehicle hurtled away at top speed, flying back toward Prague with its payload of guns. Even the StB in its relentless pursuit of the class enemy wasn't likely to stop ambulances to conduct ID checks.

Radek shared a large basement room in the city with another student, near the university. The roommate was out when Radek arrived lugging a heavy leather suitcase, which he stashed under his bed.

They abandoned the ambulance by the Vltava river, its engine red-hot and the radiator bubbling over, and split up. Each made his separate way back to Podebrady.

Once again, the rumor mills kicked into overdrive. By 10:00 AM the next day, news of the attack was flying through the capital and the surrounding towns, even though the press and the authorities maintained total silence.

"Parachutists from the West are attacking SNB policemen!"

"It is the first sally of the Third World War!"

"The Americans are coming!"

"The Americans will save the Czechs!"

After the attacks, hysterical wives pressured their husbands to resign from the state police force. That was exactly what Pepa and Radek wanted. Their psychological campaign was beginning to work.

Shortly after the Celakovice raid, Zdena Masinova had some exciting news for her sons. A group of military officers was preparing an uprising. This was the moment they had been waiting for. The counterstrike of the democratic forces was at hand, and the little group in Podebrady was ready.

On the appointed day, Zbynek, Milan, Radek, and Pepa gathered in the Masins' place in a state of high excitement. The Masins now lived in a small apartment in the center of town, next to the Tlapak Hotel. Just a few weeks before, virtually without notice, the Communist authorities had evicted them from their Na Chmelnici home to make way for a Communist Party member. Now the four youths sat by the radio in the tiny apartment with their weapons, waiting for word of the uprising in Prague. They waited all day. Night fell and they continued waiting, pacing about with pent-up energy. They waited with diminishing hope until midnight, but the call to arms never came. Later, they learned that the key players had been rounded up and arrested in Prague just before moving out.

Milan and Radek discussed the aborted uprising and came to the conclusion that the plot was too sophisticated and too large. Too many people knew about it. That was why it had failed.

The failed uprising was a turning point for the group with no name. With every month that passed, their work was becoming dramatically more difficult and hazardous. By 1951 they were out of school, living in different towns scattered throughout the republic. They held jobs and had to account for their absences. Every time they were working on a project Milan and Pepa ran into difficulties at work. Supervisors and Communist stooges asked detailed, prying questions. None of the youths or their families had any means of transportation and so coordinating their actions was a logistical nightmare.

The Communist parliament was rubber-stamping reams of new laws, rapidly turning Czechoslovakia into a Stalinist police state. Ownership of a copying machine could lead to criminal prosecution. Detailed maps were virtually impossible to obtain. Simply owning one could result in a charge of espionage. Travelers who planned to spend the night away from home had to report at the local police station to have their ID papers stamped. Police patrols and workers' militias conducted random ID checks on trains, buses, and city streets to root out saboteurs and Western agents.

Pepa and Radek became convinced that they had to leave the country and get some real training in partisan warfare in order to fight the regime. The broadcasts on Voice of America and Radio Free Europe seemed to imply that the West was maneuvering its forces into position and would strike soon. Radek was particularly impressed by one report that an American Ranger Regiment had landed in France. Radio Free Europe made it sound so ominous, even without commentary, that it seemed to be preparation for some larger action. Everybody knew that Czechoslovakia's last, best hope for liberation lay with America.

But by the autumn of 1951, leaving the country was becoming a hazardous proposition. Every month thousands of people had been fleeing the oppressive Communist regime, draining the country of its most motivated and educated citizens. To stop the hemorrhage, the government turned the country into a giant prison camp. In July 1951, the regime passed the Border Guards Act, and by autumn it was sealing off Czechoslovakia's borders to the West. Villages in the border zone were forcibly evacuated and blown up. Watchtowers went up and hundreds of miles of barbed wire and electric fences snaked out along the denuded frontier, where swaths of forest had been cut down to ensure unobstructed visibility. An unlucky step in the minefields near the fences spelled death for would-be refugees.

Pepa and Radek were sure that there would be an armed clash at the border, so they did everything to maximize the odds in their favor. Milan had a friend who had been barred from university because his father was an industrialist. This friend drove a small, four-wheel drive Peugeot for Ceskoslovenska Automobilova Doprava (CSAD), the government-owned trucking company.* Pepa and Radek hired him and his truck on a pretext. Another family friend who owned an auto repair shop cut apart old industrial steam boilers for them with a blowtorch. He didn't know it, but he was making armored plates for the truck. Their plan was to ride to the staging area in the truck. Once they arrived, they would erect the armored plates and smash through the border, stopping for nothing. They would be armed to the teeth with submachine guns and hand grenades. They would shoot anyone who blocked their path or opposed them.

Radek and Pepa decided to take along their friends Zbynek, Milan, and Egon Plech. They had carefully sounded out Vladimir, and it seemed to them that he didn't want to go. Egon, about ten years older than the others, was the brother of Pepa's then-girlfriend Hanka. He was a quiet, unsmiling fellow, a heavy smoker with a narrow face, a narrow build, and a prominent beaked nose set off by a carefully trimmed mustache. He worked as a senior engineer in a large nationalized textile factory in Jesenik.

---

* "He was lucky," Pepa recalled. "Driving a truck was actually a pretty good job for a 'class enemy' at that time."

The brothers prepared methodically, leaving nothing to chance. They tested their weapons. They maintained a rigorous training schedule. They subtly probed friends who had been drafted into the border guards for information about military operating procedures and personally inspected various sectors of the border to decide which was best for the crossing. On one such recon trip, the border guards picked Radek up, stripped him naked, and interrogated him. "Why are you so near the border?" They harangued him for hours. Unflappable, Radek trotted out his prepared alibi: "I am on my way to a friend's weekend cottage." The alibi checked out, because Radek had made sure it would, and they released him.

Then, three weeks before the scheduled departure, a calamity threatened to derail their carefully laid plans. The government, intent upon clamping down on freedom of movement, passed a draconian decree restricting all commercial vehicles to within fifty kilometers of their place of registration. The brothers worried they wouldn't be able to get the truck out of Podebrady. And without the truck, they wouldn't be able to break through the border fortifications.

The law said that when traveling beyond the fifty-kilometer pale a driver had to carry a special permit issued by local police authorities, stating the purpose of the trip and the names of everyone authorized to be in the vehicle. The band of brothers hurriedly improvised a solution. Earlier, they had cooked up a cover story for the benefit of CSAD. This they now typed up on the stationery of the textile factory for which Egon worked, and their unwitting driver submitted it for authorization. To their immense relief, the papers came back embellished with the requisite stamps and signatures. The official story was that the truck was going to pick up some machines for the textile factory.

As the time of departure drew near, Radek was approached by Alois Bezucha, a family acquaintance who ran a restaurant at the confluence of the Cidlina and Elbe rivers, near Podebrady. Bezucha dropped a bombshell in Radek's lap. He told Radek that he had been hiding an important dissident for the last six months and needed to get him across the border. Radek was taken aback: How in the world had the restaurateur concluded they could help? He gave Bezucha an evasive answer, and he and Pepa consulted their Uncle Borek, by now a major in the Czechoslovak army, about the strange inquiry. In the end they decided that, when the time came, they would take the VIP along. After all, this man had opposed the Communists too, and Radek and Pepa were ready to help him on principle. There would now be

six men in the little truck, plus Milan's friend, the driver, if he decided to
come along.

In the late afternoon of 18 October 1951, the Masins' small apartment in
Gottwald Street was crowded with men and weapons. Neat stacks of submachine guns, pistols, and ammunition filled the tiny foyer. Hand grenades
and parachute cord lay next to the radiator. In the cramped space Pepa,
Radek, Zbynek, Milan, and Egon were systematically counting ammo, filling clips, and checking out their weapons. The mood in the apartment was
businesslike but charged with anticipation. They would be setting out for
the border the following morning. In just a few hours, if all went well, they
would be in West Germany!

Borek had come over straight from duty, still in his army uniform. He
was staying behind as their contact man. Zdena was away in Olomouc, visiting Emma and Nenda at her sons' suggestion. She had said her good-byes
earlier. Her sons had told her nothing, but in her mother's heart she had
guessed what was about to happen and had asked no questions. She knew
their silence was for her own protection.

Just before sundown, Radek left to meet Bezucha and collect the mysterious VIP. The man would spend the night in the Masins' apartment and
accompany them on the train ride to the staging area the next morning,
where they would transfer to the truck and head for the border.

But when Radek arrived at the designated meeting place he was surprised to find Bezucha standing alone. The VIP was nowhere to be seen.

"So where's the guy?" Radek asked, not bothering to hide his irritation.

The thin, birdlike restaurateur looked at him oddly and then confessed,
"I have no idea. He seems to have left."

"Does he want to go over the border or not?"

"He really wanted to go." The restaurateur shrugged. "He was ready.
But then he just disappeared."

As they walked along the street pushing their bicycles, they passed in
front of the building that housed the Communist Party secretariat. Suddenly
Radek sensed danger.

"Well, I'll be seeing you," he told Bezucha, and swung his leg over his
bike. Just then several men rushed up from behind—plainclothesmen from
the StB. They had dashed out of the secretariat building.

"Hands up!" they shouted, brandishing pistols at Radek and Bezucha.

Radek had no gun and he could see no way out. He let go of his bike, which clattered to the ground, and slowly raised his hands. Out of the corner of his eye he could see the skinny restaurateur putting his hands up too. As the StB men marched their captives toward the StB headquarters, Radek wondered what on earth had happened.

Inside the building, the lobby and hallways teemed with StB. Nobody said a word to Radek, and he still had no idea why he had been arrested. He was alone now—they'd taken Bezucha away—and StB agents were frisking him, manhandling him like a piece of inanimate furniture.

"Can you please tell me what's going on?" Radek asked. "Why did you bring me here?"

Nobody would answer his questions. One of the StB men pulled Radek's apartment keys out of his pocket and took them away.

The Masins' doorbell rang less than forty-five minutes after Radek had left to fetch the so-called dissident. Then it rang again. Pepa was immediately suspicious. Radek would never ring, and certainly not twice; he had keys. Darkness had fallen, and when Pepa stepped out onto the balcony—the apartment was on the second story—he could see nothing below.

"Who's there?" Pepa called down.

"Come and open the door, please," a man's voice replied from below. Pepa could hear several people shuffling about in the recessed entryway.

"Right away!" Pepa shot back into the apartment. "State Security is here! Pack everything up and get upstairs!"

"I'll go downstairs to stall them," Borek announced.

Already Egon, Milan, and Zbynek were rapidly filling the waiting suitcases with weapons and ammunition. Everyone moved with businesslike efficiency.

Pepa went out onto the balcony again. "Someone's coming downstairs!"

He went back inside and flipped off the light, plunging the apartment into darkness. The tension was palpable. Perhaps it was an ambush. Perhaps someone had infiltrated the building, and was lying in wait for them just outside on the landing. Four fully loaded and cocked submachine guns and one pistol pointed at the apartment door.

"If they're out there, let them have it!" Pepa said in a low voice.

With one hand he reached out and pushed the door open.

A triangle of light from the landing spilled into the apartment. There was no ambush.

"Blast them if they come up to the attic!" Pepa commanded as Egon, Milan, and Zbynek raced up the stairs, lugging two bulging suitcases, cocked submachine guns in hand.

Meanwhile Borek went downstairs to open the door to the building. There were four men standing outside.

"Comrades," Borek greeted them in a measured, calm voice. "What can I do for you?"

"Hands up!" barked one of the voices, "We're from the StB!"

"I am an army officer," Borek said, trying to stall them. "What seems to be the problem?" He stood blocking the entrance, a figure of authority in his army uniform, his duty revolver in its holster.

Pepa quickly walked through the apartment to make sure it was clean. Already footsteps were echoing up the stairwell. They were on the way up. Everything looked good, but unbeknownst to Pepa four hand grenades and a skein of parachute cord had been left behind, wedged under the little radiator in the foyer.

Just then the StB agents burst into the apartment, pushing Uncle Borek ahead of them at gunpoint, his hands raised.

"You too! Hands up!"

Pepa found himself staring down a gun barrel.

Pushing him ahead of them at gunpoint, two StB men began kicking doors open and searching all the rooms in the apartment. They found nothing. Back in the foyer, Borek was trying to conduct a calm conversation with the other StB agents, asking the reason for this unusual visit. He got no answers. The StB men snapped handcuffs on Pepa and his uncle and marched them to the nearby StB station.

For hours Pepa and Borek sat handcuffed on a bench with several other prisoners. Then, in the dead of night, StB men bundled the dozen or so handcuffed, anxious prisoners into a bus with barred windows.

"No talking!" one of them barked.

Pepa and Borek took their seats in silence. Suddenly, Pepa did a double-take. There was Radek climbing aboard the bus and walking toward them! Pepa urgently sought eye contact. He telegraphed to his brother with his eyes, and a barely perceptible gesture, *The apartment is clean.* He willed his brother to understand him. Radek looked questioningly at Borek. His uncle confirmed Pepa's gesture with a look.

The bus doors sighed shut and the engine rumbled to life. The prisoners' transport trundled off into the night, its destination the infamous Bartolomejska prison where the StB had its headquarters.

After waiting in the attic for a couple of hours, Zbynek, Milan, and Egon crept downstairs. The apartment was closed. Nobody was in sight. With the Masins under arrest it was clear that there wasn't going to be an escape. The group quickly scattered. Egon hurried straight home and returned to Jesenik the next day, to his job at the textile factory. Milan and Zbynek hastily hauled the heavy cases full of submachine guns to the only safe place they could think of: behind the rabbit hutches in Vladimir Hradec's parents' yard, next door to Zbynek's house.

The next morning, Mrs. Hradec found the submachine guns. Frightened, she packed them off to a safer hiding place. Though the Hradec family never discussed their younger son's activities at home, Mrs. Hradec had a good idea that the weapons had something to do with him. Mr. and Mrs. Hradec spent the week in a state of terror, awaiting Vladimir's return home from University at Prague.

The minute he walked in the door, his mother cried out to him, "What is going on? What have you done? I found two suitcases of submachine guns here and your friends the Masins have been arrested!" The family anxiously deliberated, considering all the possibilities. If the police had planted the weapons, arrest was imminent whether they reported the guns or not. If, on the other hand, the appearance of the guns had something to do with the arrest of the Masins, perhaps one of the friends had hidden them. In that case, the police may or may not have known about them. What to do? There were one hundred more kilos of weapons buried in the garden, all sealed up in containers. That decided it. The family wouldn't say anything. It was the only option.

Now all they could do was wait anxiously. The history of Czechoslovakia and the destiny of the Masin family, so closely intertwined, seemed fated to reprise in ten-year lockstep. In 1938 the Nazis had seized power; in 1948, the Communists. In 1941 the Gestapo captured Josef Masin; in 1951, the StB seized his sons. Two totalitarian regimes. Two generations. And once again, dozens of human destinies hung in the balance.

Chapter 8

IN THE HANDS OF THE StB

The man stripped off his jacket and draped it on a stand behind the desk with meticulous care. Then he turned with slow deliberation and walked directly up to Radek, stopping in front of him and looking him straight in the eye. He was a little shorter than Radek's six feet and one inch, but he was at least twice as heavy, built like a gorilla. Now he was rolling up the sleeves of his light green shirt with impressive slowness, baring enormous, hairy forearms.

Suddenly Radek found himself yanked off the floor, gasping for air. His head bounced off the wall. The man kept at it again and again, pulling Radek's collar tight, pressing his knuckles into Radek's throat, shaking and slamming him against the wall.

"Talk!"

Wham. Wham.

"Talk!"

Radek was like a paper doll in his hands.

Now Radek was back on the floor, twisting his neck and breathing hard, all the while keeping a wary eye on the man, who was stalking around the desk like a cat, his eyes two hostile slits that never left Radek's face. Once, twice, three times he circled before abruptly stepping toward Radek and thrusting his finger under Radek's jaw. Radek strained up until he was standing on his toes trying to escape the almost unbearable pain.

"Talk!"

The pressure almost lifted Radek off the floor.

Just as suddenly he found himself crumpled on the ground, choking and coughing. "I know nothing!" he stammered thickly, as he had a thousand times before. Before the words had left his mouth, the man jumped on him again, twisting his collar with one hand and hitting his stomach with his fist. Radek slumped over and grabbed his stomach. A rabbit punch sent him sprawling.

"Get up!"

Radek didn't know the man's real name—from this point on, he would simply think of him as the Butcher. He would soon discover that there were five men on the interrogation team, but none of them exuded such an air of raw brutality as he.

Pepa, Radek, and their Uncle Borek were all going through the special kind of hell the StB reserved for its suspects. There were no Miranda rights at Bartolomejska prison, no habeas corpus, no need for the accused to have an attorney present. These trappings had no place in the People's justice system. Indeed, they would only have represented impediments to the final objective, which was to hasten the necessary, inevitable guilty plea.

Once he was photographed, fingerprinted, and all his possessions were taken away, each prisoner became a number—an anonymous cog in the system. He reported to his interrogators using that number and was addressed by that number only. One prison guard led each blindfolded man away by the arm while another guard followed—along endless hallways, up and down seemingly random elevators and stairways. Sometimes, just to keep the prisoner off balance, the guards led him smack into a wall without warning or had him step into thin air, sending him tumbling down a flight of stairs. Finally, disoriented and fearful of what was to come, he found himself in a small cell, alone. The prisoner had had his first taste of the StB's warped universe, whose sole purpose was to destroy the prisoner's sense of self and undermine his resolution. But as yet, the prisoner had only a vague inkling of what was to come.

"Get up!" the interrogator shouted at Pepa. Pepa's face was puffy with bruises and his entire body ached from repeated beatings. How many hours the interrogation had gone on he no longer knew. His body screaming with pain, he struggled to his feet and stood on wobbly legs before the interrogator, who was now lounging at his desk. Idly, with a studied casualness, the interrogator opened a drawer and pulled out a pistol. He played with it, twirling it in his hand, ignoring the teenager who silently stood before him. He took out the magazine and counted the rounds. One by one, he fed the

rounds back into the magazine, snapping it into the pistol. Then he chambered a bullet and placed the gun on the desk. Without a look at Pepa he got
up and headed toward the door. Out of the corner of his eye, Pepa watched
the door fall shut in the interrogator's wake. Now Pepa was all alone with
the gun, acutely aware that it lay just a few inches from his hand. He stared
stonily ahead. There was a two-way mirror on the wall. Pepa knew they
were watching him, testing him, trying to push him to the breaking point.
The idea was to catch him in the act, throwing him off balance and thereby
forcing the floodgates of confession open. But Pepa wasn't about to fall for
their ploy. For fifteen minutes he stood there, not moving until the interrogator came back and wordlessly put the pistol in his desk.

A wave of fury and hatred was almost choking Radek. Fleetingly he considered using the chair as a weapon, then the coat stand. He quickly dismissed
these thoughts—he was no match for this hulk of a man, even in prime
form, and now he was weak from hunger. Radek began to appreciate that
he couldn't stonewall his way out of this mess. After all, they had seized
him together with Bezucha and if Bezucha talked, Radek was implicated.
So while the Butcher was stepping on his toes and fingers, twisting his arms
and ears, and forcing him to do endless series of squat jumps and pushups,
Radek began forming a plan in his head. He would break down, but on
his own terms. First he would find out exactly how much the StB goons
knew and then he would construct a confession. It was a balancing act:
he couldn't withhold information they already knew, but he also couldn't
reveal new information that would be used to pry additional confessions
from other prisoners.

Hours later, Radek was swaying on his feet near exhaustion. A new interrogator came in. Now his adversary was a short red-headed man with a freck-
led face. This man was the "good cop," and he was patiently telling Radek,
"We know everything! Come clean! Save yourself! Never mind about the
others. After all, they talked and never spared a moment's thought for you."

Save himself—but to what end? A few miserable years in prison and a
place among the mass of faceless and honorless? If the StB really knew everything Radek couldn't save himself anyway, and he refused to die as scum.

"We know everything about your group!" the interrogator was telling Pepa
in a cold, staccato voice. "Your friends—they talked, they spilled the beans."
He put his face close to Pepa's and spit out, "You're looking at fifteen years."

He let the threat hang in the air. "But if you tell us everything, we might be able to cut that down to ten years, or even five." His words didn't have the desired effect. On the contrary, Pepa was struggling valiantly to hide his euphoria. *You don't know shit, comrades! If you did, you'd be talking about the rope and not about giving us a few years more or less.*

"If you keep on lying, your punishment will be worse," the interrogator threatened. But now Pepa knew that they had nothing on him. He could depend on his brother and uncle. Radek was made of granite and was not going to talk, and Borek was an old resistance fighter who had been baptized by fire during his Gestapo imprisonment.

"I just happened to be visiting home," Pepa sobbed, his cheeks wet with tears. "I didn't do anything. If I knew anything I'd tell you!"

Night and day, the screams of people being tortured and killed echoed through the vast Bartolomejska prison complex—sometimes the demented gibbering and inhuman howls sounded as if human beings were driven insane. Bodies were dragged groaning past the cell door like so many bags of bones, battered to the point where they could no longer walk on their own.

This was Bartholomew Street No. 4. Where time stopped dead in its tracks. Where a man learned to know himself, where his personality, beliefs, and ideals were turned inside out, dissected, ridiculed, and dragged through the mud, and the animal instincts of self-preservation and hunger lurked disquietingly close to the surface. In this place hope dangled in front of you, forever just out of reach, and men sold their honor, souls, friends for the vaguest of promises. For a cigarette butt.

"Did you talk to Bezucha on that night, about the escape to Bavaria?"

The Chief had taken the place of Freckle Face hours ago and Radek stood before him, swaying on his feet, purposely exaggerating his exhaustion when ordered to do push ups, pretending incomprehension of even the simplest questions.

Now! Now! Radek's exhausted mind screamed at him. *They've finally broken down. Now they are talking!*

Questions and verbal abuse battered down upon him, but Radek wasn't answering, just looking more nervous and frightened. His mind feverishly worked dozens of combinations with every new piece of information, trying to predict the Chief's next move and still keep the show going at the same time.

Shortly before dawn, everything seemed set for the main act. Relentlessly the Chief had been applying pressure and soon the Butcher joined in for the final assault. So far, Radek noted, they didn't appear to suspect his true role in the planned escape or his part in the attacks at Chlumec and Celakovice.

Radek still couldn't be sure about a few of the dates and the sequence of events but this was the logical climax if the breakdown was to look credible. Words began to spill out of him in a rushing torrent. The interrogators interrupted, jumping rapidly from one question to another, cross-examining him—their only purpose to find out whether they could get something more that the other prisoners hadn't revealed. For hours the interrogators bombarded Radek with rapid-fire questions. They forced their will upon him constantly, in every detail and at every opportunity.

A phone call, and a few minutes later Radek was face to face with the man who was the cause of his agony. Many times before he had asked himself what he would do if he ever had to face this man again. His feelings ran high whenever he thought of him, but now they were facing each other across the room. Bezucha's thin figure was lost in the loose prison uniform, his narrow face white and expressionless, his blue eyes dull and bulging, looking at Radek with shocked detachment. *I cannot feel sorry for this fool, but I cannot hate him, either*, Radek decided.

The interrogator motioned to Bezucha and the man parroted his piece. When they led the broken man away, the interrogator gave Radek a look of gloating triumph. Radek tried to appear the embodiment of defeat.

The interrogation dragged on into the afternoon. Well more than twenty-four hours had elapsed since Radek had last lain on his mattress, and still they didn't permit him a moment's rest, a sip of water, or use of the toilet. The interrogators worked in four-hour shifts now and continued to insist that he knew much more than he had told. By nightfall the pattern for the coming night was established. Radek had to stand at rigid attention and repeat the whole story over and over again, and woe unto him if he omitted a word or paused to catch breath! The interrogator was relaxing with his feet on the table now and just nodded every time Radek finished the story: "Go ahead. Start over." Hour after hour Radek's croaking voice recited the story verbatim. He no longer heard the words his swollen tongue formed against his parched mouth and cracked lips. Talking had become loathsome torture—a curse.

All that night and the next morning as Radek recited the story, a dull pressure expanded in his head. Nearly forty-eight hours had elapsed since he had last seen his cell and he wondered where the words were coming from, what the limit was. His mind had exited his failing body and was watching it dispassionately from a distance.

Then suddenly, early in the afternoon, the Chief changed the subject. He was not interested in this matter anymore.

It was finished.

Over with.

"Now," he announced, "we are going to start talking about the real thing!"

No! That cannot be! Radek's mind shrieked in silent agony. Had they found out after all?

The StB interrogated Pepa, Radek, and Borek for almost six weeks without mentioning concrete charges. Then one day an interrogator showed Pepa a photograph of four hand grenades, a map, and parachute lines arranged on the floor of the Masins' small foyer next to the bathroom, in front of the radiator grille. But Pepa was sure that Milan and the others had gotten everything out of the apartment. Plus he had been through the place himself. So he declared, "These are not our things. You planted those hand grenades there yourselves!" The interrogators kept insisting that the StB found these items in the apartment and Pepa stoically kept repeating that they had been planted, with such conviction that the interrogators eventually stopped asking.

Despite Pepa's bravura performance, the parachute lines concerned him a lot. Had the StB put two and two together and seen a connection with Chlumec and Celakovice? The fear that at the next interrogation they would know everything was constantly with him. The StB men made him turn around, blindfolded him, and took him up to the interrogating room without a word. They let him stand there for an hour or two and stew in his own thoughts. All the time Pepa's mind was racing. *This is it. Now they know everything.* The anticipation was terrible.

In spite of everything, Pepa was at peace with himself. He believed it was the end of the road. He wouldn't make it easy for them, but it was inevitable that sooner or later they would find out about Celakovice and Chlumec. The death sentence was inevitable. It was really only a question of time.

Soon Radek and Pepa each had a couple of cellmates. When Radek's volunteered their names and personal histories to him—a blatant violation of prison regulations—he immediately suspected that they were StB stooges sent to finagle information out of him. He steadfastly gave them the cold shoulder. Pepa, ever gregarious, struck up conversations with his two cell-mates, although he, too, made sure to tell them nothing of consequence.

One was a theater director in his early thirties who told Pepa he'd been jailed for trying to help a CIC agent.* The alleged CIC agent came to his apartment, and next thing he knew the StB showed up and arrested them both. Things looked pretty bad for him: the standard punishment for his alleged crime was fifteen years. Married for a little over a year, he was pining for his beautiful young wife and his newborn daughter. "When I get out," he lamented, "she'll be fifteen years old!" The man was completely devastated.

Pepa's other cellmate was Mirek, a well-known sprinter about two years older than Pepa who was studying at the university. Mirek ran for the Sparta sports club, and he knew Pepa's then-girlfriend, who was on the national ski team and skied for the same club. The StB picked up Mirek because a friend of a friend was allegedly part of a CIC network and had had a shootout with the StB in Prague, where they were lying in wait for him. The first thing Mirek knew of the alleged CIC agent was when the StB arrested him.

Mirek was a training fanatic who did four hundred squat jumps each day. Pepa was soon training with him. The cell was four or five yards long, four or five steps in each direction, and since prisoners weren't allowed to sit down during the day, Pepa and Mirek would walk a length, then turn, keeping count. In this way they would walk ten to fifteen kilometers a day, which amounted to quite a few thousand turns, telling each other stories or softly singing the rousing Russian marching songs they had had to learn by heart in school and which the radio and the municipal public address system broadcast all day long.

After several days Pepa and his cellmates began wondering about the constant tattoo of rapid-fire knocking on the walls around them. They deduced that their neighbors were communicating—or trying to, since Pepa and his cellmates weren't answering. They figured it was probably Morse code. Pepa told the other two, "Guys, I know A, B, C." In the boy scouts Pepa had to learn Morse code, but he only got as far as C. He and his cellmates decided they had to get in on the conversation somehow. They knew that dots were single knocks, and that dashes were two quick knocks, so they started transmitting continuously, A, B, C; A, B, C; A, B, C, until their neighbor figured

---

*The American Counter Intelligence Corps

out that they didn't know any more. Then he transmitted back A, B, C, D. They learned a few letters each day and within a week they were joining in the conversation.

The guards knew this messaging was going on and it annoyed the hell out of them. But, try as they might, they couldn't catch anyone in the act. When they looked through the peephole in the door, they only saw the inmates standing up properly, leaning against the wall. Pepa tried to find Radek and Borek using the knocking method, but they were in a different section of the prison.

By then the theater director was completely desperate about his wife and baby, so Pepa and Mirek decided to help him. An epileptic in his youth, his idea was to reduce his sentence, or at least get a transfer to a hospital and possible family visits, by simulating an epileptic attack. He prepared foaming saliva in his mouth and ran against the wall and against the metal fitting of the heater with his head. Once his head was bleeding profusely, Pepa and Mirek started to kick the door, swear at the guards, and yell that their cellmate was dying and needed to be hospitalized. The guards thought the inmates might be preparing an ambush, so they watched through the peephole for a while before ordering Mirek and Pepa to face the wall with their hands up while several guards dragged the theater director out. They never brought him back. Pepa called the man's family after his own release from prison, and they told him the ruse hadn't helped—he was sentenced to the full fifteen years.

After roughly three months Pepa and Borek were released. As it turned out, the StB were not getting anything out of Radek and Borek except corroboration of Pepa's statements. None of the three cracked and so the StB concluded that Borek and Pepa were probably telling the truth about not being involved. Radek was not so fortunate. The alleged CIC operative who was supposed to leave with them was picked up somewhere on the street. He had decided to go and say good-bye to his family and was recognized by someone who reported him as he walked downtown. When they picked him up, he confessed his departure plan to the StB. He told them everything he knew, and Radek's name was mentioned also.

Radek was imprisoned in Pankrac for eleven months before the trial was put on. He never talked to a lawyer at any time before the trial. One day, he was simply taken out of his cell and brought into a courtroom. Radek had no idea what was going on. He was there for a while. Then he was taken back to the cell. Nobody told him anything about the charges or about the sentence. Then he was taken to a large holding facility where the authorities collected all the prisoners before shipping them off to the work camps. The prisoners were packed into the cell like sardines. When they lay down for the night, they were right on top of each other. There was no latrine. There were just a couple of buckets with urine and feces spilled all around. The stink was hellish.

In this holding cell Radek learned that his crime was knowing about the escape plans of a man whom he had never even seen and not reporting them. For this crime of knowing and not telling, Radek was sentenced to two and a half years of slave labor in the Jachymov uranium mines. It was ironic, really. The StB had Pepa, Radek, and Borek in jail, and they never did make the link with the guerrilla campaign that had been under way for the past two years.

Chapter 9

THE BATTLE CONTINUED

J achymov was the Czechoslovak Communist Party's answer to the Soviet Gulag. In its confines tens of thousands of prisoners eked out a miserable existence, enduring hard labor, starvation, random brutality, and abominable living conditions. No complete record exists of those who died in this massive complex of slave labor camps. Among its victims were ex-Nazis, Jehovah's Witnesses who refused to serve in the army, hard-core criminals, simple shopkeepers and farmers branded capitalist enemies of the people, and good Communists purged for no reason they could understand. Though the mine was located in Czechoslovakia, the only free Czechs in the place were the foremen and the workers who handled the dynamite. The engineers were Russian, because Jachymov was critically important to the Soviet Union. It was one of the aspiring nuclear power's principal sources of uranium.

When Radek arrived, he was quickly confronted by the stark struggle for survival that raged in the camp. Assigned to a primitive wooden barracks, he shared a bedbug-infested bunk with two other men. Every three days he queued up with the other prisoners for a loaf of bread, a pitifully small quantity that could be eaten in a single sitting. It took real willpower to make this pittance last three days, for breakfast and supper, which consisted of nothing but this bread and watery "coffee," which was really ground-up chicory. At lunch, those who had fulfilled their quota in the mine got some potatoes or slices of dumpling with gravy, with the ubiquitous coffee. Sometimes there would be some rotten meat in a watery stew.

Wretched souls who had not fulfilled their quota a few weeks running disappeared. Radek found out that they were moved to another barracks with a stricter regimen, even less food and more harassment. It was a vicious cycle, where getting less food made a man even weaker and less able to meet his quota, the result of which was another cut in his food ration. People who got sick and couldn't work had no chance of catching up again. They were shipped out. Where, Radek never knew.

Like all the other convicts, Radek was issued a single loose-fitting uniform made of burlap. After eight hours of backbreaking work, the men emerged from the mine shaft exhausted. At the Marianská shaft, where Radek was, they waited outside for up to seven hours for the canvas-top military trucks that returned them to camp. Hypothermia was a serious problem at all times. In winter their clothes froze on their bodies as they ran around, trying to keep from freezing in the howling subzero wind. Back at camp they slept in their sodden, icy clothes, not daring to remove them for fear others would steal them.

The work in the mines was carried out under the worst conditions. Ice-cold water ran off the ceilings onto the men below, mingling with their sweat and soaking them through. The ventilation systems were perfunctory. Gases released by the blasting persisted for many hours and induced painful headaches when inhaled. Worst of all, the men worked without protection, handling uranium ore with their bare hands. Their bodies, hair, and clothes were constantly covered with a fine dust that irradiated them twenty-four hours a day, seven days a week, slowly and insidiously destroying their health. All too many of those who survived their prison terms succumbed later to cancer and various rare diseases.

Radek witnessed acts of random brutality by the guards and their stooges among the prisoners. These Kapos, inmates who had been promoted to a sort of fiendish camp police, delighted in inflicting violence on their fellow prisoners. At the slightest sign of insubordination—real or imagined—or at the guards' mere whim, a man could be thrown into solitary, where he only got half rations once every three days, was kept naked even in freezing weather, and was beaten every day.

Those unfortunates who tried to escape were invariably caught, and made to stand outside as the entire camp population filed by. Then they were summarily shot before the assembled inmates or, depending upon the mood of the camp commander, savagely beaten to death. Jehovah's Witnesses who refused to mine uranium for the war effort were forced to stand outside without food or drink in freezing weather. Radek and other sympathetic prisoners would secretly throw them a piece of bread when they passed them. To put a stop to that the camp commander moved the unfortunate Jehovah's Witnesses out between the outer and inner barbed wire fences, where the other prisoners couldn't reach them. The Jehovah's Witnesses stood day and night in the freezing wind. After about five days, it was all over for them. When the last one fell, the bodies were dragged away.

Occasionally Radek ran into familiar faces: a guard from Bartolomejska who had been caught smuggling inmates' messages out of the prison, his grammar school teacher, and one of his cellmates from Bartolomejska. But Radek kept to himself and confided in no one.

He made sure he didn't run afoul of the guards and was lucky enough to be able to meet his quota. But this inside look at the Communist class struggle filled Radek with a cold, sharp hatred—hatred for the guards, for their collaborators among the prisoners, and for the regime that brutalized its own citizens as a matter of national policy.

Though heavy labor and deprivation quickly took their toll on his health and stamina, he didn't let adversity stand in the way of his fight against the regime. Once he got his bearings and learned the routine of the place, he started a one-man sabotage campaign. The other prisoners just took a shovel and worked—they didn't look left or right. That kind of resignation was not for Radek. He borrowed books on mining from the prison library, impressing the guards with his initiative. To his chagrin, however, the pages on explosives were ripped out of the books.

But Radek watched and learned. The prime directive at Jachymov was to recover every last particle of radioactive material: Czechoslovakia's Soviet friends needed it all in their race for nuclear weapons. Prisoners working underground loaded the slag into railroad cars that ran past an especially sensitive Geiger counter located in a hut on the surface. Any car that read positive for radioactivity was towed onto a separate siding where a group of political prisoners tipped the contents onto large steel panels and sorted through it manually. The Geiger counter detected even the tiniest particles of uranium ore, and the overseers made sure they were salvaged.

Armed with this knowledge, Radek implemented his plan: Whenever a slag car passed him, he tossed in a small quantity of radioactive ore. In no time the trains backed up at the exit. Gridlock developed on the surface as huge batches of rock read positive on the Geiger counter and cars were sidelined for resorting. After he had salted several dozen cars on a given shift, output ground to a halt. The Russian mining engineers, perplexed and agitated, increased the number of prisoners sorting the slag and the number of guards watching over them. Suddenly several dozen new "miners" wearing spanking new clothes and boots showed up underground. They looked remarkably well-fed and rested and had a penchant for hanging about, half-hidden, in the darkness behind the timbering. With Radek unable to continue his sabotage work, the traffic jams at the Geiger counter came unsnarled.

Radek decided a change of tactics was in order. He acquired some of the special clay used to plug dynamite holes, wrapped a small piece of ore in the oozy mass and stuck it to the bottom of a mine car. Up at the Geiger counter the prisoners tipped out the contents but failed to find anything, so the car returned underground and the whole scenario repeated. The prisoners on the surface worked at a furious tempo, but the rail yard overflowed with mine cars. In no time, the entire mining operation at the Mariánská shaft again ground to a halt.

Meanwhile Radek was working on yet another plan. The blasting crews always began work just before the end of a shift because the air at the face took a good half hour, occasionally up to an hour, to clear enough for work to begin again. Immediately after going down into the pit, Radek looked for the latest blasting site, took a deep breath and ran to the face in darkness. Once there, he turned on his miner's lamp and started hunting. He always managed to find some fuses, unexploded blasting caps and dynamite in the rubble. Over time he amassed a significant stash of explosives, hiding them in sections of hose used for drawing compressed air to the jackhammers and closing the ends with wooden pegs to keep them from drying out. Radek wasn't deterred by the incapacitating headaches caused by gases or by the dangers involved in approaching the blasting site. His goal was to collect enough explosives to blow up the machine room and the elevator, shutting down the mine completely.

Chapter 10

THE CLASS WAR ESCALATES

Outside Jachymov, Pepa, Zbynek, Milan, and their friends watched in horrified fascination as the Communists' class war spiraled out of control. Newspapers and newsreels announced that Western agents and saboteurs had infiltrated even the highest ranks of the Party. The security services rounded up dozens of loyal founding members of the Communist Party, the so-called Slansky group, on charges of treason, and accused them of being part of a massive underground organization directed by the U.S. intelligence service.

These men were responsible for the anti-democratic coup of 1948 and the subsequent liquidation of democratic elements in society. Now, in an ironic twist of fate, they found themselves at the receiving end of their own methods: the very same brutal interrogations and torture that they considered eminently acceptable when applied to political opponents.

On 20 November 1952, after several months of brainwashing, the dramatic court hearings began. As they were marched into court, the accused unanimously parroted the Party line: "Yes. I am guilty of these heinous crimes of treason and sabotage. I am a fascist tool who attempted to subvert the dictatorship of the proletariat." They recited their lessons by rote and in turn incriminated others, according to the State's script, which led to more arrests. The audiences witnessed the phenomenon of high-ranking Party members begging for the death penalty. It was an Orwellian plot become reality. Pepa watched in amazement as the Party proceeded to cannibalize itself. He had trouble believing that some of these die-hard Communists were supposedly traitors. This wasn't symbolic posturing. This was a fight to the death. All of the Communists ran for cover to the winning faction, like a herd of lemmings, and mindlessly screamed their slogans.

Meanwhile, the effects of forced nationalization took its toll on the economy. Exacerbating the situation, in 1953 the government implemented a currency reform that wiped out people's life savings. Angry workers held spontaneous sit-down strikes in mines and factories. Shortly afterward, in a desperate attempt to forestall economic collapse, the state ordered people to work overtime and weekends without compensation.

The factory workers in Plzen went on strike in May 1953. As thousands poured into the streets, protest marches turned into riots. Strikers occupied city hall and the radio station before the protests were brutally suppressed by the SNB and the People's Militia.

The regime's forced collectivization of farms along the Soviet model had left the nation's expropriated farmers sullen and angry. In 1953 the crisis in the countryside came to a head: a mass exodus of farmers from the cooperative farms took the regime by surprise. Crops rotted in the fields and factory quotas went unmet as thousands of people laid down their tools and abandoned their workplaces in protest.

Pepa and the others were acutely aware that time was running out. They would receive their draft notices in the coming fall, well before Radek's release, and then all hope of continuing their fight would be finished. Because of their middle-class backgrounds, they were prime candidates for extended duty in the Black Barons penal battalion. If they were to continue their struggle against the regime, they would have to rescue Radek as quickly as possible and leave the country. But how?

The group had no intelligence on Jachymov—they had no idea where in the huge complex even to begin looking for Radek, much less how best to get him out. There was one obvious source for this kind of information. Everyone knew that CIC agents were active in the country, funnelling information out to the West. The Czechoslovak media were in hysterics about their total penetration of the country, and both Pepa and Borek could attest that Bartolomejska was full of them and of people who had been thrown into jail because they'd allegedly had contact with them. The Americans would know all about Jachymov and the security measures there.

Pepa decided to cross East Germany to West Berlin and get in touch with the Americans. He tapped Egon Plech to come with him. Egon was an ethnic German who spoke the language perfectly, and Pepa figured his language skills would come in handy during the trip. Pepa planned for the two of them to get some proper training in guerrilla and sabotage techniques from the Americans, and acquire good weapons and intelligence on Jachymov. Then they would spring Radek out of the camp and take off across the border.

On the appointed night they set off. Pepa could tell that Egon was getting nervous as they approached the East German border. The abandoned border villages were full of strange sounds and brooding shadows. When a dog started barking nearby, Egon, terrified, refused to go on. With Egon in a panic and unable to function, Pepa couldn't risk letting him travel back to Podebrady alone, running the gauntlet of ID checks and police questioning. Furious, Pepa called off the mission and accompanied Egon all the way back home. In Pepa's eyes, Egon had failed a crucial test—he was not someone you'd want by your side in combat.

Around this time Vaclav Sveda joined the inner circle. Vasek, as his friends called him, was an enthusiastic, upbeat young man with a ready laugh, about ten years older than the other group members. At the time he met Pepa, he was already married and the father of two small children. His wife was the adopted daughter of General Masin's cousins in Losany, whose farm adjoined the Masins' own.

Vasek was born into a humble farming family in Moravia. Shortly after he married, in 1947, his wife's adoptive parents died and the family farm in Losany passed to the young couple. They worked hard and made improvements to the farm, but their happiness was short-lived. When the Communists seized power Vasek was designated a class enemy and evicted from the farm with his wife and children.

Given no notice, the Svedas were allowed to take only the clothes on their backs. As soon as they were turned out, local Communist cadres moved in and appropriated all of the family's possessions. The young couple and their two small children were homeless. They found refuge in a small room in Vasek's parents' cramped cottage in Moravia. The four of them arrived with no blankets, no clothes, no housewares, and not a stick of furniture to their name. They slept on the floor.

To add to their troubles, Vasek, officially branded a class enemy, had difficulty finding any kind of work to feed his family. First he was assigned to tending pigs on a collective farm. It was filthy, smelly work, but he was conscientious about his job and he even won a regional prize for keeping

the pigs in tip-top condition. Then he was summarily fired—someone had
pointed out that he was a bourgeois, a "kulak." Now the family had no
income, and Vasek was reduced to asking his parents for a share of their
meager rations.

Vasek was an ardent admirer of General Masin and the Three Kings.
As a young high school student he, too, had tried to fight the Nazis. He
left home, hoping to reach England and join the Czech army in exile, but
instead spent the war in Nazi jails. Though he had missed his chance to
help his country back then, he wanted to make up for it now. He wouldn't
let himself be reduced to passive victimhood. Nobody in Czechoslovakia,
it seemed, was doing anything to reverse the Communists' hijacking of the
government—except the Masin brothers. While their peers were commis-
erating with each other in hushed voices in the cafés, the Masins and their
friends were at war. And Vasek wanted in.

When Pepa's plan to contact the Americans fell through, he and Vasek decided
to break Radek out of Jachymov by themselves. They made a couple of trips
to the Jachymov area to apply for jobs, but their applications were rejected.
Only mining specialists with the correct political profile need apply.

Next, they decided to pay off guards to obtain information on Radek's
whereabouts. But transportation by bus and train was a logistical nightmare
and they didn't have access to a vehicle, or to the kind of funds needed to
bribe the highly paid guards.

To add to their troubles, the Communist Party abruptly evicted the
Masin family once again to make way for Party members. This time they
were cast out from the relative comfort of Gottwald Street in Podebrady
to the outlying village of Cineves. Now the family home consisted of three
rooms in an abandoned farmhouse. There were good reasons no one had
been living in the place. When it rained, the roof leaked; the interior walls of
the living quarters were black with mold; the floorboards were rotten and in
one place had given way, leaving a gaping hole. The sanitary arrangements
consisted of an outhouse and a pump in the yard. But, the Party decided, for
class enemies it was just right.

By March of 1952, Pepa and his group hadn't conducted any action of
significance for five months, and they were no closer to freeing Radek. They
turned to Uncle Borek to develop a plan. After his arrest in 1951, Borek had
been cashiered from the military and expelled from the Communist Party,
even though the authorities conceded he had been wrongly accused and

no charges were ever brought against him. Through army connections he had managed to land a job as manager of a military recreation facility, the former Hotel Pupp in the spa town Karlovy Vary (Karlsbad); but later on, as the Communist Party continued its persecution of class enemies, he was kicked out of this job and only able to find work as a doorman.*

At their strategy meeting with Uncle Borek in Karlovy Vary, the group reviewed their options. Their top priority was to free Radek, but they agreed they had to restart their campaign against the regime. That entailed a delicate balancing act, because every action was fraught with danger. If anything went wrong, it could mean exposure of their past actions. With Radek completely at the mercy of his Communist captors, they had to be doubly careful. After all, the Communists, like the Nazis, were committed practitioners of *Sippenhaftung*, the premise that the whole family must suffer for the crimes of the individual.

At a minimum the group needed a motorcycle for transportation and some funds for bribes. They discussed and discarded several options until Zbynek suggested an idea everyone agreed to. Every fourteen days at the Kovolis machine manufacturing plant where he worked, the paymaster went by car to fetch the payroll, about one million crowns in cash.† The group decided Kovolis was a fair target. The company was owned by the state, and taking the money would harm only the state, as it would compensate the workers in any event.

Now they needed a police uniform to stop the Kovolis car. After several attempts to obtain one failed, Vasek volunteered to get a Communist militia uniform from his brother. This wasn't a uniform in the strictest sense. It consisted of blue overalls, a red armband, and blue beret, but it would serve their purpose as well as a police uniform. In the years between 1949 and 1954, no one dared to question or challenge a demand for ID papers from an individual in blue overalls with a red People's Militia armband. To go with the militia outfit, they made a special baton of the type used by police to stop vehicles, a circular paddle with a white and red target motif on a wooden handle. Milan would be the look-out. He would signal when he saw the paymaster's car approaching so Vasek could get out his stop sign

---

*The Hotel Pupp had been converted into an army-owned recreation center by that time.
†Roughly $140,000 in 1953 USD at the official exchange rate of 7.2/1 (Source: NARA, RG59, USFA Biweekly Intelligence Report No. 201, 31 July 1953, on Czechoslovakia, Part II, 10)

and put on his People's Militia armband. Vasek would stop the car and Pepa would be his backup, acting the part of an StB man in civilian garb.

Pepa and Vasek carefully inspected the car's route ahead of time. They took the train to Caslav, where the bank was, and walked the entire route to Hedvikov, where the company was—a distance of more than ten miles. They decided to stop the car at the intersection between the Markovice-Zleby road and the road to the village of Horky. Then they walked the entire escape route to cover all eventualities.

Two weeks later, Milan, Pepa, and Vasek took up their assigned positions. It was a warm day in mid-July and the setting was bucolic, with lovely old trees lining the sleepy country road and gently rolling fields all around. They waited and waited, then suddenly Pepa and Vasek saw the Kovolis automobile, with the paymaster inside, rushing by. There had been no signal from Milan. When they ran to look for him they found him sleeping peacefully in the grass by the ditch. They were furious: now they had to wait until the next payday.

The morning of 2 August 1952 promised to be the beginning of another lazy summer day, ideal for a drive. The head of the Kovolis factory militia,* security chief Karel Skokan, had reason to feel good about himself. He was being chauffeured in a late-model car, in a country where having one was a privilege reserved for a select few. He had a gun in his pocket at a time when the regime wouldn't even trust its citizens with maps and copying machines. This, more than anything, was the Party's badge of honor. As security chief of Kovolis he was a powerful member of the new ruling class. Security chiefs in the nation's factories outranked men in the most senior positions. Even the plant director had to watch his step or suffer the consequences.

With him in the car was Josef Rosicky, the plant's accountant and paymaster. Comrade Rosicky was in middle management, but he, too, had to make sure he stayed in Skokan's good graces. The hierarchy was clear. While Skokan got the roomy front seat next to the driver, Frantisek Koci, Rosicky sat in the back. And while Skokan had a 7.65-mm pistol, Rosicky only qualified for a smaller 6.35. Rosicky signed where he was told to sign. Still, he had cause to be happy about his station in life. The regime trusted him—he

---

*Factories in Communist countries had no unions. Instead, the militia was the party-controlled union and the internal police and security organization all rolled into one.

had a weapon—and he was making a good living, which was something worth holding onto.

The group's first stop was the bank, where the paymaster accepted the payroll in individual packets of 100 crown bills and placed them in his black suitcase. Next, Comrade Skokan asked Koci to stop at city hall so he could take care of some official business. While Koci and Rosicky waited, a corpulent woman came over to ask for a lift. Taking others along on the payroll run was strictly forbidden, but this was Ludmila Minarikova, mistress of the Kovolis factory canteen. She oversaw food supplies for several hundred men and women in a country that was racked with serious food shortages. When Kovolis exceeded its production quota, tropical fruit, raisins, and chocolate that came the plant's way were hers to distribute as she saw fit. So if she asked for a lift, perhaps the rules could be bent a bit. Koci and Rosicky readily agreed and made room for her in the back seat. Skokan made no objections when he returned, and at around ten in the morning, the car with its four occupants set off for the Kovolis factory at Hedvikov.

This time, only Vasek and Pepa were waiting. Milan had already been drafted into the army and was away in Slovakia, at the tank officer candidate school in St. Martin. When the car rounded the bend Vasek, wearing the militia man's armband, stepped out and raised the homemade stop sign. Skokan undoubtedly thought this was just another of the many militia checkpoints around the country, where vigilant groups of comrades were flushing out Western agents, saboteurs, kulaks, and other enemies of the state. The car pulled off the road.

"Honor to labor!"* the occupants called out.

"Honor to labor!" Vasek replied as he stepped up to the passenger side window. "ID papers, please."

Pepa could see that Skokan was getting ready to show this militiaman that he was a big wheel himself.

"How about you showing your identification first, comrade!?" Skokan snapped at Vasek.

Pepa quickly stepped up to the driver's side and pulled out his gun. That shut up Comrade Skokan.

"I am a member of the StB," Pepa announced. "Are any of you armed?"

---

*This greeting was to the Communists what "Heil Hitler" was to the Nazis: it identified the speaker as being of the correct political persuasion.

According to Zbynek, only one person, the security man Skokan, should have had a weapon. Pepa could see that Skokan noticed something was a little bit off—Pepa wasn't wearing a uniform—but he was still going to comply with StB and militia demands. At that time in Czechoslovakia, being stopped by men wearing civilian clothes in the middle of nowhere was nothing unusual.

"Yes, I am," he said.

"Your weapon, please," said Vasek, holding out his hand. Skokan quietly turned over his pistol.

"Does anyone else have weapons?" Pepa asked again.

"No," all four said quickly.

One look inside the vehicle told Pepa and Vasek that they had a problem. They had planned on three people, and had intended to get them out of the car and walk them to a small wooded copse, a pheasant preserve near Horky village. But now there was a fourth person in the back seat—a woman who was so heavy, Pepa seriously doubted she could manage the one-kilometer walk.

"We're involved in an investigation in Horky and we're all expected there," Pepa said. "Please get out, comrades." Pepa motioned to the driver and the security guard.

"Wait a minute now," Skokan said, his eyes narrowing. "I am head of plant security, and Comrade Rosicky here is also with the plant militia; we would have been informed!"

"It's a matter that has only just come up," Pepa said to defuse the situation. "Comrades, put up with us for a few minutes! Everything will be clarified shortly."

They looked at Pepa's gun, and that was the end of the discussion. Obediently, the driver and Skokan got out. The woman and Rosicky sat quietly in the back seat, saying nothing. Rosicky looked sullen. Pepa got into the driver's seat, put his P38 in his pocket where he could quickly get at it, and drove on. Vasek followed on foot with the driver and security guard.

Suddenly, Rosicky lunged over Pepa's shoulder and grabbed the steering wheel. The car swerved sharply. Pepa stomped on the brakes and the vehicle abruptly stopped. They had arrived in any case.

"Get out!" Pepa sternly commanded and he climbed out of the car himself. Rosicky and the canteen mistress hurriedly squeezed out on the passenger side. A glance to his right told Pepa the people were still working away in the field. They had noticed nothing. Pepa reached for the gun in his pocket. With a shock, he realized that it was gone—probably it had fallen out in the car. But Pepa kept walking around the car, toward the canteen mistress and the paymaster, without missing a beat.

With one rapid motion, Rosicky pulled out his 6.35-mm pistol and aimed it at Pepa's chest. There was a metallic clack. The safety was off, the bolt slid forward and chambered a round. All he had to do was pull the trigger and it would be over for Pepa.

"Hands up!" Rosicky spat out. His face was angry, determined. He was backing away from Pepa, toward the ditch.

In a flash, Pepa saw he couldn't reach him in time to disarm him. There were still more than twelve feet between them. So he kept walking toward him, closing the gap, smiling at him as he said smoothly, "Comrade, there must be some misunderstanding. We are police. I wanted to take you to Horky, and the situation will be cleared up shortly."

"Hands up!" the paymaster bawled, continuing to draw a bead on Pepa.

At that moment, Pepa was acutely aware of his surroundings, the people working in the field, Vasek and the two others one kilometer away. Too far away. Pepa would have to deal with the situation on his own. He looked straight into the paymaster's eyes, watching every muscle twitch in his face for sign of intent. Three feet still separated him from the end of the paymaster's pistol. Pepa held his gaze and smiled. In a split second, he sprang forward in a flying tackle, knocking Rosicky's arm from below and ramming his forearm up. As the gun jerked skyward, Pepa's hand slid up his forearm and closed firmly on his wrist. Pepa twisted the arm behind Rosicky's back and tripped him up. The paymaster fell heavily, face down. Pepa fell on top of him, holding onto his arm. It was a move he had practiced hundreds of times in the Podebrady woods. They were struggling on the ground now but Rosicky was much heavier than Pepa and was fighting hard. As they rolled into the ditch, Pepa forced Rosicky's right arm up high behind his back, loosening his grip on the gun. Pepa got his finger on the trigger, jammed the gun barrel between Rosicky's shoulder blades and pulled the trigger twice. When he leaped to his feet, Comrade Rosicky, who had sworn an oath to defend the rule of the Party, lay motionless in the ditch. It was all over for him.

The canteen mistress took one look at the motionless paymaster and ran into the woods, screaming at the top of her lungs. Pepa ran after her, calling "Stop! Stop immediately!"

She was so overweight and out of shape, he had no trouble catching up. She stopped and begged, "Don't shoot! Please don't shoot me!"

"He was lying!" Pepa said. "He said he wasn't armed!"

"Don't shoot me! Jesus Maria, don't shoot!" She was terrified; Pepa knew she would do as told.

They had planned to tie everybody down, partisan style. This was supposed to require no ropes: When the legs are twisted around a tree backward, and the person is forced down to his knees in this position, he cannot get back up unassisted. But one look at the obese canteen mistress told Pepa the partisan approach would never work.

"Stay here!" he commanded, "Don't move until I come back!"

"Yes," she stammered, nodding furiously. "Yes, I'll stay!"

So Pepa left her standing there and hurried back to the car. A quick look at the workers in the field assured him that they had heard nothing. The shots had been muffled. Pepa put Rosicky's pistol in his pocket, threw the dead comrade over the hedge, and drove back to meet Vasek.

"Get in the car!" Pepa said to the driver and the guard. "The other fellow ran into trouble because he lied. If you have any guns on you, the same thing will happen to you!"

Seeing that he meant what he said, the two complied instantly. "We have no guns!" they vigorously assured him.

They drove to the pheasant preserve without incident and found the canteen mistress still standing where Pepa had left her, sobbing, "Jesus Maria, Jesus Maria."

"Stay here! If you leave this place before the half hour is up, we will find you and you will be in trouble," Pepa warned them. There was no point in tying the other two up if the canteen mistress was free.

Vasek and Pepa hurried back to the car. They picked up the paymaster's briefcase, which lay in the ditch, and drove to the train station at full speed while Pepa hunted about for his P38. He found it on the floor, between the seats. As it was, they were running extremely late. Abandoning the car in the woods, they ran across the field to meet the train, which was stopped at a red semaphore. Luckily the train was running even later than they were. It was a close call, but this was the last time they would have to rely on public transportation to make their getaway. Vasek took the briefcase home with him and Pepa went directly to Jesenik to his job.

Before they parted ways, Pepa and Vasek tallied up the contents: 850,000 crowns in hundred-crown bills.* The group now had a war chest. They would be able to get transportation, bribe the guards, and spring Radek out of Jachymov. Now they had the resources to strike the regime where it hurt, perhaps hitting President Gottwald's personal train, or some of the special uranium transports to the Soviet Union.

Well aware that others might later accuse them of conducting robbery for personal gain, they had decided in advance that none of them would personally take any of the money. They were partisans, not common criminals. Consequently, the group designated Zdena Masinova's friend Zbynek Rousar as treasurer. Rousar was an ex-RAF officer who had served as the Czech consul to the Belgian Congo before the Communists cashiered him from the diplomatic service. He had met Zdena Masinova in 1951, when he had been sent down to Podebrady as a manual laborer on a bridge construction project. Zdena soon began accompanying the polished ex-diplomat to concerts and soirées when her deteriorating health permitted. He spoke perfect French, fluent English, and German. He had traveled extensively and, to add to his attractions, he shared Zdena's passion for music. An accomplished violinist, he often joined her in duets. Zdena decided Rousar could be trusted. But whereas Uncle Borek was passionately supportive of the boys' fight against the Communists, ex-diplomat Rousar always seemed cautious, repeatedly warning the boys to be careful. It was this caution and conservatism that, in the eyes of Pepa and his friends, made him a good steward for the group's new war chest. The funds were to be used only for operations, subject to the approval of Rousar and Borek, and to buy Vasek a sofa bed and chairs, since his family had been reduced to sleeping on the floor.

Then, in one of those unexpected twists of fate that wrench destinies into new paths, Communist President Gottwald suddenly died. His successor granted a blanket amnesty to prisoners accused of "minor" crimes, and Radek was released a year early.

He returned to his family emaciated and ill. Jachymov marked him forever. He got out and his first objective was to bring down the Communists. He had opposed the regime before, even without knowing the full truth about it. But once he had seen the insides of those prisons and camps with his own eyes and experienced them himself, he was truly committed to fighting them.

---

*Roughly $118,000 in 1953 USD at the official exchange rate

He was shocked to find his sick mother living in the hovel in Cineves. Having been expelled from the university as a subversive, he was lucky to get a job as a tractor driver at a state agricultural equipment unit.* Worse yet, his student's draft exemption automatically terminated. In a few weeks it would be fall, the season for draft notices, and both brothers fully expected to be called up into the Black Barons labor battalion, which would put an end to their resistance struggle. Milan, a year older than Pepa and Zbynek, had already been called up, but luckily the authorities had sent him to the reserve tank officers' school in Slovakia.

The brothers secretly began to prepare for departure. Not even the other group members knew of their recon trips to the border. In the meantime, they pushed their resistance campaign into high gear, planning to make best use of the little time remaining. A contact at the railroad advised them that a top secret train hauling two or three cars of uranium ore and a caboose full of StB men was scheduled on a run to the border town of Cierné. They chose a place to blow up the transport, kill the troops, and deny the Soviets their uranium. Pepa and Radek made plans to ambush a busload of StB officers that routinely took weapons practice at a nearby military base. They also considered striking directly at the president and the senior Party leadership.

For all of these operations they needed explosives, and Vasek knew where to find them. Among the assorted jobs he had held after losing the farm was one in the Kank silver mines, where Donarit explosives were used.† For this operation, Vasek traveled up from Moravia, where he was working at a sawmill. Pepa came from Jesenik with a truck, telling his boss that he was going to Prague to pick up a new tractor. Vasek led the group into the mine through a remote, unguarded ventilation shaft. Unfortunately, miners were working the night shift in that area, and they had to retreat empty-handed.

A number of weeks elapsed before they tried again. This time Pepa couldn't get away from his job, so Radek and the others went without him. Vasek asked a friend to pick them up afterwards with his car, at a predetermined time and place. It was the first time Vasek and Zbynek met Vladimir Hradec on an operation. Zbynek and Vladimir lived next door to each other,

---

*These state agricultural equipment units rented out tractors and other equipment confiscated from private farmers to collective farms and private farmers.

†Donarit, which contains dinitrotoluene (DNT), was a special explosive used in mining.

but because of the Masins' emphasis on tight security, neither had known that the other was a member of the group without a name. This encounter would later have disastrous consequences for Vladimir.

The foursome climbed down the creaky ladders into the depths of the mine, down five levels, fifty meters below ground. Vasek turned off into a passageway and the others hurried after him in single file, flashlights in hand. This time all was quiet—there was no activity in the area. Vasek finally stopped in front of a rough wooden door made of heavy planks. He played the beam of his flashlight over it. When he saw the massive padlock, he turned away in despair.

"Don't be stupid!" the others hissed at him.

They hunted about for a discarded drill bit or some other implement that could be used as a lever. The formidable-looking lock flew off on the first try. In the beam of their flashlights they saw a room hewn into the rock, packed to the ceiling with twenty-five-kilo crates of explosives. This was it! They moved quickly. Each man shouldered a crate—even Radek, although he was still weak from his stay in Jachymov. Back along the passage and up the ladder they went, lugging their crates for fifty meters in a near-verticle ascent. Exhausted, they dropped their boxes at the designated pick-up location and waited.

Time passed and the car did not show.

Shit! Radek thought to himself. *Where the heck is that guy?*

Dawn was breaking, and still the four of them were sitting by the roadside, on four boxes of explosives in the middle of open fields. At any moment an StB or militia patrol might stumble upon them. Radek began to seriously consider commandeering the next car to come down the road when Vasek's friend finally appeared. Everyone hurriedly dumped the crates into the trunk. Radek did not see or talk to the driver and purposely did not ask Vasek who he was—the less everyone knew, the better, for all concerned. The car took off with one hundred kilos of explosives in the trunk and the youths walked to the train station.

Getting the Donarit had taken much longer than expected. They would have to leave the country soon, if they were to leave at all. There was no time to develop the ambush on the uranium train or the other attacks they'd envisioned. But leaving without at least one more spectacular act of sabotage seemed like a terrible waste.

And so Vasek proposed a plan. The fall of 1953 found Czechoslovakia racked by massive shortages. In Vasek's part of Moravia, even straw was in short supply. The group decided to wipe out the straw reserves in Vasek's district. Their goal was two-fold: to help push the already-tottering socialist economy over the edge, and to prove that the Communists were lying when they claimed to have full control of the country. The Masin brothers and their friends were going to show them that their opponents were far from vanquished.

During that period, collective farms usually set up huge communal straw stacks, one per collective. Vasek had counted a total of twenty-one stacks, containing approximately five hundred railroad cars' worth of straw. The straw had a value of more than 750,000 crowns.* Vladimir and Radek—the group's technical experts—set to work cobbling together igniters.

Unfortunately batteries and clocks, which could be modified to make timers, were in short supply. Working in the Hradec family's basement, they tried using cigarettes and cigars, both of which burned for only a few minutes. Next, they tried incense sticks. These burned for twenty minutes, which still didn't give them enough time. They needed at least half an hour. Next, they pulverized the incense sticks, stabilizing the powder with glue. Still not enough time—plus the sticks broke at the slightest impact. So they wrapped wire around the glue-and-incense sticks, to restrict the flow of oxygen. This slowed the burn speed. Now it was only necessary to adjust the length of the burn stick to yield the correct time. They attached approximately 1.5 meters of celluloid camera film, which burns at a very high intensity, to each of their burn sticks, and their igniters were ready.

Igniters in hand, Radek headed off to Moravia on 7 September. This time the trip was fast and hassle free. He was riding a Java 500-cc motorcycle, one of two motorcycles purchased with the proceeds of Kovolis and the help of some well-connected acquaintances. The Java 500-cc was the fastest, most powerful machine on the road, and was used almost exclusively by police and special StB units. The engine occasionally misfired, but that couldn't be helped—parts could only be obtained through special police supply channels and were difficult to come by.

That night Radek and Vasek set off by bike. Their plan was to pass through twenty-one villages and put their explosives in the straw stacks belonging to the collective farms. The igniters were timed so that the fire would break out only after they had finished the round.

---

*Roughly $104,200 in 1953 USD

Everything was going like clockwork until the drive chain on Radek's bicycle started falling off. He had to stop repeatedly to put it back on. When the first of the straw stacks burst into flames, they had scarcely reached the village of Morice and still had a good number of stacks left to go. Already villagers were running out into the streets, shouting and pointing at the fires. Radek and Vasek pedaled by, trying to look inconspicuous, but the risk of continuing was too great. They decided to call it quits and turned back toward Vasek's house.

All of a sudden, someone in the village square called out to them, "Where is the fire?"

Radek said something in reply and immediately realized his mistake. He could have kicked himself. In the middle of rural Moravia, his Bohemian accent instantly flagged him as an outsider. They cycled out of the village and over a little bridge. Once again Radek's chain fell off. He hastened down to the stream and threw the remaining timers into the water. Then he scrambled back up the bank to his bicycle, and hurriedly tried to put the chain back on. Two men on bikes appeared behind them, gaining on them fast. In a flash Vasek jumped on his bike and zoomed away, leaving Radek to fend for himself.

Slowly Radek got to his feet. The men rode past him, dismounted and turned their bikes to block the road.

"What are you doing here?" one of them challenged.

Radek said nothing. One look told him these two were militia types. He pulled out his gun, took quick aim and fired twice. One in the chest, one to the head. The man let go of his bike and fell to the ground. The other man instantly flung away his bicycle and sprinted off into the cornfield, his back illuminated by the glow of the bicycle lamp. Radek fired twice at the receding silhouette.

Now Radek stood alone on the country road. All along the horizon, as far as he could see, fiercely burning fires lit up the night sky. He hoisted his useless bike onto his shoulder, guessed the direction of Vasek's house and hurried across the field toward it. After a while, in the almost-total darkness and rough terrain, he popped out of the corn. To his surprise, he nearly ran into Vasek, who was peacefully marching along the road pushing his bike.

The next morning Radek fired up his Java and headed for home. It turned out that the two men were heads of the local fire department and in fact were members of the local militia.* Police had swarmed into the villages, setting up roadblocks at every intersection in the district, but to Radek's amazement, they waved him through. His Java 500-cc gave him a free pass.

As he neared Olomouc, the Java's engine was repeatedly stalling and misfiring. Radek knew he'd never make it back to Podebrady. He asked for directions to the local police garage and coasted in, his engine coughing and sputtering.

"Honor to labor!" he hailed the first policeman he saw. "Comrade, I have some problems with my motorcycle. Could you take a look at it?"

The comrade did. No charge and no questions asked. Radek thanked him and hopped back on the motorcycle. As he roared off to Podebrady he couldn't get over his amazement: he was the guy they were looking for and they had just fixed his motorcycle for free!

Vasek reported that the media, true to form, maintained total silence, but for weeks the rumor mill ran hot with fantastic tales.

"Do you know what's happening? Those were the partisans. Guerrillas. They shoot incendiary ammunition into straw stacks!"

"Guerrillas are moving in from Russia, heading West through the Czech Republic!"

"The partisans have special boots that allow them to jump over tall fences in a single leap!"

"The Americans are on the move!"

"U.S. Special Forces are already in Czechoslovakia. The invasion is under way!"

There were even reported sightings of black troops all around rural Moravia. After months and years of hoping and waiting, something, finally, was happening.

What was more, the Communist regime's foot soldiers were running scared. Pepa and Radek knew people who had joined the police because they thought it was a good job: good pay, the chance to be big wheels in town. Now their wives were telling them to get out because they could come to a bad end.

The brothers heard that a number of SNB men quit the service in the wake of the operation, thinking that the day of reckoning was coming. Pepa and Radek were pleased. The rumors, they believed, hurt the regime more

---

*Every collective farm, like every factory of a certain size, had its workers' militia, an internal armed guard whose function was to ensure compliance with the regime's directives. Radek had hit the first man in the chest and right eye. He survived.

than the economic losses. In totalitarian societies where people cannot trust the media to report reliably, rumor takes on a power unknown in societies with a free press. Pepa and Radek concluded that a few hard-hitting sabotage actions could unleash the power of rumor and bring about popular rebellion to coincide with the expected American invasion.*

The regime quickly took countermeasures. It was decreed that every collective farm had to post guards at every straw stack. Needless to say, this was not a popular measure among the farmers, who were already disgruntled about losing their land. They had to work in the fields all day long and then work as guards at night.

During September pressure on Radek, Pepa, and their friends began to mount. A number of eyewitnesses at Morice had seen Radek and Vasek, and it was only a question of time until the authorities matched names to faces. Militiaman Blazek, one of the men Radek had fired on, told the police that he recognized one of the two mystery men. The police had him reviewing line-ups and mug shots. Already the SNB had gone door to door in Vasek's home village of Pivin, showing pictures of suspects, questioning and arresting people. They had stopped by Vasek's house twice—the last time Vasek escaped over the backyard fence, fearing they'd come to get him.† Pepa got his draft notice and was ordered to report for service with the Black Barons in one week. In a few weeks Radek would likely receive his notice as well.‡

Meanwhile, in the United States, Dwight Eisenhower, the World War II hero and victorious D-Day commander, had been president for nearly nine

---

*Siegfried Kracauer and Paul L. Berkman's interviews of East European refugees led them to conclude that: "The interviews show that many who caution against active resistance are convinced of its desirability and success in the event of an open East-West clash. War, or perhaps even the imminence of war, is the only crisis which in their opinion will call forth, and justify, active resistance. The interviews are replete with misgivings about untimely action and useless sacrifices, and with indications that most Satellite non-Communists would be ready to consider active resistance only when they thought the U.S. was fully prepared and willing to aid in liberation." Kracauer, Siegfried, and Berkman, Paul L., *Satellite Mentality: Political Attitudes and Propaganda Susceptibilities of Non-Communists in Hungary, Poland and Czechoslovakia*, New York: Frederick A. Praeger Publishers, 1956, 125. Significantly, the Mašíns and their friends began their campaign to obtain weapons and launch active resistance in 1951, soon after RFE began broadcasting, when they became convinced that war was imminent.

†Recollection of Lidka Švédová, as told to Joseph Mašín in 1991

‡Vladimír Hradec was later jailed for thirteen years and after his release was promptly drafted into this forced labor battalion. It was imprisonment by another name. "What saved Kikina's butt," Pepa later opined, "was that he knew how to type, so he worked in the commander's office."

months. During his campaign, he had outdone President Harry Truman in his hard line toward Communism, denouncing him for having "abandoned friendly nations such as . . . Poland and Czechoslovakia to . . . Communist aggression which soon swallowed them."[1] Throughout the 1952 presidential campaign, RFE and VOA reported that Eisenhower had promised to free the Eastern Europeans. Pepa and Radek knew that East European refugees were already enlisting in the special commando unit that had been set up in West Germany for behind-the-lines action in the coming war.* With the Third World War about to start, possibly in a matter of weeks, he and Radek decided it was finally time to leave the country.

Five would go this time: Radek, Pepa, Milan, Vasek, and Zbynek. Egon Plech had disqualified himself the year before by his conduct during the abortive escape attempt. Radek and Pepa had sounded out Vladimir in a roundabout way, and it seemed to them that he didn't want to leave. Neither Egon nor Vladimir knew the true origin of the group's new submachine guns and pistols, so Radek and Pepa thought they wouldn't be directly at risk. The brothers carefully sounded out others among their friends whom they thought might want to join them, but in the end it was back to the core group.

There was a question about Zbynek. He was getting unruly and rebellious. He wanted to do more sabotage actions and argued that the group was not doing enough. On Friday and Saturday evenings he was drinking more than Pepa and Radek thought prudent. Pepa and Radek, who believed in the need to stay clean and in total control of your mind and mouth, were teetotalers and didn't smoke. They did not want nicotine dependency to weaken their resolve during the next interrogation, and they did not want to risk a run-in with the police for something stupid like drunk driving. On one occasion several people had seen Zbynek riding one of the two motorcycles purchased from the Kovolis proceeds under the influence, and they told Radek the motorcycle was dented. Vasek put in a good word for him, claiming that his youth was a mitigating factor, but Zbynek was jeopardizing everyone in the group. Pepa and Radek decided they couldn't leave him behind. They would take him along, but with a condition: he wouldn't get a weapon. The brothers didn't tell him why, but they believed he might misuse it, fire it for no reason, and jeopardize them all.

---

*A small U.S. Army Special Forces unit was set up in 1952. It was stationed in West Germany, consisted mostly of Eastern European refugees, and had begun training in guerrilla warfare (*New York Times*, 18 January and 24 March 1952, as quoted in Kovrig, *The Myth of Liberation*, 105).

Lieutenant Colonel Josef Masin shortly before World War II. *Courtesy of Zdena Masinova*

Captain Vaclav Moravek. *Courtesy of Jaroslav Cvancara*

Lieutenant Colonel Josef Balaban. *Courtesy of Jaroslav Cvancara*

Ctibor "Borek" Novak, Josef Masin's brother-in-law and fellow underground fighter, before World War II. *Courtesy of Zdena Masinova*

Josef Masin holding a brace of pheasants, circa 1937. He was a passionate hunter. *Courtesy of Zdena Masinova*

Josef Masin in 1914, as a young recruit to the Austro-Hungarian imperial army. *Courtesy of Zdena Masinova*

The long way home: Captain Josef Masin with his company during a troop review in Manchuria, circa 1919. Sixty thousand Czechoslovak troops fought their way across Russia to the Pacific Ocean. The saluting officer is a Russian general. *Courtesy of Zdena Masinova*

Adolf Hitler meets President Hacha in Prague castle after the German invasion of 1939.
Courtesy of Jaroslav Cvancara

Czechs express grief and anger as German troops
enter Prague on 15 March 1939. *Courtesy of Jaroslav
Cvancara*

Waffen SS troops of the *Leibstandarte Adolf Hitler* parading in occupied Prague. *Courtesy of Jaroslav Cvancara*

Gestapo Commissar Oskar Fleischer. *Courtesy of Jaroslav Cvancara*

Paul Thümmel (aka Agent A-54) with his wife. *Courtesy of Jaroslav Cvancara*

Kdo ho zná?

Do pražské nemocnice byl dne 13. V. dopraven těžce zraněný muž, který tam zakrátko zemřel, aniž přišel k vědomí. Jeho totožnost nemohla býti dosud zjištěna. Měl u sebe osobní doklady na jméno Václav Seidl, 3. ledna 1901 v Praze rozený, do Zbraslavic, okres Kutná Hora příslušný, a další doklady na jméno Josef Novotný z Prahy XII. O dokladech však bylo zjištěno, že nepatří zraněnému muži. U muže byl nalezen větší peněžitý obnos.

Tempo   Snímek ČTK

Left: "Who knows him?" This newspaper article was part of the Gestapo's campaign to determine whom they had shot in Prague on 13 May 1941. The mystery man was Lieutenant Colonel Josef Masin. *Courtesy of Jaroslav Cvancara*

Below: The Pankrac Testament, Josef Masin's 1942 farewell letter to his children. Written on toilet paper and hidden in a crack in the wall of his prison cell, it would remain undiscovered for four years, until 1946. *Courtesy of Zdena Masinova*

The Masin family in 1944. Clockwise from left rear: Josef "Pepa" Masin Jr., Ctirad "Radek" Masin, Zdena Masinova, Emma Novakova, Zdena Masinova Jr. *Courtesy of Zdena Masinova*

After the war, Radek and Pepa found several Steyr command cars in a depot of abandoned German military vehicles near Kolin. From three wrecks they and their friends built one complete vehicle. Here a group from Podebrady is on the way to support the volleyball team during an away game. Milan is driving; Vladimir "Kikina" Hradec is fourth from left. Radek, Pepa, and Milan sold this prized possession in 1951 to the Chlumec fire department in order to finance their first, failed escape attempt. *Courtesy of Milan Paumer*

Chapter 11

TERRA INCOGNITA

With Czechoslovakia's borders to the West impassable, the group opted for the much longer route across East Germany to West Berlin. After the border crossing, the trip would be 180 kilometers long, most of which they planned to cover on foot or by train. What lay beyond the border in East Germany was a complete unknown. Of the five friends only Vasek spoke German fluently. Radek and Pepa spoke broken German and the others spoke none at all. None of them had ever seen the area they were to traverse. They had no maps and no prospect of getting any.

The German Democratic Republic, like Czechoslovakia, was run by a paranoid Stalinist government that did its utmost to isolate its population from the West, as well as from its brother socialist states. But despite the strictly censored media, the East German population had a growing sense that while the United States was pumping money into the Western occupation zones via the Marshall Plan, the Soviet Union was plundering its occupation zone. The Soviets shipped everything from automobiles, art treasures, and telephone cable to railroad tracks and even entire industrial plants back to the Soviet Union as war reparations. Although many workers believed fervently in socialism and the Communist ideology, they saw that living conditions in the Communist German Democratic Republic lagged far behind those in the capitalist West.

Meanwhile, the doctrinaire Communist government under Secretary General Walter Ulbricht started a systematic campaign to destroy the private sector of the economy. The campaign would have led to massive economic dislocation in any event, but then Moscow also ordered a dramatic

defense buildup, insisting all the while that the flow of reparations continue undiminished.

As the economy reached the breaking point, supply chains collapsed
and the nation was plunged into crisis. Business owners and entrepreneurs
fled the country in droves, seeing no future for themselves and their families
in the GDR.[1] Farmers abandoned their farms and their villages.[2] Dramatic
shortages of food and basic necessities were the result. Fruit and vegetables
were virtually unavailable in the stores and there were acute shortages of
potatoes, sugar, rice, meat, butter, fats, and cooking oil.

In late 1952 wildcat strikes and work slow-downs sporadically erupted
in nationalized factories around the country. On 16 June 1953 a strike broke
out in the Stalinallee construction site. The construction workers were the
vanguard of the progressive proletariat according to Communist ideology
and the Stalinallee construction project was its showcase. Although the
workers dispersed by evening, word spread like wildfire.

Rundfunk Im Amerikanischen Sektor (RIAS), the West Berlin radio
station which enjoyed enormous prestige and a huge audience throughout
East Germany, broadcast news of the Berlin protests far into the provinces.
The Ulbricht regime was caught completely unprepared as massive strikes
and protest marches broke out on the following day in Berlin and the large
industrial centers of the nation. The Soviet *Kommandatura* declared martial
law in the greater Berlin area. Soviet troops moved decisively against the
unarmed marching workers, deploying hundreds of tanks throughout the
city, firing rubber bullets and ultimately live ammunition against workers
and housewives who carried signs calling for free and secret ballots during
elections, resignation of the Ulbricht government, reduction of prices, and
removal of border fortifications.

The Kasernierte Volkspolizei (KVP), East Germany's proto-army, moved
into action only when the Soviet military authorities authorized it, and only
in the wake of Soviet troops. In the following days it deployed without
Soviet oversight in mop-up operations. Contrary to the Party leadership's
fears, the KVP didn't fraternize with the workers. It proved to be politically
reliable, yet a lack of training and experience limited its effectiveness. A
total of 8,133 KVP troops saw action on 17 June.[3]

With more than five hundred thousand people participating in the uprising on 17 June and the following days, many of them of working-class origin,
any illusions the Ulbricht regime might have cherished about its popularity
were shattered. Until October 1953 the KVP was beating down the strikes

that continued to flare up sporadically,[4] and the Communist leadership was fully aware that only the decisive intervention of the Soviet military had saved it from certain destruction. The Party leadership and the Volkspolizei brass rushed to overhaul training programs and procure new weapons. They rolled out an early warning system to give advance notice of future trouble. They also developed a series of graduated responses to internal unrest. A new network of *Abschnittsbevollmächtigte* (ABVs)—local police officers assigned to community policing—would keep a finger on the nation's pulse.[5] In the event of a disturbance, the ABVs would call on the newly formed *Schnellkommandos,* motorized rapid deployment units that represented the regime's first line of defense.[6] The regime's final bulwark would be the KVP, which it hastily began equipping to oppose internal revolt and to strengthen its rapid response capability.

Blinded by its own ideology, the leadership refused to acknowledge that this revolt was a spontaneous, homegrown phenomenon. According to the leadership's Marxist-Leninist worldview, western provocateurs and agents had seduced and misled "their" workers. Workers simply did not revolt against Marxist-Leninist governments. This conviction shaped all of the regime's plans to counter future unrest.

When the Masins and their three friends crossed the border into East Germany in October 1953, they walked into a country only barely beaten into submission. Under the quiet surface, it was roiling with discontent. Though the five men didn't know it, conditions in East Germany were in fact closer to the boiling point than they were in Czechoslovakia. The East German Communist regime feared its own people and sat with its finger nervously on the trigger of a massive repression mechanism. Its nightmare scenario was an armed uprising of the people, instigated and led by foreign provocateurs.

Chapter 12

"HAVE THE WEDDING
WITHOUT ME"

Radek and Pepa knew that the way to Berlin was fraught with danger. The border districts were heavily patrolled by armed guards. All of Czechoslovakia was swarming with SNB and workers' militia spot-checking travel permits. They guessed that the situation in East Germany was no better. What was more, navigation was going to be a serious problem. Detailed maps were considered classified state secrets, and they had none. In fact, being caught with a map near the border meant an automatic three years in prison—more if the Party decided to press charges of espionage.

Then in an unexpected stroke of good luck, a friend of their mother's gave them a map of the Mount St. Katherine area. It was a few years old, but it showed every road and forest trail in the immediate vicinity of the East German border. Leaving nothing to chance, Pepa made one more scouting trip all the way to the border fence. He had to talk his way through police ID checks and he observed patrol activity in the abandoned border villages, but he judged the approach doable. Finally they had their route!

Because the mail was not secure, Pepa traveled all the way to Slovakia to brief Milan. He explained that he would send a coded letter with the exact date of departure. If he couldn't come, Milan was to reply by telegram, "Unable to participate. Have the wedding without me." Pepa also visited Vasek and Zbynek, giving them different code sentences and swearing them to absolute secrecy.

While the others waited tensely, Radek and Pepa packed all of the guns and the Donarit explosive in sealed tanks and buried them in the woods near Podebrady. When they returned at the vanguard of the American liberating armies, their weapons would be ready. Only two others knew the location: Uncle Borek and their mother's friend Zbynek Rousar.* Finally Pepa wrote to Milan, Zbynek, and Vasek using the agreed-upon code.

Vasek left his home in Pivin on the morning of 1 October. His heart bursting with emotion, he kissed his wife good-bye. He told her that he was going to see a doctor about a bothersome old hip injury. Then he lovingly hugged his two small children, assuring them that he would be back in a couple of days. He consoled himself with the thought that the separation wouldn't be for long. After all, the American invasion was imminent, and if General Masin could endure separation from his family, then he could too. He had packed a change of clothes, an extra pair of shoes, a razor, some handkerchiefs, and a German-Czech dictionary in a briefcase. In his pockets were a watch and silver cigarette case. He took the train to Kolin, near Prague, where he spent the night with a friend. The next day he continued on to Prague, where Zbynek was already waiting for him in a state of high excitement.

Like Vasek, Zbynek wore city clothes—his black leather jacket, of which he was very proud, and pressed trousers under a military-style greatcoat. He too had his cigarette lighter and cigarettes in his pockets, plus a watch and pocketknife. While Zbynek went off to buy five train tickets to Chomutov, Vasek furtively slipped a farewell letter to his wife into the mailbox. This was in express violation of Pepa's security instructions, but he simply couldn't bear the thought of leaving Lidka without word of any kind.

Milan forged his leave pass and went AWOL from the officers' school in St. Martin on 2 October, just days before graduation. He was just a little sorry to miss graduation, which would have made him a full-fledged tank commander, but for him there was no turning back. Deserting from the Czechoslovak Army carried a two-year jail sentence, and forging the pass another five years. When he arrived in Podebrady he was still in uniform. Inside his briefcase, he had stashed the essentials: a brown civilian suit and a pair of civilian shoes; his watch, driver's license, and military documents; his military graduation picture; a membership card for the Czech youth organization; his girlfriend's ring and picture; and eight speeding tickets.

---

*The weapons, unearthed from their woodland hiding place, were exhibited in the Prague police museum, at Na Karlově, from the mid-1950s until 1991 or 1992.

"Be careful, boys!" Zdena Masinova entreated her sons. Her eyes were unnaturally bright and Pepa saw that she was fighting back tears.

"It'll be a piece of cake," Pepa assured her, with more bravado than he felt. "A question of a few days and we'll be over there."

"As soon as war breaks out, we'll be back," Radek promised. "Don't worry, Mama. Uncle Borek and Rousar are here to keep an eye on things."

"And if there's a delay, we're coming back to get you and Nenda out," Pepa added.

"Godspeed. I know you'll make it." Zdena was determined to be strong. It was what her husband would have wanted and what her sons expected. Pepa and Radek had not told her the exact day of departure and she had not asked. One day they would just be gone, and that would be that.

Radek stood next to Pepa on the Podebrady station platform as Milan's train roared in. Under their cool, controlled exteriors anticipation surged. They monitored the platform and the train unobtrusively for any sign of police surveillance.

Radek was wearing a greatcoat and black raincoat over his gray suit and brown sweater. He had wanted to take something that had belonged to his father with him, so he had put on his father's hunting shirt. Pepa was wearing his father's gold wristwatch. His black raincoat matched Radek's. Underneath it he wore a brown sweater, a necktie, a gray sports shirt, and pants. He had his ID papers and driver's license in his pockets, along with a season bus pass, twenty-five U.S. dollars that he had bought on the black market, 135 Czech crowns, and a doctor's note stating that he was ill and unable to work.

Pepa also carried a briefcase in which he had put a spare pair of shoes, a flashlight of the type used by the Czechoslovak police—it might come in handy to stop cars—a Czech-German dictionary for coded communication with Borek, and, in the dictionary, a picture of his father. He and Radek had decided against bringing shaving gear since neither one was shaving on a daily basis and the trip would be short anyway.

To aid in navigation, they were bringing along a road map of the Czech Republic, the detailed map of the border, two compasses, and a map taken from a popular magazine showing East Germany in outline and the main highways to Berlin. Well aware that after crossing into East Germany they would be operating blind, they planned to bear north using the compasses and, once they hit a highway, to orient themselves by posted signs. They hoped to cover part of the way by train, but there they faced another problem. They had no East German money, which was impossible to get in Czechoslovakia.

But the most valuable element of their inventory was not in their brief-cases or in their pockets. It was the information that their father's old friend Frantisek Vanek, a former general in the Czechoslovak army, was ready and waiting for word from the Americans. Vanek himself, a silent man of simple tastes and humble origins, had been purged from the army in 1952. But his associates still retained their commands. He had been tapped for the failed 1951 uprising and now he knew the Masin brothers intended to leave the country. When the Americans invaded, his group could deliver a whole frontline division—fourteen thousand men. If this division stood down and didn't fight, the western forces could pour through the breach and attack the Soviet bloc troops to the north and south from behind, decimating them with deadly speed, cutting off their supply lines and wreaking havoc in the rear. If some or all of Vanek's forces joined in the assault, the resulting may-hem in the Soviet bloc's ranks would be truly impressive.*

The brothers would establish a communications link between Vanek's group and the Americans in the West. Only Radek, Pepa, and their Uncle Borek were privy to the secret, and they hadn't breathed a word to the others—not even to Milan, Zbynek, or Vasek.

Zbynek and Vasek met the train from Podebrady in Prague's main train station.† After a quick greeting the five youths went to the men's room, where Radek handed out the weapons each had previously requested. For Vasek he had a brand-new Czech 7.65-mm with twelve rounds, and for Milan a STAR pistol, a Spanish 9-mm military model. Pepa already had a Walther 7.65-mm, along with a spare magazine and some loose rounds, and Radek had chosen a German 9-mm P38 Parabellum with two magazines and twenty-one rounds.‡

---

*There were no Soviet troops stationed in Czechoslovakia until they invaded in 1968 after the Prague Spring.

†The five men met at the Wilsonovo Nádraží (Wilson Train Station) named in honor of U.S. President Woodrow Wilson, whose Fourteen Points and advocacy of national self-determination were instrumental in the creation of the Czechoslovak state at the close of WWI.

‡Pepa's Walther was the gun he had taken from Skokan. Both Vašek's and Milan's weap-ons came from the police station at Čelákovice. Radek's Parabellum was a German weapon from WWII.

Zbynek was the only one without a gun, and he was not happy about it. To make him feel better, Radek and Pepa put him in charge of the chloroform, the parachute line, and the food, which he grumpily stashed in his briefcase. They were traveling light, taking only minimal provisions: a little ham, two cans of condensed milk, some bread, and a dry salami. Since the trip to Berlin would be short—the friends estimated no more than four days at most—they had decided to take a calculated risk, trading supplies for speed.

Radek quickly reviewed their MO one more time. "We've got to expect at least one police check; probably more. We'll try to talk ourselves through, but if there's trouble, group A backs up group B. Jump the bad guys, chloroform them, and tie them up with the parachute line. Remember, the guns are a last resort only, if all else fails!"

There was one additional insurance policy, which he left unspoken. Radek would be in one group and Pepa in the other. Each brother trusted the other's judgment and leadership ability implicitly. Each knew he could depend on the other to pull the trigger.

The youths boarded the 7:00 PM train to Chomutov. As the train clattered through the dark, cold October countryside, the five friends relished the warmth of their well-lit railroad car. They warily monitored the railroad car and station platforms at each stop, but only a few travelers were abroad and, to their amazement, they encountered no patrols. When they arrived in Chomutov, the last major town before the border, it was already 11:30 PM. Now it was time for their first cover story: they were visiting friends who, unfortunately, were not home. The local address was genuine and the friends in question really were out of town. Everything would check out.

The two groups, one trailing the other at a distance, marched from the train to the bus station. According to the posted schedule there would be no bus until early the following morning. Bad news, for they would have to spend the night in Chomutov. But where? Checking into a hotel was out of the question; they had no travel passes and no authorization to be in the area. So they walked along the dark streets, in their two groups, to the edge of town, where they crawled into some shrubs. Once everyone had squeezed in, they huddled under an overcoat.

Pepa pulled out the map of the border area and briefed everyone on the route they would take the next day. "The last four to six kilometers before the East German border are the most dangerous. The place is crawling with patrols, and they take their security measures seriously. One border guard'll get on the bus to check ID papers. Two to three others will be hiding in ambush outside—behind trees, in ditches, around corners. All of them will be armed with submachine guns. If the first guy doesn't buy our cover stories, we'll have to shoot our way out."

"They can fire 50 rounds for every one we fire," Radek added. "That means we've got to fire first and make every bullet count. We've got to neutralize our targets with a single shot."

"If there's shooting, there'll be casualties," said Pepa.

The others grimly digested this information. Everyone studied the map by flashlight until they had memorized the routes.

The study session over, they pressed together in a futile attempt to keep warm and get some rest. Temperatures dropped below freezing. As the hours dragged by, sleep eluded them and they felt themselves getting progressively colder and stiffer. Every so often one or another of them got up and did squat jumps to warm up. This was their first night on the road, and despite their discomfort, they took great pains to keep their pants and jackets unwrinkled.

In the chill morning, they ate sparingly from their small stash of provisions and marched back to the bus station. How different the place looked in daylight! It was teeming with workers heading off to their jobs. They purchased tickets and went to look for their buses. Radek, Vasek, and Zbynek were traveling on one bus, Pepa and Milan on another. The Sudeten border areas were almost totally depopulated and five young men in one bus would excite immediate suspicion. The cover story was that they were looking for jobs with the state forest administration. Milan, in uniform, was on leave and accompanying Pepa.

Each group placed one man near the front of the bus, as a decoy for police patrols. The backup would intervene as necessary. Everyone was well aware that this leg of the trip was the most perilous.

Pepa and Milan were the only passengers on their bus as it meandered through abandoned Sudeten villages. Vandals had smashed most of the windows, leaving shards of glass jutting out of peeling window frames. Doors stood ajar. In the dark interiors of the houses, Pepa could make out smashed crockery and the odd piece of furniture. Everywhere there was rust, dirt, and decay.

Wordlessly he and Milan gazed at this desolation. The silence was oppressive. At any moment a patrol might burst out from a dark doorway or from behind a house. Both Pepa and Milan became increasingly tense and jumpy. When the bus arrived at the end of the line, to their immense relief, the stop was deserted.

They set out on foot, leaving the forlorn huddle of houses behind and continuing into the pine forest on a logging trail. Whenever they spotted men in civilian clothing they melted in among the pine trees. No cover story would pass muster this close to the border.

Radek's group was first to reach the jumping-off point: the summit of Mount St. Katherine. It was late morning. The sun shone overhead and the day was growing pleasantly warm. All around them they could see the round-shouldered Ore Mountains cloaked in wooded green. They tried to make out the border, but it was down in the valley, invisible among the trees. Steering clear of a log tower in the middle of the clearing, they retreated into the woods. If they could see the valley, then watching eyes could see them, too. After settling down in the deep moss behind some large boulders, they posted a rotating guard and spent a few more hours committing the map to memory. Finally they put away the map and relaxed.

"It'll be great to sign up with the American commandos," Vasek said.

"Yeah, I can't wait either," Zbynek replied. "Finally we'll get some real commando training. There'll be no more of this fucking about, we can go back home and blast all the comrades to hell."

"I wonder what American commando training is like?" Vasek asked.

A dog barked in the distance.

"That's down in the valley, near the border," Radek observed.

"How long d'you think it'll be till they notice we're gone back home?" Zbynek asked.

"I told Lidka I was going to see the doctor in Prague about my hip injury. She isn't expecting me back till tomorrow," Vasek answered.

"My parents don't give a shit. My stepmother hates my guts anyway," Zbynek replied.

"Well, how about your girlfriend?" Vasek prompted.

"Yeah, she'll worry. If she doesn't hear from me, she'll probably check with my parents."

The dog barked again.

"I bet that's a canine patrol," said Radek.

"Great. Dogs, too," said Zbynek. "What do you think they'll do when they miss us?"

"They'll put two and two together. They'll guess we're off to join the American army," Vasek speculated.

"There'll be quite a commotion. No question," Radek added.

Noon came and went. Every so often the dog barked. Gradually the afternoon spent itself and they began worrying about Pepa and Milan.

Running hours behind, the two laggards finally reached the top of Mount St. Katherine. When Radek spotted them circling the tower, they were scanning the woods for their buddies. Finally they noticed Vasek, Zbynek, and Radek gesturing frantically at them. They hurried over.

"Where were you two idiots?" Radek demanded. "We thought they caught you!"

"Our way was longer than yours," Pepa said. "And we had to lay low a few times. We had a few close calls with woodcutters."

"Hey, we know the truth. You guys got lost. Fess up!" Vasek teased. "Glad to see you, despite your sorry map reading skills."

Eventually everyone settled down for another study session with the map. They were keyed up and ready to go. Just ahead of them was the riskiest part of the whole trip. The border was guarded, and an encounter with an armed patrol was a distinct probability. Once more they went over their tactics. Then Radek reached for Pepa's briefcase. He produced a wad of worn dollar bills and started counting them out. "Five dollars for each of us, " he said. "That should be plenty to tide us over when we get to Berlin." Pepa had bought the dollars on the black market and they had cost a fortune. From their price he concluded that $5 should be enough to tide a man over for at least a week.

Chapter 13

ACROSS THE BORDER AND INTO THE UNKNOWN

As the sun sank behind the horizon, the five friends set off, moving down the mountain in single file in ten-meter intervals. Pepa was in the lead. The weaponless Zbynek came second. Radek, with his 9-mm, followed; then came Vasek and finally Milan with the second 9-mm. Anticipating an ambush, they had concentrated the group's firepower toward the rear of the line. The shadows lengthened across the narrow logging trail. Then the last rays of light disappeared. They were walking in the dark. A dense fog rolled up from the valley and a fine, cold drizzle began falling.

The fog thickened as they descended. Before long each of them had a hard time making out the trail, let alone the shadowy silhouette of the man ahead. The dirt track had become a muddy morass. They stumbled over massive roots, deep ruts, and tree stumps that had been yanked out of the ground and now lay strewn all about. They narrowly avoided falling into several large, treacherous holes full of water that lurked along the trail. In a number of places they had to detour around massive barriers of dead branches, piled up to stop vehicles from crashing across the border.

Suddenly, the sound of their heavy breathing and squelching footsteps was drowned out by a loud, droning roar. In a split second everyone catapulted off the trail. Hyperalert, fingers poised on pistol triggers, they scanned the woods for signs of the danger.

"Hey, everyone!" Vasek called out in a low voice. "That was only a stag calling!" Vasek, a hunter, recognized the red deer's distinctive mating call. "Come along. Don't worry!"

Everyone relaxed. Only then did they realize they were standing in a little stream that seeped along beside the road in a series of muddy holes. They regrouped on the trail and set off again. Pepa scanned the darkened forest around him, straining his ears to catch the sound of a footfall or snapping branch. Everything was black and silent. But he couldn't shake the feeling that the night was filled with hidden eyes.

All at once, Vasek cried out. Pepa and Radek whipped around, raising their guns. They strained to make out figures in the fog. Nothing. Radek carefully backtracked, pointing his gun straight ahead. He made out a silhouette and then spotted Vasek next to Milan.

"What happened?" he snapped, lowering his gun.

"Milan ran into me!" Vasek gasped, shaken.

"I fell behind in the fog," Milan panted. "When I noticed I'd lost you guys, I ran. Then I crashed into Vasek."

"Milan, you cowboy!" Vasek joked, his voice still shaky. "You just about knocked me over!"

By then Pepa and Zbynek had joined them. They gathered in a little knot and conferred. "We're too far apart. We need to close up!"

"It's safer to keep the intervals. If we run into a patrol we're not all bunched together."

"Well, if we lose each other it totally defeats the purpose."

Everyone agreed. The risk of losing each other in the fog was too great. They reduced the spacing between walkers and silently moved out again into the dark mist.

After slogging on for a while Pepa began to feel uneasy. The road was inclining to the left. That didn't match his recollection. He stopped and the others came up one by one until they stood together in a huddle.

"Hey, guys, this can't be right!" Pepa whispered. "The road is veering left. I don't remember seeing anything like it on the map."

Radek pulled out the map, Pepa got the flashlight out of his briefcase and all of them gathered underneath Vasek's overcoat to examine the map. They had a worried discussion and decided that the only explanation was that the terrain had probably changed since the map was issued. They set off again, slogging on through the mud in tense silence.

"Here it is!" Pepa suddenly called out in a low voice. He had finally located the tenth firebreak that, according to the map, would lead them straight to the border.

As they crossed the muddy little stream that hugged the right side of the trail, Vasek accidentally slipped and fell into the water.

"Vasek, you dummy!" Pepa teased. "You're not planning to swim all the way to Germany, are you? You must be soaked."

Vasek laughed softly. "I don't mind. I only hope it'll be this dark on the night I come back for my family. I'll carry my little boy on my back and lead my little girl by the hand. It'll be a real family outing."

They huddled at the crossroad as Vasek wrung out his soaked pant legs.

"We've got to change tactics," Pepa said in a low voice. "With this damn fog, we can't see enough to tell friend from foe."

"In case we run into a patrol, everyone hit the ground and open fire," Radek said.

"Yeah, anyone standing up is a fair target," Zbynek said. "Take those assholes out!"

"I'll be point man," Radek declared.

"Keep quiet, you guys," Vasek urged. "Let's get out of here before we alert every border guard in the district."

Radek set off, followed by the others. Each man kept his eyes glued to the dark shadow ahead of him. As they stumbled on, the forest thinned out. They entered a clear-cut area pocked with hundreds of uprooted tree stumps and deep holes filled with water. They floundered through the mud, scrambled over piles of bark and tripped over half-peeled logs that suddenly loomed up out of the fog. By now their shoes and trouser legs were heavy with mud and no one thought of pressed clothes anymore. Every time someone accidentally stepped on a branch, all of them jumped. The sharp cracking sounded like gunshots. Several times they stopped, sure they had lost the trail, until Radek pulled out his compass and brought them back on course.

The clear-cut ended. Ahead of them large trees loomed up, merging into the black sky. Radek caught sight of a light-colored strip among the tree trunks. He moved toward it with extreme caution, deliberately placing one foot in front of the other, carefully shifting his weight to keep from making noise. Grasping his pistol firmly in his right hand, he paused, straining to hear. The forest was completely still. Light filtering down through the forest canopy illuminated the white strip ahead of him. It was a dirt road!

When he was sure there was no patrol, he darted across and stopped fifty yards into the woods, waiting for Pepa to move into sight. The trees crowding up to the road behind him stood sullenly, a black inchoate mass shrouded in fog. Pepa didn't emerge. After a while Radek backtracked and found his brother standing on the other side of the road, apparently waiting as well.

"There you are, you ox. What's going on?" Radek demanded. "I've been waiting for an eternity!"

Pepa shrugged, exasperated. "Milan fell in one of the holes back there. He went in up to his waist. One of his shoes is gone and so's his pistol."

"What the hell? If you all would pay attention, our tactics would work!" He followed Pepa back to the scene of the accident. In the middle of the trail was a deep hole. Vasek and Milan were both floundering in its black, icy water. They gasped from the cold as they plunged in up to their necks, groping around the mud at the bottom. Zbynek was squatting next to the hole, minding the briefcases and Vasek's coat.

"Got one!" Vasek announced triumphantly. He hoisted a sodden, mud-caked shoe out of the water. Eventually they retrieved the second shoe as well. But the gun was nowhere to be found. In one stroke 25 percent of their firepower had vanished, swallowed by the mud. Everyone was furious at Milan.

"You jerk! Couldn't you be more careful?"

"Hurry up, you idiot!"

As Milan laced up his sodden shoes, the others quietly continued cursing him for his carelessness.

On the far side of the white road was a dense, virtually impassable stretch of forest. The ground between the tall, wide-girthed trees was carpeted with a thick layer of dead leaves that crackled loudly underfoot. Now nothing seemed to matter except that next step. They moved with extreme caution, their progress agonizingly slow. Each footfall threatened to give away their presence to the listening woods.

The tension in the group was electric as they came to an impenetrable barricade of fallen trees and branches. It was quite old, and the dry wood broke off noisily at the slightest touch. Pepa recognized the place from his run to the border two weeks earlier.

"This is the border, guys!" he whispered.

Already Pepa was squeezing through the dense thicket that abutted the barrier. As he disappeared from view, the others waited in ready positions.

"All clear!" he called after a while.

One by one, the others squeezed through the thicket. Behind it, running perpendicular to their trail, was a wide, well-maintained path. Pepa was already on the far side, crouching before a high wire fence. They darted across the path to him and huddled beside the fence. As they waited with beating hearts, Pepa pulled up the bottom wires and held them. One by one they wriggled through. They were in East Germany.

This was the land that had spawned Heinrich Himmler, Adolf Eichmann, Willy Abendschön, and Gestapo Commissar Fleischer. The five Czechs believed that Germany's inhabitants had willed the destruction of Czechoslovakia and the murder of its citizens. From now on they would be moving through enemy territory.

As if to make the point, a formidable wall of pine trees barred their way. If anything it was even less penetrable than the wood on the Czech side. The low-hanging branches were dry and brittle, and broke at the slightest touch. To their startled ears the noise sounded like .22-caliber shots, advertising their presence to any border guard within miles. Radek dropped to his hands and knees and began crawling forward on all fours. The others followed his example. Branches jabbed at their eyes and faces. They used their hands and briefcases to try to protect themselves, chastising each other for making a racket.

A leaden rain began falling from the unseen clouds above. It beat a driving tattoo on the forest canopy overhead, forced its way through the branches and spilled down from the trees onto the five shivering forms on the forest floor. Dense, thorny thickets forced them into wide detours. After a while someone said in a low voice, "You sure you're on course, Radek?" The last thing they wanted was to lose their bearings and circle back to the border. They squeezed into a space between the tree trunks and waited in the pouring rain while Radek fished out his compass.

It said they were heading back toward the border.

"Goddamn compass!" Radek cursed. He tapped it, but the heading didn't change. "It's not working!" he declared. He fumbled in his pocket and pulled out the other compass. Holding it next to the first one, he brushed the rain drops off for a closer look. It pointed in exactly the same direction. "Son of a bitch, it's right after all."

"Jesus Maria," Milan groaned, "we're crawling right back to the boys at the border!"

"Come on, let's have a look at the map," Vasek said.

Once again Pepa got the flashlight out of his briefcase. Vasek struggled out of his wet coat and they all huddled under it. As Radek unfolded the map, Pepa pointed the flashlight at it.

Zbynek pointed to a spot on the map and said, "Isn't that a border guard barracks?" It was indeed, half a mile to their right. There was no margin for error. They decided they'd better put their stock in the compasses. All of them had heard stories of people who made it across the border only to wander back into the arms of the border guards.

Thoroughly worried, the bedraggled procession wriggled off again, each man keeping his eyes riveted to the soles of his predecessor's shoes. No longer trusting his sense of direction, Radek stopped frequently and got his bearings from the compass.

They crossed a deep, narrow ditch and entered a new forest whose trees had never been thinned. Radek stood up and the others followed suit. As they plunged through the dense growth, head and arms first, the branches whipped their faces and splashed water into their eyes. It took enormous effort to break a path. Soon they were covered with scrapes and scratches, sweating in spite of the cold.

Rain was sweeping across the forest in unbroken curtains now, pouring down on their heads. Through the rush of the falling water they heard a motorcyclist gunning his engine nearby, stopping at frequent intervals. The sound became fainter as he drew farther and farther away. After a while the motorcyclist seemed to return and repeat his tour. After the third time, Pepa was sure of it: this was a motorized patrol moving along posted guards up ahead. The others appeared to have drawn the same conclusion, because no one spoke, and they tried to keep as quiet as possible as they struggled forward.

They stumbled out of the trees and stopped, breathing hard. It took a moment to register the silent ribbon of asphalt before them. It was a road, but they had no idea which one.

Pepa and Vasek dashed across and scouted in both directions to make sure it wasn't guarded. On their signal the rest of the group rushed over, crouching low. They tried to shadow the road, staying in the woods, but that proved impossible because of the many holes and the heavy underbrush. So they gave up and marched on the blacktop, plunging into the woods to take cover on the rare occasions the beam of car headlights appeared ahead. The road meandered up and down forested hills, frequently changing direction. Other roads crossed it, winding off in different directions. It was strenuous going. Though they tried to maintain a northerly heading, they knew they were lost.

Some miles later the road emerged from the woods and they stood facing a village. The rain had stopped. The houses, high and large, every one of them as big as an inn in a typical Czech village, consisted of a barn and dwelling in one unit. All the windows were dark. No cows mooed, no dogs barked, and the village stood cloaked in silence.

"This place looks completely dead."

"You think anyone still lives here?"

"Maybe the Krauts are hard up for food. They probably ate all the animals!"

"Even the dogs?"

"Yeah, even the dogs."

Pepa contemplated the silent village and thought about how desperate people had to be to resort to eating their dogs. Then he and the others swiftly moved out, grateful that no barking called attention to them.

As 4 October dawned, gray and cold, they came to another village and tried the doors on a few barns only to find them locked. Lights were already going on in the dwellings. Time to disappear.

They looked around. "How about the thicket up there?" someone suggested, pointing. Up on the hill stood a cluster of young birch trees in a blaze of gold and red fall foliage. Since it was the only hiding place around, they didn't waste any time hoisting themselves up the retaining wall that flanked the street. They scrambled uphill on the wet, slippery grass and squeezed into the thicket of raspberry canes below the birch trees. Squatting among prickly canes, the five Czechs settled in as best they could.

"We made it! We fucking made it!" Zbynek hissed excitedly.

"Yeah!" Milan punched the air exuberantly. "We didn't even run into one lousy patrol!"

"That was supposed to be the hardest part of the whole damn trip." Vasek was grinning from ear to ear.

"From now on, it's a piece of cake!" Pepa enthused. "All we have to do now is head north. In three days we'll be safe in Berlin."

They said little as they polished off the last of their food. Soon the rain started again. They tried to quench their burning thirst by lapping up the raindrops that clung to the leaves, but finally gave up. They tried, unsuccessfully, to get some sleep. All day long, the rain drummed down on them. Though they were sopping wet and their teeth chattered from the cold, the five Czechs were overjoyed.

The contours of the land were fading into grays and blacks as the fugitives squeezed out of the thicket. The rain had stopped. Empty stomachs growling, they slithered down to the road. At this early hour, near the little town, foot traffic wouldn't attract attention. So they marched along the road in their two groups without bothering to hide from passing cars.

They were making good time, but by now they were intensely thirsty. A dark stream rushed swiftly alongside the road, and in the shadow of a small stone bridge they finally decided it was safe to scramble down to the waterside. They had come prepared: each man popped a water purification tablet, saved from the military-style UNRRA* rations distributed after the war, under his lip and drew the water very slowly through his teeth. During the Second World War, they had watched Russian soldiers sip their tea through sugar cubes in exactly the same way.

Greatly refreshed, they set out once more. As the hour grew late and traffic on the road diminished, the five men took care to keep out of sight. Each time a car passed, they dropped into the ditch, ducked behind a bush, or ran into the woods. Still, they were happy with their progress.

All at once, a loud ringing noise startled them. Bing! Bing! Bing! It was coming after them and gaining fast. They hurtled into the ditch in high alarm. Had someone reported them?

Crouching down, they waited tensely, fingers on triggers, their eyes scanning the darkness. Suddenly a large black shape burst around the bend with a deafening roar, smoke billowing from two funnels.

"It's a steam engine," Zbynek whooped. "Can you believe it?" He pointed. All of them laughed aloud, giddy with relief. And on the engine was a clanging cowbell! That sent them into paroxysms of laughter.

"You ever see anything like it? How primitive can you get!" Still chuckling, they climbed out of the ditch and set off again in high good humor. They were making good progress and their clothes were drying out. Things were looking up.

The rain started again after midnight. Water ran down their necks and backs as they stoically plodded along, and every time they dove into the ditch to avoid the headlights of a passing car they landed in icy water. Soon all of them were swearing at the weather and the cars.

As a dreary morning dawned on 5 October the only shelter in sight was a solitary barn. They trudged across the soggy fields, wet soles squishing, and found it unlocked.

"Man, this place is great!" Milan exclaimed.

---

*The United Nations Relief and Rehabilitation Agency, established on 9 November 1943, was intended to give aid to areas liberated from Axis occupation.

"A definite improvement over last night," Radek agreed.

"And don't forget the Hotel Chomutov the night before that!" said Vasek.

"Yeah. Make that the last *two* nights' accommodations." Pepa laughed and made a face at Vasek.

At first they were pleased with their choice. Not only were they out of the rain with a roof over their heads, but the place was packed with straw. Clambering all the way to the top of the straw pile, just under the roof, they undressed and wrung out their clothing. Though the straw was full of scratchy awns and the air was chilly, no one was eager to put the wet clothing back on—it stuck to their skin and felt like a cold compress against their shivering bodies.

"I'll show you how the partisans used to operate during the Second World War!" Vasek joked. Wearing only his drawers, he plunged into the straw and began burrowing. The sight of Vasek's butt up in the air and the straw flying made the others laugh, in spite of their misery. They followed his example. A watch, they decided, was unnecessary: they'd have plenty of advance warning if anyone approached the barn, which stood all by itself in the middle of the water-logged field.

Before the hour was up, everybody was wide awake and on top of the straw again, teeth chattering. Vasek's teeth were clacking so hard that he was unable to talk. That day they learned the hard way that straw, unlike hay, is drafty and retains no heat. They tried to burrow deeper but it made no difference. By noon they gave up. They crawled out of their holes and huddled together under the roof, shivering and miserable, vowing never again to spend the day in straw.

They decided to set off again well before sundown. The thought of sitting inactive for another hour in the cold barn was unbearable. Hungry, chilled, and exhausted, their euphoria replaced with ill humor, they slowly pulled their wet clothes back on and collected their things. Pepa looked around for the burrow where he had hidden his pistol, wrapped in his raincoat. He rummaged through the straw, increasingly frantic.

"Hey guys, my pistol's gone!"

"Jesus Christ! First Milan, now you," Radek reproached him.

"Well, I'm looking."

"Look harder, you ox. We can't afford to lose that gun," said Zbynek.

"Well, if all of you are so smart, why don't you help me look for the damn thing!"

Radek was bristling. "That's a good idea," Vasek said quickly, in a pla-cating voice. "We'll help you look."

He dropped to his hands and knees and began to search the straw near where Pepa had lain that morning. Straw and dust were flying, Radek was chewing Pepa out, and still the gun and the raincoat were nowhere to be found.

Finally Pepa's hand brushed against cold metal. It was the pistol, but the raincoat and compass had disappeared and not even the combined efforts of the whole group could turn them up. There was no help for it: Pepa had to go on without a coat and a compass.

Before the sun had fully set, the five men were on the road again, each absorbed in his own thoughts. The countryside lay wrapped in somnolent quiet. Grass was growing between the cobblestones on what was obviously a little-used stretch of road. But suddenly, at the foot of a small hill, two girls on bicycles appeared out of nowhere. The Czechs were startled. Taken completely by surprise, they had no chance to hide. Forced to keep on walk-ing, they warily tracked the progress of the approaching girls. Luckily the girls pedaled past, intent on their own business, and eventually disappeared from view.

"Hey, look! Apples!" Radek, the pointman, exclaimed excitedly.

Instantly everyone perked up. The Czechs enthusiastically swarmed toward the trees and began knocking down as many apples as they could, eating a few and stashing the rest for later. The small, shriveled fruit, their first food in twenty-four hours, was barely enough to tease their stomachs. "The first three days are bad," Vasek jokingly advised as they returned to the road. "After that we'll feel nothing." As always, Vasek got the others to smile in spite of themselves.

Their maps were useless. They had long ago moved beyond the border and their stylized map of East Germany showed only the principal high-ways. At every crossroads they chose the most northerly road. But more often than not, after a few hundred yards it would veer off into an entirely different direction. They became increasingly frustrated as they realized they were walking a lot of redundant miles. They tried to take cross-country shortcuts, but their feet sank deep into the muddy ground and they found they made better time on the roads, despite the detours.

Temperatures dropped steadily. The water in the ditches began to freeze and the cold nipped at their exposed noses and ears. Walking briskly warmed them up, and after a few hours' marching their clothing had almost dried. But with no food or sleep in twenty-four hours, they all felt miserable, achy, and tired.

"Maybe this is a good time to stop," Pepa suggested. It was long before dawn, but nobody disagreed. They clambered up a slope by the side of the road, into a pine wood. Underneath the tall trees the ground was strewn with stones of all sizes. Innumerable circular depressions pocked the slope. It looked as if large artillery shells had fallen here eight years before during the last hot war to move through the area. The friends lay down in one of the bigger craters and tried to sleep, to no avail. It was cold, and they had to huddle together for warmth. When anyone tried to turn, the movement woke up the others. Small, sharp-edged stones continually dug into their sides and somebody was always squirming about, trying to get comfortable. At least those in the middle had their buddies warming them from two sides.

In the distance they could hear cars going by on a busy road. Zbynek, unable to sleep, was listening to the sounds of traffic. All of a sudden he caught his breath. He turned over and strained to see. Close by, among the trees, a light was shining.

"Wake up!" he hissed urgently, elbowing his neighbors. "Wake up! There's a light. Somebody's out there!"

Instantly the others snapped awake, pulled out their guns and flicked off the safeties. All of them were scanning the dusky forest.

"I see nothing . . . No, wait! There it is!"

"No. No. Over here!"

Before long, everyone saw lights. But in different directions.

"This is crazy," said Vasek finally. "We're seeing things. We're all just too tired. I'm going to sleep!" He stuck his gun in his pocket, wrapped his coat around him and lay down again. Radek scanned the horizon warily. The light he had seen before was gone.

"You're right. There's nothing out there," he finally agreed. "We're tired, it's just an optical illusion."

"Let's get some sleep," said Milan with finality. Everyone put their guns away and settled down again into a shivering, soaked huddle.

Pepa felt a soft touch on his face. He put out his hand and saw that dim, white flakes of snow were settling on his glove. "Guys," he announced, "it's snowing!" The others greeted this news with muttered curses and morose grunts. Soon the snow was falling faster, filling the air.

When dawn broke nobody was sleeping. Pepa got up, neck stiff and back sore where the stones had dug into him. "Vasek and I are going to scout uphill," he announced. "Maybe we can find better shelter."

The two young men trudged off into the swirling snow. Not far away they found a dense stand of pine trees. It was the work of fifteen minutes to assemble a rude roof of branches in it, and the rest of the group soon joined in to help finish the job. By the time they squeezed underneath, snow blanketed the ground in a thin layer of whiteness. Their gloves were wet through and their fingers freezing, but everyone was happy—they now had some protection from the sleet that was beginning to come down full force. They lay down again and tried to sleep a little, setting a watch to keep an eye on the woodcutters who had begun working only a few hundred yards away.

Before long, sleet gave way to heavy rain. Their makeshift roof proved to be far from watertight, and sleep was impossible as they shifted about to avoid the worst leaks. Gradually, the ground under them turned to frozen mud.

Chapter 14

FIRST CONTACT

As the freezing rain ran down their necks, Zbynek and Vasek despondently smoked their last cigarette. Zbynek produced one of the two cans of condensed milk he still had in his briefcase. Split five ways it did not go far.

The fugitives discussed their predicament at length and reviewed their remaining options: One, keep walking north. They were in bad physical shape, and the weather seemed likely to get worse. They had covered surprisingly little ground so far and, with their stamina deteriorating sharply, the long road ahead of them was daunting. Two, try to take the train. They had no money, and no prospect of getting any. Scratch that. Three, liberate a car on the highway and drive it all the way to Berlin. There was some discussion about the dangers: the checkpoints, the risks involved if the hijacking went wrong. But it all came back to their present state and eventually everyone agreed. They would requisition a vehicle.

Zbynek categorically refused to participate without a weapon. Radek thought that the action would prove uneventful. After all, they had practiced their method quite a few times and had their moves down pat. So he gave Zbynek his gun. Zbynek visibly perked up. He was a trusted member of the team again.

They did a weapons check and then left their rustic shelter, heading for the highway in the driving rain. On one side of the road sat a small toolshed, a board and batten hut belonging to the road works department. The door was padlocked. They tried to break inside, hoping to shelter there until a car stopped, but the wall was sturdy and wouldn't give way. So they stood under the nearly nonexistent overhang as the rainwater poured off the roof directly onto their chests and reviewed their plan.

Pepa and Vasek were to pose as hitchhikers, stop the car, and pull the driver and passengers out. They would only flag down cars heading away from town. Zbynek was to stand guard about fifty yards down the road. Milan and Radek would chloroform and tie everybody up, and they'd be on their way.

Things were looking up—everyone felt better. They could already see themselves speeding along in warmth and comfort. In four hours they would arrive in Berlin.

Several cars rushed by. The odd cyclist passed. But none of the vehicles stopped on Pepa's signal. Then for a long while the road lay silent under the incessant drumming of the rain. "Where the hell are all the cars?" Pepa wondered. Finally, a pair of headlights appeared in the distance. He and Vasek waved their arms and prayed the vehicle would stop. Indeed, it slowed, then pulled over. It was a military-style amphibious VW with a canvas top—a very tight squeeze for the five of them.

The man opened his window as Pepa and Vasek approached. A searching look inside the car; he was alone. They drew their guns.

"Get out! We're taking over the car," Vasek ordered in German.

"I'm a medical doctor from Freiberg. I'm on my way to see a patient," the man protested in Russian.

"Get out! We're taking the car!"

"I'm not going to get out. Look, how about if you and your friend hop in and I give you a ride to Dresden?"

That was the last place Pepa and Vasek wanted to go.

"What's the matter? What's taking you guys so long?" Radek yelled, exasperated, from behind the shack.

"The guy doesn't want to get out!" Pepa yelled back.

Radek sprang over.

"Heraus!" he bellowed in German, grabbing the man by the collar and yanking him out of the car. Together with Vasek he led him into the woods, well away from the road, and began to administer chloroform.

"Don't! I won't report you," the man protested. "Please don't chloroform me and leave me in the woods. It's so wet!"

Meanwhile Pepa was in the VW searching for the car key. In the ignition. On the dashboard. On the floor. Between the seats. It was nowhere to be found. He jumped out of the car and searched the ground. Still nothing. Now he ran into the woods. There was no trace of the others.

"Guys! Where are you!?" he called.

Suddenly he heard the footsteps crunching in the fallen leaves. Vasek appeared, beckoning him. Pepa followed him to where Radek was kneeling in the pouring rain, next to the unconscious driver.

"The key's missing!" Pepa announced.

The friends greeted this news with curses. They frantically searched the inert man's pockets.

As they bent over him, a shot cracked through the woods.

"Shit! What the hell was that?" Radek exclaimed.

Alarmed, the three of them whipped around, straining to see through the falling rain and tree trunks. It had come from the highway.

"Hilfe! Hilfe!" (Help! Help!) a man screamed.

Radek jumped up, Pepa and Vasek following suit. A pair of head-lights had stopped behind the parked VW. Suddenly a whole bunch of cars appeared, slowing down, pulling over. Doors banged. Excited voices shouted. One of the vehicles started down the rough logging trail, its head-lights bouncing crazily.

Leaving the sleeping doctor prostrate, Radek, Pepa and Vasek flew toward the road. Zbynek and Milan, his briefcase in hand, erupted from among the trees running toward them.

"What the fuck happened back there!?"

"It was Zbynek!" Milan shot an accusing glare at Zbynek.

"An old guy came uphill," Zbynek panted, "—he was pushing his bike—I just went to him and he started hollering."

"You idiot, you grabbed the bike and fired a shot in the air for no good reason—"

"Shut up, Milan, it was a warning shot!" Zbynek said. "Then a car came and we had to get out of there fast."

Already the car bouncing along the logging trail was gaining on them.

"Shit," Pepa exclaimed. "They're coming after us!"

They threw a last, desperate look toward the shed—there was no way to retrieve the briefcases. There was too much commotion. They turned tail and ran, tripping over branches and falling into ditches and holes.

"Give me that gun, idiot!" Radek barked. He was furious at Zbynek for firing the weapon, and even more furious at himself for having trusted him with it. Chagrined, Zbynek handed it over.

They'd been running full tilt for just a few seconds when suddenly Zbynek gave a yelp of pain and pulled up short.

"What's the matter?" Pepa asked impatiently, stopping beside him.

"I sprained my ankle." He had jumped into a ditch between the rows of trees and stepped into a deep hole.

"Run on it. It's nothing. It'll go away." Pepa took off again.

Zbynek kept going, but soon his ankle was swelling up painfully and would hardly bear his weight. The hijacking had turned into a fiasco. They were on the run, with the police on their tails, with no idea where they were or which way to go.

They had to get away as fast as possible. After their first headlong flight they settled into a pattern of running fifty steps at a time, followed by an equal number at a rapid walk, in an Indian-style run. They knew it allowed a man to cover long distances quickly.

They saw a sign pointing to the town of Freiberg. Keeping the lights of the town to their right, they navigated around it. A guard at a factory gate yelled something at them, but they paid no attention and kept going.

Eventually they came to a wide, level stretch of concrete that looked like a runway. Was this a Russian airfield? Why wasn't there a perimeter fence? And where were the security measures?

Jogging alongside the runway they looked for a way around it and wondered about the strangeness of it all. After a while, they paused and listened. There was no sign of life. They rushed across.

"Guys, guess what?" Vasek called out. "That's no runway! That's the autobahn!"

The autobahn? But of course! Yet it was completely devoid of traffic.

They checked the map and deduced their approximate location. The question now was whether to follow the autobahn or stay away from it. They decided to stick as close as possible, heading north along forest trails and dirt roads that ran parallel to it. The rain ceased after a few hours and the sky, now clear, was strewn with stars. Vasek pointed out Polaris, the North Star, and showed them how to orient themselves by it.

In the meantime, the doctor emerged from the woods, dazed, his glasses askew and his hair and clothes full of pine needles. Two cyclists and three automobile drivers at the scene accompanied him to the Mönchenfrei Inn five hundred yards up the road. One of the cyclists telephoned the police. Within a half hour the police wrapped up the crime scene investigation and finished interviewing the witnesses. There wasn't much to go by, except the doctor's sketchy eyewitness description of four athletically built men, about 5 feet 9 inches tall, one of whom wore no coat, despite the weather, and the other a dark leather oil coat. Three briefcases abandoned behind the maintenance shed yielded a couple of Czech-German dictionaries. The criminals were apparently fugitive Czechoslovak nationals. Inside one of the dictionaries was a photo of a man in his early 40s in a Czechoslovak officer's uniform. There were no names. The tracking dogs didn't pick up any scent, and the police, though they searched the area, didn't find any spent cartridges.[1]

The authorities proceeded at a leisurely pace. It took them an hour and a half to advise a manhunt in the Branderbisdorf district. Later, at 9:30 PM, the Volkspolizei (People's Police) declared a level III search alert for several neighboring districts.* By 11:00 PM, they added a couple additional districts to the alert roster. But nothing happened after that.

As far as the police were concerned, they had put out the word and it was merely a question of waiting until the wanted men turned up somewhere.

When they stopped for a brief rest, the fugitives talked longingly about the warm Red Cross blankets waiting for them somewhere in a West German refugee camp. Zbynek was limping badly. "My leg's really messed up," he complained. "I can't go on like this."

It was the morning of 7 October and they had been on the move for more than ten hours.† The eastern edge of the horizon turned pink, then red, and they stood exposed in the middle of open fields with no woods or buildings in sight. Soon it would be day. They were so exhausted they could hardly put one leaden foot before the other. Happening across another tool shack by the roadside, they decided to break in. A piece of board was missing on the rear, but no matter how hard they tried, the solid workmanship defeated their efforts to pry off more boards. They gave up and plodded on in broad daylight.

About half an hour later they came to a village. It looked exactly like a Bohemian village, with its pleasant single-story houses and walled gardens.

---

*Whereas a level I alert could be effected by regional commanders, levels II and III had to be decreed by the Head of the German People's Police or his operational second in command (BArch, MdI, DO 1/11/776, p. 65).

†That night alone, they made approximately 26 km headway toward the north, more than the distance they had traveled the two previous nights together.

The cobblestone streets glistened wet, and a low fog hung just above the ground. No one seemed to be out yet, so they hurried on in single file in their two groups. With rising apprehension they headed through the village, searching for a place to hide. Buildings and low garden walls hemmed them in, rendering escape impossible. There were no hiding places. When at last they emerged on the far side of the village, they saw that the road wended its way up a long, bald hill. Several people on bicycles were coming down it straight toward them. Behind them, the village was beginning to stir. The air was filling with the sound of voices and morning activity.

Thoroughly alarmed, they turned off the main road and hurried down a lane flanked by meadows on one side and a high, gated wall with barbed wire on the other. They slipped around the end of the wall, pressing themselves against an adjoining chain link fence. Then they waited, expecting any second a shout or some other sign they'd been compromised. But the cyclists cruised right past.

Behind the chain link fence was the municipal swimming pool with a row of cabanas. Walls surrounded three sides of the compound and on the fourth, facing open fields, was the chain link fence topped by barbed wire. They'd have to hide here. At least the walls shielded them from view.

With some difficulty they negotiated the fence and the barbed wire. Though the cabanas were locked and boarded up, they managed to squeeze through a broken window. Everyone began struggling out of their drenched clothes and wrung them out as best they could.

"Ouch!" Vasek exclaimed, playfully shielding his eyes. "Cover your butt, will you? The light shining off it is blinding me!"

Pepa, at whom this was directed, laughed aloud. He obliged and pulled his drawers back up. The others guffawed, too. They were tired, but Vasek was still joking and able to make them laugh in spite of everything.

"Should I put this wet stuff back on? Or do we try sleeping in the nude?" Zbynek asked.

Everyone was standing around in their shorts, hugging themselves for the cold and shivering.

"This stuff is soaked," Radek decided. "It's like a cold compress. I'm not wearing it!"

"With that cold wind whistling through here, maybe it's better to keep on some clothes," Zbynek said.

"Sheesh, maybe I'll just put on my shirt. It's a little dryer than the other stuff," Pepa said. His teeth were chattering.

Vasek reached over and fingered it. "Imperceptibly," he quipped. Pepa laughed and smacked his hand away. Vasek turned around and pointed at Milan, who hadn't said a word the whole time. "Hey! Look at him!"

Milan had calmly extracted his dry civilian suit from his briefcase and was putting it on. He had discarded his wet uniform onto one of the benches.

"Hey, you whore!" Pepa said enviously.

"Yeah, you're a whore mascarading as a friend!" Zbynek said.

"Am not!" Milan defended himself.

"Well, what do you call that?!" Vasek gestured with dramatic flourish. "At a minimum, you could've offered me your suit. Now that would've been the charitable thing to do! The least you'd expect from a friend."

"Yeah, and what if you'd accepted?" Milan shot back. They all laughed.

The cabana was so full of benches they couldn't move around to keep warm. So they lay on the benches and froze.

"Damn the cold!" said Vasek.

"You ass, Zbynek, firing that gun for no reason," Pepa said angrily.

"I shouldn't have given you the weapon in the first place," Radek added.

"Look, I already said I was sorry," Zbynek said defensively. "And besides, the guy was going to compromise us."

"Jeez, you know he wasn't," Milan retorted.

"Hey, it was the right thing to do! I was covering your butts!"

"Fuck covering our butts," Pepa snorted. "Just think, we could've been in Berlin by now."

"Man, I don't even want to think about that," Milan groaned. They all fell into a despondent silence.

"Well, look at it from the other side," Vasek said diplomatically. "Just think of all the checkpoints and patrols. Plenty of Vopos all over the place! Maybe they'd have picked us up at the next roadblock."

That thought comforted everyone a little.

It had been forty-eight hours since their last meal. Starving and bone-tired, they dozed fitfully. As the afternoon wore on, they grew increasingly chilled and were shaking uncontrollably with the cold. Desperate for something, anything, with which to warm themselves, they decided to break through the partition into the neighboring cabana, in the hope of finding some sort of cloth or cover. But their scuffing and pounding made such an alarming racket that they had to abandon the project for fear that someone might hear the noise and come to investigate.

At long last night fell, and they prepared to set off. They'd leave behind the wet overcoats. Milan decided to leave his uniform, removing only the little tank insignia from the jacket as a souvenir. Later, to his great sadness and distress, he would discover that he'd forgotten his girlfriend's gold ring in the pocket. What, Pepa wondered, would the local people say when they found the Czech uniform and overcoats the next summer? They climbed over the fence out of the pool compound and resumed their march.

They came to a stretch of road torn up by road crews. Potholes and deep yellow mud forced passing vehicles to a slow crawl. Zbynek was in bad shape—he had difficulty walking, let alone running—and everyone's strength was rapidly ebbing. They guessed they had more than a hundred miles still left to go and they were deeply worried about their ability to make it on foot. They debated stopping another car. But so many pedestrians, bicycles, and automobiles were moving in both directions that they abandoned the idea and decided to keep on walking, maintaining tactical spacing of roughly fifty yards between walkers to blend in with all the foot and bicycle traffic. Practically every other car appeared to be a new BMW limousine.

"Hey, look at that license plate!"

"Yeah, so what?"

"On that BMW! It says 'GB.' You know—GB, like Great Britain!"

With mounting excitement they noted that several of the passing cars had license plates beginning with the letters "GB."

"Maybe those cars belong to the British delegation!"

It was possible. Their spirits rose. Here was another potential fast pass to Berlin! They considered flagging one of the cars down. But then more and more vehicles with "GB" plates passed.

"Guys," Radek said, "do you know how many of those GB cars we've been seeing? The Brits would never have so many official vehicles cruising the East German podunks." Their spirits plummeted.

"You're right. GB—maybe that's GB like Groß-Berlin (Greater Berlin)."

"Yeah, and you know what? These Krauts are poor, man. I mean, you've seen it. There's no food in the shop windows. They're still wearing what's left of their Nazi uniforms. And it's eight years later! They can't be driving all those luxury limos. It doesn't compute. I bet these're all government cars."

"No shit. Just think if we'd stopped one of them—we'd really be screwed."

A well-finished hardtop road lined with tall trees began where the construction site left off. Their nightly marches through the East German provinces were falling into a routine. After 8 PM people in the villages turned off the lights and went to sleep. From then on the Czechs had to keep a low profile and stay off the roads to avoid attracting attention. At first they ran far out into the fields, returning only when the headlights had passed. But this cost them a lot of energy, and with every passing car they stayed closer to the road.

"Vehicle! Get down!" someone would call out as headlights approached.

Zbynek almost invariably squatted instead of lying flat like everybody else. Sometimes he didn't squat at all.

"Hit the dirt, damn you!"

"Get the hell down!" a chorus of angry voices would hiss at him in the darkness.

"Fuck you!" Zbynek replied.

"Get down, you ass—it might be the police!"

"My foot hurts! It doesn't make sense to jump into the goddamn ditch!" Zbynek was defiant, truculent, and sore at heart. Afraid of being discovered, the others told him off and made him get down, pointing out that most cars traveling at night were police and military cars. But in fact all of them were exhausted and fed up with crawling in the mud and falling into water-filled ditches.

After a while, nobody went beyond the ditch when it was deep enough to hide in. If it wasn't, they hid behind piles of manure in the fields. Though tired and cold, they continued to watch each other closely to make sure nobody got careless.

As the hours crept by, traffic became progressively lighter and they started making better time. They were leaving the hill country. The road grew level with fewer twists and turns. Now they walked two by two with one point man in front. Pepa and Vasek walked together, softly singing rousing tunes about the victorious march of the Red Army, nostalgic ballads about traveling a long way from home and leaving love behind. Pepa had learned the songs from the Russian troops who had liberated Podebrady. Vasek didn't know all the words, but he was a quick study and he fudged the parts he didn't know. Both Pepa and Vasek had good tenor voices. The stirring melodies, which they sang in two-part harmony, lifted everyone's spirits and they marched at a good clip.

A heavy fog rose out of the fields and the friends began to feel the cold in spite of the brisk pace. They came to an intersection that appeared to be guarded. After lying in wait for a seeming eternity, hoping a car would come by and illuminate it, they finally skirted it and continued on. As they marched northward, the fog thickened to the point where they could hardly see across the road.

Presently they were startled by the yellow glow of headlights probing the fog behind them. It was a slow-moving vehicle. Someone must have seen them and reported them to the police! All thoughts of cold, hunger, and pain were banished. They leaped across the water-filled ditch, sprinted out into the fields and flung themselves to the muddy ground. Sixty yards behind them the vehicle was advancing, a searchlight mounted next to the vehicle's driver playing across the field. They waited breathlessly. The car stopped. A rifle shot cracked, loud in the cold night air. The friends didn't know what to think. Another crack, this time closer, and then the car resumed its slow forward crawl.

"Keep your heads down so they don't see the light reflecting in your eyes!" Vasek said softly.

Five faces went into the mud as the car stopped right before them. Several sharp cracks, each followed by a harsh whistle. That sounded like .22-caliber rifle fire! The shots seemed to be zeroing in on them. Pepa froze. He had learned to think like a hunter: shadow, shape, shine, silhouette, and, above all, motion were lethal giveaways. By not moving, they stood the best chance of escaping notice. Several more shots cracked, but this time into the field on the other side of the road. The car started off again and quickly disappeared into the fog.

The friends dared to breathe again. But no sooner had they picked themselves up out of the mire than another pair of headlights emerged from the fog. Down they went again, flat out in the mud, facedown. Once again a searchlight played over the field and rifle shots cracked. Then the second car resumed its crawling progress into the fog.

"Russian officers," Pepa thought. Those had to be Russian officers out for an evening hunt. Nobody else in East Germany had weapons and the impunity to use them that way.

Jittery from their scare, the friends resumed their march and at length came to a sizeable village with a few streetlights strung along the main drag. The fog was almost gone and the air was noticeably warmer. On the right side of the main street was a bakery with some pastries displayed in the window. That was unusual; the shop windows they had seen along the way, almost without exception, had been empty. There were no bars in front of the window, only a roller blind, but they resisted the strong urge to help themselves. The noise of shattering glass would alert the entire neighborhood.

As they approached yet another village a large sign loomed up ahead of them: Berlin 160 kilometers.*

They stopped and stared at the words in disbelief. It was as if someone had punched them in the solar plexus. This was Thursday—seven days into their trip—and they were a mere twelve miles closer to their goal! They had thought they had covered at least twice that distance. Their plan to live off the land and complete the trip in a few days was a complete bust. There was nothing to eat in the fields because the workers on the collective farms had already brought in the harvest. Zybnek was injured and had trouble moving. All of them were in a bad way: exhausted, starved, cold, and footsore.

Weighed down by their discovery, they trudged glumly through the village. They had settled back into a numb marching routine when a dull droning started up from somewhere along the road behind them. Presently a short convoy of battered American-made Studebaker two-and-a-half-ton trucks appeared. The bedraggled friends double-timed it off the road, Zbynek hobbling as quickly as he could. From the protective darkness they watched the trucks roar past, full of well-fed Russian soldiers singing and playing harmonicas. Their voices rang out, strong and clear in the frosty air. With a sudden pang, Pepa was acutely aware of their deteriorating physical condition.

When the trucks had gone and the singing had faded away they stood on the road and looked at each other. They would somehow have to get money and try to negotiate part of the way to Berlin by train. Everyone agreed on that. It was risky, but the roads were under constant surveillance and "liberating" another car wouldn't get them anywhere.

The road sloped down into a valley toward another good-size village illuminated by a few streetlights. Still divided into their two groups, they rounded a curve. The shock was like a physical blow: there, walking straight

---

*100 miles

toward them, were three armed people's policemen! Tension rising in his chest, Pepa kept on going, as did the others, making every effort to act as casual as possible, and tightened his grip on the gun in his pocket. Steadily the policemen drew nearer, staring at the five disheveled forms in the wan light that shone up from the valley. Any moment now, the Czechs expected to hear a sharp "Halt!" or "Hände hoch!" But whatever the policemen thought, they didn't say a word as they passed the first group and then the second. Pepa kept walking without looking back, concentrating on putting distance between himself and the policemen.

At the bottom of the hill they crossed an intersection with a traffic light. At the railroad station Vasek went in to look at the schedule and check the group's position on the map. But they still had no East German money, and they walked on regretfully.

About two or three miles beyond the village, they passed a construction site where several unfinished apartment blocks jutted up into the night sky. A truck roared up from behind. When it drew level with Pepa and Vasek, it stopped.

"Do you want a ride?" the driver called down in broken Russian.

"Wir sind Griechen!" (We're Greeks!) Pepa called back.* Vasek's Russian was not good enough to pass muster.

"Ach so! Wollt ihr mitfahren?" the driver repeated his offer in German.

"Nein. Danke schön!" Vasek called back, smiling and waving. The truck driver waved back and pulled away as Pepa stared after him wistfully. They would very much have liked a ride, but it would have meant leaving the others behind.

Now they were absolutely determined to get some money and cover some ground by train. Vasek produced his empty silver cigarette case, cigarette lighter, and watch.

"I won't be needing these anyway," he said.

They selected a house with a light in the windows despite the late hour. After the others positioned themselves strategically to cover him, Vasek approached the house and rang the doorbell. From their hiding places, they watched warily as the door opened and light spilled out. The people inside spoke with Vasek. Vasek showed them his items. There was more talk and the people in the house shook their heads. Though they obviously took

---

*The explanation was plausible. After the failed Communist uprising in Greece, many of the exiled insurgents fled to Eastern European countries.

pity on him, they were afraid he might be a police provocateur and didn't want to have anything in their possession that could be used against them. Every foreigner was by definition a suspected foreign agent in the eyes of the Communist police, and helping foreign agents was a crime that carried a stiff prison sentence. One of the people inside disappeared from view and came back with two little rolls, handing them to Vasek and making him eat on the spot while they watched. Vasek quickly polished them off; he couldn't tell them he had four hungry friends.

Vasek returned to his buddies with nothing to show for his effort. Everyone was disappointed, and they felt their weariness more than ever. Though it was only about midnight, they started looking for a hiding place. When they came to a solitary farmhouse they checked the doors and windows, but the place was locked up. They trudged on through a wood and through another village with some newer dwellings, most still without plaster. Most of the houses were dark. Vasek tried to sell his items at another house, but the people inside were terrified and refused to open the door, calling out to him to keep moving.

Finally, they came upon a bakery with lit windows in the living quarters upstairs. This time Pepa accompanied Vasek. It didn't make sense to carry two weapons because there was always a possibility of somehow being disarmed inside the house. Vasek left his pistol with Zbynek. They were doubly careful about security, in case the people in the other house had called the police. A detachment might already be on the way. Milan, Zbynek, and Radek hid behind the house in the orchard and covered the road in front of the house.

Nobody answered Vasek's knock. When Pepa finally found and rang the bell, a good-looking blonde girl, about eighteen years old, opened the door and looked out.

"Papa!" she called.

Her father, a man in his late forties with a sharply featured face, came to her side and spent a moment sizing up the two visitors. Then he appeared to make up his mind.

"Come in," he said in German, holding open the door and standing aside, "but don't tell anyone you've been here." Pepa and Vasek followed him into the house. Pepa understood only snatches of the conversation. Vasek had to fill him in on the details later. "Our neighbors are all right, but they don't have to know who you are," the man went on.

"We're armed and we won't tolerate any tricks," Vasek told him.

The man didn't seem to take it amiss. He understood that Vasek just had to make sure that there was no misunderstanding.

The girl was very excited and Pepa kept stealing glances at her, thinking she looked very nice.

"What would you like to eat?" the father asked.

"We're going to Berlin and haven't had any food for a long time. Please, could you do us a favor and give us something for the road?" Vasek wanted to share the food with the others who were waiting outside, but of course he couldn't say so.

"No, I'm sorry, but we can't do that," the father countered. "You understand, with things being as they are nowadays. . . . But we'll make something for you to eat here."

While the girl prepared some food, Vasek talked to the father about their personal situation and the general political situation in the Eastern bloc. Pepa stood back with his back to the wall and his hand on the gun in his pocket, ready to cover Vasek in case of trouble. The man spoke calmly, with determination, his entire manner expressing an understanding for his visitors' predicament. He explained that he had been in the POW camp at Podebrady after the war and had been badly treated by the Czechs. "But," he remarked, "all that should be forgotten now. Both sides made mistakes. The situation has changed." He said it sincerely and with feeling. It was clear that the man opposed the Communist regime.

Vasek related that he had spent a few years in Nazi prisons himself and told him about the Masin family's plight under the Nazis.

The girl came back with the food and two cups of hot coffee. The coffee was marvelous. It was their first hot sustenance in almost a week of freezing and it did wonders for them both.

"How long have you been on the road?" she asked.

"We haven't had anything to eat for at least five days," Vasek replied.

When she heard this, the girl insisted with tears in her eyes that they stay overnight. Pepa and Vasek were touched by the kindness but, mindful that their three friends were anxiously waiting for them outside, they regretfully turned down the invitation and prepared to go.

"Here, take these rolls with you," the man urged. It was a brave gesture in a time and place where any stranger could be a police provocateur. Pepa and Vasek were touched.

"We won't tell anybody about your help," Vasek assured their benefactors as they stuffed the food in their pockets. "Even if we are caught."

Pepa nodded in agreement. They offered to pay with one of their sweaters, but both the baker and his daughter vehemently refused and instead gave them ten marks each. After the man gave them some walking directions, Pepa and Vasek took their leave, with profuse thanks, and promised to send a short message via Radio Free Europe upon their arrival in Berlin, to let them know they had made it.

"What took you guys so long?" Milan complained. "You were in there forever!"

"Pepa was busy picking up the guy's daughter," Vasek teased. "I had a hard time getting him out of there!"

"You did not," Pepa retorted. He was thinking of the pretty girl's tearful eyes and of the food. He wouldn't have minded staying longer.

"You should have seen the sparks flying. I had to intervene before he assailed her virtue."

Pepa protested and punched him in the arm. The others laughed. Pepa could be a shameless flirt.

"Well?" said Zbynek.

"I think you noticed," Pepa said expansively to Vasek, covering up his embarrassment with bravado, "the sack she wore was hiding some nice goods. I'm definitely changing my mind about Germany!" All of them had observed and commented on the fact that the East Germans wore clothing that was downright shabby: threadbare, sacklike garments. In spite of the recent shortages, Czechs wore fashionable clothes of better-quality material. In all respects, people in East Germany seemed much worse off than the Czechs.

"The girl is safe, thanks to me. Now, let's eat!" Vasek announced, as he produced the food the baker had given them.

They divided everything equally. The amount, meant for only two people, was ridiculously small when divided into five parts.

"Jeez, look at that!" Zbynek groaned. "My portion fits in a thimble. Best not to eat at all rather than eat *that*."

"Fine, if that's how you feel, I'll have your share," Milan volunteered. Zbynek smacked away his hand.

"No. I meant we'll only be teasing our empty stomachs, and we'll end up feeling as bad as we did during the first few days, half crazy with hunger."

"I don't want my whole share," Vasek said. "I already had two buns, back in the other village!"

They redistributed his portion and quickly ate.

The kind treatment Pepa and Vasek had received from the two Germans surprised the Czechs immensely, and they spoke of it many times thereafter. Though aware that in many instances the Czechs had not treated the Germans kindly after the war, until now they had been convinced that all Germans were bastards. After their encounter with the baker and his daughter, they revised their opinion. They agreed that it was possible to find a few good people among the Germans also.

Though it was well before dawn, they were exhausted and ready to call it quits for the night. They located a barn in the very next village, broke in with some difficulty and went to sleep. It was 8 October. All day the Czechs rested. When night had fallen and everything was quiet outside, they set off again, passing through large stretches of woods, constantly on the lookout for something to eat. By now, their thoughts revolved exclusively around food. A short walk exhausted them: they realized they couldn't continue much farther without eating. Encountering a *Waldschenke*, a solitary pub in the woods that was closed for the winter, they tried all doors but the place was locked up tight. Glumly they pressed on.

It was still early when they neared Riesa, an important railway hub and garrison town. The road was busier now and the friends had to hit the dirt often to avoid being seen. Closer to town, with other pedestrians on the road, they stopped hiding. The suburbs, with their poorly lit streets and shabby gray houses, seemed endless. The friends were acutely conscious of their scruffy looks, which made them stand out uncomfortably, and when they came to a railroad crossing with the crossing bars down they hid rather than joining the cluster of waiting pedestrians and vehicles. Standing behind a building that looked like some kind of a machine shop or agricultural equipment repair station, they waited until the bars clanged up and everyone dispersed.

As they moved into town they passed one barracks complex after another, each surrounded by board fences about twelve feet high. They were amazed by the sheer vastness of the Soviet military presence. A Soviet artillery battalion had camped in Podebrady in 1945, and Radek and Pepa had visited Ruzyne, their father's old regimental command, but what they saw here exceeded anything they had ever seen before by orders of magnitude. From the deeply rutted streets and the chewed-up sidewalks they concluded that Riesa housed a tank outfit. Almost all the windows in the barracks buildings were lit and they could see numerous soldiers lounging in them, looking out. The light was dim and yellowish.

"The comrades are very economy-minded," someone observed drily. "They're using such small light bulbs!"

In the yard, the public address system was in full-throated cry.

"What're they saying?" Vasek asked Radek.

"'For the motherland, against the imperialists!'" Radek translated.

The Czechs listened as slogan after slogan rang out, showing no signs of abating in spite of the late hour.

"When are these people going to get some sleep?" Radek finally asked. "It's got to be hell to listen to that political nonsense even in your sleep!"

They didn't dare ask for directions to the railway station. Radek had vivid memories of the last time he had asked for directions, back in Czechoslovakia. To avoid attracting attention, they turned onto a darker side street lined with tall trees. A cluster of several Soviet military staff vehicles attracted their attention. The vehicles stood in front of a rundown villa. A soldier patrolled back and forth with a submachine gun. No question about it, this building was occupied by high-ranking Red Army personnel. The friends walked past trying to make themselves inconspicuous and taking care not to show any interest. But in fact they were taking a precise mental photograph of the place—its features, its size and layout, its position relative to the barracks and other landmarks. They would report it to the CIC in West Berlin. Another useful piece of information for the Americans when they finally blasted through and kicked the Soviets' collective ass.

In fact, the friends had stored up a whole treasure trove of intelligence on Czechoslovak military units, armaments factories, power plants, and the like, filing it all away in their heads. During their long hours of marching they tested each other's recall. It was a way to pass the time and put the cold and the painful, gnawing hunger out of their minds, for a while at least.

As a mental exercise, they put together a tactical plan to take out the villa, deciding how many hand grenades they would need and what type of firearms they would use. In Czechoslovakia, whenever two or more group members had gotten together they had made a point of running through hypothetical ambush and assault scenarios. During these discussions and continuous mental rehearsals they covered every conceivable contingency, and Pepa and Radek were confident that everyone would respond quickly, as one well-oiled machine, when crisis struck.

Once they reached the railroad station, Vasek left to try to sell his cigarette case and watch. The others decided to begin exploring the empty lot opposite the station building. It was slightly elevated above the road, set behind a retaining wall and surrounded on all sides by tall bushes. Suddenly two heads with military caps appeared above the retaining wall. The Czechs froze and watched in tense silence. Slowly the new arrivals moved into view. They were Russian soldiers armed with submachine guns. The friends waited with bated breath until the patrol had moved away.

Resuming their exploration, they came upon a wooden shack made of used lumber. They enlarged a hole in one wall just above ground level and crawled in, posting a guard outside to intercept Vasek when he came back from town. Inside they found a few old shovels, a bunch of birch brooms, and a pile of rags. The rags were old, dirty, and full of holes. They put the brooms on the floor and the rags over them. The brooms were hard, but better to lie on them than on the cold, filthy floor.

Vasek returned after about an hour, at 11:00 PM, sporting a smile and a clean shave. The others greeted him with relief. He obviously had a story to tell. But first he produced a piece of blood sausage, which, divided equally among the friends, yielded a tiny sliver the size of a finger for each man. As they ate, Vasek told them what had happened.

"I went to an inn and sat down behind the bar, where the light was dim. When the proprietress came to take my order, I told her, 'I cannot order anything because I have no money, but I'd like to sell my watch or cigarette case or cigarette lighter.' She looked at me. She could tell I had an accent. She saw the beard on my face and my dirty, wrinkled clothing and she knew instantly what was up. She asked me if I was on the run.

"In the end, I admitted that I was going to Berlin with my friend. She came back with a beer and explained the conditions in Berlin to me, and the security arrangements they had there. Then she gave me that piece of blood sausage to take with me and told me to wait for her husband. When he came, he looked around and gave me a signal to follow him upstairs into their apartment. He let me shave there. They offered to let us stay with them for the night," Vasek finished, and looked at the others.

"It's a trap!" Radek said.

"I don't think so," Vasek countered. "She said that during the war she was a refugee herself. Her husband was in trouble with the Communists; something to do with the Berlin uprising. I don't think she was trying to deceive me."

"It's a crappy idea," Radek insisted. "The inn's in the middle of the town. There's no cover. You'd be totally exposed."

"Radek's right," Pepa said. "We can't take our usual security measures. You know we can't trust anyone."

"Look at Milan's beard," Vasek pointed out. Everyone looked. Milan, whose stubbly beard was heavy and black by now, looked back sheepishly. "He looks like a wild man from the woods. He's got to shave if we travel by train."

"Forget it, "Radek insisted. "If we don't have total control of the situation, we don't do it."

"I think Vasek's right. Milan needs to get cleaned up," Pepa said.

Milan looked happy at the thought of spending a night indoors.

"Okay," Radek agreed. "But you're on your own. Show up by 4 AM on the dot. If you don't, we're leaving without you."

"Okay, fair enough," Vasek replied.

"If they pick you up, make sure you tell them you two are traveling alone," Pepa added.

The decision made, Vasek and Milan made their way back to the inn, looking forward to some warmth and a nice rest. They had brought along Radek's sweater to exchange or sell and sat down at an out-of-the-way table for two, feeling slightly nervous. The proprietress brought each of them a glass of beer.

"Wait here for my husband," she told them quietly. "Don't talk to anyone else."

Vasek and Milan nursed their beers and waited. At 2:00 AM, a man came in, had a brief word with the proprietress, and approached their table. Vasek recognized the husband.

"Come with me," he told them.

Vasek and Milan followed him upstairs into the couple's tiny one-room apartment while the proprietress closed up for the night.

Upstairs, she fixed a cup of coffee and a slice of bread with butter and jam each for Milan and Vasek, then hurried over to the railway station to check the train schedule. The two Czechs polished off their small meal, which was gone much too quickly for their taste. Then Milan shaved. He and Vasek pressed their suits and cleaned them up as best they could. The husband gave them an alarm clock, which they set to a few minutes before four. He got into bed with his wife, and Milan and Vasek lay on the rug. For the first time in days Milan and Vasek felt cozy and warm and they quickly fell into a deep, restful sleep.

The alarm shrilled a scant one and a half hours later. As Milan and Vasek hurriedly adjusted their clothes and prepared to leave, the bleary-eyed innkeeper and his wife got up to see them off. The woman gave each of them some bread for the road. Vasek gave them the watch and the cigarette case, but the German couple refused the sweater, pointing out how bitterly cold it was outside. The couple also gave Vasek fifty marks. It was all the cash they had. Vasek and Milan knew it was a substantial amount of money, especially considering the couple's obviously destitute state.* And these people certainly had no pressing need for a cigarette case or a watch. Vasek and Milan were fully aware that they had "bought" these items only to help them.

Deeply grateful to the couple, Milan and Vasek thanked them profusely, said their good-byes and set off into the night. The generosity and kindness of the German couple gave all of the Czechs something to think about. Here was a second instance where total strangers had helped them. Clearly the encounter with the baker and his daughter was no exception.

---

*According to Torsten Diedrich, the monthly salary of an industrial worker was 318 marks per month in 1952. Torsten Diedrich, *Der 17 Juni 1953 in der DDR. Bewaffnete Gewalt gegen das Volk* (Berlin: Dietz Verlag, 1991), 26.

Chapter 15

TROUBLE WITH TRAINS

Freshly spruced up and rested, Milan and Vasek rapped on the wall of the maintenance shed at precisely 4:00 AM. The others had spent the night worrying about these two. Now they heartily envied them. While Milan and Vasek had slept in comfort, they had had a rough time of it, freezing and virtually sleepless on the pile of birch brooms. While Milan and Vasek waited, Pepa, Radek, and Zbynek tried hard to straighten up their clothes, clean their shoes with their socks and generally make themselves more presentable. But they were forced to admit that their efforts didn't do much to improve their seedy appearance. At 6:00 AM they filed across the street one by one, trying to blend into the busy morning crowd inside the station. Vasek went off to buy tickets.

The commuters wore drab civilian clothing, many in old Wehrmacht uniforms or parts of uniforms dyed black. The station was swarming with troops and police. Several Vopos and Russians stood around in twos. There seemed to be two kinds of Vopos, some in black uniforms, others in olive green. The Czechs had no idea what service the green uniforms represented, but in fact they belonged to the new Kasernierte Volkspolizei, East Germany's proto-army. A Russian lieutenant holding a small brown suitcase was waiting on the platform. He had a shaved head and wore a gray overcoat, black riding breeches, and knee-high black boots. A couple of women in Russian military uniform stood nearby.

All the local men wore military-style hats with visors. As the Czechs looked around they were painfully aware that they stuck out like sore thumbs in their berets. People were staring at them. They removed their berets and stuffed them in their pockets. But that didn't help. There wasn't a single bare-headed man in the station. Since most people were moving through the building with a sense of purpose, their idle waiting made them feel even more conspicuous. What was taking Vasek so long, for God's sake? Police were everywhere and disaster was just one wrong move away.

At last Vasek walked out of the ticket office. He had used up all of their money and still the tickets would take them only as far as Elsterwerda, the next stop up the line. He asked for directions and led the way out to the waiting train, which consisted of a few beat-up cars. They selected a car of the old German type, its compartments each with a separate door facing onto a wide running board outside the car, which provided the only communication between them. Once again the group split in two—Pepa, Vasek, and Zbynek in one, Radek and Milan in the other.

The train was almost full, and as they sat on the uncomfortable, straight-backed wooden benches they tried to maintain a low profile and avoid all conversation. Radek and Milan looked fixedly out the window at the fog-covered countryside and occasionally faked sleep. In the same compartment, a few seats away, Pepa, Vasek, and Zbynek sat together. Two girls tried to engage Pepa and Vasek in a conversation. Vasek limited himself to a few jokes and Pepa's German vocabulary was not up to the demands of flirting, so the conversation quickly died. Then the conductor appeared, an older woman who let herself into the compartment from the running board. She checked the friends' tickets, smiled at them, and said, "Sehr gut."

"Excuse me, ma'am," Vasek asked, "is this train going to Elsterwerda?"

"Ja, ja," she assured him, smiled again, and moved on.

The train, like most others in Germany at the time, was powered by a steam engine and had a top speed of forty miles per hour. It chugged through the fog, slowing to a crawl now and again for reasons that were unclear. The Czechs sat inside the warm railway car feeling replenished. They were sitting in a train, it was warm inside, and this train ride was taking them a good step closer to their goal. Zbynek was happy to be sitting, his weight off his injured leg.

After leaving Riesa, the train crossed a bridge high over the River Elbe. Finally a great number of rail switches indicated that they were approaching a big station. Vasek asked a passenger once more whether the train went to Elsterwerda. Whatever the answer was, the friends stayed on the train after it came to a halt. All the passengers in the compartment got off. Pepa threw Vasek a questioning look, but he assured him that everything was all right.

The station PA system crackled to life with an announcement, which Pepa didn't understand clearly because the door and windows were closed. He thought it said "Der Zug fährt weiter." (The train is departing.) And indeed, the train lurched off a few minutes later. There was just one problem—it was headed back the way it had come. A bit uneasy, Pepa rationalized that perhaps it was pulling off onto another track. Then all of a sudden the friendly conductor showed up again and asked in a surprised tone, "Was machen Sie denn hier?" (What are you doing here?)

Vasek explained: "Wir fahren nach Elsterwerda!" (We're going to Elsterwerda!)

"Well," the conductor answered, "you've made a mistake then: you should have gotten off at the last stop. This train is going back to Riesa!"

She smiled kindly, looked over the down-on-their-luck, scruffy young men, and moved on. The friends were stricken when Vasek translated this piece of bad news. Luckily the conductor didn't insist on payment for the return trip. They wouldn't have had the money to pay.

When the train pulled into Riesa they disembarked, sorely disappointed. It was now almost 9:00 AM and they were back where they had started. They made their way out of the train station singly and started the trek to Elsterwerda on foot, following the railroad tracks. Ahead of them lay an eighteen-mile march in full daylight, during which they would be completely exposed to prying eyes.

After walking through town they came to a big steel-beam bridge with the Elbe River far below. The most striking feature about the bridge was that it was guarded—and they had to cross it to get to Elsterwerda. In fact there were two soldiers in black overcoats on the bridge, both armed with heavy StG44-type assault rifles.* One stood on the side of the bridge closest to town and the other patrolled back and forth in the middle of the span.

The friends retreated to a small park by the bridge and hid behind a locked wooden shack that looked like a newspaper kiosk. There they held an animated debate.

"What do we do now?" Milan asked helplessly.

"If the first guy decides to stop someone and we disarm him, the other guy has the situation covered," Pepa replied.

"Our three pistols are no match for his submachine gun," Radek said.

---

*The StG44 was a precursor of the AK-47, used by the Soviet army.

"Fuck those assholes!" Zbynek announced. "Just let them try us. I'm getting myself one of those submachine guns, and then they'd better look out."

"Don't be an idiot," Vasek said soothingly. "We can't risk a run-in with those guys."

Zbynek looked sullen. He was still smarting that the others had not seen fit to provide him with a weapon.

"There aren't many bridges over the Elbe," Radek said. "Most got busted during the war. We could walk a long way and run into exactly the same thing at the next bridge. We have to try here."

With half the way to Berlin still ahead of them, the situation was serious. None of the friends, with the possible exception of Zbynek, looked forward to a run-in, but they had little choice. They had to try.

They started off one by one, at intervals, with the unarmed Zbynek and Milan walking together. The two of them pretended to be Germans and feigned an animated conversation, consisting mostly of *ja* and *nein*, as they passed the guards. Odds were that at least one of them would be stopped and requested to produce ID. As it turned out, the soldiers didn't pay them any attention. They were guarding the bridge against sabotage and not checking who crossed it.

By the time they reached the first village, Pepa was exhausted. The early start that morning, the emotionally taxing river crossing, and the lack of food and sleep exacted a toll. The country was flat and almost treeless, offering little cover between villages. For more than a week they had traveled exclusively under the cover of darkness. At night, safety lay just a few steps off the road on the other side of the ditch. They unanimously decided that this would be their last leg of daytime travel.

They helped themselves to water from a pump in someone's yard. The cool, clean liquid felt like heaven on their parched tongues and throats. Refreshed, they set off again. The road stretched on straight and seemingly never-ending through flat, featureless terrain. They trudged through a couple of nondescript villages. The fields were mostly bare and Pepa began to despair of finding any food. But then they came to a single patch of tomato plants. Immediately hope revived. The plants were brown—they had been killed by the year's first frost a few days earlier—but maybe there were still some tomatoes on the vines? Everyone quickly scattered into the field. But all they found were a few small, shriveled specimens. Most were inedible. Despondently they trudged back to the road.

At the edge of the next patch of woods Pepa spotted blackberry plants. But the blackberries were few and far between on the prickly canes. Reluctant to waste time hunting down the tiny berries, they quickly resumed their march. By now Pepa was light-headed with hunger.

Some hours later a Soviet military truck loaded with troops roared past them. One of the soldiers was playing the harmonica; the others were singing and laughing. It was a picture that filled the Czechs with a pang of bittersweet nostalgia. Pepa remembered scenes just like it from 1945 when the Russians had chased the Germans out of their country. Back then, Czechs and Russians had made common cause against the enemy. How times had changed! As the truck barreled past, one of the soldiers threw a cigarette butt on the road. It was a *machorka*, the ubiquitous Russian soldier's cigarette he remembered so well from eight years earlier: a big chunk of tobacco wrapped in a piece of newspaper, about a finger thick and four to five inches long. To all appearances, nothing had changed in the Red Army. The soldiers were provisioned as scantily as ever. The ZISS truck itself looked old and battered, as if it had come to East Germany all the way from Stalingrad.

The condition of the road deteriorated as they walked, the blacktop torn up and criss-crossed with tread marks made by heavy, tracked vehicles. From up ahead came the throbbing noise of powerful motors. Soon a thick cloud of dust appeared in the fields to their left and from it, like some sort of apocalyptic vision, emerged a platoon of tanks. They were T34s, all buttoned up with their guns in ready positions, each pointing in a different direction. Though he had seen tanks like these before, Pepa thrilled anew to the size and sheer power they projected. Immediately he and Milan started conjecturing about what they would do if they had one.

"I'm driving!" Milan finally announced.

"The hell you are," Pepa retorted.

"I'm almost a full-fledged tank officer. So I'm the only qualified guy here."

"*Almost* is the key word," Pepa shot back. "I spent years driving logging rigs off-road."

"You're not even qualified to look at the damn thing!" Milan retaliated.

Pepa bristled. "What do you know about anything, jerk!"

Before long they were calling each other names. The repartee barely disguised frayed tempers. Once past the training ground, the five retreated into the woods for a few minutes to rest.

"So what do you think of the Vaterland so far?" Vasek asked.

"Doesn't look all that fabulous," Milan grunted.

"Nope," Radek agreed. "And it looks worse by daylight. The fields are poor and sandy. Those Krauts are poor as church mice."

"Yeah," said Zbynek. "They're even worse off than we were back home."

"No wonder they invented *Eintopf*. Yuck!" Milan said. All of them knew *Eintopf*, a one-pot soup, and they regarded it as something unimaginably horrible: a meal good only for people on the verge of starvation.

In another village Radek spotted some plum trees with a few plums still clinging to the highest branches. They began shaking the nearest tree vigorously. The fruit was sweet and tasty, but there were no more than two per man. Though sorely tempted, they decided that five vagabonds shaking all the trees along the road would look too suspicious. Again they pressed on.

Behind the village, the road stretched on straight and seemingly endless. To their left a railroad track ran parallel with the road, separated from it by a strip of fields. Suddenly they saw three Vopos walking along the track toward them. The Vopos left the track and crossed the fields, making a beeline for them. Although the Czechs were walking at fifty-yard intervals, Pepa had no doubt that a sharp-eyed policeman could tell they belonged together. But he could do no more than tighten the grip on his pistol and keep going. To his amazement, the Vopos walked past Radek without showing the slightest interest. They walked past Vasek, then Milan, then Zbynek, then past Pepa himself. They didn't turn. The Czechs didn't turn either. Gradually, as the distance between them increased, Pepa relaxed his grasp on his weapon.

Several hundred yards later the railroad track passed over their heads on a simple trestle bridge with high fills on either side. Turning back, Pepa was shocked to see a lone Vopo standing on the span. Just then, a *Steyr* military truck roared past and halted at the bridge. The guard scrambled down and hopped aboard. Another dismounted. Then the Steyr headed off toward Riesa. Pepa breathed a sigh of relief. How long would their luck hold?

Presently they came to a large compound surrounded by a high hedge and perimeter fence. It appeared to be a derelict public swimming pool. The main entrance to the pool area was visible from the bridge, so Radek walked to the far end of the compound, turned right, and followed a narrow dirt road into the fields beyond the pool area. The others followed him.

"Fuck," Zbynek exhaled. "That gave me a heart attack."

"Me too, man," Milan said. "I need a drink. My throat's parched."

"Time to lie low for a bit," Radek agreed. "Too many damn Vopos popping out all over the place. We can hide in there and get a drink." He pointed to the pool compound.

Out of sight of the guard on the bridge, they crawled through the fence.

They inspected the cabanas, which were vandalized, the doors torn off the hinges. Crouching at the edge of the pool, they saw that it was empty, except for twigs and branches littering the bottom. The concrete lining was cracked and at the deep end was a little puddle of black, dirty water. Milan found a deep, concrete-lined hole housing valves for the pool. The handles had been removed and there was no way to open them.

Burning with thirst and bone tired, they washed their feet in the swimming pool and hid in the cabanas.

"Nothing to drink. Nothing to eat. It's fucking freezing, " Zbynek complained.

Radek looked at Zbynek's grotesquely swollen foot. "We can't go on like this. We need to eat something. We need money for train tickets."

"I'll go recon the next village," Vasek volunteered.

"Here. You can sell my cigarette case and my watch." Zbynek pulled out the items.

"Take my sweater," Radek said. "In this bombed-out country they need decent clothes more than they need silver cigarette cases." He took off his sweater.

"And mine," Pepa said. "The wool's good quality." Pepa pulled his sweater off too.

"You two are crazy," Vasek said. "You'll freeze to death."

"Look," Radek said. "We don't have much choice. Either we cover some ground, fast, or we starve. We've been fucking around in this goddamn country for eight days now, with nothing to eat."

Vasek didn't contradict him. He collected all the items.

"Right! Time for a visit to the bazaar."

As Radek and Pepa hugged themselves and shivered in the cold, wearing nothing more than their sports jackets and thin shirts, Vasek set off.

After a while, Vasek returned. The others were huddled together, shivering. "Okay, guys," Vasek announced. "Lunch is served."

Vasek handed each man two sweet rolls, keeping one for himself.

"I sold the sweaters for thirty-two marks," Vasek informed them. "There's enough money left over for train tickets."

"Man, you're great!" Milan croaked enthusiastically.

They eagerly bit into the rolls. But their mouths were so parched, they had trouble chewing and swallowing. All of them needed water.

"My tongue's so parched, I can hardly swallow," Zbynek croaked.

"We've got to go on and get some water," Radek finally said. Everyone grunted in agreement. They got up and stiffly made their way to the door of the cabana. Suddenly, very near by, a two-way radio crackled to life. The Czechs dropped to the ground. Through the almost leafless hedge Pepa spotted a military command car sitting on the road with a Vopo inside. The radio crackled again.

A series of loud cracks, the sound of branches breaking, emanated from the bottom of the swimming pool. The Czechs waited tensely.

Presently a second Vopo emerged from the pool. He circled the compound and approached the cabanas. Then he stopped moving. Everything was quiet. His gaze swept over the open cabanas, passing right over the heads of the Czechs who were lying flat on the ground. But he didn't approach. Then he walked away, kicked a few branches, and headed toward a cluster of bushes. He searched them with his eyes, then turned away.

Moments later he got into the command car, which drove away.

"Fuck!" Zbyna exhaled.

"I didn't even hear that car coming. Did you?" Vasek said. None of them had.

"The people at the bakery must've reported you!" Radek said.

"Maybe it was the Vopo on the bridge," Pepa said. "Or the three guys we saw before that."

"This place is crawling with police!" Zbynek said.

"Let's move on while we can," Radek said. "Keep your eyes peeled, everyone. And for god's sake stay out of sight of the Vopo on the bridge!"

They arrived in Elsterwerda for the second time at five o'clock that evening, having walked nineteen miles. They were so exhausted and thirsty they were on the verge of hallucination. Zbynek was limping badly. After quenching their thirst from water faucets in residential gardens, they made their way to the railroad station. Vasek and Radek entered the small terminal building to check the schedule and the map hanging on the wall, calculating how far their money would take them. It wasn't far—just a couple stops up the line to a place none of them had ever heard of. The name was Uckro.

They kept moving through the streets of Elsterwerda until the town was claimed by the gathering dusk. Then they returned to the railroad station to check the schedule again. There were not many options. Only two trains headed north. One was leaving in a few minutes, but it didn't stop in Uckro. The other was due at 2:00 AM. This was the one they would take.

They found a little shack just a short way from the railroad track. A ladder leaned against the wall. Radek moved it over to reach the door in the gable. When the last man was safely inside the empty hayloft, he moved the ladder back to its previous position. Anticipating another public appearance, they tried to press creases back into their pants, rubbed dried mud from their clothes and smoothed their hair.

"Hey, Zbynek. What time is it?" Vasek asked.

Zbynek checked his watch using Pepa's flashlight.

"11 PM."

"I'll go get the tickets now. Pepa, coming with me?"

"Yeah, sure."

They opened the door and disappeared down the ladder.

It was a small, provincial station, not much frequented. While Vasek approached the ticket counter, Pepa covered the exit.

"Fünf Fahrkarten nach Uckro, bitte," (Five tickets to Uckro) said Vasek. He pushed the money through the window.

The surly-looking middle-aged woman behind the counter looked at him sharply. "Warum brauchen Sie fünf Fahrkarten?" (Why do you need five tickets?)

Vasek gave an indirect answer. The ticket seller turned her sharp gaze away and with agonizing slowness issued the tickets.

"Danke," Vasek nodded. Vasek and Pepa walked toward the door with unhurried steps, the distrustful gaze of the ticket seller following their every move.

After slipping back into the loft, Vasek and Pepa described the encounter with the ticket seller to the others.

"I have to tell you, that old hag gave me the creeps," Pepa said.

"What do you think, Vasek?" Radek asked.

"She gave me a really bad feeling. She was a snoopy old busybody and I wouldn't put it past her to make trouble," Vasek replied.

"That doesn't sound good at all."

"All I can say is, I'm glad we're doing a few clicks by train," Zbynek said. "Let's stay on after Uckro. Every mile on the train is one mile less to walk."

"I second the motion. It's a god-given opportunity," Milan chimed in.

"We're screwed if they catch us fare-dodging," Vasek said.

"Let's not run any unnecessary risks," Radek said. "We'll go as far as Uckro, and continue on foot."

In the end they decided that being caught fare-dodging would only land them in a mess. The plan, then, was to go as far as Uckro and continue on foot. This decided upon, they set the watch and went to sleep.

Chapter 16

GUN BATTLE AT UCKRO

It was Zbynek's watch. A few minutes before 2:00 AM he moved through the loft, prodding everyone awake. The steam engine was already snorting and chuffing its way into the railroad station as the five friends groggily scrambled down the ladder and hurried across the street in their customary two groups. Inside the terminal stood a solitary Volkspolizei officer. They walked past him warily.

Don't go too fast.

Act normal.

But he didn't seem to be paying them any attention.

The train was already waiting at the platform, a motley collection of beat-up passenger cars. Some were in the old style, with the running board outside; others, in the newer style, had no running boards. At the front of the train, the steam engine was spewing out dense clouds of condensation that curled back along the platform. The friends chose a new-style railroad car without any interior lighting and hurried toward it. Open seats instead of compartments made it easier to see approaching Vopos. There were only two doors: one at each end of the car. Warily they took their seats and waited. The seconds crawled by. Footsteps resonated on the platform as they sat in the dark in their two groups, mentally rehearsing their standard operating procedure. Suddenly, the whistle shrilled. Doors banged. And finally the train lurched and they were off. As Pepa watched the station building slowly fall away into the night, the train rolled past a solitary figure standing on the platform, observing the train. It was the Vopo.

They tried to get comfortable on the high-backed wooden seats and pretended to sleep. Though they were the only passengers in the car, it was best to play it safe. This time around, they were determined not to repeat the accident of their last ill-fated train trip. They carefully counted the stops. Suddenly, the door at the end of the car burst open. Everyone startled, but the figure that materialized was wearing a conductor's uniform. The man came down the aisle, grasping the seat backs to steady himself as the train swayed and clattered along. "Fahrkarten, bitte," he grunted. Two in the morning was too early for pleasantries. One after another, the five friends wordlessly handed him their tickets. The less said, the better. He shone his light on the tickets, punched them and handed them back. The five companions nodded at him each in turn and immediately turned away, tired travelers eager for some sleep.

In the darkness outside, indistinct black masses that represented houses and trees trundled by. One stop. Then the train slowed once more. A two-story brick building slid into view. "Uckro," said the sign on the station wall. There were a couple of platforms, the one abutting the station building covered with a metal roof.

"We're here!" Vasek announced as the brakes squealed and the train pulled to a stop.

"Okay, everyone," Radek said. "Maintain visual contact. We meet up on the road out front."

The others were already on their feet and moving toward the exit. Doors flew open. People began moving past toward the terminal building. The Czechs got out and tried to blend in among the two dozen or so passengers who had disembarked. It was still dark outside, and the platform was only dimly lit by ramp lights.

During the short walk across the platform, Radek saw a Vopo in the crowd, but thought no more of it. After all, the whole country was crawling with police. He passed the ticket checker who was sitting in his small wooden cage to the right of the door and handed him his ticket with the left hand; the right one was in his pocket, on his gun.

Pepa disembarked with Vasek. Then, among the rushing travelers they were separated and he continued on by himself. He saw five Vopos on the platform, spread along the whole length of the train. Inhaling sharply, he straightened up and looked around for his friends. He could only see Vasek just ahead of him in the crowd. Warily, he looked toward the Vopos again. They were armed and seemed to be waiting for something. He handed his ticket to the ticket checker, like everyone else, and rushed, now with Vasek again, toward the main exit of the terminal building.

"There are five armed Vopos on the platform," he murmured to Vasek under his breath. For a second their eyes met. Trouble. Maybe this was for them.

Ahead of them was the exit, a narrow, high wooden door with glass panels, a style much in vogue around the turn of the century. Several people had already disappeared through it into the night. Five steps. Two steps to the door. The door was swinging shut. One more step. As Vasek reached out to push it open, a young Vopo jumped in front of them.

"Personalausweis, bitte!" (ID card, please!) the Vopo said, his hands on his belt. The wooden door fell closed with a heavy thunk. Vasek's eyes darted down and saw that the Vopo had a 9-mm automatic P38 in a black holster.

Vasek smiled, "Ich bin Grieche," he began, his tone relaxed, apologetic. "I am a Greek laborer at the tile-making plant in Dresden and I've forgotten my pass." Pepa slipped past Vasek, making for the door, but the Vopo thrust out his arm, stopping him short. "Und Sie sind auch Grieche?" (And you're Greek, too?) Pepa felt the sarcastic sting in his voice. He said nothing and the Vopo laughed at his own joke. By now, a group of passengers, including Radek, Milan, and Zbynek, had piled up behind Pepa and Vasek.

Radek appeared at Pepa's side. "Was ist denn los?" (What's the matter?) he demanded.

The Vopo looked at Radek: "Und Sie auch?" (And you, too?)

He quickly picked Milan and Zbynek out of the crowd, "Sie und Sie, bei Seite treten. Hier rein." (You and you, step aside. In here.) He motioned all five of them into a hallway to his right. This was not the place to resist: too many people around. They obediently filed into the passageway. There were a couple of doors and two barred windows, a bench against the wall below each window. It was a dead end.

The Vopo said, "Warten Sie!" (Wait here!), and motioned to someone around the corner in the main hall. Pepa moved quickly to check the doors. They were locked. No way out. But he wasn't seriously worried. This was a situation they had rehearsed many times, to the point that every reaction was automatic and required no conscious thought. They would follow the guards to their duty room or someplace out of the public eye, overpower them, and put them to sleep with chloroform.

The Vopo turned back to face the five friends. He watched them, his eyes sharp, his face betraying no emotion. A few of the passengers had dispersed into the street, but a cluster of gawkers had gathered around: civilians mostly, and a uniformed soldier with jackboots and a small suitcase. Suddenly the friends heard the pounding of many booted feet.

A mass of eight to ten policemen holding pistols and StG44 submachine guns rounded the corner and completely blocked the passage—many more policemen than the group's contingency plan was designed to handle. The plan was dead in the water. Bolts rattled as the Vopos armed their weapons and safeties clicked off. The senior Vopo officer, an older man with sharp, leathery features wearing knee-high boots and cavalry pants, stood slightly in front of the other black-clad Vopos.

"Hände hoch!" he barked, pistol raised. The entire phalanx slowly approached, their weapons trained on the friends.

Milan pulled his reluctant hands out of his pockets. Slowly he inched them up, looking about furtively to see what the others were doing. Almost all of them seemed to have their hands up, too. The commissar roared "Hände hoch!" a second time and threw himself upon Radek, who still had his hands in his pockets, knocking him back against the bench and onto the floor. A moment later, there was a deafening report followed by staccato bursts of heavy fire. The mass of Volkspolizei quickly retreated. Milan looked down and saw a man lying on the floor, face down, with a gaping red hole in the back of his skull. Milan bolted, hard on the heels of one of his buddies. He joined a knot of passengers and Vopos pushing and shoving at the exit, all struggling to get out the door at the same time. Another burst of gunfire erupted behind him as he rushed outside. There were shrieks and screams from the crowd fighting to get out the door.

In front of the building stood a tarp-covered police truck. A few Vopos were milling around in confusion. Milan flew down the stairs, but the person in front of him was still ahead, running like hell.

"Who is that?" Milan yelled.

"Milan?" It was Vasek.

"Yes!"

They both kept running. On the right side of the street, two or three street lamps cast a weak yellow glow over the area, but a little farther down the road lay a welcome black darkness. The two of them tore down the street toward it. A man came out of a house to the right and shouted at them, "Was ist los?" (What's the matter?). They ignored him and ran on.

As if in slow motion, Pepa watched the Vopo turn his back and beckon his comrades. "This is it!" Pepa thought. All of a sudden he felt calm and hyperaware of his surroundings. He knew he could rely on Radek and his friends. Each of them knew what to do. Radek's right hand was still in his pocket. With a casual motion, Pepa reached for his breast pocket and flipped off the safety on his gun.

A mass of black-clad policemen charged around the corner, readying their weapons. A short one, clearly the officer in charge, roared, "Hände hoch!" When there was no response, he pointed his P38 pistol straight at Radek: "Hände hoch!" Pepa slowly moved his hands up his chest. Out of the corner of his eye, he saw the short officer lunging at Radek. Radek would have to deal with that guy. Just in front of Pepa was another Vopo training an armed StG44 assault rifle, capable of firing twenty rounds in one burst, straight at Pepa. All at once Pepa snatched his pistol out of his breast pocket, aimed at the Vopo and fired once, then once more. The reports blended with an outburst of fire that sounded like thunder in the small, enclosed space. Pepa saw little clouds of pulverized plaster where bullets ricocheted off the walls. The man with the StG44 was down. The Vopos' faces registered surprise and shock. They were retreating in disorder. Pepa quickly aimed and fired once at the officer struggling with Radek, then jumped over three bodies that lay on the floor in puddles of blood and dashed into the main hall of the terminal.

The sharp odor of cordite was everywhere. The hall was empty, except for a panicked crowd around the exit at the far end, toward the trains, where a bunch of policemen and civilians were trying to get through the narrow opening at the same time. The ticket checker had abandoned his cage. Pepa pointed his pistol toward the retreating crowd and fired a shot. He had never seen so many people rush through such a small door in such a short time. He turned around and saw Radek standing alone at the far end of the dead-end passage. The sound of shooting at close quarters had been absolutely deafening. Now that it had stopped, the quiet was total. A pall of smoke hung thickly in the air.

Pepa burst through the door. In front of the building stood a tarp-covered police truck. Nobody was around. There were two flights of stairs, one going down to the left and the other to the right. He leaped down the left one, firing one more round into the bush next to the truck to keep the Vopos down. Someone on the truck called out, "Was ist denn los?" Pepa saw two figures running away down the street to his left. He turned and sprinted after them, quickly closing the gap.

When the second order came, Radek still had both his hands thrust deep in his pockets. He gripped the P38 firmly with his right hand. Without warning, the commissar stepped forward and punched him in the chest. The blow knocked the air out of Radek and sent him sprawling onto the bench. At that moment, he noticed another Vopo right behind the commissar, aiming a P38 directly at him. Radek leaped up, pulled his gun out of the pocket, pointed it at the Vopo and pulled the trigger. There was only a loud click. A misfire! The ammunition was old, from the war, and the cartridges were cheap ones, made of steel instead of brass. Quickly, Radek pulled back the slide and chambered the next round. He pointed at the same man and fired a second time. In that instant, the commissar punched Radek again. Hard. Radek went down as the commissar threw the full weight of his body across Radek and grabbed his right hand. *Did I get that guy?* flashed through Radek's mind. The commissar maneuvered himself until he was sitting on Radek's chest and pinning Radek's arms down on the ground, spread-eagled. Radek writhed fiercely against the commissar's viselike grip, the crushing weight of the other man's body on his chest.

Above them gunfire thundered, the sound of individual shots merging with their echoes into one big, ear-splitting boom. Radek and the commissar were intent only on each other. Radek's breath came in short gasps. The commissar let go of Radek's left arm and grabbed his throat. Using all his strength, Radek twisted around and managed to get on top of his adversary. The commissar let go of Radek's other hand and began choking Radek with both hands, crushing his windpipe. A big mistake. Radek jammed the muzzle of his gun onto the left side of his opponent's chest and pulled the trigger. He felt the commissar's body jerk and then go limp. Jumping up, Radek saw two more bodies lying between him and the exit, with big puddles of blood spreading across the width of the hallway. The air was full of gun smoke as he stood alone in the dead-end passage. Leaping over the motionless bodies, he ran toward the exit, pistol in hand.

Nobody was in the main hall. The total silence was disturbed only by the sound of Radek's footsteps as he ran out the door. In front of the exit the truck with the tarp-covered bed was deserted. To his left he could see his friends running down the street. He turned to follow them.

Pepa, who was some distance ahead, turned around and yelled, "Hurry up!" Radek caught up moments later.

"Pepa!" he gasped.

"Yeah," Pepa said. "Milan? Vasek?"

"I'm here," said Milan.

"Me, too!" said Vasek.

"Zbynek's missing!" Radek panted.

They slowed down, running sideways, briefly backward.

"Zbynek! Zbynek!" they shouted as they ran. No answer.

"Zbynek! Zbynek!" Silence.

They were now in the darkness, out of the wan glow of the streetlights. Tall chestnut trees on both sides of the street cast deep shadows over the cobblestone road and they almost stumbled in the dark. They looked back but couldn't see anyone in front of the station. The deserted police truck stood alone with its red tail-lights glowing.

"Where is that asshole?"

"Jesus, this is a major fuck-up! There were too many of those goddamn Vopos!"

"We've got to find Zbynek!"

"Are you crazy? The fuckers are regrouping!"

"No, wait for chrissake! We hide here! Right under their noses! They'll never think of looking for us here."

"Fuck no. Let's get the hell outta here!"

"Those Vopos don't think we have the balls to stick it out right here. It's the opposite of what a normal person would do."

"Fuck the psychology. Let's clear out!"

"They'll put guys on all the roads to Berlin. We have to divert for a few days."

They knew it was a sound idea, but no one was prepared to turn their backs on Berlin, even for a little while. It was decided. They sped up, racing north along the railroad tracks as fast as their legs would carry them. All of them were pumped on adrenaline, excited and anxious after the firefight. Their breath was ragged, their lungs and limbs ached. Radek was in terrible shape and he was lagging far behind.

"Radek, you ass, keep going!" the others urged him on.

Radek had fired two shots and lost one round as a misfire. Pepa was almost out of ammo, having used up five rounds out of eight in the magazine. They had kept count as they fired. Even though it was hard to do in combat, keeping track of the number of bullets you had left was vital in a situation where getting caught with an empty magazine was a death warrant. They'd used up a total of eight bullets out of their meager cache.

"Hey Vasek," Pepa called, "Let me have some of your rounds! I need five!"

Vasek counted off the rounds as he ran and passed them to Pepa.

"Where the heck is Zbynek?" Radek gasped. "I saw three guys on the ground, maybe Zbynek was one."

None of them had an answer—it had been over too quickly.

They ran along a trail in the woods, navigating by the noise of trains passing on their left and by the North Star when it occasionally appeared among the scudding clouds overhead. When anyone showed signs of flagging, the others urged him on. The terrain was rough, and in their headlong rush they repeatedly stumbled over protruding tree roots. Afraid that the police would put dogs on their trail, they took off their shoes and waded up a stream for several hundred yards.

Hours later, they were in a country of small fields and tamed woodland. The light was broadening quickly in spite of the overcast. There would be no sunrise. Already people were at work in the fields. It was time to drop out of sight. Everyone agreed that they had come far enough to evade the dragnet. They had run nonstop in the most taxing race of their lives and guessed they had covered between ten and fifteen miles since Uckro.* Now they were totally spent. The initial adrenaline rush was over. They stopped to pull a few carrots in a field, then began looking for a hiding place.

They came to some woods, but the young forest was not thick enough to provide good cover. The tall grass was completely wet. Finally they crawled onto an overgrown tree farm, where the pine trees grew on ridges, spaced only about one and a half feet apart. The branches hung all the way down to the ground and seemed to offer reasonably good concealment. They squeezed in between the trees and perched on the ridges.

They conversed in low, urgent voices. What had happened to Zbynek? None of them could recall seeing him run outside, and they were not even sure who was standing where at the moment the gun battle began. Was he one of the three bodies lying on the floor? It was possible. Zbynek was wearing a dark leather jacket, and the Vopo uniforms were also black. Or had he run out to the trains? Or down the street, heading south? Or had he run out the back? Vasek said that he heard shooting that seemed to come from the platform as he ran away. The whole gunfight had lasted only a few confused, action-packed seconds, and it was difficult to reconstruct

---

*They had actually covered 5.6 miles, as the crow flies.

what happened. Radek had obviously shot the commissar, but it wasn't clear whether Pepa or Radek had shot the other two casualties. At least one of the Vopos might have been shot by his own people. There was no good explanation accounting for all three bodies on the ground.

In spite of their heavy loss, a feeling of exultation energized them. Against towering odds they had managed to extricate themselves from a terrible predicament. But Vasek was subdued. His hands were shaking and he looked ravaged, exhausted.

"I'm sorry," he finally said, his voice breaking in remorse. He looked at Radek and Pepa in turn. "I . . . I don't know what to say! I shouldn't have run out on you guys back there!" He put his head in his hands, then looked up again. "When I heard the first shot, I thought you were all dead. I just ran like hell. I didn't see who shot at whom. I thought to myself, *I'm the only one who got out alive.* I thought that the Vopos had shot you all. I'm so sorry."

"Hey, chief, don't worry about it now," Radek said. "It was a pretty wild situation back there."

Pepa gave Vasek an encouraging grin. "It's okay, chief. Just make sure it doesn't happen again."

Milan said nothing.

Vasek turned toward Radek. "Thank you for saving my life. If you hadn't started shooting they would have gotten us all."

And they knew exactly what he meant. Had they allowed themselves to be captured and brought back to Czechoslovakia, certain death awaited them. They had suffered three months of interrogation hell on the mere suspicion they had known about someone else's planned escape. What would the Communists do to them if they caught them in the middle of East Germany? And what when they learned of Celakovice, and Chlumec, and Hedvikov, their raids in Czechoslovakia? Not just their own fates were at stake; there were patriots—friends—waiting back home whose lives hung in the balance. They *had* to get through to the Americans, whatever the cost. General Vanek's group might well be holding the key that would change the course of the coming war. Getting caught was not an option.

As the day wore on they tried to get more comfortable by digging deeper into the furrows between the ridges with their bare hands and lying down in them. For camouflage, they stuck a few twigs in front of their heads and feet and also in some of the unoccupied furrows. They ate the carrots and tried, unsuccessfully, to get a little sleep. The cold, damp sand chilled them to the marrow, but they didn't dare to get up.

It was 10 October, eight days since they had left home, and Zbynek was missing. Their strength had come from their togetherness. With Zbynek gone, maybe dead, there was suddenly a profound void in their midst. Pepa missed the sound of his voice, his cocky charisma, his eagerness for action, and his sometimes unfounded enthusiasm. He even missed Zbynek's sore ankle. His thoughts turned to his mother and sister and the others they had left behind. He missed them terribly. And always, in the back of his mind, loomed the fateful contact at Uckro. They had been irrevocably compromised. No question, the Vopos would be looking for them.

A light sleet started falling.

"Hey, Vasek!" Radek finally said. "Tell the story of your escape!"

All of them were eager to hear it. Not that they hadn't heard it before, but it was an inspiration to them in their plight.

Tormented by the thought that the others had written him off as a quitter, Vasek looked visibly relieved that they were still willing to include him in the group. "When the Germans occupied our country," Vasek began, "I was just in high school, but I wanted to fight them. I decided to go to England to join the Czech pilots in the British Royal Air Force. I didn't get very far; the bastards caught me and locked me up in Brno. They put me in a work gang assigned to the fifth floor of the courthouse. A locked partition kept us from escaping. But one day the guard left for a while. I seized the opportunity; I opened the window overlooking the courtyard and crawled out. There was a four-inch ledge running all the way around the building, connecting the windowsills. The ground was a hell of a long way down, but I screwed up my courage and stood up on this ledge, pressed my back to the wall, and inched over to the window on the other side of the partition. When I got to the window, I jimmied it open and jumped into the hallway. Then I opened the door in the partition and let out all the other prisoners. Most of them took off, except a few old guys who didn't think they could make it out of the country.

"This time the Germans didn't catch me. Even getting across the border into Switzerland was no problem. I was so happy that I had made it! Since Switzerland was a neutral country, I knew I'd be safe from the Germans there. I reported to the nearest Swiss police station and told them that I wanted to go to England to join the RAF. What I didn't know was that the

Swiss were in bed with Hitler and his thugs. They clapped handcuffs on me and handed me over to the German authorities the very next morning. Everyone who made it to Switzerland, and I mean everyone—Jews, political exiles, underground fighters, people who faced certain death—was handed over to the Germans. I was no exception. I spent the next three years in a German jail, pressing uniforms in the prison laundry.

"I never did get to fight the Germans," Vasek closed with a rueful little laugh. "But I guess one good thing came out of it—I sure can press a set of overalls now!"

"Two things, chief!" Milan corrected him. "You picked up German pretty good!"

"You know," Vasek added, "I even spent a few of those years in the Marienburg penitentiary. That's pretty near Uckro."

Pepa grinned at him. "Feeling right at home, are you?"

All day long there was unusually heavy traffic on the nearby roads, even on the dirt roads in the woods. They tried to explain it away: lots of people working in the woods nearby. But their rationalization did nothing to allay their nagging worry that something big was afoot. Finally they crawled to the tree line to get a better view. Within minutes, several military vehicles passed by. An astounding number of motorcycles were zipping back and forth.

"Shit. This doesn't look very good," Pepa whispered. "We've got to move out and put distance between us and all these goddamn Vopos."

They crawled to the edge of the nursery and prepared to rush across the dirt road. But far to their left a man in a black uniform was walking to and fro on the dirt road.

"The Vopos have posted sentries!"

"We can cross while he's got his back turned."

"No shit. What if there are others hiding in the wings?"

They withdrew and waited, restless with worry, until nightfall. Pepa studied Vasek. His friend was still subdued, still haunted by the thought of having failed his buddies.

In fact, the Transportpolizei, the East German railroad police, had been on full alert since 6 October, the night of the attempted vehicle heist at Branderbisdorf. With no new leads forthcoming, the alert was downgraded to level I two days later, and due to expire at 5:00 PM on 9 October.

The Trapo were operating on sketchy information. They only knew they were looking for five armed Czechoslovak nationals. But at 1:30 PM on 9 October one of the patrols along the Riesa-Elsterwerda railroad line reported a definite sighting.[1] The Transportpolizei now knew that the party of Czechs was on the Elsterwerda road. Only the friends' lucky decision to seek refuge in the abandoned swimming pool saved them from discovery by the motorized patrol searching for them along that very stretch of road. Then the ticket seller at Elsterwerda, whose suspicion had so worried Pepa and Vasek, made her report. But the Trapo wasn't sure these were their men. They dispatched the solitary Vopo to the station to confirm the sighting, and only the friends' decision to stay clear of the station until their last-minute dash for the train ensured that a force was not on hand to intercept them.[2] The Vopo, however, telephoned ahead to the Uckro station master, advising him that a group of five men and one woman had boarded the train and were on their way to Uckro.

In Uckro the local ABV officer, Hermann Grummini, was the man in charge. The position of *Abschnittsbevollmächtigter* (local authorized officer) was one of the post-uprising reforms, designed to embed the police force in the populace and monitor local sentiment. Lieutenant Grummini* did not feel up to confronting five men and one woman who were armed and dangerous by himself, so he called in reinforcements.

At 3:45 AM on 10 October an eight-man *Schnellkommando*, the quick-response strike force that was another post-17 June innovation, moved out in response to Grummini's call for backup. Fifteen minutes later, at 4:00 AM, the Schnellkommando, headed by VP-Unterkommissar Helmut Strempel, pulled into Uckro train station in a canvas-covered military truck. Grummini was already waiting for them with the stationmaster. Grummini and Strempel discussed the disposition of their troops and the men assumed their positions to await the train.

The train from Elsterwerda arrived punctually at 4:14 AM. Grummini, Strempel, and a third man boarded the train; four men guarded the station platform, and two men stood on the far platform, behind the train, to intercept anyone who might jump off in that direction.

The suspects managed to evade the four men posted on the platform and had passed the ticket checker when the stationmaster told the nearest Vopo,

---

*Kommissar Grummini. All East German ranks have been translated to the nearest American equivalent, insofar as there is one.

Corporal Wittkiewicz, to intercept them at the exit. Wittkiewicz, realizing he had missed the men after moving away from his assigned position by the ticket checker, hurried over to the exit, arriving there just before the mass of train passengers. In short order he rounded up the five suspects and called for reinforcements. The other troops arrived en masse. Then the gun battle erupted. Within seconds it was over.[3] By 4:20 AM Grummini was dead, felled by a single shot to the head. Strempel lay on the floor seriously wounded, having taken six bullets. He would later claim that his Communist Party membership booklet had saved his life: it deflected a potentially fatal shot to his heart.[4] Wittkiewicz suffered a grazing shot as he dashed out the back door to the trains.

The official East German accounts of what happened at Uckro contradict each other. One maintains that "only Comrade Strempel had cocked his submachine gun, while all the other comrades still had their pistols in their pocket."[5] Another claims that the attending Vopos were armed with three submachine guns, one "pistol 08," and four rubber truncheons.* On the other hand, the Czechs had counted eight to ten men (there were eight), all of whom bore firearms, plus one man with a rubber truncheon at the door. Ewald Fitzek, the young Vopo candidate with the rubber truncheon, remembers it this way: "I started [with the Volkspolizei] in September, and the others were already in longer. And that's why they gave me a rubber truncheon, because I still hadn't had weapons training. And the others, they were already in for two more years, and they had live firearms."[6]

Strempel, who had taken several grazing shots and a shot through the lungs, was hospitalized. His small intestine was perforated ten times, his large intestine twice, his bladder punctured, his right kidney destroyed, and he had a bullet lodged in his buttock.†

---

*BArch, MdI, DO 1/11/777, p. 0077. The Volkspolizei records speak of two casualties on the ground: Strempel and Grummini. Pepa and Radek Masin reported that they jumped over three bodies. Who was the third body? Somebody faking death so he wouldn't get shot by the Czechs?

†BArch, MdI, DO 1/11/777, p. 0078. The friends' count of their remaining ammunition confirmed that they had fired only seven shots total, plus Radek's misfire. Radek had fired one of his good shots at Grummini and one at Strempel. Pepa fired twice at Strempel, once at Grummini, once after the retreating Vopos (when he probably hit Wittkiewicz), and once outside, into the bushes. According to this tally at least some of the six bullets in Strempel would have to be from friendly fire.

Meanwhile, the colossus was stirring. At 5:00 AM news of the gun battle at Uckro reached East German Central Command in Berlin.[7] Five Czech men and possibly a woman had smashed through a Schnellkommando, the regime's first line of defense, without taking any damage. Now these armed and dangerous individuals were on the loose—individuals who did not hesitate to shoot point-blank at forces that outnumbered and outgunned them, individuals who shot to kill. Such a thing was unheard of in the annals of the GDR. Not even during the June uprising had determined opponents dared to shoot at the regime's armed troops. Moreover, these fugitives were foreigners, in a country controlled by an utterly xenophobic regime that lived in fear of the next uprising fomented by foreigners.

Within fifteen minutes, Central Command ordered the highest response level—a level III alert—for the districts north of Uckro.[8] Level III alerts were serious propositions, directly under the command of the head of the East German armed forces by definition. Yet the initial response to the Uckro incident was disjointed and piecemeal.

It took a couple of hours for six hundred Volkspolizei men to deploy in a blockade line, denying the fugitives access to the north. Volkspolizei also lined the southern part of the Berliner Ring, the major autobahn artery that encircled Berlin, more than sixty miles away.

The head of the Manhunt Department, a major, arrived at the Luckau regional police headquarters at 9:00 AM, nearly five hours after the shootout. He presided over a hastily assembled command staff that incorporated members of the Criminal Investigations Department (Hauptabteilung K), the so-called Protective Police (Hauptabteilung S), the infantry (Hauptabteilung A), the border police, and the transport police (Trapo).[9]

Meanwhile Major General Dombrowsky, head of Criminal Investigations, had already ordered a full-scale deployment of every available resource in the area. All available Trapo, all of the Cottbus Schnellkommandos, and the entire Potsdam Vopo complement rushed into action. But Dombrowsky believed this was still not enough. He called for a third blockade line and a total of fifteen hundred troops. "With deployment of 800 KVP members security would be ensured," he promised.[10] He was asking for infantry, for fifteen hundred troops to stop five men. He got them and more.

By 10:00 AM, troops had formed a security perimeter around the town of Uckro with a five-kilometer (roughly three-mile) radius. The first army infantry units (KVP) appeared on the scene as troops deployed in a second blockade line to the north. This was no longer a standard police manhunt, even in the sense understood by the East German Communist authorities. Although they didn't know it, the friends faced a formidable series of obstacles. Despite their excruciating run, which they had hoped would put them beyond the reach of the dragnet, they had managed to clear only the first obstacle—the encirclement of the town. Two blockade lines, plus the secured autobahn ring, still lay between them and Berlin.

Meanwhile the central command in Berlin kept a close watch on the western allies' movements. A vehicle from the British mission* was reported to be moving toward the operations area.[11] In the early afternoon a second British mission vehicle was sighted at Rangsdorf, just south of Berlin. When it failed to show up at the Potsdam checkpoint, the central command in Berlin notified the Secretariat for State Security (Stasi). Now two British mission vehicles were presumed en route toward the operations area.[12] Were the Brits attempting to rendezvous with the five Czechs?

The crisis was becoming too serious to be entrusted entirely to one major. At 2:00 PM, Dombrowsky dispatched Colonel Karl Mellmann to Uckro to assume command of the operation from Major Treczoks.[13] Dombrowsky's third blockade line had already finished deploying south of Uckro.[14] Now a second perimeter ringed the town, roughly six to nine miles from "ground zero" at the Uckro train staion. The four Czechs were hiding just inside this perimeter.

Then Karl Maron, head of the East German Armed Forces, issued an order throwing more troops into the hunt—in total 2,604 men—to form a third perimeter outside the first two. He put his deputy, Lieutenant General Willi Seifert, in charge of what was now code-named Operation Uckro.[15] Colonel Mellmann would report to him. Command had passed from a major to a colonel and now finally to a lieutenant general, who was reporting directly to the head of the East German Armed Forces.

During the course of the day increasing numbers of Vopo and KVP from all over East Germany converged on the core mobilization area. Search teams deployed inside the perimeters.[16] The countryside was crawling with thousands of Vopos and infantry. Several times troops fired at suspicious individuals who ran away rather than stopping.

---

*Quoting from http://www.brixmis.co.uk/contents.htm: "BRIXMIS was set up on 16 September 1946 under the Robertson-Malinin Agreement between the chiefs of staff of the British and Soviet forces in occupied Germany. The agreement called for the reciprocal exchange of liaison missions in order to foster good working relations between the military occupation authorities in the two zones."

The shock waves of Operation Uckro washed outward in all directions.[17] By 3:50 PM all the districts on the fugitives' presumed path to Berlin were on alert. Districts far to the east and south also went on alert.[18] Volkspolizei units continued streaming into the core mobilization area throughout the night as the alert levels in ever more distant districts ratcheted up from level I to level III.[19]

Since large-scale deployment of East German forces couldn't take place without Soviet approval, a Soviet colonel visited the Operational Command Center in Luckau that evening. He reviewed all the measures and approved them on behalf of his commanding general.[20]

And what of Zbynek? As soon as the barrage of deafening gunfire exploded around him, he broke and ran, making for the door in a burst of speed and shouldering his way past the young Vopo, who was still off-balance from the last person who had collided with him in headlong flight. He ran out the door, its two wings slamming shut behind him, down the right-hand flight of stairs in bounding leaps. The door flew open once more and footfalls pounded behind him, but they turned left at the top of the stairs and clattered down the other side. Zbynek didn't turn to see who it was. No time! He found himself on a cobblestone road and just kept running—blindly, as fast as he could go, putting as much distance as he could between his unarmed self and the Vopos in that train station. He covered 650 yards in a dead sprint before veering off and heading into the fields. He splashed through an icy stream and kept running. Here was a road: the going would be easier on his gimpy leg. He jogged along, and then slowed to a walk. Clearly, the others weren't coming. He was alone.

His adrenaline rush had gotten him through the field and across the icy stream and he had completely ignored his injury. Now he was anxious and scared. He limped slowly down the road, not quite sure where to go and what to do now. The sky was cloudy, the North Star nowhere in sight. And his ankle hurt like hell.

"Damn it all!" he cursed. When a huddle of houses materialized up ahead, he stuck to the road and headed straight through the village. No more dodging about in the muddy fields for him. After all, the other guys weren't here to tell him what to do, so he'd just as well do it his way. About six hundred yards on he came upon a large pile of wilted potato greens by the roadside. It was the best hiding place he'd come across so far. He wormed his way deep into the tangled mass of vegetable matter and curled up, shivering.

After a seeming eternity, a cheerless gray dawn crept over the country-side. Zbynek lay in the potato greens, the hours dragging on in agonizing slowness. Again and again he heard motorcycle and foot patrols pass by, some within feet of where he lay hidden. The roads and fields seemed to be swarming with Vopos. It was cold. He was hungry. He was thirsty. And his sprained ankle still throbbed with pain. Last night's run hadn't done it much good at all. He was alone. From the footfalls behind him, he thought that at least one other person had gotten away. . . . But who was it? He didn't speak a word of German, he had no gun, and he was injured. Berlin was sixty long miles away.

Zbynek's luck held, and he had picked his hiding place well. All that day he escaped the attention of the searching Volkspolizei. After nightfall he scrambled out of his hiding place. Cold, stiff, and hungry, he took his bearings and limped away northward. He crossed a stream, some footpaths, and a railway line. His leg hurt too much, so he decided to continue on the road. His progress was slow as he limped through a village and, as he came to the last houses, he saw three forms approaching him on the road. His heart leaped—and then sank. "Halt! Stehen bleiben!" They wore black uniforms and they were pointing guns at him. Zbynek slowly raised his hands and he surrendered himself to the Vopos. At 8:20 PM in the little village of Pelkwitz, two short miles northeast of Uckro train station, Zbynek's road to Berlin came to an end.[21]

Once the twilight had segued into total darkness, the four remaining fugitives did a quick equipment check. They crawled out of the nursery and moved off in single file, continually scanning the silent woods for the smallest movement. But the night was utterly still.

Eventually they reached a swampy flatland, where a light fog floated ghostlike above the ground. A hard slog through the mud eventually brought them to a sandy track on a high embankment. It was as wide as a highway, lined with tall poplar trees and flanked by deep ditches on either side. They moved warily, scanning the area, ready to hit the dirt at the slightest sign of danger. Oddly, the path was completely deserted, although the hour was still early.

"Where're all the people?" Pepa whispered.

"Maybe they locked the doors and went to sleep at sunset."

They walked on in silence.

"There aren't too many villages around here," Radek offered. "It's all swamp."

When the sandy track veered west they left it. Now they continued north along a stream, gingerly picking their way around large pools of water. The swampy ground subsided under their feet and they began sinking into the mud up to their ankles.

"Run across it!" Radek called in a low voice.

They tried running, as light-footed as possible, but with every step they only sank deeper. There were muffled curses and grunts.

"Spread out!" Radek hissed.

Everyone immediately complied. They knew they would all go down at once if they hit quicksand.

They were wading shin-deep, then knee-deep in water. Suddenly the ground fell away. Gasping from the cold, they floundered up to their waists in the icy water, hearts thumping in their throats.

"I bet the Vopos'll never think of coming after us in here!"

"They'd be crazy to!"

On all sides water stretched away in an unbroken expanse. Only the occasional soggy hillock or odd tuft of swamp grass broke the surface.

"Hey, Radek! How do we know we're not going in circles?" Milan said.

"We don't!" Pepa snapped.

"We need to get out of here."

"That's great advice. You have any suggestions?"

No one did. They struggled on in silence, increasingly worried.

"Solid ground!" Radek finally called out softly, relief in his voice.

The others breathed sighs of relief as they sloshed out of the water and back onto marshy land. "No more shortcuts!" Milan swore.

"We stick to roads!" Vasek agreed.

Numbly they plodded through the fields, shivering inside their sodden clothing. Their feet squelched loudly in waterlogged shoes. Not long afterward, some strange-looking hayricks on stilts materialized out of the fog. As they silently trudged past them, Radek looked them over curiously and thought to himself that they resembled strange, three-legged African huts.

The stars kept appearing and disappearing behind thick banks of clouds. They had been forced to leave their last compass behind when Zbynek fired his weapon, and now they were reduced to navigating by guesswork. Their only guide was the sound of the occasional train passing on their left. In the long intervals of total silence they began to worry, certain that they were veering badly off course. Soon they came upon another sandy track and a quiet village loomed in the darkness to their left. Continuing past it, they were thoroughly disoriented. At least, they comforted themselves, their wanderings were confined to the area between the autobahn on their right and the train tracks on their left.

They stopped and listened. Voices carried toward them. There were men ahead—and a noise that sounded like a large number of motorcycles idling and revving.

"I'll check it out!" Pepa said in a low voice.

He moved off into the fog to reconnoiter. Soon he came upon a cross-roads. A sign pointing right said "Autobahn," and a convoy of motorcycles and trucks was parked nearby. Pepa was reminded of a bunch of boisterous village teenagers out for a ride. Not long ago, he and his friends had enjoyed many such evenings in Czechoslovakia. Now, those troops were the hunters, and they were searching for him.

Grimly, he turned and retraced his steps. He made a hand signal to the others and they followed him as he silently moved away from the autobahn. Then they rushed across the road unobserved.

The terrain was still swampy and dotted with dense willow thickets that made the going difficult. They crossed an irrigation ditch via a small bridge and walked across a large meadow in single file. The fog was denser here, the grass hard and short, stiffened by white hoarfrost. In a little birch grove they came upon a burned-out, rusting half-track. They huddled briefly behind the half-track.

"Shit!" Pepa breathed.

"We've got to hide!" Radek said.

"Thanks for stating the obvious, smartass."

They set off again.

Fifty yards on, Radek signaled "stop." Everyone froze and listened. A strange, rhythmic clicking sound was coming from up ahead. A moment later, the sound of a voice drifted over, muffled by distance. Then another noise, like rifle butts hitting the hard top of the highway. The cold air seemed to carry sounds easily over long distances. They yawned to ease the pressure on their eardrums and cupped their ears to guide in the sound. After a while a man coughed behind them. A rifle bolt clacked.

The fog started rising in a perfect layer, exposing their feet. Behind them a truck engine growled, slowly advancing. It passed by, headlights moving through the fog in a weak yellow glow.

"Halt!" a loud, fog-muffled command rang out.

The truck kept going.

"Halt!" two or three other voices bellowed. A rifle shot rang out.

The truck immediately stopped. Voices rose in animated discussion and soon the truck took off again.

The fog was still rising and by now the Czechs' legs were completely exposed. Again and again the four men crept toward the road only to be driven back by the sound of sporadic coughing. Though the guards were quiet and didn't move around, the road was obviously completely occupied. At last they turned back and slowly headed away from the road. Back at the wreck, in the little birch grove, they huddled and turned back to look the way they'd come. Every step they'd taken had left a clearly visible dark print on the frost-covered grass.

"Shit," said Radek.

A trail of black footprints lead across the meadow, where the layer of fog was progressively rising, and pointed straight to their hiding place in the birch grove. The road, on top of a high fill, was still enveloped in fog, but the meadow below was completely clear. They were in imminent danger of discovery.

"How big is this dragnet?" Vasek asked.

"How do we get out of here?" Milan wondered.

"That road is only one piece of it," Radek said. "It's got to be huge."

The Czechs waited at the wreck for the fog to descend again.

Far ahead of them, vehicles were still moving. The Volkspolizei were still at work. The trap was not yet ready to be sprung.

Chapter 17

GOING TO GROUND

As soon as the fog dropped down to ground level again, the foursome retraced their steps to the ditch in search of the little bridge they'd crossed before. They found the ditch, but where was that bridge? The whole area looked different. Was this even the same ditch? They began to have serious doubts. For quite a while they had not heard any trains. They debated what to do next.

How about hiding in the hayricks?

No. The Vopo would search those.

What about following the canals, and trying to cross under the autobahn by swimming down the canal?

No. Too risky; they'd undoubtedly be guarding those, too.

They were all getting testy, and tempers flared. They needed a hiding place to get them through the next couple of days. Clearly this troop deployment wouldn't be over in a few hours or even a day. It would be kept up until every last haystack in the district had been thoroughly searched.

"Let's go back to the village and hide among people," Pepa suggested. "We're better off there than taking our chances in an open field."

"Yeah, sure," Milan said. "But where the fuck's the village? There are no lights—it could be anywhere!"

"It's back over that way," Pepa retorted, pointing.

"Like hell!" Radek countered. "There's fog all around and you said you don't recognize this place either."

"It's that way! I'm sure of it," said Pepa, pointing.

"You dumbass, it can't be that way, we came from the other side."

"I suppose you have a better idea?"

"Hey, how about we vote on this?" Vasek intervened.

"I vote we follow Pepa," Milan said quickly.

"Pepa, you lead," said Vasek.

"Fine," Radek agreed. "Off we go. You lead the way, know-it-all."

Driven by a sense of impending peril, the group quickly moved off, following Pepa. They found and crossed the bridge, then pushed on through the swampland and willow thickets with utmost speed. Suddenly a wide canal yawned at their feet. They hadn't seen this one before. It was almost thirty feet across and they had no idea how deep.

"We've got to swim it," Pepa said.

"It's too cold," Milan complained.

"You see a bridge anywhere?" Radek replied.

Radek started stripping down. They all undressed quickly.

"Your butt is glowing in the dark," Vasek joked.

"Good! Just follow the light . . . that way you won't get lost."

They bundled up their clothing and waded into the icy water, holding their bundles above their heads. By the time they were knee-deep in the water, they had lost all feeling in their legs. In seconds their bodies were completely numb. Soon the water was up to their armpits. Luckily there was no current to speak of, and they clambered out on the far side feeling strangely detached from their unwieldy, chilled limbs.

"My pistol's gone!" Radek suddenly exclaimed.

"Piss on it!" Pepa snapped.

"Hurry up, chief," Vasek said.

But Radek wasn't about to abandon his weapon. "I'm going back to find the gun," he announced firmly.

"You ass!" Pepa hissed.

Pepa turned and headed off into the darkness, followed by Milan and Vasek. Radek turned back by himself. He waded back across the freezing canal and hunted about on the ground. He finally found his pistol at the spot where he had undressed. It had fallen out of his bundle. As he recrossed the canal he could hardly move for the bitter cold. He pulled his clothes on while running to catch up with the others, who were already far ahead.

There was the road! Pepa could see it dimly through the fog. Just then he heard the rumble of truck engines. A convoy was quite close, heading toward them. The Czechs broke into a flat-out run. Already they saw headlights piercing the fog, slowly advancing. They were racing the convoy now. They rushed up the embankment and onto the road just as the beam of the lead truck bore down on them, wanly illuminating their legs.

.es hit the ditch on the far side. A second later the lead truck

.k. A pair of heavy boots hit the ground no more than seven feet
.pa's head. They were attached to a Vopo armed with an assault rifle.
.et farther another pair of boots hit the ground. Then another. It was a
.urity cordon.

So that was why the convoy was moving so slowly! Pepa and Radek exchanged looks of concern as one truck after another throbbed loudly past.

Scarcely daring to breathe, the four Czechs crawled away from the road using the willow bushes as cover. In a plowed field they finally dared to get to their feet, but their progress across the deep furrows was hampered by the soft, loose dirt, and they were constantly falling. Who would be the first to break his legs?

The fog-enshrouded swamp now lay behind them. To their left, jagged treetops reached up toward the sky. "The highway's on the other side of those trees," Vasek said in a low voice.

"Let's try crossing," Radek said.

Milan and Pepa nodded in agreement. They turned and headed toward the highway.

Someone gunned a motorcycle engine on the highway.

The Czechs stopped.

"The highway's occupied, too." Vasek said, an edge to his voice.

The motorcyclist stopped, then revved the engine again. Then he stopped and started again. Gradually he drew ahead of them in his peculiar stop and go rhythm. Then he stopped. A red signal flare blossomed in the sky.

What did it mean? Was some sort of troop deployment complete? They were arguing in low, urgent voices. Where to go? What to do? Going near the road, they decided, would be a waste of time. They turned away and waded through the loose soil of the field.

Finally they staggered out of the plowed field onto a rutted dirt trail and elected to follow it, hoping it would eventually bring them to the village, or any village. They walked as quietly and carefully as possible. Desperate thirst plagued them after their long march. Their tongues stuck to the roofs of their mouths and their voices were so rough and hoarse they could scarcely speak.

Presently a little pond appeared to the left of the trail. The banks were muddy, covered with cow hoof-prints. The water reeked of manure and algae. Undeterred, the Czechs dropped to their hands and knees and greed ily sucked up the water.

When they'd drunk their fill they looked up. All around them stood the black silhouettes of houses. They had stumbled right into a village! The whole place was blacked out. All the windows were dark and the nearest dwellings crowded black against the skyline. Silently they crept into a farmyard. A big can of milk stood near the gate, waiting to be picked up the next morning. Each of the friends took a little drink, and the last man carefully wiped off the telltale ring of cream.

On the far side of the yard, opposite the house, the barn loomed black and silent. Radek tested the large sliding door. It was locked. In the end they hauled the lower part of the door away from the wall and squeezed in one by one. Inside, the darkness was close and thick. Exploring by touch, they found that the right side of the barn was completely full of straw.

"Let's burrow deep," said Vasek. "All the way to the ground."

"If each of us has his own hole, it's better," Radek said. "If the Vopos decide to poke through here with poles, we've got a better chance of avoiding or deflecting them."

They started digging. Pepa and Milan stayed together and burrowed down by the wall, where the straw was deepest. It was bitterly cold. As they shivered in the drafty straw, straw dust enveloped them, stinging their eyes, biting their skin, and burning their throats.

The next day Pepa woke up to find he could hardly breathe. He tried to find the tunnel to the surface, but it had collapsed overnight. Close to suffocation, he struggled desperately to get out. Sputtering and coughing straw dust, he finally flailed up to the surface, Milan following close behind. "Shit, man, this is horrible stuff!" he sputtered.

Radek and Vasek swam up to the surface, coughing.

"What was that we said about never sleeping in straw again?" Vasek asked. "I'm freezing my butt off!"

The four of them sat atop the stack, straining to hear what was going on outside.

This was 11 October, the ninth day of their odyssey, but it seemed more like the ninth week to them. The future did not look good. They were weak with hunger and far from their goal; one of their buddies was lost and the Volkspolizei was out in force pursuing them. How long it would take before

Berlin was anybody's guess. They'd have to wait until the pulled the troops off the roads. That couldn't take more than

...

...ter dawn Pepa heard voices shouting orders. "Vorwärts, marsch!" "Dalli, dalli!"

Hurriedly Pepa, Milan, Vasek, and Radek scattered and burrowed back into the straw. Troops were moving through the village. Officers shouted. Fences squeaked and cracked as soldiers climbed over them. Metal clinked against metal. The tromping of booted feet came closer. The search moved up to the barn, then past it. No one came in.

At midday a police car equipped with loudspeakers rolled by.

"Achtung! Achtung!" the tinny speakers blared. "Hier spricht die Volkspolizei! Attention! Attention! This is the People's Police! Four bandits who have committed several assaults and murders are in your district! The population is requested to cooperate with the People's Police and to report any unusual observations to the police. The harshest punishments in accordance with People's Law will be imposed on anyone harboring these bandits!

"The description of these individuals is as follows:

"Vaclav Sveda is the only one who speaks German. He is 5'9" and 140 pounds*, brown eyes, oval face, regular teeth. He is dressed in dark gray pants, a sports coat, and brown shoes.

"Ctirad Masin—6' tall, 145 pounds, light blond, blue eyes, oval face, dressed in a gray suit and black shoes.

"Josef Masin—5'10", 130 pounds, brown hair, blue eyes, oval face, dressed in a gray suit and brown shoes.

"Milan Paumer—5'10", 130 pounds, black hair, brown eyes, oval face, dressed in a brown suit.

"They are armed! They have been living in the open for an extended time and their clothing is unkempt. The four are hiding in the immediate vicinity. Report their whereabouts to the closest Volkspolizei police station!"

They got Zbynek! The dreadful realization hit Pepa like a ton of bricks. They had exact physical descriptions. They had names. Feeling newly vulnerable, he lay numbly in the straw. The vehicle meandered through the village, repeating its message in and out of earshot.

---

*These are metric pounds. For U.S. equivalents add 10 percent.

That night after dark, the four friends emerged from their hiding places i the straw. The mood was despondent.

"They got Zbynek!" Vasek said.

"They've got exact physical descriptions," Radek added. "They've got names."

"Poor bastard. They're already putting him through the wringer."

"Did you hear those Comrades? They called us bandits!" Pepa said, trying to make light. "Who are those fuckers to call us bandits? We'll pay them back for that."

Nobody laughed.

"They'll make him talk," Milan agonized. "They'll find out everything. He'll drag everybody else into it. My parents. Your parents. Then, off to the camps."

"Cut it out!" Radek said. They were silent. Everyone thought about poor Zbynek and how his capture had compromised them.

"Let's recon the area," Radek finally said. "We have to find some food, somehow."

They waited until the village had gone to sleep. Then they groped their way to the barn door. As Radek stepped into the opening, a ferocious growling made him freeze instantly. Radek peered out, scanning the barnyard. There, in the middle of the yard, stood a very large, very mean-looking dog. It stared right at him. Another menacing growl rumbled in its throat. The Czechs beat a hasty retreat.

"What now?" Vasek asked.

Radek tried again. He stepped into the doorway. The growling started. Radek retreated.

"We're stuck here," he said.

Every time they stepped into view, the beast resumed its growling. Finally they sat down just inside the barn door, waiting.

At about 11 PM somebody fetched the dog inside. Carefully the Czechs eased out of the barn. It was pitch black outside but every so often a flare exploded in the sky, bathing the area in phosphorescent light and long shadows. They crept toward the water pump in the farmyard. The dust from the straw had made them wretchedly thirsty, but when they pressed down the handle, an ear-splitting screech shattered the silence. They looked at each other in consternation. Milan reached for the rusty tin under the spout. There was a little water in it. He sniffed it and grimaced at the smell.

..hey were all so thirsty, they drank up the contents completely,
their faces in distaste.

..stopped in front of the milk can that awaited collection in front
..arn and looked at each other. Radek shook his head in warning—it
.. safe to drink from. They couldn't take any risks.

They explored, carefully avoiding the entrance and windows of the
..rmhouse, which faced the pump. At intervals a powerful beacon swept
the sky. What did it mean? They hurriedly debated, but to their knowledge
there was no airfield around and they had not heard any airplanes. Perhaps
the Volkspolizei were using the light to illuminate some large open field, or
maybe the autobahn?

It was late in the season and the small gardens behind the barn had been
picked clean. They collected some frostbitten apples, a few frozen green
tomatoes, and some carrots, spreading out their efforts over several gardens so that no one family would become suspicious. They found an empty
bottle and filled it with water from a pump in another farmyard. Reluctant
to stay outside any longer than necessary, they soon retreated to the safety
of the barn.

For an entire week they were pinned down in that barn. Troops moved
through the village during the day, in skirmish lines or patrols, while the
four Czechs lay in the straw, shivering and listening intently to the activity
outside. Volkspolizei automobiles patrolled once or twice daily, blaring the
all-points bulletin from their loudspeakers. At night colored and white flares
exploded all around. Vasek was suffering acutely from nicotine withdrawal,
experiencing nausea and headaches. He was anxious and irritable.

After the first few days, they got to know the daily routine of the farm
and could identify all the family by their voices. Every day a middle-aged
woman in widow's weeds came into the barn and fed some straw into the
cutting machine, while a young girl operated the hand crank for her. As the
days went by, the Czechs felt confident enough to spend the day on top of
the straw, covered with bits of straw for camouflage and listening through
a ventilation hole near their hiding place. They dozed fitfully, startling at
the slightest unusual noise. At night, once the family took the dog inside at
about 11:00 PM, the Czechs would send out two foragers to scrounge up
some carrots and fill the bottle with water. They dared not go far, fearing
that the village collectives had posted guards to protect farm equipment,
stock, and forage from sabotage by dispossessed farmers and other enemies
of socialism.

The few bits of food were divided among them precisely and fairly. Nobody would think of cheating. They were famished. Moving around became increasingly difficult. With every passing day, they grew weaker, and at last the grim specter of starvation stared them in the face.

Chapter 18

THE HUNT

A special Vopo detachment had rushed Zbynek straight to Luckau,[1] where interrogators immediately went to work on him. This was the break they had been looking for! Within hours the Volkspolizei were connecting the dots. Names. Identities. Biographies. The East German authorities immediately requested information from Czechoslovakia.[2]

Meanwhile the clampdown on the Luckau district continued in full force. By the morning of 11 October, 5,972 East German troops had swarmed into the Uckro area.[3] Walking patrols and checkpoints monitored the roads, while forces systematically scoured the entire countryside in cordon-and-search operations. The town of Luckau itself, the regional administrative center, was a hub of chaotic activity. The place looked like an armed camp. All the roads were closed. Volkspolizei, KVP, and Soviet units were encamped all around town.[4] Central Command sharply boosted the number of troops, stepped up patrol activity along the country's borders, and upped the number of boat patrols in the lake district southeast of Berlin.[5]

Sightings of suspicious persons triggered massive Vopo responses. On the afternoon of 12 October, three people who looked like the wanted Czechs fled from a Vopo challenge near the Berliner Ring. Two hundred infantry troops chased after them.[6]

In Karl-Marx-Stadt district, a man reported that a stranger had attacked him, throwing rocks. More than four hundred Vopos and forty-two dogs surrounded and combed the area. They didn't catch the perpetrator, but a young enlisted man was fatally wounded by friendly fire.[7]

In Leipzig district, a civilian auxiliary volunteer ordered two men pulling a handcart to produce their ID papers and asked them where they were going and why.* They answered, in broken German, "To Berlin." The volunteer challenged them and one of the two foreigners pulled out a pistol, sending the auxiliary volunteer packing. This time 735 Vopos, five hundred Soviet troops, fifteen armored personnel carriers, and four troop transport trucks descended on the area.[8] One of the two men was arrested by the Soviets, and the city of Leipzig was ringed by a security cordon to prevent infiltration by the remaining fugitive, who was apprehended later.[9]

The districts on level III alert represented a growing cancer on the situation map in Luckau, gradually spreading outward in all directions from the core mobilization area. It didn't take much to attract the Vopos' attention, as many a hapless refugee found out. A stubbly face and foreign accent were enough, and asking for directions was always risky. In the town of Meissen two men in their forties were fingered as suspects, even though they were at least twice as old as the men seen at Uckro train station, because they asked for directions in broken German and looked unshaven and unkempt.[10]

The police arrested another man who claimed to be on the way to visit his parents in West Berlin—it was enough that he spoke broken German, didn't have ID papers, wore a beret and carried a compass. Major General Dombrowsky requested that he be rushed straight to Luckau.[11] Numerous other unfortunate Polish and Czech refugees were also caught up in the dragnet willy-nilly.

Why were so many foreign refugees asking directions to Berlin? The Central Command's assessment was strictly doctrinaire: "One can conclude that the class enemy has instituted efforts at deception."[12] In other words, the exodus of tattered and desperate Polish and Czech refugees was a massive diversion intended to distract the authorities from the real danger—the brazen shooters at Uckro. All the while, the Volkspolizei continued to keep careful tabs on the western allies' activities. News of an American mission vehicle passing through Jüterborg on 11 October, heading northeast toward the core operations area,[13] was reported to Central Command.

Soon Operation Uckro encompassed the districts of Cottbus, Potsdam, Leipzig, and Karl-Marx-Stadt; most of the southern half of the country. At night troops along the perimeters and roads shot at anything that moved. The ammunition expenditure was so substantial that in the morning hours trucks had to travel the lines replenishing the troops' exhausted ammo supplies.[14]

---

*The German term for these civilian auxiliary volunteers is "Freiwilliger Helfer." They were proregime enthusiasts who volunteered to help the Volkspolizei in its work.

On 13 October the command reorganized the inner perimeter around the core mobilization area, shifting the center of activity northeast of Uckro, ordering troops posted at fifty-yard intervals, and putting 120 dogs at their disposal. At 9:00 AM that morning Vopo searchers scoured the secured area once more, to no avail. Then Colonel Karl Mellmann and Lieutenant General Willi Seifert planned another intensive search, of a small triangular area around the town of Reichwalde, for the next day. By chance, this was exactly where the Czechs were hiding.[15]

On the morning of 14 October, skirmish lines began moving through this triangle a third time. At the Pietzschen shepherd's hut they hit pay dirt. Three people rushed out of the hut and ran off, but not before the Vopos had identified them through their binoculars as the wanted men. The Volkspolizei forces quickly encircled the wooded area into which the three suspects had disappeared.[16]

That night troops formed a double perimeter in the Uckro area.[17] Just before midnight, inside the encircled area, Vopo guards observed two individuals moving from the Pietzschen shepherd's hut toward the perimeter. The shepherd's hut was turning out to be a veritable hotbed of suspicious activity. Fifteen yards to the north, troops sighted a third person. All three were moving at a crouch and returned into the center of the encircled area. Additional motorcycle patrols were ordered and the perimeter was reinforced pending daybreak, when a search could be launched.[18]

The Volkspolizei spent most of the following day chasing down dead-end leads—and chasing after itself. Not far from Uckro, at a small village named Liebesdorf, searchers found tracks leading away from the Dahme River that had been made by several people crawling. One of these individuals had heeded the call of nature and had evidently been eating raw potatoes.

Two tracking dogs were immediately rushed in. Ten guard dogs stood by in the event the tracking dogs lost the scent. All the surrounding roads were secured. Ten hours later Berlin headquarters learned that the tracking dogs had been hot on the trail of troops who had passed through the area earlier.[19]

The Volkspolizei had spent four days spinning its wheels, and now the trail was growing cold. Head of the Armed Forces Karl Maron submitted a six-page summary of the known facts surrounding the Czech fugitives to Interior Minister Stoph, beginning with the attempted vehicle heist at Branderbisdorf and ending with the "armed attack" on Volkspolizei members at Uckro. It drew principally on Zbynek's testimony. Since Zbynek didn't know Vasek's surname or place of residence, Vasek remained a cipher to the East German authorities, but they pegged Radek the "leader of the gang." According to Zbynek's testimony, the Masins' motive was to seek out acquaintances of their father in the West. "Allegedly these are well-situated individuals who were formerly important persons in public life. They explained several times that they had to reach Berlin 'at all costs.' Janata stated that he himself wanted to have a skin rash treated in Berlin and then find work. Paumer wanted out of the military and allegedly also wanted to find work in Berlin. There was no report on why 'Vaclav' wanted to reach Berlin."[20] According to the lead interrogator, "the reasons given for . . . their immigration to West Germany hardly seem plausible."[21]

While the interrogators continued working over Zbynek, Central Command began winding down the operation. Volkspolizei and KVP returned to their home bases. At 9:00 PM, Colonel Karl Mellmann and his staff departed Luckau for Berlin.[22]

By the following day, 16 October, only the nine-hundred-man security cordon at the autobahn ring around Berlin remained in place. It was the eye of the needle: the fugitives would have to pass through it to reach Berlin.*

---

*Arrests of refugees at the ring continued all that day.

Chapter 19

WHICH WAY TO BERLIN?

Sixteen October was the fourteenth day of their odyssey, and the sixth day since they had lost Zbynek. Lying on top of the straw, the four friends debated their predicament. The roving searchlight was still shining every night, but the police patrols seemed to have ended. Life in the village appeared to be back to normal. Traffic on the road had abated. People no longer spoke of the police and the bandits. The old standbys, work and family, once again dominated conversations in the farmyard. The Czechs started feeling cautiously hopeful that they had outlasted the dragnet. That night they would move on.

In the afternoon Milan emerged from his hiding place in the straw and announced: "I'm going to take a look at what's going on in the yard."

"Hey chief, come back here!" the others hissed at him in dismay. "Take cover! Someone might come up!"

There was no straw in that part of the barn, and Milan would be completely exposed if someone surprised them.

Milan waved them off and stared fixedly through the ventilation hole. All of a sudden he tensed. He turned around and frantically motioned Vasek over. Now the two of them crouched by the ventilation hole.

"I saw them!" an old man was telling two other people in the yard. "For sure those were the bandits. They were foraging in the garden last night."

Vasek didn't understand everything, but he heard the words "Ich werde die Beamten holen"—"I will get the authorities."

They had hidden themselves for a whole week to shake off the police. All for nothing! Vasek turned back to the others.

"Fuck! He's getting the Vopos. He saw us."

"We're trapped," Milan exclaimed. "We need to get out of here!"

"It's still broad daylight," Radek said quickly. "If we leave now, they'll see us for sure. Maybe Vasek misunderstood?"

"I don't think so," Vasek said darkly.

"Let's stay put in the barn for another hour," Pepa said. "It'll take the old guy a while to scare up the police, if he's in fact doing that."

"If the Vopos catch us in here, we hold them off for as long as possible," Radek said.

"Take out as many as possible before the end," Pepa added. "Make sure to save a bullet for yourself."

"What about me?" Milan asked.

"I'll save one for you," Pepa assured him.

Milan was still looking out the window every so often, keeping an eye on the yard outside.

"Shit! The farmer's wife is coming," Milan suddenly exclaimed. This was not part of her daily routine. All of them dove into the hay. Halfway up the ladder she stopped and looked around, wary. Suddenly her face and posture tensed. She had noticed that something was off. Quickly she clambered down and hurried out of the barn.

"Shit," Pepa hissed.

Everyone burst up out of the straw. Now they had nothing to lose.

"We've got to find out if that old guy made the report!"

"Where'd that asshole go?"

"Vasek, go find out!"

Vasek was already hustling down the ladder while the others staked out firing positions in the barn. They would cover him in case the Volkspolizei showed up.

Vasek burst into the kitchen, stubble on his chin, uncombed and dirty, gun in hand. "We're the wanted guys!" he cried, highly agitated. "Tell the truth! Has anyone gone to the police?"

"Yes, yes! It was the old man. He went to make a report." The woman was hugging herself, terrified.

"Where are the Vopos? Are they still in the village?"

"It's not my fault," the woman stammered, naked fear in her eyes. "Please don't shoot! I beg you, please don't shoot! I'm a widow. My husband died in the war. It's just me with the children now." She began sobbing.

"We're here because we're fighting the Communists," Vasek explained, more calmly now. He tried to ease the woman's fear. "We're only trying to get to Berlin. We don't want to hurt anyone. But we don't want anyone to cross us."

"We had no idea . . . we thought you were bandits . . . criminals. That's what the police are saying." She was still tearful, but her panic was subsiding. "Had we known, we wouldn't have reported you."

The others spotted Vasek running back across the farmyard. They crowded forward impatiently.

"What the hell's going on? Are they coming?"

"Everything is fucked up. Let's get out of here!" he said tersely. "The woman isn't hostile."

The four of them hastened over to the house, following Vasek into the kitchen. There was the woman, more composed now. A young boy, perhaps twelve years old, stood off to the side. Quickly the Czechs scanned the kitchen. Starved as they were, it looked like the family was not much better off. The only food in the place was part of a loaf of bread and some lard.

The friends gave the youngster some of their German money.

"Buy bread. Please," Radek told him in German. The boy looked up at him, nodded and ran off. But all too soon he was back—without the bread.

"The night watchman told me I can't buy bread now," the youngster said, handing back the money. "He told me to go back home."

What the hell was the night watchman doing, patrolling during daytime?

"Have you had anything to eat?" the widow was asking. She was curious now, even concerned.

"No," said Vasek, who was their spokesperson. The others shook their heads. She reached for the family's sole loaf of bread and cut a few slices of bread for each of them, smearing them with lard.

"I don't think that the Volkspolizei are in the village anymore," she explained as she handed them the slices of bread. "You must leave immediately. I'll send along the remaining two slices of bread with my boy." She indicated the two slices on which she was still working. "Go north." Through the window, she pointed out the direction the friends should take. "From here to Berlin the area is forested. Maybe you'll be able to hide in the woods."

"Thank you, ma'am," Vasek said. "Thank you so much!" There was no time to lose. "Auf Wiedersehen!"

Filing out of the house, they threaded their way through the kitchen gardens behind the farmhouses and out into the fields, then broke into a jog, hungrily devouring the bread as they ran. Moments later the boy appeared behind them. He quickly caught up, clearly excited by this adventure and happy to be helping them. Handing them some more slices of bread, he continued running with them, guiding them to the best place to cross the deep drainage canal that cut across the field. In the middle distance people were working in the fields and cows were placidly grazing the meadow.

"Danke!" Vasek finally told him in German. "Thank you. You must go back home now."

"Nein!" The youngster insisted that he wanted to continue with them to show them the way.

"He's got to go back now." Radek urged. The worst obstacles seemed to be behind them. The last thing they wanted was for this youngster to compromise himself and his family.

"You must leave," Vasek said adamantly. "Go now! It's dangerous. You cannot come any farther."

Finally the boy acquiesced. He nodded and smiled at them, "Alles Gute!" (All the best!) And he was off, loping home across the fields.

They were jogging along a dirt path, unable to move fast because of hunger-induced dizzy spells. After six days of inactivity and food deprivation, Pepa felt as if he was learning to walk all over again. His eyes, used to constant darkness, were aching, and excitement shortened his breath.

Suddenly, a big BMW police car roared onto the trail behind them, a motorcycle in its wake.

"Here they come!" shouted Vasek.

Still stuffing bread into their mouths, they leaped off the rutted path and set off across the fields. The ground was sandy and they floundered, unable to get traction. Back to the path. The BMW was gaining. They ran as fast as they could, but the car was hurtling toward them, closing the gap.

"Let's leave a rearguard behind the bushes! One man can take care of the car."

"Forget it. There's the motorcyclist!"

The car was almost on top of them now. The motorcyclist, with his StG44 assault rifle slung across his back, was lagging behind, not able to move as quickly on the sandy path.

The four Czechs struck out across the field again, floundering through the sandy soil. The car stopped, unable to follow. Two men in civilian overcoats jumped out and ran into the field.

"Stuj! Stuj!"(Halt! Halt!) they shouted.

The Czechs didn't slow down. Radek risked a glance back. The Germans had pulled out handguns. A couple of shots cracked and sharp whistles zinged by. The Czechs ran as fast as they could. More shots. Some of the bullets whined past them alarmingly close. Too close. A massive surge of adrenaline pulsed through their bodies and they ran for their lives, desperate for breath, their lungs burning inside their chests and threatening to burst. Radek, weak from his ordeal at Jachymov, was falling father and farther behind. The plainclothesmen were catching up with him. Up ahead Vasek, Pepa, and Milan reached the woods, forced their way through the thicket, and were gone.

Radek reached the edge of the woods with a supreme last effort. He tried to break through the brush, thick with blackberry canes. Thorns cut into his clothes and hands like barbed wire, but he couldn't take another step. He was hanging helplessly in the thicket, plainly visible, his pursuers a mere twenty yards behind him. Exhausted, he fell to the ground. Only a very few more steps and they'd have him. Radek knew he was finished, but still he fought on. Feeble and dizzy, he struggled to his hands and knees and groped forward on all fours. He was vaguely aware that his pursuers were not coming any closer. Were they afraid?

When Radek finally crawled through the thicket and stood up, swaying unsteadily on his feet, the others were gone. His ears ringing, his vision blurred, he tottered deeper into the woods and tried to call out. Not a sound came out of his mouth. Then his friends swam into focus. They were standing in a group of tall birch trees. Their mouths were moving, but he couldn't hear what they were saying. Gradually his hearing returned.

"We were calling you, you idiot! Where the hell were you going!?"

"I couldn't hear you," he croaked. "They were right behind me."

"We've got to get out," Milan gasped.

"Let's go back for the police car," Vasek said.

"No, we're totally outgunned," said Pepa.

"We've got to make for the big woods," Radek panted.

Their only hope was to reach the big woods to the north. They had to avoid getting pinned down. They had to evade the Vopos until nightfall.

"What time is it?" Milan asked.

"Heck if I know," Pepa said. "Zbynek had the last watch."

"Probably only about 4:00."

"Two hours until sunset."

They set off again. The woods turned out to be no more than a big patch of pine and deciduous trees. Before them lay an open field and a two-lane highway. They'd have to cross it. Off in the distance the great forest beckoned, a dark mass along the horizon.

They crept out toward the highway in single file, crouching low inside a reed-choked ditch, hyperalert, pulsing with adrenaline. To their right, a Vopo on a motorcycle was struggling toward the patch of woods, his wheels sinking deep into the sandy soil. He gave up and returned to the highway.

"Go!" commanded Radek.

The four Czechs dashed out of the ditch, running full tilt toward the highway, arms and legs moving like pistons, powering them across the sandy soil. The Vopo spotted them at once. He turned and rode away from them, then stopped, propped the motorcycle against a tree, grabbed hold of his rifle and opened fire.

Another motorcyclist arrived and began shooting.

In single file the friends sprinted across the highway. They were fully exposed in the wide-open field. A third Vopo pulled up. Now there were three of them, blazing away like marksmen at a shooting range. Bullets zoomed around the Czechs, kicking up puffs of sand in front of their feet, ricocheting off the ground with an angry buzz. They strained forward, willing their tired bodies to continue, but Pepa began faltering. He fell in the sandy soil. He sucked for air. Behind him, he could hear the others gasping, stumbling, and picking themselves up.

"Zigzag! Run zigzag!" Pepa yelled, picking himself up.

They tried but quickly gave up, instinctively fanning out to present a more diffuse target. Behind them the force of shooters was growing. Over a dozen automobiles and motorcycles had discharged black-clad troops onto the highway.

In front of them and to both sides, motorcycles, squad cars and trucks were popping into view. A couple of military buses roared up the road and threatened to overtake them. A pack of motorcycles and squad cars passed the buses, gaining rapidly. The Czechs ran on as if possessed, refusing to give in to the pain, driving on their arms and unwilling legs.

Just ahead a little grove beckoned—a harbinger of the great forest to the north. The Czechs reached the first trees. The motorcycles, temporarily out of sight, were loud on the road behind them, closing fast. The Czechs crossed the road. A pair of yellowish, low-slung buildings appeared among the trees. Then a neat picket fence, and behind it, a man, staring, open-mouthed in amazement. His green forest warden's jacket flapped open.

"In welcher Richtung geht's nach Berlin?" (Which way to Berlin?) Pepa yelled.

"Da!" (There!) cried the forest warden. He turned and pointed excitedly.

Pepa sprinted past, grateful for this small gesture of help from a stranger, Milan and Vasek hard on his heels. Radek was again lagging far to the rear, just ahead of the first of the squad cars and motorcycles.

In the grove, Pepa, Milan, and Vasek slowed to a walk, gasping for breath, every muscle in their bodies aching. Radek stumbled up to them a few seconds later. Feverishly they ransacked their brains for options. Trucks churned slowly through the muddy fields outside. Buses lined up in front of the forest warden's station, discharging troops.

A lone Vopo on a motorcycle was struggling along the rutted dirt trail to their left.

"Let's get that Vopo! We can get away on his cycle," Milan said.

"Yeah, how are all four of us going to fit on there?"

"We have to try. Two on the back. . . ."

"Forget it. It's not going to work."

They stopped at the far edge of the little wood, their eyes wide with shock. The field ahead was swarming with troops and vehicles. They couldn't continue forward and they couldn't go back. They were surrounded. This was their last stand.

Chapter 20

THE DRAGNET SNAPS SHUT

Their gaze broke from the Vopos and trucks massing before them. Frantically they searched for an escape.

"We can sneak out along that ditch!" Radek whispered. A shallow, brush-filled ditch started in the woods and extended north through the field.

"Are you out of your mind?" Pepa snapped.

It was in fact sheer suicide, in view of the massive deployment going on. They crossed the ditch, desperately hunting for a defensible position, while behind them bus after bus roared up the road. Troops disembarked and readied their weapons. Officers shouted orders.

The little wood measured a scant 150 yards across. Trees and shrubs stood leafless and bare. A thick layer of fallen leaves covered the ground, crunching loudly with every step. Depressions, probably made by heavy artillery shells during World War II, studded the ground. Each was a yard deep and six to ten yards across, the edges softened with dead grass, fallen leaves, and branches.

"Here?" Radek said.

"You see anything better?" Pepa replied.

"Okay—I'll take the field, you guys cover the woods."

They ducked into a depression near the edge of the woods where some sparse undergrowth and fallen branches offered some concealment and arranged themselves in a circle on their stomachs, peering out over the lip of the crater. Pepa faced the ranger station, Vasek covered the right flank, and Radek covered the field ahead of them, as well as the left flank, where the unarmed Milan lay. Pistol shots popped and automatic weapons stuttered somewhere near the ranger station. Shadowy figures were moving among the trees.

And then Vasek, who was trying to get into a better position, froze and stared. A skirmish line of uniformed Vopos was advancing, systematically firing pistols and submachine guns into the grass and bushes. Some were firing from the shoulder, others sprayed bullets from the hip. NCOs barked orders to keep the advancing line straight as additional troops moved up. The gunfire was becoming heavier by the minute.

"Hold your fire, everybody!" Pepa urged, his voice sharp. "Wait until they actually see us." The 7.65-mm pistols he and Vasek carried had an effective range of thirty feet. To make each shot count they had to wait until their target was virtually about to step on them.

Vasek was kneeling behind a birch tree, pistol in hand, watching the oncoming troops.

"Hit the dirt, idiot!" Pepa hissed.

Radek had also noticed Vasek. "Get down, you dumbass!"

But Vasek didn't appear to hear. The brothers' warnings were overpowered by deafening volleys of small-arms fire.

Vasek was watching the advancing skirmish line intently. Aiming his pistol at an advancing Vopo, he fired. The shot went wide; the Vopos were still well out of range of his 7.65-mm. He fired a second time. Suddenly a searing pain exploded through his right upper arm. He fell to the ground and lay there, stunned. A dark stain was spreading rapidly on his jacket.

Meanwhile Milan lay in a textbook prone position, his feet flat, his arms stretched out to the front. When you were in a correct prone position, he had learned in his military tactics training, no bullet was going to get you.

"Get down! Press your body against the ground!" he whispered.

In front of him a Vopo with rolled-up sleeves was on one knee, firing round after round into the grass above his head.

Suddenly two huge, vicious-looking German shepherds bounded up. Pepa froze and forced himself to breathe shallowly, hoping to look dead and uninteresting. The beasts ran back and forth, sniffing and stepping all over the Czechs. In all the shooting and commotion the canines seemed confused, unsure of what to do. Finally they ran off.

Radek glanced over at the birch tree. He was glad to see that Vasek had hit the dirt.

Pepa hid his face in the dry grass as bullets cracked and whistled above his head. Twigs and grass smacked down on him.

Looks like it's curtains for us, he thought. *Any second now. . . .*

He was pressing his left arm to his side. His right arm stretched out before him, pistol in hand. Intently he searched the faces of the approaching Vopos for a sign that they'd been compromised. He would get himself a Vopo before he died.

Slowly turning his head, he looked over to Vasek's position. He was relieved that his friend was finally down. "Hold your fire until the last possible moment!" he urged once more. Then thoughts of family, friends, and home rushed through his mind.

Partially hidden by tall grass, Radek lay motionless and intently focused. He was hunting for a target. Troops had formed a security cordon around the copse, fifty yards back from the tree line. An officer and a group of subordinates stood almost directly in front of him, about twenty yards away.

Not those guys. If I shoot them, I'll give away my position, he decided.

He turned his attention to his left toward the far side of the ditch. About sixty yards away stood a Volkspolizei trooper in the regulation black uniform and black overcoat. The man was idly gazing at the wood, his arms casually crossed over the muzzle of a rifle propped on the ground in front of him. His two companions were talking together, their backs to him and the woods. They looked unconcerned. After all, their opponents had nothing but handguns. Short-range weapons.

Radek raised himself up on his elbows, firmly grasped his right hand with his left and aimed. The single sharp crack from his P38 merged with the ear-splitting barrage of small-arms fire. The Vopo toppled over. At first, his two companions kept talking. Then one of them turned around and spotted his comrade lying motionless on the ground. He rushed over. When he saw that the fallen man was dead, he started yelling and hit the ground next to the corpse. Everybody in the vicinity went down like ninepins. The group around the officer didn't notice and kept talking, but those troops nearest the ditch saw that something was amiss and looked indecisive. Evidently the Vopos believed them to be on the *other* side of the ditch, a good sixty yards from their actual position.[1]

It took another moment for the officer to notice all the men on the ground. But just then a messenger pulled up to him on a motorcycle, demanding his attention.

Radek was sorely tempted to put a bullet into the cycle's gas tank. But the group was too close. The firing behind him was getting heavier and alarmingly close now. Radek glanced back and found himself looking up into the pale face of a young Vopo, standing in what should have been Pepa's position.

Pepa will have to take care of it, he told himself. He tore his gaze away and resolutely faced forward.

In fact the troops had come so close that Pepa could make out every detail in their faces.

They don't see us yet, Pepa thought in disbelief. *How is it that, with all those bullets flying around, I'm still alive?*

The enemy was in range. But there was something Pepa had to take care of first. He turned to Milan.

"Do you want it now?" he said softly.

Before setting out, they had made a pact that no one would be caught alive. Since Milan had no weapon, Pepa had promised to save one bullet for him.

Milan's eyes met his friend's.

"Wait a bit," he croaked.

Radek's pistol had jammed. Quickly opening it up, he saw that the magazine was full of sand. As he pulled it out, the topmost bullet fell to the ground. He desperately hunted for it in the grass, loath to lose even one round of precious ammunition. Finally he found it, but at just that moment it seemed to him that he had lost another one. Abruptly he abandoned the search; a young Vopo was creeping along the edge of the woods, pistol in hand. The Vopo crouched low, peering into the undergrowth as he advanced. Radek hardly dared to breathe. The Vopo passed by, no more than seven yards away. Then he turned to the officer in the field.

"I don't see anybody!"

He turned around again and came still closer to the edge of the wood, peering into it as he crept along. Once again he overlooked Radek, who lay absolutely motionless. When the Vopo was about sixty feet away, Radek raised himself up a little on his elbows, aimed between the man's shoulder blades, and fired. The Vopo fell flat on his face without a sound and did not move again. Nobody seemed to notice.

The volley of gunfire abated slightly. Suddenly a few German shepherds overran the Czechs again. Once more the dogs excitedly stepped all over them, nudging motionless bodies and faces with their cold, wet noses.

Radek pressed his face into the grass.

Am I going to die here? he agonized. *What a terrible blow for Mom to lose both of us. . . . This can't be happening to me! It can't be over yet! I should have killed more of those Commie bastards while I had the chance. That whole wing in Pankrac, full of people those fucking bastards were going to murder. Those SOBs aren't putting me behind bars again!*

Suddenly he remembered the fortune-teller. His mother had visited her in Prague shortly after the Communist takeover.

"Radek," the fortune-teller had said, "will attain old age, but he'll live dangerously and go through a lot of suffering. He will reach his goals by pursuing them ruthlessly and walking over dead bodies. He will go abroad."

That part about the suffering had already come true. If he got out alive, Radek swore he'd believe the whole prophecy to the last letter. *If I die, I swear I'm taking as many Commies with me as I can. They'll never get me alive.* Meanwhile another part of his mind stood aside, observing dispassionately, *So these are the ideas that occur to people seconds before they die.*

The score is six to five, Pepa thought as he lay motionless, the dogs walking over him. *Six comrades for the five of us.* He didn't know that Radek had shot two more. *Those fucking bastards aren't catching me alive! And I'll take enough of their hides with me to make them sorry they tried. We should have done those SOBs back home. The police bus. The police training school. The uranium train from Jachymov.*

Vopo officers were stopping segments of the line. They seemed to be having trouble coordinating the advance and the line of troops was ragged by now, though the officers shouted their orders in quicker succession.

"Alle zurück!" (All fall back!) someone suddenly barked.

The skirmish line halted. Pepa could almost touch the man standing closest to him.

What the hell! Pepa thought in disbelief. *This can't be true.*

But the Vopo in front of him slowly dropped the barrel of his submachine gun. As the order was repeated up and down the line, the weapons fire diminished and finally petered out. The dog handlers called their charges back. One by one the animals left. Already the Vopos were retreating. Most moved cautiously backward, their weapons at the ready; a few slung their weapons over their shoulders and casually turned their backs.

It was true, the Vopos were pulling back! Pepa felt a rush of relief.

Then Vasek's strained voice whispered, "Guys, I've been hit!"

The others were shocked.

"How bad?"

"It's pretty bad. I'm bleeding a lot."

With troops all around, watching the edge of the woods, Pepa and the others couldn't go to him. They could only whisper words of encouragement.

The Volkspolizei knew for sure that the four fugitives were hidden in the narrow strip of brush and grass at the edge of the woods, and they were coming after them. The officer in charge issued a few orders and a second skirmish line formed out in the field.

"Wir haben hier einen Gefallenen!" (We've got a body over here!) a Vopo called out from the far side of the ditch,

A plainclothesman approached and discovered the man Radek had shot between the shoulder blades.

"Another one over here!" he called.

"Who? A bandit?" the officer shouted back.

"No! A policeman!"

The officer began to curse aloud.

"Move out!" he ordered brusquely.

The rank and file looked at each other but not a man moved.

"Advance!" the officer yelled again.

"Scheiße!" someone shouted from the ranks. "Shit! We're not moving!"

"They have other weapons, not just pistols!"

"We need machine guns!"

"You call yourself People's Policemen? Forward!" The officer was apoplectic.

"Kiss my ass!"

"Do it yourself!"

"Just wait!" the enraged officer hollered, "you're going to catch it later on!"

"Asshole!" voices shouted back.

Nobody moved. Faced with mutiny, the officer finally gave the order to withdraw. The attack was over.

Out in the field the Vopos milled about in disorganized confusion.

"Wir bestellen Maschinengewehre!" (We're ordering machine guns), officers called out. "Tomorrow morning we'll smoke out those bandits."

They ordered their men to encircle the grove fifty yards from the tree line and called for trucks. The troops lay down a few steps apart, pointing their assault rifles at the woods and assuring each other that the machine guns would arrive soon.

"The sun will set at about six," Milan whispered softly. The minutes dragged by. Both sides waited.

In the gathering dusk dozens of trucks growled onto the field. They parked end to end around the wood, each about two lengths from the one ahead of it. When they switched on their headlights they formed an unbroken ring of light.

Troops mounted machine guns, some on anti-aircraft tripods, onto the trucks. Ammo belts rattled into the feed trays. Teams of Vopos hauled big searchlights up. After some time the commotion died down. The Volkspolizei were ready.

Darkness fell. "Go check on Vasek," Pepa whispered to Milan. Milan nodded and crawled off while Radek and Pepa stayed behind to guard against a surprise attack. Milan found his buddy lying on his back in a pool of blood, fading in and out of consciousness.

"I feel awfully weak," Vasek whispered. He looked at Milan with pleading eyes, "If I have to stay behind, please don't forget about Lidka and the kids."

Vasek was bleeding heavily and was in excruciating pain, though he bore his suffering bravely and didn't complain.*

Pepa soon crawled over and helped Milan ease off Vasek's sport coat. The bullet had entered below his elbow and exited near the shoulder, traveling some ten inches through flesh and bone. The sport coat was drenched with blood, so they threw it away. They hurriedly rigged a makeshift tourniquet under Vasek's shoulder using Pepa's necktie and a piece of wood. The bleeding stopped, but help had come too late. Vasek hung limply in their arms and could hardly talk. Tears were running down his cheeks and the others had lumps in their throats as they contemplated their helpless friend.

After a while, when it was clear the Vopos had settled down for the night, Radek crawled over to join them. Radek, Pepa, and Milan sat in a dejected huddle around Vasek.

---

*It was clearly a stray bullet. The official East German record Barch, MdI, DO 1/11/777, p. 00105 states: "The main witness is the head of the criminal division at HDVP Cottbus, Comrade Major Rebentisch, who himself lay six meters opposite one of the fugitives and was engaged in a gun battle with him, which he had to interrupt after two shots because his gun jammed." The command appeared to accept this testimony at face value. Had the cordon of searchers been able to establish the exact location of their opponents, it is unlikely that they would have withdrawn when and as they did.

This is it. All of us will die here, was the unspoken thought in all their minds.

They talked of their parents and families with desperate longing, deeply sorry for the pain they were causing them. Each in turn apologized for past wrongs. They said emotional, wrenching good-byes.

This was the end of the line. Totally surrounded and with no way out, Pepa felt no fear. There was just a grim sense of reality, an awareness that the odds were impossibly stacked against them. The thought hardened him, and Radek too.

"We don't know if you want to give up, but we won't," Radek declared, absolutely resolute. The brothers had firsthand experience with the StB's methods, and they knew how much credence to give Communist promises: exactly nil. While they were still capable of fighting, neither brother would even think of coming out with his hands up, voluntarily putting himself into their power.

Everyone hastened to reaffirm the vow to commit suicide rather than be caught alive. In the morning they would exact a heavy price from the Vopos coming in to get them.

Outside the wood, troops walked about joking and chatting. The glimmering tips of their cigarettes glowed and faded in the darkness as they smoked. The Vopos had their whole lives before them. The Czechs knew they were about to die.

Suddenly, the loudspeakers boomed, "Sie werden aufgefordert sich zu ergeben! (Give up!) You are surrounded. Your situation is hopeless. Nothing will happen to you if you give up!"

That only reaffirmed Radek and Pepa's commitment to fight to the last. They knew it was a lie.

When the loudspeakers fell silent the Czechs could hear idle conversations in German once again.

Another broadcast blared out into the night, this time in fractured Czech. "Give up! Nothing will happen to you!"

Again the Czechs renewed their pledge to fight until the end.

They began reminiscing about their unfinished business—the actions they had planned but hadn't gotten around to executing. They were sorry they wouldn't be able to kill more Communists. Then they talked about what would have happened if they had brought along their submachine guns and hand grenades. They debated this point for a while and finally agreed that the hand grenades would have been useful but the submachine guns would have been too bulky and heavy to carry around.

The tantalizing scent of hot meals and coffee wafted over and made their mouths water. A field kitchen had been set up near the forest warden's house and was distributing chow to the troops along the line. Pepa listened longingly to the clinking of mess tins and the sounds of the troops eating.

To get their minds off food, they discussed how to spend the night. Should they sleep or stand watch?

"I'm not going to sit here until the Vopos come in tomorrow morning and shoot up our asses," Radek finally said. "We should do something. We should try to break out. It really makes no sense to sit around."

"Yeah. You've got a point," Pepa agreed. "If we try to get out, our best shot is under cover of darkness."

"Let's go for it," Milan agreed. "We've got nothing to lose."

The first priority was to try to pinpoint the troops' exact locations.

"I'll do recon," Radek announced and crawled away toward the ditch.

Pepa and Milan followed him. The woods were black, but the ring of trucks blazed with light. Occasionally the searchlights were turned on and panned over the woods. Every time they swept by, the Czechs closed their eyes to protect their night vision. As Pepa crawled after Radek, along the edge of the wood, he peered out at the bright lights, the trucks and the troops, trying to make out the weak point in the circle. He heard Vopos moving behind the trucks, subdued conversations, the occasional cough and laugh, and the crackle of radios in command cars parked behind the trucks.

Not seeing much of anything, Radek finally gave up and they all crawled back to Vasek. Vasek was so weak that when he wanted to relieve himself Milan and Pepa had to hold him up. He couldn't even undo his fly by himself. Pepa couldn't find the words to say what all of them knew: Vasek was not going to make it.

"Leave me here," Vasek said calmly. "I'll just slow all of you down. I know I can't make it. After you break out I'll try to get to a village or back to the forest warden's house. I'll hide somewhere, maybe in a well. Hopefully the Volkspolizei will follow you. After the commotion dies down, I'll try to move on."

The others agreed. But they all knew that the water wells in that area had concrete covers several feet in diameter. Vasek couldn't even stand up. How was he going to move a concrete well cover? His only chance was to throw himself on someone's mercy in one of the villages. But with all the troops in the area, they were cut off from the villages. No one would grab the bull by the horns and address the question of their pact. No one could find it in his heart to force Vasek to take his bullet. After all, there was always an outside chance that he could make it. Milan was living proof. So they agreed on a fallback plan. Anyone caught alive and unable to commit suicide would blame everything on those killed in the breakout.

They decided to break out after midnight. By then the guards would have tired of the monotony of waiting and would be less vigilant. At Radek's command they'd take off from the ditch, passing right in front of the closest truck. There the beam of the headlights was narrowest, and they would be moving under cover of darkness until the last minute. Any Vopos looking directly at them would be blinded by the light. They wouldn't dare shoot toward their own trucks. Milan and Pepa would shoot at the open driver's compartment, Radek would aim for the troops on the ground. The Czechs would have at best a few seconds' head start before the *Vopos* grasped what was happening and swung the searchlights around to track them. The rest of the plan was simple: run like hell. Beyond the trucks they would be the only people standing and all the troops would be firing at them. They would be exposed across 150 or so yards of open field.

As the time for departure approached, Milan took Vasek's pistol from him.

"Come on, chief!" Pepa urged Vasek. "Run with us."

"No, Pepa. I'll stay behind. I can't move," Vasek insisted.

"At least come to the ditch with us."

"No, I can't make it."

"Come on. You can do it! At least to the ditch!"

Eventually Vasek let himself be persuaded to come with them as far as the starting point of their run. The others helped him into the ditch. After a last-minute equipment check, they put their arms around Vasek, kissed him, and said a last, wrenching good-bye. As the searchlight swept over them for the last time, they closed their eyes to protect their night vision.

"Now!" Radek said in a low voice.

Away they went.

A strange feeling of lightness winged Pepa's steps. Pepa didn't expect to last halfway across the fifty yards to the trucks. He listened for the rattling sound of machine-gun fire, fully expecting to be mowed down at any second. Pepa heard Milan running hard on his heels, Radek close behind. As he burst into the headlights, Pepa fired a couple of rounds toward the driver's compartment. Milan, beside him, was firing also. A fraction of a second later they were past the truck and back in the dark, running in the open field. Behind them, Radek fired at the two sentries sitting in the ditch.

The Vopos were caught totally by surprise. But their paralysis didn't last long. Excited shouts filled the darkness. Abruptly the searchlights swung around and swept across the field, catching the three fugitives in their beam within seconds. The Czechs were twenty to thirty yards beyond the trucks, clear targets in the middle of a flood of bright lights. They spread out, running, pumped up on adrenaline. Behind them officers bellowed orders. The machine guns opened up a fraction of a second later.

A first burst of machine-gun fire slammed into the ground just to Pepa's left. The next burst was long, but closer. Burning phosphorous streaked between their legs, in front of them, above them. Tracer bullets. Pepa was running as fast as he could. He stumbled and fell in the sandy soil, scrambled back to his feet, then staggered and fell again. A hail of bullets hit the ground directly in front of his head, flinging sand into his face. He pulled the muzzle of his pistol out of the sand and continued onward, thinking grimly that it was useless now. Milan, on his right, fell down and scrambled forward on all fours, driven on by naked fear. Behind them there was a loud whoosh and a flare erupted above them in a phosphorescent explosion, bathing the entire field in a harsh white light.

"Run zigzag! Run zigzag!" Pepa hollered.

But it was no use, they could barely run straight. They continued on a direct course, hoping against hope that the machine gunners wouldn't get a fix on them. Another flare went up. Then another. By this time the entire line of machine guns was firing in long bursts. The rounds hissed over their heads, between their legs. Finally, as they moved beyond the range of the searchlights, they began zigzagging.

Pepa heard someone fall heavily in the darkness in front of him. There was a prostrate body. Vasek! By some miracle he had managed to cover 150 yards faster than everyone else. But now he was unable to get up.

The angels must have carried him, Pepa thought.

Milan and Pepa began dragging Vasek toward the woods ahead of them, gasping from exhaustion. A deep ditch yawned under their feet and they tumbled down, landing in a stunned heap. Milan accidentally discharged his weapon as he hit the bottom but luckily nobody was hit.

Pepa picked himself up. "Radek!" he hollered. An answering shout came from their left: "I'm here." It was a miracle: they had all made it.

Though totally exhausted, they dared pause only briefly to catch their breath and take stock of the situation. The ditch was well more than four feet deep and had steep sides. Out in the field officers were bawling orders and the machine-gun fire sputtered to a stop. Excited shouts rang out in their wake.

". . . sind durchgelaufen!" (. . . ran through!)

Then, as dozens of truck engines revved up, "How many?"

"All four!"

They couldn't wait. A few more yards still lay between them and the shelter of the forest, so Pepa grabbed one of Vasek's arms and gasped, "Milan, grab the other one!"

Milan complied and they scrambled out of the ditch, awkwardly dragging Vasek's limp form between them, struggling under his weight. Vasek half-walked and half-hung onto them, his head lolling on his shoulders. Behind them heavy military vehicles ground laboriously through the sandy soil, heading for the roads on the east and west sides of the field.

Another flare exploded above them, throwing its harsh white illumination over the landscape. In the now brightly lit field Pepa could see frantic activity in and around the trucks as black-clad Vopos milled about, antlike, clambering onto the vehicles. There were scuffling sounds and muffled thuds as men jumped aboard, weapons banging against the sides of the vehicles. Officers were excitedly shouting into their radios, and replies crackled back.

Slowly Milan and Pepa tottered into the dense brush on the outskirts of the forest, dragging Vasek between them.

"I can't go on," Vasek protested weakly. "Just leave me here!" He stumbled again, grunting in pain.

"You're doing great!"

"Put me down," Vasek said.

"Hurry . . . we've got to get him deeper into the woods. We can't stop here!" Radek gasped.

"Then get over here and help us, you idiot!"

"I can't, guys. I can hardly move myself. You'll have to do it."

Radek's legs were shaking so badly he could scarcely walk. Milan and Pepa continued dragging Vasek onward. After about thirty yards they passed the first trees of the forest and came to a small pond. Exhausted and at the end of their strength, they stopped and let Vasek's inert form down. Vasek lay on the ground among the thick ferns and moss-covered tree stumps, looking more dead than alive. He was unconscious.

Milan sat down with him and cradled Vasek's head in his lap, but with the weight he couldn't breathe, so the three friends propped Vasek up against a tree.

Finally he came to.

"Can you walk by yourself?"

"No." He was slumped against the tree. It was clear that he wouldn't be able to rouse himself again. "Leave me here," Vasek said weakly. "Go on by yourselves. I'm tired. I just want to sleep."

"You can't sleep now! You're doing great."

"Just come on with us."

"I can't do it. I'll just slow you down."

Another flare shot up into the sky and exploded, throwing harsh shadows from the trees onto the ground. As the flare drifted down, the patterns of light and shadow wavered and fled across the ground and the faces of the four fugitives.

"You can't wait around anymore," Vasek murmured. "Leave me the gun and I'll delay the police when they come through here."

He was obviously in a lot of pain and too weak to hold up the weapon, let alone shoot with it.

"We'll have to take the gun," Radek said.

"It's a question of half an hour, maybe less, till we have another shootout with those guys. We'll need all the firepower we can get." Pepa added.

"We'll distract their attention," Radek went on. "Meantime you can get back to the forest warden's house."

There was a momentary silence. If they took the weapon Vasek would have no way to kill himself. Now was the time to act on their pact, if it was to be acted on at all. Vasek lay there against the tree trunk, breathing with difficulty.

"Do you want us to do it for you?"

He looked at them and after a moment replied, "I'll try to make it out. I'll pull myself together after I rest a while. I'll try to get back to the forest warden's place."

Vasek had made his decision, and the others couldn't bring themselves to force him to comply with their pact. They put the awkward moment behind them, offering advice and suggestions. Vasek's eyes were closed and they weren't sure if he heard what they were saying. Even as they spoke their encouraging words, they were thinking that the Communists would kill him if they caught him. What was worse, they would break him with torture and would involve many more people in his fate.

The shouts and orders continued back in the field. Already trucks rumbled along on the paved roads on either side. Two seemingly interminable processions of headlights blinked through the tree trunks and branches, moving inexorably northward. One flare after another climbed into the sky, casting its eerie pattern of stark illumination and distorted shadows over the four hunched forms under the trees. The dragnet was closing in on them. In a question of minutes they'd be cut off in this patch of woods, facing exactly the same predicament they had just escaped.

Pepa was hurriedly cleaning his pistol, trying to get out the sand, but still the weapon wouldn't fire automatically and he would have to reload by hand after each round. After making several fruitless attempts to get the pistol fully functional, he abandoned the effort. All of them knew that the moment of parting had come.

"Go!" Vasek urged them, pain in his voice. "Go now! And please, don't forget about my Lidka and the children," he implored, tears in his eyes.

"No. We won't forget."

"Hey, chief—next thing you know, you'll be in Berlin."

"Long before us! Just like in that ditch back there! You got across that field like a hare."

"The Vopos will be after us. You'll have a clear path the whole way!"

"If we should get to Berlin before you, we'll wait up for you. . . . And if you make it first, chief, wait for us, okay?"

They went through his pockets to make sure there was no compromising material. Milan took off his sweater and gave it to Vasek. It was their last sweater. Radek placed the few bills of German money he had left into Vasek's pocket. Pepa and Milan followed suit. Another flare exploded above them. In its light, Vasek's eyelids flickered open briefly. He saw the pale, somber faces of his friends leaning over him. His buddies were talking, but he didn't hear their words. He saw their faces, very close to his own. Then he felt their stubble graze his forehead. Silent tears ran down his cheeks. *Good-bye, my friends!*

Milan, Pepa, and Radek each in turn gently kissed Vasek's forehead. Then they got up and stumbled away into the woods. As they left him there, slumped against the tree in the darkness and bitter cold, they knew that he faced certain death. All three of them were near tears. They were leaving their best friend and courageous comrade behind. Alone. Hungry and thirsty. Wounded. Weak from the loss of blood. It was Saturday, 17 October, exactly one week since they lost Zbynek. Fourteen days on the road and Berlin was still far away.[2]

Chapter 21

HOT PURSUIT

A fter passing out of Vasek's sight, Pepa, Radek, and Milan began a desperate dash through the woods. Myriad lights were winking dimly at them through the trees, an ominous number of glimmering specks. Were they village lights? Or, more likely, vehicle headlights from convoys on the road?

With mounting alarm, they pushed on as quickly as their tired legs would go, over a little bridge and a wire fence, across a cow pasture, over another wire fence, through a clover field. The clover and, in the next field, the sugar beet plants stood tall and uncut, despite the advanced season. Now they walked with difficulty, the tall plants grabbing their legs and slowing their progress.

"Seems the comrades can't get the harvest in on time!" Radek observed.

"What else is new?" Pepa said acidly.

Anxious about the lost time, they broke into an Indian-style run as soon as they left the beet field behind. With Pepa as the pointman in front, they hurried on in single file, fifty or a hundred steps at a run and then an equal number at a walk, almost blind in the thick darkness. Occasional trees and fence posts loomed up, weird shadows in the nocturnal landscape. Above them the sky stretched away, black and featureless. Not a single star was visible through the heavy layer of clouds. They had no sure means of orientation to keep them from wandering off course.

They were running with a fixed purpose now, the sound of their breath loud in the stillness, the crunch of frost-burned foliage underfoot and grasses rustling against their trouser legs. Little clouds of condensation puffed from their mouths and nostrils in the cold night air, and always the pinpricks of light shimmered mysteriously in the distance.

Leaving the beet and clover fields, they staggered across a sandy flat. The next field was full of knee-high vines, wilted, drooping, and bearing shriveled little orbs.

"Tomatoes!" Pepa cried joyfully. Another failure for the Communist command economy, this was a stroke of unexpected luck for the three starving fugitives. They fell voraciously upon the shrunken specimens that clung to the frost-burned plants. As they moved through the field, they stuffed their mouths and their pockets with as many as their greedy hands could grasp.

Suddenly a loud, mournful wail shattered the night. It was quickly joined by others, and in no time a cacophony of banshee wails was pressing in on them from all sides. They froze in midstride, their hands outstretched, their hearts in their throats.

"Shit, what's that?" Pepa whispered.

"Air raid sirens," Radek said. "From fucking World War II." All around them villages were popping into relief, ablaze in lights. "It's the fucking Vopos. They're putting the alarm out for us!"

The Czechs were filled with alarm, surrounded now by illuminated settlements where before there had been an unending expanse of blackness. All thought of food vanished. What in the hell were the Vopos up to? Were they charging in to the hamlets, pounding on doors and rousting people out of bed? Were villagers being ordered to watch the barns and buildings upon pain of punishment if the fugitives turned up on the premises?

All around them lines of lights were on the move, convoys of vehicles moving bumper-to-bumper at a fast clip. Either the vehicles were setting out cordons of troops or, more likely given their speed, they were headed to drop-off locations. *We'll be cut off,* Pepa thought with dread.

At that moment the clouds broke and a few stars appeared in the sky. They took their bearings from the North Star and started running, desperate to cross the last road separating them from the big woods to the north before the Vopos got there. They sprinted north, racing to keep up with the rapidly advancing columns to their left and right. Every passing minute, every second could mean the difference between life and death. As they tore across the shadowy fields of clover and stubble, tired legs pounding on, their lungs threatening to burst, once again Radek fell behind. The three small figures seemed to crawl across the black countryside as the speeding lines of trucks moved purposefully to cut off their escape.

There was a road ahead. Already several convoys had traversed it east to west, moving at a fairly rapid clip. The friends ran on, hopeful that none of the trucks had discharged troops. With a last burst of speed they bore down on the road, but a slow-moving convoy beat them to it: they could only watch helplessly from nearby as troops jumped off the moving trucks to form an impenetrable cordon. Just as Pepa had feared: cut off.

As precious minutes ticked by, they turned west and ran toward a stretch of road over which several convoys had passed earlier, apparently without discharging troops. From the black, still woods on their right the road emerged, several feet above the surrounding fields on a bed of fill. Using a small spur of young pine trees as cover, they advanced cautiously toward the road. Radek's shoes were squeaking loudly. He took them off and hastily cut holes in the tongues to pass his belt through them. Barefoot now, the shoes firmly attached to his belt, he resumed his advance with Pepa and Milan. They slowly crept toward the road at a low crouch, halting every few steps to listen with their mouths open.

The trees stopped fifty yards short of the road. They halted and waited a long while, watching the road for any sign of movement. Everything was absolutely still. Several cars passed, and in the conical beam of their headlights the friends saw only the piles of gravel that loomed up at intervals along the road. Off and on, the moon peeped through holes in the quickly scudding cloud cover, but the three friends could see no sign of the enemy in its pale light. A light fog lay between the woods and the road, giving Pepa a glimmer of hope.

Satisfied that all was clear, they finally left the protective cover of the woods and moved noiselessly toward the road in a V formation, with Pepa as pointman. Twenty yards from the road, they all heard the unmistakable clack of a machine-gun bolt being drawn back.

"Halt! Wer da?" (Halt! Who goes there?) a sharp voice demanded.

Pepa fired a shot toward the voice. In the same instant the whole length of the road blazed with gunfire. Automatic weapons chattered. The fill was dotted with red muzzle flashes and the air was cross-hatched by red tracer lines. Bullets whizzed all around them, between their legs, past their heads. Radek felt a powerful blow to his stomach that almost knocked him off his feet. Straightening up, he turned and dashed back toward the tree line, hit the ground and rolled underneath the low-hanging pine branches. Pepa and Milan threw themselves to the ground nearby, breathing hard. Suddenly a terrible shriek rose above the thundering automatic gunfire. A second after it died off, the weapons ceased firing.

"They must have hit one of their own guys!"* Pepa whispered.

"I think they got me," Radek replied breathlessly. Apprehensively he palpated his midriff looking for the bullet hole, but found nothing.

Lying under the trees with his heart pounding, Pepa saw searchlights trained on the area in front of the road. Several Vopos were walking about, studying the ground. One of them stooped to pick something up and the others crowded around him. A number of cars arrived and the Vopos carried their find over to one of them. The commotion was short-lived. Soon the whole road fell silent again. Only one car remained, its standing lights turned on.

"What did they find?" Milan whispered.

"Heck if I know!" Pepa replied. "They sure made a big deal about it, whatever it was."

"Let's get moving," Radek urged. He groped for his shoes. Then he suddenly announced. "Guys, I know what they found!"

The others looked at him. He was holding a solitary shoe in his hand. "They shot the other one clean off my belt!"†

"Jesus Maria!" Milan exhaled sharply. "An inch over and that hole would've been in you."

Radek grimly put his remaining shoe and sock back on. They were still many days' march away from Berlin, and he had to cover untold miles wearing only one shoe. It was a daunting prospect. But they had more pressing problems.

"We have to find a spot to break through the line," Radek said. "Someplace where the woods come very close to the road, so the guards don't have much time to react when we come running out."

"Forget it!" Pepa snapped. They were all tense, and tempers were rising. "Breaking through will just get us into another compartment. Can't you see what they're doing out there? It's a huge dragnet."

"We don't have a choice. We have to keep moving. If we stay here, they'll pick us up by morning."

---

*In fact, the Vopos shot their own major. East German propaganda attributed his death to the Czechs.

†The Volkspolizei records make no mention of this find.

"We can't outrun them, chief! They're motorized. They've got trucks."

"Sitting down and waiting like a fucking bunch of sitting ducks isn't an option!" Radek countered heatedly. "Let's find a stream or something. Maybe we can get into the next sector by crawling along the streambed."

Grimly they continued walking east along the road, hoping against hope that they would come to a stream. No stream appeared, however, and soon they drew near the autobahn. Judging by the noise, large numbers of military trucks and motorcycles were moving along it.

"Shit!" Pepa whispered. "They've got the whole place locked down."

They turned back. "Let's go back and hide in the village!" Milan urged.

"Why the hell d'you want to do that!? There's at least one road between here and there. The Vopos hold all the roads!"

"Then let's go back to the little forest!"

"The one where Vasek is? That's cut off by now, too!" Pepa said dismissively.

Racking their brains for a way out, they continued walking through the woods until they came to a dirt road. On the far side was a sand pit, surrounded by scrawny pine trees. They were about to cross over to it when the sound of powerful motors stopped them short. The threesome hit the ground behind the trees and waited tensely.

A truck appeared, kicking up thick clouds of dust as it crawled through the sandy terrain. Behind it was another one, followed by an entire convoy. All the trucks had canvas tops. Inside, troops sat rigidly on benches, their submachine guns and rifles wedged between their knees. *Just like back home, during the war!* Radek thought. *If only we had our hand grenades and submachine guns! It's the perfect place for an ambush.* The convoy passed.

"Let's take out a straggler!" Radek whispered as the trucks receded down the road, leaving a cloud of choking dust in their wake. They waited a long time for single cars or motorcycles that they could ambush to get weapons, uniforms, a vehicle.

"It's no use!" Pepa said, picking himself up. "There're no more coming."

They got to their feet and ventured across the road into the sand pit. Standing on the far lip they could see across the field behind it, toward the autobahn.

Milan pointed. "Look at that!"

A deep ditch cut diagonally across the field—a potential escape route. Quickly they dropped into the ditch and advanced toward the autobahn.

But the ditch got progressively shallower and halfway across the field it disappeared almost entirely, now nothing more than a partition between the fields on the right and left. When the troops on the autobahn began firing illuminated flares that turned night into day, the three fugitives abandoned the effort and crawled back to the sand pit.

"Fuck! What do we do now? We need a hiding place."

"How about climbing up into the pine trees? We can hide in the crowns!" Milan suggested.

They considered this. But these pine trees were such skimpy specimens, they would be clearly visible at the first glance.

"Forget it! It'll be a turkey shoot for the Vopos," Pepa said.

"Let's find a stream or pond or something. When the Vopos come, we jump in," Pepa suggested.

"And we can breathe through hollow bulrush stems," Milan added eagerly.

"We'll freeze to death in a matter of minutes. It's below zero," Radek said dismally.

He turned and strode purposefully over to the sand bank. It was home to a large and evidently thriving rabbit colony and he started digging at one of the large rabbit holes with his bare hands. The others saw what he was doing: it was like the sandbank at Kouty, where the Russian POWs and Jewish camp survivors had hidden during the war! They sprang over and began scrabbling at the hard, cold sand in a desperate effort to enlarge other rabbit holes in the pit. Soon they fetched some large branches to help make headway against the freezing, solidly packed dirt. In spite of their best efforts, however, progress was agonizingly slow. Radek threw down his branch in frustration.

"It's not going to work!" he said. "The sand's as hard as a rock, and camouflaging the openings is going to be impossible. And what if we have to stay here for several days? The sand is freezing!"

Kowing they wouldn't live through such an ordeal, they gave up and carefully covered the rabbit holes. Then they raked the whole area with big branches to hide all traces of their activity, and moved on to look for some other hiding place.

At length they came to an intersection of two trails, in the middle of which sat a dark mass. A stray beam of light shone out and muffled chatter emanated from it. A radio car.

Retreating into the shadows, they skirted the crossroads and continued cautiously along the trail, keeping to the shadow of the trees. By and by they came to the edge of a clearing. The Vopos were still shooting flares up from the autobahn, a mere hundred yards or so to the left. In the bursts of bright phosphorescent light, the threesome silently observed the clearing, which was large and surrounded by marching rows of scrawny pine trees. In its center were three large piles of dead branches and along the eastern edge was a tree farm, consisting of closely spaced young trees.

All three were tense. Their predicament was impossible and their options nonexistent.

"Let's keep going!" Radek argued. "We've got to find someplace we can break across the autobahn."

"Forget it—the Vopos hold all the roads," Pepa snapped.

"All right, wiseass. You have a better idea?"

"Yeah. Let's stay right here in the tree farm. Just like after Uckro."

"That's just plain dumb. They'll search the entire forest after last night."

"Hey, guys, cut it out!" Milan interjected.

Pepa ignored him. "I suppose you want to just run into their blockade and get shot to pieces?" he said.

"It sure beats sitting here and waiting for them to pick us up!"

"Fuck it, I'm sure as hell not letting them shoot the stuffing out of me at the next road."

They sorely missed Vasek's mediation. The dispute unresolved, they retired to the tree farm and sat huddled together, sullen and shivering among the young fir trees, waiting for an idea or some better opportunity.

A thick fog began to close in. From the autobahn the sound of clinking mess tins drifted over. The troops, at least, were getting hot refreshment.

"I've got to take a crap," Pepa announced sullenly. Thanks to their starvation diet, it was his first bowel movement since the border crossing fourteen days earlier. He went off to relieve himself, using half of his old bus-ticket book in lieu of toilet paper. As he carefully covered everything with sand, Radek and Milan trailed over and watched him, volunteering liberal advice on how best to camouflage it. When they returned to the edge of the clearing their gaze was drawn by the three piles of branches that hulked in the clearing. Each was approximately four feet high, fifteen to twenty feet long and eight to ten feet wide.

"Let's tunnel under the branches," Pepa suggested.

"Jesus, that's about as bright as your last idea!" Radek said.

"But if we get under these branches they won't be able to see us at all."

"We'll be sitting ducks! You'd have to be crazy to hide there. They're the most obvious landmarks in the whole damn area."

"Exactly!" Pepa defended himself. "*No sane person would hide under those piles.* They're in the middle of the clearing—and that's precisely why they're a good hiding place."

In the end everyone agreed. There didn't appear to be a lot of other options.

They started work right away, tempers running high. Each man was to dig a tunnel for himself under the middle woodpile. They lugged displaced sand to the tree farm in their berets and scattered it around. They pressed some of it in among the branches on both sides of the tunnels, but soon they ran out of places to get rid of it all, so they broke off some of the branches and widened their tunnels upwards, into the pile.

It was hard work and they made little headway. The bottommost branches were wedged into the sand and over time had jammed into an intertwined mass. Realizing that completing even one tunnel would be a major task, they abandoned the two others and concentrated their efforts on Pepa's. Pepa dug while Milan and Radek scattered sand. Progress was agonizingly slow.

"I'm going on recon," Radek finally announced. "We've got to find a way out of here."

The others acknowledged his words with grunts and kept working as Radek set out toward the autobahn, crawling a long way through the thick ferns and moss. The ferns were heavy with moisture, soaking him through, but he got close to his objective. From among the ferns, he saw that the troops were standing just a few feet apart, firing flares continuously and spraying the edge of the woods with bullets every so often. No—crossing the autobahn was unthinkable, despite the heavy fog that limited visibility to a few feet.

By the time Radek returned to the clearing, Milan and Pepa had made some progress on the tunnel, but it was far from finished. All three men took turns tunneling. Every time a thick branch got in the way, Pepa had to wriggle into the tunnel and break it because he had more strength left than the others.

Some of the branches were too thick to break and had to be bent out of the way. To the keyed-up fugitives, the cracking of breaking branches sounded as loud as gunshots. They finally settled on a technique whereby Milan and Radek hung onto the branch both in front of and behind the place where Pepa was breaking it. That reduced the noise, but it required more strength and Pepa did the brunt of the work. They worked at a feverish pace, afraid that dawn would surprise them before they had finished the job.

At long last, they stood back to inspect their handiwork. The tunnel would scarcely fit one thin man, let alone three. They gathered large, heavy branches and piled them up by the entrance, then scoured the clearing, collecting the small twigs and residue that had scattered during construction, stuffing everything into the pile. Systematically they crawled back and forth in the darkness, reduced to using what sense of touch was left in their cold, numb fingers. Last of all, as they backed up toward the woodpile on all fours, they raked the sand with branches to remove their prints.

Pepa and Milan crawled into the hole first. It took them at least half an hour to squeeze in. They had to bend the protruding branches back and could only move a fraction of an inch at a time, wriggling forward slowly, scrunching and expanding their bodies like two worms. When they were in, headfirst, Radek began to crawl in feetfirst, Milan and Pepa pulling him by his feet and pants. Several times they had to stop and rest. When Radek was in, he pulled the big branches on top of the entrance and camouflaged the hole with small branches and twigs. Now all they could do was wait.

The waiting was far from dull, thanks to the Vopos, who continued firing flares and shooting bursts of automatic fire into the woods. The three friends watched searchlights sweep across the sky and listened to jet planes landing and taking off at a nearby Russian military airfield.

They remained pinned together in their small hole, bodies shivering and teeth chattering, through the rest of the night and the whole next day. Even the slightest movement was impossible. Itches developed into horrible, unreachable agonies. Just before daybreak a clammy fog settled in. Eventually the sun rose and the fog dissipated.

As the minutes and hours crawled by they could only guess the time of day by the periodic feeding of the troops on the autobahn, where the Volkspolizei had set up a field kitchen upwind from their hiding place. The odor of food that wafted over at mealtimes was acute torture to the famished fugitives. All day long they heard sporadic gunfire; a few shots every so often, but every once in a while a wild outburst of automatic weapons fire made them wonder what had provoked it. They were exhausted and, unable to sleep for the bitter cold, they occasionally fell into a dazed stupor.

Pepa Masin, circa 1951. *Courtesy of Joseph Masin*

Radek Masin, circa 1951. *Courtesy of Joseph Masin*

Zdena Masinova Sr. in 1950. *Courtesy of Zdena Masinova*

Milan Paumer, circa 1951. *Courtesy of Milan Paumer*

Vaclav "Vasek" Sveda, circa 1949. *Courtesy of the Sveda family*

Zbynek Janata. *Courtesy of Milan Paumer*

On Podebrady's promenade, 1953. From left: unknown friend, Vladimir "Kikina" Hradec, Milan Paumer in uniform, Pepa Masin. Kikina is wearing a beret and great coat of the type the five friends wore when they left Czechoslovakia in October 1953. *Courtesy of Milan Paumer*

Czechoslovak General Frantisek Vanek, whose secret message the Masin brothers brought west. *Courtesy of the Vanek family and Pavel Pobrislo*

Werner and Marta Grunert helped the surviving Czechs escape from the second encirclement. Here they are pictured, circa 1955, with their son Björn and baby girl. *Courtesy of the Grunert family*

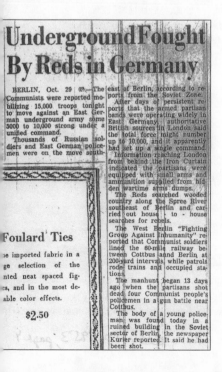

An underground army of five. On 30 October 1953 the *Washington Post* claimed that an "underground army some 5,000 to 10,000 strong under a unified command" was "operating widely in East Germany." For a ten-day period wild speculation and fantastic rumor about the Uckro manhunt flew in the Western media.

1000 DM Belohnung

für zweckdienliche Angaben, die zur Ergreifung der drei wegen
mehrfachen Mordes und Raubüberfalls gesuchten Banditenführen!

Maczin, Czirard
etwa 22 Jahre alt
Gestalt: untersetzt; etwa 1,85 groß;
Haar: blond; Augen: blau; Nase: normal;
Gesichtsform: oval; Bekleidung: grauer
Anzug, schwarze Schuhe, graues Hemd

Maczin, Joseph
20 Jahre alt
Gestalt: untersetzt; 1,75 groß;
Haar: dunkel; Gesicht: oval; Nase: nor-
mal; Bekleidung: grauer Anzug, graue
Halbschuhe, graues Hemd

Baeumer, Milian
etwa 21 Jahre alt; etwa 1,76 groß;
Haar: schwarz; Gesicht: länglich;
Augen: grau-grün; Nase: normal;
Bekleidung:
brauner Anzug, braune Halbschuhe,
hellgrünes Hemd

Die drei Mörder sprechen nicht deutsch, nächtigten mehrere Tage im Freien
und sind verwahrlost. Bekleidung kann gewechselt sein.
Die Bevölkerung wird aufgefordert, bei der Festnahme der drei gemeingefähr-
lichen Verbrecher mitzuhelfen. Zweckdienliche Angaben sind bei der nächsten
VP-Dienststelle oder VP-Angehörigen zu machen.
Achtung! Die Mörder sind im Besitze von Schußwaffen!

Chef der Deutschen Volkspolizei
Maron

(87/11) 10. 53

Ag 67/53

Most wanted poster offering a one-thousand-deutschmarks reward for evidence leading
to the arrest of the three Czech fugitives. The mug shots of Pepa and Radek were taken
upon their arrest by the StB in 1951. The picture of Milan is his official graduation photo
from the reserve tank officers' school. Note the misspellings of the names. *Courtesy of the
Grunert family*

Josef "Joe" Masin in the U.S. Army
Special Forces, 1955. *Courtesy of
Joseph Masin*

Ctirad "Ray" Masin in the U.S.
Army Special Forces, 1955. *Courtesy
of Joseph Masin*

Josef Masin in the U.S. Army Special Forces,
preparing to liberate Czechoslovakia.
Courtesy of Joseph Masin

Milan Paumer in the U.S. Army,
serving in Korea, 1957. *Courtesy of
Milan Paumer*

Clockwise from upper left: Joseph Masin, Eva Masin, Sandra Masin, and Barbara Masin in 2001. *Courtesy of Barbara Masin*

From left: Radek Masin, Czech Senator Josef Pavlata, Joseph Masin, and Milan Paumer in 2005 in Halifax, Canada, when the Masin brothers and Milan Paumer received the Czech and Slovak Association of Canada's Masaryk Award. *Courtesy of Barbara Masin*

Chapter 22

VASEK'S ROAD

The old man rushed straight from the farmyard to Reichwalde's mayor. At 3:35 PM the mayor was hollering into the telephone in feverish excitement: "The four gangsters are here!" Headquarters immediately dispatched a motorized patrol.

An hour later the patrol reported back that the four wanted men were heading toward the village of Waldow. They left unsaid that they'd closed to within a few feet of them and let them escape. Headquarters sprang into action, ordering troops to occupy the autobahn and National Road 115. It was too late. The fugitives had dashed across before the troops deployed fully.

By 6:20 PM the Czechs had reportedly barricaded themselves in at the Waldow Forest ranger station, and the Volkspolizei surrounded them. In the official version of events, a gun battle pitting Vopos against the Czech fugitives was under way. Already one comrade had been shot dead and another seriously wounded. Twelve hundred troops were rushing to the scene.[*]

Head of the Armed Forces Karl Maron was formally notified that the Czechs had resurfaced.[1] Within two hours Lieutenant General Seifert, Colonel Mellmann, and six staff members hurried back to Waldow and were urgently requesting troop reinforcements from as far afield as Frankfurt an der Oder by the Polish border.[2]

At 9:00 PM[†] East Berlin learned that the Czechs had attempted a breakout through the inner ring toward Rietzneuendorf. "They opened fire,"

---

[*]BArch, MdI, DO 1/11/777, p. 00090. The 6:20 PM report stated incorrectly that a second individual was wounded. Both were dead.

[†]No longer in possession of a timepiece, the friends did not know what time they broke out; they thought midnight, but it was actually before 9:00 PM.

said the report. "In the process Comrade Lieutenant Lehmann Martin was lethally wounded and VP-Major Hoffmann was seriously wounded. The gangsters were able to successfully break through the inner ring."*

An hour later three armored vehicles set out from Potsdam. A fourth got into a traffic accident and was disabled. As troops poured into the area, a twenty-kilometer (roughly twelve-mile) perimeter was formed around the scene of the firefight: 2,104 Vopos, posted in pairs twenty yards apart. Additional troops secured every railroad line and road within the perimeter.

Vopos in the cordons spotted unidentified individuals approaching roads and canals and shot at them while they ran for their lives. At the commanders' meeting that morning, two officers reported that in each of their respective sectors of the autobahn perimeter, one person had attempted to low-crawl across. In each instance, when the individual noticed that the autobahn was occupied, he withdrew into the woods.[3]

In the early morning hours of 17 October Volkspolizei investigators examined the depression where the four friends had hunkered down for their last stand. The report noted that two individuals had fired their weapons. One had fired once or twice from behind a large fir tree about twelve yards from the edge of the woods, before which lay the dried crown of a fallen birch, about nine feet long, shielding the bandit from view from the field. The other had hidden fifteen yards away from the first one, behind a birch. The distance from this tree to the woods' edge was six yards. Two expended 7.65-mm cartridges lay here, plus a page torn from a Czech magazine that showed the map of greater Berlin on one side and all of Germany, with its four occupation zones, on the other. A trail of blood led from the birch toward the ditch and terminated in a pool of blood. One yard away lay a blood-soaked, gray-patterned jacket.[4]

Reviewing the findings, Lieutenant General Seifert concluded that the early report of the successful breakout was probably incorrect, and that "the criminals must still be in the inner ring." He ordered the woods south of Waldow combed and detailed 350 Vopo troops, four tracking dogs, and four armored vehicles to search the entire area and encircle the town of Waldow. All farm buildings and other possible hiding places were to

---

*BArch, MdI, DO 1/11/777, p. 00091. The report was wrong on almost all counts. Hoffmann was killed by friendly fire and Lehmann was killed more than two hours earlier at the forest warden's station in Waldow. Also, the fugitives did not manage to break through the perimeter; they were in fact forced to turn back.

be thoroughly searched. The troops were to check treetops, and spacing between men in the encirclement and in the search chains was not to exceed three meters.[5]

Vasek lay under a fir tree, just outside the Waldow village cemetery. He had hardly moved since his friends had left him. Now he lay in the grass, drifting in and out of consciousness. Spotting a line of troops moving toward him, he shrank behind the fir tree, and presently they moved on past him toward the village. Unaware of the passage of time, he had not moved from the spot when they returned two hours later, heading the other way. Again he shrank behind the fir tree. They were moving toward him, then parallel with him, then passing him. . . . Then a voice called out, "Halt! Hands up!"

Vasek didn't react immediately. "Yes, you! Hands up! Throw away your gun!" With a dull sense of inevitability, he knew it was over. He was too weak to raise his hands and so he just lay there. The young soldiers came running up excitedly. They had caught a bandit! They roughly tied his hands behind his back. An officer came, a car arrived, and soon they had bundled him inside.[6]

He was taken directly to the Brandenburg/Görden prison where he was bandaged and pronounced fit to be interrogated. The interrogators lost no time getting started.[7]

Two down. Three to go.

The troops combing the area inside the perimeter attacked their assignment with renewed vigor. Their commitment was soon rewarded when forces securing the perimeter northwest of Waldow reported three people in the willow thickets. The three fled at top speed and four armored vehicles were called in. Two and a half hours later the armored vehicles surrounded a hayloft in Waldow, trapping the fugitives inside.[8]

It took one and a half hours for the troops to determine that the gangsters were not in the hayloft after all. They had definitely been sighted in hayricks north of the village, however, where troops opened fire but did not succeed in apprehending them. The area perimeters were secured with additional forces. One mile north of Waldow, from Sorge to the autobahn, a second, supplementary security cordon was thrown up and National Road 115 was sealed off by three hundred Soviet soldiers.[9]

The entire operation had taken on the aspect of a military deployment. Troops lay in ditches with their guns trained on the roads, and the locals didn't dare go outside their houses unless they absolutely had to. Trains passing through didn't make their scheduled stops. Nobody was permitted to leave or enter the villages, even to go to work. All civilian traffic in the area ceased as uniformed infantry and policemen armed with submachine guns patrolled the streets. Armored vehicles churned through plowed fields and woodlands, accompanying skirmish lines of men who fired into bushes and at everything that moved.[10]

Chapter 23

THE WAIT

Night came and temperatures plummeted below freezing. The three Czechs could see their breath condensing on the branches above their faces, where it froze into a white velvet coating. Though again shivering uncontrollably, they dared not leave their hole to move their cramping arms and legs. That evening the smell of food was painful and they tortured themselves with mouth-watering descriptions of banquets, which they stocked with their favorite dishes. Sporadic shooting continued from the road and from the autobahn throughout the night. The Vopos fired white flares, occasionally interspersed with colored flares.

After they had exhausted the topic of food, the friends talked about their breakout. What could they have done better? Was there anything they could have done for Vasek?

In retrospect, Vasek should have taken his own life or one of the others should have taken it for him. Surely he would have had much greater peace of mind on the last day of his life had he taken his destiny into his own hands!

What was more, the Communists had Zbynek. If they caught Vasek, too, they'd have two captives to play off against each other, leveraging the testimony of one against the other, extracting details about the group's activities back in Czechoslovakia, step by excruciating step. The Communists had time on their side. All the time in the world. Vasek was a courageous and dependable person, but nobody knew the limits to an individual's tolerance of physical and psychological suffering until they were tested. Pepa and Radek were under no illusions about the efficacy of the Communists' interrogation methods. They knew what lay ahead for Vasek and his family, and for their own family and the friends who had stayed behind.

By the second day the three had come up with a plausible explanation for the outbursts of heavy fire that had puzzled them during the day. The soldiers and police appeared to have divided the countryside into a number of consecutive compartments and combed each in succession. As the troops approached thickets and areas overgrown with tall grass where somebody might be hidden, they were raking them with automatic weapons fire. This was the same tactic they had used back in the little copse where Vasek was wounded. Odds were high that the Vopos would simply shoot up their woodpile.

"Don't open fire unless we're discovered!" Pepa urged.

"If anyone's hit, don't scream," Radek added.

For a while, they kept themselves busy estimating how much the manhunt was costing in ammunition alone. They also kept making and revising guesses of when the troops would get around to combing their sector. Although the hiding place was carefully camouflaged, they wouldn't bet a penny on their hides.

Chapter 24

THE LUCKAU WAR

In Brandenburg prison, Volkspolizei Colonel Weidlich had a second prisoner to work on. But the initial interrogations didn't yield much compelling new material: Vasek testified that he and his friends were at the end of their strength and had completely lost their orientation. He himself had last eaten on 9 October, and since that time they had subsisted exclusively on carrots and sugar beets. The Volkspolizei also learned that each of the three Czechs still at large had a pistol with only eight rounds, except for "Maczin, Josef," (*sic*) who had a few extra shots.

Weidlich reported that his subject had not volunteered a word about the attack on the doctor from Branderbisdorf. One item must have made Weidlich's ears perk up: Vasek testified that on the morning of 16 October the fugitives "received a piece of bread from a shepherd boy and divided it among themselves." The Volkspolizei immediately launched an all-out search for this mysterious shepherd boy. They presumed that he lived in Waldow."[1]

Volkspolizei investigators were also grilling the unfortunate widow in Reichwalde village several times a day. They bombarded the anxious, terrified woman with questions. "You helped them!" they accused her. "You gave them food!" The widow desperately denied the charges. Every night her three children heard her crying, afraid for her life, thinking that she would be bundled off to prison, never to return.[2] Though they persecuted her for weeks, the authorities never seemed to make the connection between Vasek's shepherd boy and the widow's young son in the village of Reichwalde.*

---

*In another omission, the official Volkspolizei report makes no mention of the widow and her children (the Luehmann family), and the intensive grilling to which they were subjected.

With KVP, Vopos, and Soviet troops all deployed in the same action,* Operations Command was experiencing problems: friendly fire incidents, poor communication and coordination between the different units, and, in the absence of concrete information from headquarters, the frontline troops were spreading fantastic rumors about their elusive opponents. The Czechs were crack shots. They had killed more than eight Vopos with single shots to the heart.[3] They had managed to shoot a Vopo off his moving motor cycle.[4] They had appropriated submachine guns from Vopos they had killed.[5] They were armed with heavy weapons.[6] In another variation indicative of the strained relations between German troops and their Soviet "friends," Corporal Heinz Sunkel had been shot by Soviet soldiers, not the Czechs.[7]

Not surprisingly in light of the wild rumors, the rank and file were afraid of their elusive and invisible opponents. As in the previous week's mobilization, there was shooting everywhere, at anything that moved. And the fugitives' determined resistance also impressed the central command, which dispatched a number of armored vehicles to the mobilization area. These accompanied the lines of infantry that combed the countryside.[8] People called it the Luckau War, for good reason.

On the morning of 18 October, the day after the cordon-and-search operation had turned up Vasek, the Volkspolizei combed the inner perimeter yet again in sectors.[9] A seventy-member task force descended on the village of Waldow,[10] ransacking every house and barn in the place. "They looked under the beds and under the blankets, even into our baby's crib," a resident recalled. "They wouldn't go into the hayloft, though, and wanted to make my husband go up instead. My husband refused. He told them flat out: 'You're crazy. I'm not going up there!' In the end the Vopos went themselves: stuck their heads over the edge, quickly looked around, and ducked down again."[11]

---

*The documentation is fraught with discrepancies in numbers: adding up individual troop strengths of deployed units as stated per MdI DO 1/11/777 yields numbers approaching 10,000 Vopo troops for the days around October 17, plus a presence of 500 Soviet troops on October 16 and 300 Soviets on October 18. MdI DO 1/11/1184, 0209, gives a tally of 3,968 Vopos, 100 "Schutzhunde" (trained protection/attack dogs), three tracking dogs, and three armored vehicles at Waldow, plus 900 Vopos in Potsdam district. BArch, MdI, DO 1/11/1184, 0210, gives a tally of 2,496 for the same day. Neither document gives totals for Soviet participation. The East German records make very scant reference to the Soviet deployment. There are only four passing references to the involvement of Soviet troops. Eyewitnesses report that at least equal numbers of Soviet and East German troops were deployed in the core area around Waldow and, in later days, farther north near Berlin.

The search was over by late afternoon. The Vopos came up empty-handed.[12] There were some leads, but nothing concrete,[13] and at the evening's situation conference it was decided that the Volkspolizei would comb the entire inner perimeter yet a third time, in smaller sectors.

Chapter 25

LYING LOW

Nineteen October dawned pale and cold. Judging by the noises from the autobahn, Radek thought that the field kitchen was feeding more troops than usual. The smell of coffee assaulted their frozen nostrils and made their stomachs ache at the memory of a square meal. After a while, the rattling of mess tins stopped and officers began bellowing out commands along the length of the autobahn.

The distant winter sun slowly warmed the air above freezing. Now time could be measured in the droplets of water that dripped down onto their gaunt, hollow-eyed faces, from the ice created by their own breath. It was maddening torture, for they couldn't move aside or wipe their faces. From the distance came the sound of sporadic gunfire, carrying far in the cold morning air.

All of a sudden they were startled out of their frozen stupor by a barrage of snapping branches and the tramping of hundreds of feet. It sounded like a herd of bison approaching. This was it—they were coming!

All three pulled their weapons out of their pockets and switched the safeties off. Each man reported how many rounds of ammunition he had left. Each would save the last bullet for himself.

As the troops moved into view among the trees, Pepa stared at them through the branches of the woodpile. "Halt!" shouted the officers.

The line of troops stopped at the edge of the clearing. Before them an expanse of dirt and withered grass glistened with hoarfrost. Any living thing moving through the clearing during the night would have left a visible trail, but on that morning the silvery expanse was unbroken.

"Check the treetops!" the senior officer bawled. "And watch where you shoot! Don't shoot each other!"

The Czechs congratulated each other on their decision to stay out of the trees. Adrenaline kicked in. Pepa realized with a jolt that his fingers had grown stiff from the cold and that he wouldn't be able to pull the trigger. "My trigger finger is numb," he whispered urgently. "Exercise your index finger to get the blood flowing!"

It took the Vopos a few minutes to reorganize.

"Move out!" shouted an officer. The line rolled forwarded, officers and NCOs bellowing orders to keep it straight.

"Remember, don't scream if you get hit!" Pepa warned.

Now Radek was wriggling, struggling to get his pistol into position.

"Hold your fire, you ass!" Pepa hissed at him furiously.

"I'm getting a few more of those bastards before they get us!"

"Cut it out! You'll give us away!"

"They're hosing this pile down either way. At least make them pay!"

The firing had stopped, but the troops could shoot up their woodpile at any moment. And the Czechs had no way to respond in any meaningful fashion. They were trapped.

"Shut up, both of you!" said Milan.

"Shut up yourself, Milan!"

They fell silent as the tromping boots bore down on them. Some of the Vopos let loose war whoops.

"Du blöder Tscheche," one shouted. "Komm' 'raus! Ich geb' dir eine Fatzka!" (You stupid Czech, come out! I'm going to slap your face!) Laughter greeted his sally.

Bitterly, Pepa thought it was easy for the Vopos to feel safe and heroic, outnumbering the Czechs by hundreds to one.

The line halted at the first woodpile. Then a group of officers walked forward and stopped right next to the Czechs' pile.

"What are we supposed to do about those piles of branches?" a voice called out.

"Let's try lifting them," suggested an officer standing next to their woodpile.

"Move up, comrades!" the ranking officer called out. "Lift the branches!"

Several more pairs of boots walked up and surrounded the Czechs' pile, stopping just a couple of feet from their heads. Hands reached down and grabbed branches. The men strained in unison. The branches shifted slightly, but the lower ones were partly buried in the sand and the rest were firmly wedged together. Finally the men let go and the branches crunched down. The boots stepped back.

"Let's fire a few rounds into each of the piles!" someone called.

Pepa held his breath and readied his finger, the blood now flowing, on the trigger.

"That won't be necessary," the officer said. "Just get on the piles and jump up and down."

Several soldiers clambered up onto the wood pile and began jumping, the soles of their boots crashing down to within ten inches of Radek's face.

"Hier ist etwas!" (There's something over here!) a voice suddenly shouted from over by the tree farm. Excited voices conversed.

"Boy, you're never going to use your bus pass again!" Evidently someone had discovered Pepa's bowel movement and bus pass.

"Halt!" the officer shouted. "Get off and break for five!"

The boots scrambled down the woodpile. Everyone's attention turned to the tree farm, where a detail was digging up the evidence in a time-consuming fashion with plenty of commentary and wisecracks about bowel movements. At last a motorcyclist roared off, taking the evidence with him.*

"Form up!" the officer shouted. The skirmish line re-formed just behind the Czechs' woodpile.

"Move out!" The line rolled forward. Soon it disappeared into the woods beyond the clearing. Suddenly a concentrated barrage of fire erupted. For about sixty seconds the Vopos seemed to be firing all their weapons. Then they moved off, the sound of their voices gradually receding in the distance.

All three Czechs were elated. Incredibly, they were still alive—they had won this round! But there was no time for rejoicing. They still faced major problems, beginning with hunger and the terrible cold. In their thin shirts and sport coats they were entirely exposed to the elements, and hypothermia was taking its toll. Pepa was missing a sock. Radek was missing a sock and a shoe. They had no watch and no compass. They didn't know how far it was to Berlin, or even where they were. And they hadn't had a proper meal for over two weeks.

---

*This incident is not recorded in any of the official reports on the manhunt. Considering that Pepa's bus pass was the first concrete evidence found after 17 October and that the find was widely broadcast to the public—to the extent that people later reported to Pepa that the authorities knew he had dysentery—it is one of several glaring omissions in the East German record.

The remaining daylight hours dragged by. When one of them had to urinate, which happened with increasing frequency since three days in the cold sand had chilled their kidneys, the other two helped him turn around. Every such ordeal left them exhausted. Every change of position required a long period of maneuvering, because they couldn't use their arms to move in the cramped space. They had to help each other with buttons and clothing adjustments before and after each operation. In the afternoon Milan announced that he had cramps in his bowels and diarrhea. That was the last thing they needed, and the others cursed him out. But there was no help for it. Pepa helped him dig a hole and pull his pants down. After a long effort, his excrement was buried in the sand.

Another night brought more tantalizing smells from the field kitchen and the cruel clink of mess tins and spoons. All night long the Vopos put on their fireworks as untold numbers of flares exploded in the sky. But the following morning, 20 October, all was quiet. By midday it seemed that the main enemy force had pulled out. But the three youths remained in their hole, fearful of running into a patrol.

After sunset, they started clawing their way out. It took them at least an hour of agonizing effort. Weak from starvation and numbed by the cold, even the smallest movement exhausted Pepa, forcing him to stop and rest. When he tried to stand, acute dizziness forced him back to his hands and knees. Spots danced before his eyes, and like Radek and Milan, he had to crawl on all fours. They were completely vulnerable, unable to defend themselves if anyone should happen upon them. Feebly supporting each other, they got to their feet and tottered over to the place where Pepa had relieved himself. All that remained was a hole.

"They took your shit as a souvenir!" Radek exclaimed. "Christ, the comrades have got to be desperate." As miserable as they were, they had to laugh about what the Vopos were going to do with Pepa's shit.

The moon was up, the skies were clear, and once again the temperature had dropped below freezing. They shivered in their thin shirts, and their breath was smoking in the cold night air.

"I'm going on recon," Radek announced, and tottered off along the edge of the tree farm. He didn't get far. After about ten yards he sat down, unable to take another step from sheer exhaustion. Stones and sticks on the ground jabbed the sole of his bare foot. He put the sock on his left foot and the remaining shoe on his right. They decided to skip the reconnaissance.

Food was uppermost in their minds. From the glow of lights they glimpsed through the trees and the sound of cattle lowing, they figured a village was close by. Slowly and painfully they staggered through the woods, sitting down frequently to rest. The ground was frozen hard and frost covered everything. High above them stars twinkled in a cloudless sky. The forest was completely still. They came to several large piles of pine needles, about four to five feet high. The piles were in shambles: pine needles had been blasted across the forest floor in clumps. Here was a possible explanation for the crazy bout of weapons fire they'd heard the previous day: the Vopos had been firing on these piles. The Czechs were silent for a moment, contemplating how close they had come to dying under their woodpile.

Eventually they reached the edge of the woods and peered out across the field at the village. Approximately halfway across stood a large stack of straw.

"What about hiding in there? It's got to be warmer in there than in that godawful woodpile!"

"Yeah, but look at that!" Pepa pointed. They strained to see in the darkness. "Isn't that someone walking? And there's a bicyclist."

"Shit—that's some kind of a trail!"

As they watched, they saw that the dirt road was heavily trafficked, with people moving along it on bicycles and on foot. The straw stack was on the far side—unreachable. They decided to turn back. Their decision turned out to be fortunate. Later they would find out that every straw pile and haystack in the district was manned by a rotating three-person, round-the-clock guard for a full week.

They retraced their steps along the edge of the woods, looking out across the empty fields that stretched away from the wood.

"There's nothing to eat here!" Milan said glumly.

The sandy soil, typical of the country, had been tilled into small, smooth furrows that stretched away, achingly bare, before them.

"I'll see if there's something closer to the village," Radek volunteered. "No sense in all of us running into a trap."

"Okay. We'll wait here for you."

"If I'm caught, I'll tell the police that I don't know where you two are."

"Right. Say you got separated from us and you hid in a village well."

Radek nodded and disappeared into the darkness as Pepa and Milan watched. He hadn't been gone long when they noticed a military vehicle crossing the field, apparently along a dirt trail they had overlooked in the darkness. The vehicle proceeded slowly, with only its parking lights on. When it was directly in front of Milan and Pepa, it stopped. The two of them stood there, their hearts pounding.

"They've got Radek!" Milan gasped.

Noises came from the dirt road, and now they noticed that troops were still posted all along it. Several people got out of the vehicle and began doing something to it. As Pepa and Milan strained to see, they concluded that the vehicle was stuck in a hole and that the crew was struggling in vain to get it out. Eventually another truck showed up and towed it out. After that everything was quiet again.

After a long while during which they became increasingly worried, a dark figure appeared to their right. Radek! They signaled and he came toward them, struggling to carry a few frozen heads of cabbage and some shriveled carrots. "That was a close call!" he panted. "That truck got stuck in a rut just a few yards ahead of me."

"We thought they caught you!"

"I couldn't move. I had to get flat on the ground and wait until the Vopos dragged the damn thing out."

Milan was inspecting Radek's haul. "You're a hell of a scavenger—don't they have anything but carrots and cabbage in that village?"

"You didn't have to carry this stuff. You have no idea how heavy a head of frozen cabbage can get. I had to stop every few feet and rest." They divided up the cabbage and carrots equally. "The Vopos are still sitting on the road," Radek went on. "They've got people staked out around the perimeter of the whole goddamn village. I couldn't get near it. And then I missed the damn trail on the way back, so I couldn't find you guys."

Slowly retracing their steps to the piles of pine needles, they gnawed on the bitter cabbage and rock-solid carrots full of ice crystals. They were glad to have something, anything, to eat. Burrowing into the pine needles, they covered themselves up to their chins in the sweet-smelling warmth. It didn't matter in the least that the needles pricked and scratched them all over.

Shortly before first light they reluctantly made their way back to the clearing and shoehorned themselves back under the woodpile, camouflaging the entrance as before. The temperature rose slightly after sunrise and a persistent drizzle started falling. Soaked and shivering, they endured until darkness, dreaming all the while of the comforts of the pine needles.

In the evening, when the woods were dark again, the trio inched back out of their hole. Once again Radek went off to get some cabbage and they returned to the pine needles as quickly as their condition permitted. Though wet on the surface, the stacks were dry inside and wonderfully toasty. It began raining again after midnight, but they still got a little sleep before they had to retreat back to the frozen safety of the woodpile.

Chapter 26

ETERNAL HONOR AND GLORY TO OUR HEROES!

O nce again thousands of troops were scouring large tracts of country-side, sealing off entire districts and turning the town of Luckau into an armed camp. At the epicenter of the upheaval, skirmish lines combed the wooded areas around Waldow village for three consecutive days. Though they returned empty-handed, Major General Dombrowsky remained confident that he had trapped the Czechs inside his gigantic dragnet. On 20 October he assured the Interior Ministry, "It seems impossible that they would have succeeded in breaking through the encirclement to Berlin and one must assume that they are still in the sealed-off area."[1]

Meanwhile the beleaguered regime's public response was total silence. Not a word was breathed in the press. As if nothing out of the ordinary had happened, the media continued proclaiming the party line: fraternal relations with the Soviet Union; the success of class struggle; and the population's gratitiude to the Party for the "New Course," which pumped food-stuffs and consumer goods into the shops (thanks to emergency imports of foods and massive loans by the Soviet Union) while reducing work norms to levels prevailing before 17 June.

Then the regime abruptly reversed course. The Party had to acknowledge the massive mobilization or risk further damage to its already tarnished credibility. When the three dead Volkspolizei men were buried on 20 October, the Party turned the funeral into a massive propaganda event.

The three Vopos were given heroes' send-offs. Flags flew at half-mast in the town of Cottbus, where the lying-in-state and funeral procession were held. A Volkspolizei honor guard accompanied the coffins. A color guard marched. All factories and shops closed for the day. The local paper exhorted the entire population to turn out and attend the "mighty funeral demonstration that will make the enemies of our republic tremble."[2] All three men, the Party proclaimed, had died heroes' deaths at the hands of "fascist murderers"—even the major who had been shot and killed by friendly fire.

"Eternal honor and eternal glory to our dead heroes!" the official eulogy trumpeted.[3] The local paper explained that all three men had sterling Party credentials and had professed their unwavering dedication to the Communist cause. These were role models that the Party wanted the people to follow.

"We know that the order for this murder was issued in Washington and Bonn," the district secretariat of the Communist Party in Cottbus thundered. "The shots upon our comrades are no coincidence. . . . After they [Washington and Bonn] suffered an ignominious defeat with their fascist putsch-attempt on 17 June, they are trying it this way now."[4] Specifically, that meant, "On orders of foreign and West Berlin agent centers, armed fascist terrorists were infiltrated into the territory of the German Democratic Republic. . . . Their goal was to organize sabotage and murder in our republic."[5] This was the Party line, and it was reprised verbatim by all the GDR's principal papers.

Despite the news media's full-throated cries about the population's "resolute hatred of the fascist bandits," the Vopo high command was not at all sure it could count on grassroots support.[6] Two Vopos attached to the Operational Command at Lübben were dispatched to conduct an attitude survey among area residents. The pollsters interviewed blue-collar workers, white-collar workers, and women to find out how they really felt about "the murders of the policemen and the measures taken by the police." The pair reported back that everybody was "outraged at the murder of the policemen and welcomed the police measures. . . . In the Waldow community there exists a profound hatred toward the bandits."[7]

Even without the leading questions, it is unlikely that the population would have dared to voice honest opinions to Vopos on such an explosive subject. The truth was that the authorities didn't trust the locals or, for that matter, the results of their own survey. In the Waldow area most farms had been small family operations. The state was turning these proud smallholders into indentured servants, confiscating their land, their plows, their tractors, and their harvests. These people had good reason to hate the regime and empathize with those who ran afoul of it. The fact was that the Czechs had the courage to resist and the villagers admired them for it.[8] The people in the villages would have willingly provided them with food and shelter, given a chance, as resistance to the state.[9] Popular sentiment was with the Czechs.[10]

Rank-and-file Vopos on the front line bore the brunt of this widespread antagonism. Locals provided an unending stream of bogus leads, which sent the police on wild goose chases all over the countryside.[11] With the motives of so many alleged eyewitnesses suspect, the Volkspolizei resorted to a crude system of triage. When the sister of a 17 June activist reported seeing two men in the woods to Colonel Mellmann, she was sent packing with the remark, "You're nuts." But when the son of the head of the local collective farm reported a sighting the following day, a perimeter was formed around the area in question.[12]

The Volkspolizei plastered community bulletin boards with most-wanted posters featuring head shots and vital statistics of the three fugitive Czechs, offering a cash reward. One morning in the village of Alt-Golßen, a wreath appeared around the young Czechs' faces. "Eternal Honor and Glory to the Courageous Heroes," the attached ribbon declared,[13] an ironic reprise of the Communist Party's eulogy to the dead Vopos. The message was unmistakable: the regime had its heroes and the people had theirs. Though the wreath was whisked away, the rumor of it raced through the district. A few days later another wreath appeared around a different poster, only to be whisked away again.[14]

Volkspolizei Central Command was well aware of the implications of such overt solidarity with the Czechs. Concerned about possible fraternization between the Czechs and local regime opponents, the Volkspolizei targeted "negative elements," including the pastor and the forest ranger of Waldow, on the assumption that they might be harboring the fugitives.[15]

In fact, virtually the entire local population was already actively defying and disobeying the government. The fact that the East German public was enthusiastically availing itself of American food aid that was being freely distributed in West Berlin, and which the Communist government derogatively labeled the "begging package action," greatly embarrassed the East German regime. It drove home the point that the regime was not able to feed its own people, and the authorities discouraged popular participation as much as they dared.[16]

The authorities tried to deter the villagers from making common cause with the Czechs by threatening dire reprisals. "Any support of the terrorists will be punished according to the law,"[17] loudspeakers and news-papers blared at every opportunity. Everyone knew that the unspecified punishments would be harsh.

Even with the make-work leads volunteered by obliging locals, by 21 October the Volkspolizei was covering ground it had already gone over numerous times before. A new, slightly smaller inner perimeter, ranging from the forest warden's house up into the woods north of Waldow, stopped just short of the Czechs' clearing.[18] The following day Vopo skirmish lines combed the encircled area while twenty-five detectives descended on the ranger station, searching it for over an hour.

On the afternoon of 22 October the command dissolved the perimeter. A drastic overhaul in tactics was in order. No more massive cordon-and-search operations. No more combing of woods and fields. The new tactic was to "reduce the visibility of uniformed Vopos to a minimum, so that the fugitives gain the impression that their pursuit has been terminated."[19] Sentries disappeared from the forest trails and the troop cordons surrounding the villages vanished.

Only a low-profile Volkspolizei presence remained on paved roads. Plainclothesmen walked the fields during the day, observing all movement with binoculars.[20] The forces freed up by this new disposition were to retire outside the perimeter and wait in reserve.[21] Accordingly, after nightfall on 22 October, the troops billeted in Waldow and Dornswalde left for new accommodation in other villages. A few K- and S-forces and Stasi remained to keep tabs on nightly traffic into and out of Waldow.*

As added insurance, a second security cordon went up about ten kilometers north of the first one. The Trapo invested both north-south railroad lines, as well as Highways 96 and 101, the two major north-south arteries. Now four parallel lines of troops ran north to south and two security cordons intersected them east to west. Beyond all of these measures waited the Berliner Ring, where Vopo sentries stood at seventy-five yard intervals along thirty miles of the Ring's southern sweep.[22] That was the eye of the needle.

---

*BArch, MdI, DO 1/11/777, 00159. K- and S-forces were the criminal investigations division (Hauptabteilung K) and the so-called protective police (Hauptabteilung S).

Chapter 27

FIRST-CLASS ACCOMMODATIONS

The woods brooded in silence as the three fugitives wormed their way out of the woodpile for the last time. It was the night of 22 October. They had spent six hellish days in that miserable hole, but it had saved their lives. Fully aware it might do so again, they camouflaged their hiding place with great care before heading out. After creeping into the cabbage field and picking as many of the bulky red cabbages as they could carry, they made their way to the straw stack they had spotted two nights earlier. The Volkspolizei had torn apart the top of the stack and scattered quantities of straw about the field. What was left was tightly machine-packed and they gave up the idea of tunneling inside. Eventually the Czechs turned toward the village. Perhaps they could shelter among people for three or four days until the search was over.

It was after midnight. The village, completely blacked out, appeared unguarded, but they decided to play it safe by inspecting the houses from behind rather than entering the village via the road. They scrambled across fences from one outlying farm to the next, searching for a suitable barn or hayloft. Presently they came to a farm with an outbuilding a stone's throw away from the main house.

While the others covered him from a distance, Pepa warily approached it. He tried the first door, which creaked open unresistingly. There was no lock. Several cows turned a placid gaze on him. Carefully he closed the door and opened the next one. Judging by the noise and the smell, a few large pigs were snuffling about in the darkness. He closed the door softly. The third door revealed a kitchen, and through a window Pepa saw a fourth room, a workshop of some kind. He retraced his steps and signaled for Radek and Milan to join him.

The threesome entered the cow byre, where Pepa decided to help himself to some milk, straight from the source. He bent under a cow and tried to milk it directly into his mouth. But since the animal didn't appreciate Pepa's clumsy efforts and wouldn't stand still, most of the milk squirted wide of its mark. Abandoning the effort, he hurried after the others, who were already inspecting the pigsty.

The pigs grunted softly, exuding contentment as they tucked into their supper of potatoes mixed with bran. It smelled heavenly. Without further ado the Czechs joined the pigs at the trough, greedily digging into the swill and stopping only to quench their thirst from the pigs' water trough. A fair amount of sand and dirt was mixed in with the potatoes, but no one minded. The pigs, however, did mind their uninvited guests. They got progressively more and more agitated until they were indignantly squealing their objection at the unwelcome intruders. Afraid that the ruckus would wake up the people in the farmhouse, the youths interrupted their meal and fumbled about blindly in the dark, looking for the ladder to the hayloft. It was leaning against the wall.

The hayloft looked empty, but on further inspection the rear half turned out to be filled with hay up to the roof. They wasted no time scrambling onto the pile, all the way to the back of the gable. They dug into the soft, sweet-smelling hay, leaving an opening above their heads for air and keeping some hay close at hand for short-notice camouflage. That night, they didn't move again. Not even the kitchen could tempt them. After freezing outside for almost a week in the rain and frost, they congratulated each other on stumbling into such first-class accommodations. Exhausted as they were, they remained vigilant and posted a watch.

Eventually first light probed through the cracks between the roof tiles and the household started to stir. The Czechs lay hidden in their hay nests, listening to the voices and noises drifting up from the yard, occasionally nibbling from their stash of cabbage. All day long conversations outside revolved around the gangsters and the manhunt. A motorcyclist stopped by several times to ask whether anyone had seen anything suspicious. It was clear that the search was still very much on.

When the sun set and the interior of the barn faded into a formless gray under the coming night, the three emerged from their hiding places and ventured outdoors. Everything was dark and quiet. Their first wary stop was the little garden behind the farmhouse, where they harvested several heads of red cabbage. The only other edibles they found were a few potatoes the pigs had left in their trough inside the barn. As they polished them off, the furious pigs started rushing about and squealing. The friends left quickly, heading into the kitchen.

Their first move was to cover the windows with paper. One man stood guard at the door while the other two searched for food with the help of a flashlight they had discovered. The battery was nearly exhausted and the beam dimmed rapidly. Food was in short supply; only a few crusts of bread lay on the kitchen table. The flashlight died. Pepa found a candle and a box of matches. As the flickering light of the candle threw long, leaping shadows across the room, the friends broke a tiny piece off each of the crusts, watching each other closely to make sure no one took too much. These few crumbs merely teased their empty stomachs. Desperately they searched the empty cupboards and bare shelves for more food, to no avail. Hunger, it seemed, was stalking the family in the house, too.

When the candle flickered out, they had their next light source ready: an empty shoe polish tin into which they had stuck a piece of tallow and a string. After thoroughly searching the whole kitchen, they were forced to recognize that there was nothing else to eat. Their stomachs crying out for food, they removed the paper from the windows and returned everything to the state they had found it, then retired to the hayloft for another day's wait.

The little party awoke on 24 October to the same routine on the farm. The talk outside was still centered on them. The motorcyclist still made his rounds. All the while, they lay low in the barn, which they jokingly called their hay hotel.

That night the three friends headed straight to the kitchen. As on the first night, they posted a rotating watch. Taking extreme precautions to leave no trace of their presence, they established ground rules for themselves. Only one item could be moved at a time. No two people could move objects at the same time. One man always had to watch the person moving an item to ensure that it was replaced exactly.

And then, when Pepa turned around, he saw Milan bent over a bowl of potatoes.

"Milan, you've got no business gobbling up those potatoes," he whispered fiercely.

"I didn't even touch them," Milan retorted, deeply offended. "I was only sniffing them!"

"Don't even *think* of eating them!"

"I wasn't, you asshole!"

"Hey guys, cut it out—look what I found here." Radek was pointing at a can of condensed milk. The squabble stopped as the three of them contemplated this find. It was made in England. How had these farmers in the middle of the East German provinces gotten ahold of it? They decided they couldn't risk touching it—such a rarity would surely be missed immediately. They ate a few small pieces of potato and then decided to inspect the garden to see if anything edible could be found there. After some deliberation they decided to take a box of matches back with them. When they closed the kitchen door behind them, they had left no trace of their visit.

The garden contained nothing but red cabbage, which the three friends could no longer stomach. It left a burning sensation in their mouths and eating even the smallest amount made them feel ill. With their sole sustenance that night the little bit they dared take from the kitchen, they were grimly aware that such miniscule amounts wouldn't sustain them.

As the days crept by, the friends lay about weakly and dozed almost continuously. They learned the routine of the household and the people who frequented the farm almost as if they were members of the family. The young farmer's wife had a beautiful voice and often sang. The police patrol came by every day like clockwork, inquiring whether anyone had seen the gangsters. But now a new problem arose: shortly after nodding off, the sleepers snored so loudly that the person on guard duty had to wake them up. None of them could understand why this was happening. None of them had ever snored before. Unable to sleep continuously for more than a few minutes, they were short-tempered but too exhausted to argue about it for long.

They passed the time talking about the future and trying to decide which branch of the U.S. military they would join. Pepa and Milan opted for the Air Force, and Radek wanted to join the "commandos." They thought a lot about Vasek and wondered what had become of him. They also discussed the refugee camp. What would it be like? They looked forward to it yearningly. There they wouldn't have to worry about hiding. They would be nice and warm at night under thick UNRRA blankets, and they would at least be assured a few slices of bread each day. Not once did it occur to them to fantasize about anything more elaborate than plain bread and an occasional piece of cheese—they had been hungry for so long.

Every morning an old woman climbed up to the hayloft and threw a pile of hay to the ground floor. The hay supply in the loft was rapidly diminishing, and they worried that she might end up discovering her uninvited guests. So they pushed and pulled some hay toward the ladder every morning, to keep her from climbing all the way into the loft.

They spent each day carefully monitoring conversations in the barnyard. Whenever someone left the farm they became alarmed, fearing that they had somehow been discovered and reported. The memory of their recent debacle still fresh in their minds, they developed a contingency plan. The three of them would hold their fire until all the troops were upstairs in the loft, and then take out as many of them as they could before they themselves were killed. It was not much of a plan, but they couldn't see a way out for themselves.

They continued raiding the kitchen, but it remained depressingly empty. When they found a piece of bread, it took immense self-control to take just a sliver. Even so, after two days or so, they heard the old lady berating the old man for eating too much. So the family had noticed the missing food!

They decided they had no choice but to practice even greater discipline. They had to revert to the frozen cabbage again. Every night, they delegated one person to go out and collect some. A few days later, the monotony of red cabbage and paper-thin bread slices was relieved by the appearance of a pot of plum jam. Thrilled at their discovery, the three friends put a little bit of the jam into an empty jar and mixed it with groats, a bag of which they had discovered in the barn. These groats were also excellent with salt and sugar and, later on, when the sugar was gone, rapeseed oil helped make them a little more nourishing.

One day, a big bowl of cinnamon plum compote appeared in the kitchen. At first, they allocated themselves two plums apiece, but later voted to take two more each on the grounds that there were lots of them and no one could tell the difference. Nothing had ever tasted so good before. The plums lasted several days. Sometimes they discovered a pot of leftover soup or coffee. They would drink a little and wipe away the ring that indicated the liquid's former level on the inside of the container.

For four consecutive nights they dined on miniscule quantities of pulverized dried pears, which they relished. One night, they found three apples on the table, and after a lengthy deliberation and carefully thinking things over, decided to eat one of them. From the discussions they overheard in the kitchen, they knew that there wasn't even enough food for the people who lived in the house. Feeling compassion for their unwitting hosts who had so little themselves, they decided to leave some money for them when they left.

But then, noticing the heavy traffic into and out of the house during the daylight hours, and what looked like a number of award placards hanging inside the workshop, they concluded that the man of the house must be some sort of Party official. Then there was the Vopo who came every day by motorcycle. They surmised that he was either the son or the son-in-law of the old couple living in the house, because he usually stayed longer than necessary and talked to the people a lot.

The three told themselves that having a Vopo in the family was a good thing, because that put them beyond suspicion of harboring criminals. But it killed the Czechs' compassion and they summarily voted to punish these despicable people. That night, they drank all of the remaining English condensed milk.

Chapter 28

EAST GERMAN REVOLTS

While the three Czechs had their hands full trying to stay alive and out of sight, the Volkspolizei were rushing about the country on wild goose chases. Both civilians and Vopo sentries continued to report sightings and rumors. Unshaven men. Men without hats. Men crouching in ditches by the road and making mysterious signs to others in the woods. Men crossing railroad tracks. Men firing guns. All of them melted away into the woods without being identified. After each report smaller detachments were sent out to investigate, and smaller perimeters were established and combed. They seized hapless Polish and Czechoslovak refugees and East German labor camp escapees whose unfortunate timing had put them in the way of the dragnet. The Masin group was not alone in wanting to join the allied forces in the West.

Although leads continued to trickle in from all over the south of the country, the Operational Command decided that their quarry was still pinned down in the Waldow area. "According to verifications done thus far," it pronounced, "the only leads that deserve special attention are those from the Waldow area."[1]

Near Groß-Radden, ten miles southeast of the friends' actual location, a farmer's wife reported three persons camping in her barn. Volkspolizei and Soviet troops were immediately dispatched, but the advance guard, two SfS* men on motorcycles, was afraid to go in and confront the fugitives by themselves. They marked time by driving back and forth in front of the farm until

---

*SfS—Staatssekretariat für Staatssicherheit, aka Stasi (State Secretariat for State Security), was the East German secret police.

the main force arrived and surrounded the barn. By that time the transients were long gone, leaving behind a smattering of broken eggshells from purloined chicken eggs. The report concluded: "The m.o. of the bandits is to hide in remote barns."[2]

Once again the trail was growing cold. On 24 October several hundred troops were shipped back to their home bases and the eye of the needle at the Berlin Ring was reinforced.[3] Additional troops were deployed in depth to the south.[4] The following day barns, haystacks, and other potential hiding places surrounding Waldow in a sector measuring roughly forty square miles were scoured one last time. Once again the Volkspolizei came up empty-handed.

Over the next three days, new leads clustered in an area northeast of the autobahn. Operational Command concluded that the fugitives had escaped the Waldow perimeter, somehow managed to cross the heavily guarded autobahn, and were now moving northeast. Acting on this mistaken assumption, the Volkspolizei shifted its resources from the western to the eastern side of the autobahn. It threw up a containment perimeter thirty miles northeast of the Czechs' actual location,[5] and it deployed armed guards all along the eastern railway line from Schönwalde to Königswusterhausen.[6] To free up troops, it simply dissolved the security cordon on the western railway line that the Czechs had been following.

While the Volkspolizei groped about blindly trying to reestablish contact with the fugitives, the West took belated notice of the massive deployment. Visitors to the East German provinces came back bearing breathless accounts of heavily armed Volkspolizei patrolling trains and guarding streets and railway lines; of troops lying in camouflaged foxholes with shoot-on-sight orders; of a huge troop deployment, unprecedented in scope.[7]

There were rumors of pitched battles between Volkspolizei and partisans. Twenty-eight Vopos were supposedly wounded or dead; sixteen resistance fighters had been arrested. Partisan bands were said to be trying to reach Berlin.[8] The respected *Frankfurter Allgemeine Zeitung* reported that five hundred to a thousand Czech, Polish, and German partisans were allegedly trying to break through to Berlin, having fought their way as far north as Cottbus. The Berlin-Cottbus autobahn was reportedly lined with machine gun nests at hundred-yard intervals, with vehicle checkpoints installed every twenty or so miles.[9]

In the United States, major dailies ran stories about revolts behind the Iron Curtain. The *Boston Daily Globe* reported a spreading revolt by "Red Army deserters, anti-Communist East Germans and Czech partisans," and went on to say, "It is not clear whether there is liaison between several reported bands. It is known, however, that their numbers are large enough that they have engaged Soviet and East German peoples' police units in pitched battles and that 10,000 or more Red Army troops and Communist police have been ordered out in the Berlin area alone in an attempt to root them out."[10] The partisans allegedly were "on the offensive," armed with "machine guns and other automatic weapons seized in raids on Red Army and police barracks."

In West Berlin the *Neue Zeitung* spoke of a "growing resistance army . . . comprised in part of Soviet deserters, including the commandant of a Soviet air base."[11]

An unnamed London source breathlessly revealed to reporters that an "East German underground army some 5,000 to 10,000 strong under a unified command"[12] was fighting "some 3,000 crack Soviet Army troops . . . sent into East Germany with orders to crush an anti-Communist resistance movement operating a 'hit and run' guerrilla warfare."[13] The government source conjectured that the commander of the antipartisan campaign was no lesser a man than Feldmarschall Friedrich von Paulus, the German army commander captured at Stalingrad.[14]

The East German authorities, meanwhile, remained tight-lipped. The only nationwide press coverage was an "advisory of the Volkspolizei District Authority at Cottbus," printed on 21 October in all the major East German papers. The text was reproduced verbatim in all newspapers. The advisory fulminated about "foreign and West Berlin [intelligence] agent directorates" which had "infiltrated armed, fascist terrorists into the territory of the German Democratic Republic. . . . The brutality of the criminals arises from the death of four People's Policemen in the fight against the terrorists. The People's Police has taken all necessary measures to liquidate the remainder of the terrorist group. The population of the Kottbus and Potsdam districts are called upon to actively support the measures of the state organs. All instructions and directives are to be strictly followed in your own interest. Every support of the terrorists will be punished according to the law. Any observation, even the smallest, concerning the whereabouts of the terrorists and their accomplices and abetters is . . . to be reported immediately."

Western analysts were reduced to reading between the lines. "That is new language," the *Süddeutsche Zeitung* pointed out. "In the past eastern propaganda only spoke of 'American' intelligence services. This indefinite formulation 'foreign' seems to confirm the Czech origin of the fugitives."[15]

As the massive troop deployment dragged on and mushroomed in size, Western analysts had trouble accepting the official East German explanation that the authorities were attempting to liquidate five Czech youths armed with pistols. Journalists and government analysts groped for more plausible explanations: military training maneuvers[16]; detachments of several hundred partisans fighting their way to the West from Poland and Czechoslovakia[17]; a major uprising in East Germany[18]; an "East German underground army"[19]; a "growing resistance army comprised in part of Soviet deserters including the commandant of a Soviet air base."[20] Arrests of escaped convicts and 17 June leaders reported by the East German authorities during this period seemed to substantiate the interpretation of a large-scale roundup of the opposition.[21]

The mysterious disturbance even boiled over the sector border into West Berlin. The night of Wednesday, 21 October, ten Vopos rushed across the sector border brandishing carbines and submachine guns. They chased two West Berlin policemen fifteen yards into the British sector. As the East Germans shouted, "You murderers, we are taking revenge on you for Cottbus," the two West Berliners hastily beat a retreat to an emergency telephone to call for a radio car and reinforcements. Reinforcements arrived and the Vopos retreated into the Soviet sector. The West Berlin policemen barely avoided abduction.[22]

Meanwhile, American officials in Berlin were attempting their own explanations. Something was afoot. But what? Cecil Lyon, director of the U.S. High Commissioner's Office there, reported to the Secretary of State on 23 October: "Associated Press filed story stating: 500 to 1000 armed Polish, Czechoslovak and German partisans clashing with *Volkspolizei* in Bezirk Cottbus near Polish border in last forty-eight hours; partisans executed by KVP; and Berlin-Cottbus-Forst autobahn heavily patrolled with KVP reportedly entrenched at places with machine guns. We have no confirmation of report. CIC has no report."[23]

By 28 October, the swirling rumors and breathtaking stories in the press had Secretary of State John Foster Dulles impatiently wondering why the press had more details on the disturbance in the Soviet sector than his own people in Berlin. He dispatched a curt request for more facts.[24]

Cecil Lyon responded promptly the following day: "Only substantiated element of special police action so far relates to escaped Czech youth. CIC has copy of East German police notice offering reward for capture three armed, 20-year-old youths with Czech names. . . . Current Communist political line, absence any overt moves against West Berlin, prevailing mood of East Germans and proven capabilities of Soviet military forces are factors which lead us to conclude unlikelihood of any partisan activity in Soviet Zone at present."[25]

Contrary to the Masin brothers' belief in an all-knowing CIC, the Americans faced this new turmoil in East Germany virtually blind. CIC intelligence sources in East Germany appeared to be limited to unsubstantiated reports in the *Neue Zeitung*, a copy of the most-wanted handbill that had found its way to Berlin, and one trusted source in the East Berlin Social Democratic Party office, a Mr. Koerner, who volunteered a mix of fact, fiction, and personal opinion when the Americans approached him for insight on the ongoing mobilization and whether it signaled another uprising.[26]

Chapter 29

SILENT HEROES

The young men who were the cause of all this upheaval remained totally oblivious to the vast scope of the mobilization and the wild speculation it spawned. They were battling troubles of their own. The supply of hay that hid them was dwindling rapidly, the food shortage continued, and after a few more nights in the hayloft they decided they had to move. But several taxing recon missions didn't turn up any better hiding place. Most of the buildings in the area were locked and the few barns were empty or inadequate for some other reason. Their level of exhaustion after these small excursions alarmed them: if they didn't leave the village soon they would starve to death.

But was it safe to move on? They had to find out whether troops were still posted in the village. Radek volunteered to go out on recon. According to their usual practice, he went alone; the others would follow when he signaled all clear.

That night, the moon shone brightly in a cloudless sky and by its light Radek could see clearly for a considerable distance. A light fog hung just above the ground so that the sleeping houses, barns, and trees looked as if they were floating in it, illuminated by pale moonlight. It was a hauntingly beautiful scene.

Radek was just about to leave the deep shadow of the barn and hurry over to the next building when he heard a faint noise coming from the road in front of the house. Seconds later a six-man Vopo patrol rounded the corner, armed to the teeth with StG44 submachine guns. A police dog accompanied them.

His heart pounding, Radek shrank back into the shadows and flattened himself against the wall. He had already been gone longer than usual. What if Milan and Pepa became impatient and came out to look for him? With every fiber of his being he willed them to stay in the barn. The patrol stopped a few yards away and stood talking quietly. The seconds crawled by. Radek scarcely dared to breathe. By some miracle, the dog didn't pick up his scent, and presently the patrol moved away.

Radek returned to the loft in a highly agitated state. When Pepa and Milan heard about his close call, they instantly shelved their decision to leave the village. They would have to tough it out in the barn until the manhunt ended.

By now their limbs were so weak they had trouble climbing into the hayloft. In fact, it took them longer than the old lady who came every day to fetch hay. They didn't even have the energy to burrow into their holes. Rationalizing that no one came upstairs during the day anyway, they lay about all day in a dizzy stupor.

On 29 October, they lay on top of the hay, as usual. Milan, whose watch it was, must have fallen asleep, because suddenly they all woke up to find the old woman moving around the hayloft. Usually the woman panted and rattled the ladder loudly on the way up, but this time nobody had heard her. It was too late to crawl into their holes, so the three friends just held their breath and froze, waiting to see what would happen. Apparently there was not enough hay at the front of the loft near the stair, so she climbed on top of the pile and began raking up some more. She thrust the rake all the way to the wall, but it hit the wooden floor. So she thrust the rake out again, flattening out the little mounds of hay as she dragged it toward her.

Suddenly, there was Milan! With a squeal of surprise, she dropped the rake and quickly disappeared down the ladder. The Czechs were wide awake now.

"We're screwed!" Pepa hissed. "I'm going to check the kitchen. Radek, you check the house!"

Pepa took Milan's weapon from him, leaving his own for Milan; it had never been quite right since it falling in the sand during their breakout.

"Stay here and make sure no one leaves the house!" Radek hissed to Milan. "Keep an eye on that guy in the field!" A man was working in the field behind the farm and there was a good chance he would see the two brothers running from the barn.

They were off, down the ladder. Radek raced toward the main house while Pepa chased after the old woman, who had fled to the kitchen. Flinging open the kitchen door, he saw her announcing breathlessly, "I saw 'the man in the brown suit' up in the hayloft!" She stopped short as Pepa burst in.

"All of you! Hands up!" Pepa shouted in fractured German. "Who left the house!?"

There were five people in the room—the old woman, the old man, the young couple and the baby. In a state of shock, they put their hands up.

"Nobody left!" they cried. "We swear! Upon our souls, nobody left!"

"If anybody went to call the police, I'll shoot everybody and burn this place down!" Pepa pointed his gun at the terrified family.

Radek burst in.

"I've rounded everyone up!" said Pepa quickly in Czech.

"There's no one in the house," Radek replied.

"Leave! Please, go away now!" the family begged. "Somebody might come in at any time and see you! We won't report you! Just leave. Quickly!"

"You're crazy," Pepa snapped. "It's daylight and everybody will see us. Did somebody go to the police? Tell the truth! You've heard about us. You know we'll do whatever it takes and that we don't give a shit about anything. If the police show up, you've had it. We've got more than enough bullets for all of you. And we're saving the last bullets for ourselves."

"No! Nobody went to get the police!"

The two youths kept their guns pointed at the family.

"This is a fucking mess," Radek said to Pepa in Czech. "We take them with us to the hayloft, so nobody changes their minds afterward."

"Okay, everybody. Upstairs. Let's go!" said Pepa in German, motioning with his head toward the door. The brothers knew they had to maintain the psychological momentum and impress on these people that they had no option but to cooperate.

"No! Please listen!" said the old man urgently. "You should go back to the barn and leave us in the house. People come by here to call on us every day. And the police are checking several times a day. If nobody is here they might get suspicious."

Radek and Pepa understood his logic.

"If we only take one of the women with us, that's not enough of a disincentive. The others could still pull a fast one on us," Pepa said in Czech.

"Okay. You, come!" Radek said in German and motioned to the young man.

"I can't! I've got to go to work. If I don't show up, that will make them suspicious," replied the young farmer.

"All right. You three, then!" Pepa motioned to the young woman holding the child and the old man huddled by her side.

"No, please don't take the child!" cried the old woman. "I'll go with you instead."

Radek looked at Pepa. Their eyes met with a small nod of agreement.

"Okay, then. You and you! Let's go!" He motioned the two women toward the door with his head, his gun still trained on the huddled family group.

The Germans had become calm and cooperative. The two women slowly moved toward the door.

"Did anybody see you in the yard?" one of them asked.

"No, not as far as we could tell," Pepa replied. "Who's the man working in the field behind the house?" He was the only one who might have seen them running around in the yard.

"He's a farmer from the village." To all appearances, the man in the field was attending to his work and had noticed nothing.

The question of who was to go with the brothers to the hayloft was settled, but there remained the question of political allegiance.

"Are you Communists?" asked Radek.

"No!" the family replied vehemently. After some questioning, Radek and Pepa decided that the family's explanation of their friendly attitude toward the police was plausible.*

"Go outside and make sure that nobody is in the street," Pepa instructed the old man. "Be sure nobody is in sight."

The old man left on his mission. A few seconds later he was back.

"All clear," he reported. He looked tense, but his attitude was cooperative.

Radek and Pepa led their hostages out of the kitchen, around the house, and into the barn. The women wanted to stay on the ground floor, but Pepa and Radek ordered them up to the hayloft, assuring them that nothing would happen if everyone cooperated.

Up in the hayloft, the two women initially eyed the Czechs with apprehension. The older woman was slightly stooped and had a wrinkled, care-worn face. She wore the head covering and conservative dark dress typical of older country women, with a work pinafore. The younger woman was in her

---

*Today neither Radek nor Pepa can recall what it was.

midtwenties and had blonde, curly hair. She was wearing a faded work dress. The two women sat down, and the Czechs were as courteous and respectful to them as possible, reiterating that they had nothing to worry about.

Before long the women felt more at ease and even began putting questions to the Czechs. Since none of the Germans spoke Czech, and Radek and Pepa spoke only broken German, the conversation was challenging, but everyone was curious. The young mother asked whether they had hidden in the barn from the beginning. The Czechs implied that they had hidden somewhere in the village. They didn't disclose their real hideaway, in case they needed to retreat to it again.

When the two women began to relax, they started talking about themselves. They told of the extremely difficult time during the war and under the Soviet occupation, and the Czechs saw that they had suffered. The women explained that a battlefront had passed through the area in 1945. They had hidden in the woods for days while the Russian troops came through. Many men had died in the war, and many were taken away by the Soviets, never to be seen again, including an older relative.

Radek and Pepa asked about the condensed milk they had discovered in the kitchen and the women told them that it was from West Berlin, from U.S. care packages. The younger woman told them she had gone to West Berlin several times and brought back food packages that the American and British aid organizations were giving away to the starving East German population. She also explained the mystery of the traffic in the yard: the old man ran a tailor shop and did work for the villagers and the Soviets at the base nearby.

After a while, a timid voice called up from downstairs. "Hello!" It was the young husband. "Can I come upstairs so my wife can take care of the baby?"

The friends assented. He climbed up to the hayloft and his wife climbed downstairs. The man was friendly and outgoing and explained the extent of the manhunt in animated detail.

"How did you ever manage to get into the village?" he asked, shaking his head in amazement. "The policemen who saw you were telling stories that you ran like Zatopek and that you shoot like Finnish sharpshooters!"*

All of them had to laugh at that one.

---

*Emil Zatopek won the five thousand meters, ten thousand meters, and marathon in the 1952 Olympic Games, setting an Olympic record in each event. The Finns dominated shooting events during the 1950s.

"Which one of you has dysentery?" he asked.

Radek laughed aloud again and commented to Pepa: "It seems the whole East German population knows about your shit, chief."

Unable to contain his curiosity, the young man asked, "What did you eat this whole time?"

"We have a confession to make," said Radek. "We have been helping you out with your supplies."

Everyone laughed at this and the old woman said, "That explains a lot of things! We did think the food was disappearing rather quickly. We noticed that one of the three apples just disappeared, and we had no explanation for it. We'd been wondering what had happened to it!"

"I need some shoes," Radek said. "Do you have an old pair you can give me?"

The farmer nodded. "Sure. I think we can get you something."

"We heard screaming when they shot off my shoe," said Radek. "What happened, do you know?"

The young man told the Czechs that either they or the police had shot a police major. Later, he brought Radek a pair of elastic-sided boots that was several sizes too small. Radek was able to put one of them on after cutting the back of the boot open. It was not an ideal solution—his whole heel was exposed—but it was definitely better than nothing.

"Why in the world did you take off your shoes when it was so cold?" the farmer asked. Radek couldn't explain because the word "squeaking" was not in his German vocabulary, so he pantomimed it and in a short time everybody was laughing again.

The husband also told them that the police had found Vasek in the woods the day after the breakthrough, at 11:00 AM, and had put him in the prison hospital. The man knew nothing about Zbynek. He said that a high-ranking StB officer had come from Czechoslovakia to take custody of them all once the Russians and East Germans caught them, adding that the boss of the East German armed forces, Karl Maron, was personally in charge of the manhunt.

Then he explained that the entire district was plastered with most-wanted posters showing pictures of the three Czechs and offering a reward for their capture. Every family in the district was required to have one at home. The young man showed them his. The friends got a big kick out of the mug shots, which showed Radek and Pepa glowering and unshaven. The family asked them when the pictures were taken. The brothers explained that their pictures were taken when they were jailed in Czechoslovakia, and asked if the young man would give them the poster as a souvenir. He refused, telling them that in case the police decided to check he had to keep his on hand.

They chatted on with increasing goodwill and bonhomie, curious and eager to learn more, but the friends never asked the family for their names or the name of the village. They didn't want to be in a position of knowing these things should they be caught.

The young wife returned to the hayloft early in the afternoon and announced that she had made potato pancakes for lunch. She asked the three friends if they wanted some. Enthusiastically they agreed and on her next trip to the hayloft she brought one potato pancake for each of them. The smell was heavenly, but though they felt like devouring them instantly, the Czechs refrained. Pepa and Radek politely insisted their hosts take the first bite. The request was put as a courtesy, but the real objective was to make sure that the food was not somehow tainted. Then the three Czechs quickly ate up. The meltingly delicious pancakes, made with plenty of fat and a crispy brown crust, were gone before the famished Czechs were able to properly savor them. When the young woman saw how hungry they were, she went back to the kitchen and made a modest-size bowl of potato salad for them. It was tasty, but they could hardly eat any because their stomachs had shrunken so badly.

By that time their young host was completely relaxed and conversing with them on the friendliest terms. Talk had moved on to the political situation, his problems, and the friends' as well. He began drawing a rough map for them and explained what kind of precautions the Communists were taking to stem the stream of refugees disappearing into the western sector of Berlin every day. He drew the autobahn, and then he sketched two railway lines that ran parallel to it: one to the west of the village, and the other to the east, beyond the autobahn.

"You've got to take this one," he said pointing at the western railway line. "The eastern one goes into the Russian sector of Berlin."

Pepa exchanged a glance with Radek. All along they'd been trying to cross the autobahn and reach the eastern railroad line! They would have missed the American sector entirely without the man's advice. All of them were convinced that nothing better could have happened to them than the encounter with this friendly family.

"Get on a northbound freight train and look for open railroad cars carrying potatoes," the young man was saying. "All of those go directly to Berlin. Don't even try to catch the train around here. There's still heavy patrol activity in the area. And the Vopos are guarding the railway lines. Even when you get further north you've still got to be very careful. I know about the situation around here, but I can't tell you what's happening up there." He destroyed the map when he was through with his explanation, and the friends commended him for his caution.

Then he made an offer that they had not expected at all. "I'll guide you out of the village," he said. "I'll show you the way past the Vopos to the railroad tracks."

As they talked, the three friends fieldstripped and cleaned their guns one at a time so that they were never completely defenseless. Radek found that the tiny gear spring on the right side of his 9-mm was slipping out of engagement and that the screw holding the two halves of the pistol grip together was stripped. He didn't know it at the time, but the pistol would never fire again. They were down to one reliably functioning weapon: Milan's.

Later that afternoon, the young man went out on his bicycle to do some reconnaissance. Upon his return, he explained that he had stopped by to see some friends of his who were Vopos, in order to find out more about the disposition of the troops. Most of the roads had been cleared. However, the Berliner Ring, the autobahn surrounding Berlin, and all roads converging on it were still occupied. The authorities believed the fugitives still had not reached Berlin.

The Czechs spent the rest of the day talking with their newfound friends. The German family's lives were not easy. A relative had been hauled off to a Russian prison camp—the friends thought it had something to do with the uprising of 17 June 1953—and to that day the family had no idea where he might be. Radek and Pepa told them about their own family and how their father had been executed by the Nazis. Everyone wholeheartedly agreed that people of all nationalities had to work together to oppose totalitarian regimes. But despite the developing closeness, the Czechs never let down their guard, still fearing betrayal.

As evening slowly fell outside the barn, they got ready to leave. The family gave them a loaf of bread to take along. Before the departure, they agreed on a special code, which the Czechs would arrange to broadcast on RIAS, Radio Free Europe, and Voice of America once they got to West Berlin. After promising their friends that under no circumstances would they ever disclose their help, they said their good-byes to the old couple, the younger couple, and the little baby. The young man offered again to walk them through the fields. This time the Czechs accepted.

The darkness was total. The moon wouldn't rise for a few hours more. Everything was quiet in the village as the young man set off to make sure the coast was clear. A short while later, the Czechs left the hayloft and joined him in the fields to the north. As they marched, he showed them the tracks left by tank treads and explained that tanks had been posted around woodlands to provide fire support to the infantry searching them.

"The police don't plan to take you alive," he said. "They plan to chase you down with tanks once the foot troops find you."

The rotating beacon from the nearby military airfield lit up the sky from time to time, and each time it swept over them they dropped down to the ground.

The time for taking leave was rapidly approaching. Radek, Pepa, and Milan debated, in Czech, what to do about their benefactor. They still carried their chloroform and ropes; should they really be as trusting as they were? They considered putting the young man to sleep, then discarded the idea. They believed the man to be genuine, and anyway, chloroforming him wouldn't prevent a betrayal. They decided to trust their instincts, even though such conduct went against the rules of military engagement.

When the group had arrived at the next stretch of woods, their guide didn't want to continue. He told them which way to go to avoid a nearby Russian airfield.

"Danke schön!" said Pepa. "Vielen, vielen dank!" The thanks was heartfelt. Each in turn shook hands with the young German.

"Good luck," their benefactor said with feeling. Then he turned around and vanished into the darkness.

Chapter 30

POTATO TRANSPORT

The three Czechs continued plodding north. Every couple of minutes the airfield beacon swept the open fields and they dove to the ground. It dogged them for miles. Then they were overcome by terrible nausea. Their bowels started cramping ferociously. Their limbs felt weak and heavy at the same time. One potato pancake and a few spoonfuls of potato salad apiece! That was all it took to wipe them out after three weeks without a square meal.

Fortunately, their old friend the North Star was shining down on them and accompanied them into the woods, where it winked at them through the trees' bare branches. All too soon, though, it disappeared behind a thick bank of clouds and did not reappear.

Slowly they trudged on, trying to orient themselves by the sound of the trains that occasionally passed in the distance. The noise was faint and echoed among the trees, seeming to come first from one side, then from another. Before long they were thoroughly confused.

Splashing through a small stream, they came to a meadow and a cluster of haystacks. Although it was well before midnight, they were exhausted and decided to call it quits for the night. They would burrow inside the hay. But when a dog started barking on a nearby farm they became alarmed and decided to press on.

They followed the edge of the woods as it fell back from the stream until they came to a sandy road. The loose sand smothered the sound of their footsteps. Absorbed in their misery, they didn't notice the bicyclist who approached them rapidly from behind.

Milan saw him, but not until the cyclist was already sixty feet away. "Cover!" he hissed. They quickly stumbled into the woods and hit the ground. Had the guy seen anyone? He came abreast of them, puffing and panting as he struggled to propel his bicycle along the sandy path, seemingly intent on his own progress, then passed on and was swallowed up by the darkness.

"Hey, chief, you were last in line!" Pepa said. "Sleeping on the job, idiot!"

"You try to hear tires in the sand," Milan snapped back.

"Screw it. Just pay attention and make sure nobody sneaks up on us like that again."

A few isolated farmhouses, quiet and dark, emerged in the broad expanse of sandy fields crisscrossed by drainage ditches. Enviously Pepa thought of the people inside, snug in their warm beds with supper in their bellies.

They entered another leafless forest where ghostlike trees stood in total stillness. A fine, noiseless drizzle was falling, soaking the walkers and the thick layer of dead leaves that squelched underfoot as they advanced. Their feet were encased in great clumps of mud. They tripped over deep ruts made by logging trucks. Every once in a while a train rushed by, its sound ricocheting off the trees in a disembodied, disorienting way.

Finally the woods ahead started to thin. They halted at the edge. Before them lay a deep ditch full of water. They jumped over it and continued across the fog-enshrouded meadow at a low crouch. Soon Pepa and Radek were arguing fiercely about where north lay. They bickered, then started punching and kicking each other. Milan tried to mediate.

"Forget about it," he pleaded. "We made it this far and if somebody hears you, we're all screwed!"

A small farmhouse had emerged from the fog. Without warning, its front door swung open, framing a human silhouette in light. A dog catapulted past, barking furiously. Instantly the fighting stopped. The three Czechs froze, hoping to blend into the shadows of the trees. The dog's chain rattled and the animal jerked to an abrupt stop. It bayed viciously, rushing the fence as if it meant to break it down.

"Komm, Hasso! Komm zurück! Das ist nichts." (Hasso, come back! That's nothing!) the man's voice called. Much to the Czechs' relief, the dog retreated into the house and the man closed the door again. Recovering from their fright, the trio moved on in silence at maximum alert.

After reaching the far side of the meadow, they entered a coniferous forest and then passed a small pond and a cluster of dwellings. Before them, in a shallow cut, lay a band of gravel and two thin rails of steel. The railway line! Fir trees came to within thirty feet of the track on both sides. They dropped on all fours and crawled along the edge of the woods till they reached the last of the trees. Then they sat down and rested, their backs against the trunks.

It seemed to Pepa that hours went by. No train appeared, so they picked themselves up again and trudged on. They were numbly plodding along beside the tracks when two human shapes materialized out of the darkness before them. The Czechs fell to the ground and lay motionless as the shadowy figures drew near, now no more than a stone's throw away, feet crunching on gravel, butts of StG44 submachine guns clanking dully against buttons on their uniforms. An armed Vopo patrol—already the third close call! The two troopers passed on wordlessly and receded into the distance.

It took Pepa a while to come down from the adrenaline rush. When the Czechs finally dared to pick themselves up off the ground, they furiously chastised each other for their growing carelessness. Exhaustion was wearing them down. Their alertness was slipping. Vowing to redouble their vigilance, they headed into the protective shadow of the trees, despite the dense, wet brush that soaked their clothes and impeded their progress. They would shadow the tracks at a distance.

They neared a small village, its diminutive railway station deserted and all the houses dark except for an inn just behind the station. A military truck stood in front of the building. The driver was behind the steering wheel, but the rest of the crew appeared to be inside, where a dance band was playing lively music. Lots of people were milling around. Behind the inn was a large, dark barn. It was still early and they had covered little ground that night, but they were dizzy with exhaustion. The next village might be far away. They had to rest.

Pepa went ahead to recon, while the other two spread out to cover him.

"It's the perfect makeout place!" he announced on his return. "Hey, Milan—that band could use a good drummer."

"Casanova!"

"You're in no shape to check out the chicks tonight," Radek said.

"You're right. We'll have to wait till Berlin," Pepa said wistfully. "I need new threads anyway. I don't cut the right figure in this getup."

They laughed in spite of themselves. It was the understatement of the week. The usually stylishly attired Pepa really did look awful. His hair was matted, his clothes were soiled and smelly, and his face was covered with three weeks' stubble.

Weapons in hand, they sneaked into the barn and began to feel their way through the pitch-black interior. It seemed to be half-empty. On the right side, hay was piled almost to the roof in a steep, almost vertical stack. Over in the empty half of the barn one of the friends ran into a heavy ladder.

Radek volunteered to climb up.

"Don't fall, you idiot!" Pepa hissed. "Watch out!" Pepa kept up a steady stream of good advice to Radek as he ascended. When the ladder finally ended more than twenty-five feet above the ground, Radek discovered that he was on a plank loft. The boards were loose, few and far between, and flexed disturbingly as he moved over them. Pepa was still dispensing advice and instructions when Radek arrived on top of the haystack.

"It's okay. Come on up!" his voice floated back down.

Pepa and Milan followed him up the ladder and across the catwalk. When they reunited on the haystack after their hair-raising experience, they felt very safe; certainly no one would dare come up into their hideaway at night!

Each man dug a burrow in the hay and crawled inside, reveling in the sweet scent and springy softness of the hay. But their happiness was short-lived.

"I've got cramps," Pepa announced. "I've got to take a crap."

The others heard him rustling about in the hay. Not long afterward, a terrible stench assaulted their nostrils.

"Christ almighty," Milan swore. "Do something about that god-awful smell!"

Pepa got out of his hole again and scrabbled about in the hay for a while.

"Sorry, it's too dark," his voice came back apologetically. "Can't find it!"

"Try harder, you dumbass," his brother shot back.

When Pepa finally gave up, the three friends attended to the serious matter of the bread. They sat in a circle in the dark. The loaf lay invitingly in the middle.

"We could lose it, you know."

"That would be a terrible waste."

"There's no telling what'll happen tomorrow."

"Besides, if we run into trouble, they'll ask us where we got it."

They sat in silence. The mouthwatering scent of the bread tempted them.

"We've lasted without food for twenty-eight days. It really doesn't matter if we eat tomorrow or the day after." The vote was unanimous. They polished off the entire loaf.

Shivering and soaked to the bone, they stripped off all their clothes and spread them out on top of the hay. Pepa even pulled off his shoes, which, the others pointed out, was very risky—once they were off it was impossible to get them back on over wet socks and swollen feet. He stuffed his shoes with hay to help them dry out and announced that he had them in a safe place in a special cavity inside his hole.

They buried their noses in the hay and tried to get some sleep. Music from the inn drifted up along with shouts of laughter. Every time the door opened, warm light and the sound of clattering beer mugs surged outside. The three men listened wistfully. On a few occasions, drunks staggered out and took a piss against the side of the barn before heading back inside.

After a while a boy and girl came in and made love in the hay below. The Czechs kept quiet, listening to the noises.

"Your smelly shit might have its uses after all," Radek observed wryly. But the amorous couple below them didn't seem to notice.

30 October dawned hazy and cold. Several children played briefly in the barn. A middle-aged man worked downstairs and left after about twenty minutes. Otherwise everything was quiet. In the evening, as soon as darkness had settled in and all was still, Radek and Milan were dressed and ready to head out.

But Pepa was still frantically hunting around in the hay for his shoes. When at last he found them and tried to put them on, the leather had shrunk and he couldn't get his feet inside. He tried to walk without them, one foot in a sock, the other barefoot, but the ground was too cold. So he tried putting them on again, this time without the sock, and succeeded. He tied his one soaked sock around his neck and hobbled after the others, the wet, stiff leather rubbing painfully against his swollen feet.

Outside, a thin, icy wind was blowing and they shivered in their light suits, buttoning their collars as high as they would go. After struggling up a hill they were overcome by leaden exhaustion, and they decided to catch a train behind the village. A road cut through the hill. All they had to do was cross it and the railroad tracks beckoned on the far side. They slid down the rain-soaked, grassy embankment. As Pepa reached the bottom he heard a sound that filled him with dread: rapidly approaching car engines. Two military vehicles burst around the bend, headlights bearing down on the Czechs as they hobbled across the road and scrambled up the opposite embankment.

The cars roared past, then abruptly halted. The trio dropped to the ground and waited, shivering and tense. Had they been spotted? The car engines idled, but nobody got out. Just as suddenly, both vehicles roared off to the station. The Czechs watched several uniformed men get out and talk for a while before disappearing into the terminal. They quickly scuttled their idea—hitching a ride on the train from this place might not be such a good idea after all.

They shuffled on through the fields. The shrunken shoes were pinching Pepa's feet, and he could feel blisters forming on his heel and along the sides. Radek, wearing the rubber boot the German family had given him, was rapidly becoming footsore as well. His toes, half frozen, no longer had any feeling in them.

A straight drizzle fell softly and steadily, veiling the fields, trees, and houses in the distance. They passed another sleeping village and waded through a field grown high with beets. By now they were too spent to speed up, even when crossing open fields where they were completely exposed. The ground was rising, and the gentle grade was sapping them of their last remaining strength. As they passed through a cabbage field they harvested a few heads, which they ate as they slogged on through the mud.

From atop the ridge, they spotted the railroad tracks running through a shallow valley. Several hundred yards away a semaphore was glowing red.

"Look! A train!"

A northbound train was approaching, pulling mostly open freight cars. Just as the young husband had said, they were filled with potatoes. The men broke into a run, their numbed legs giving out repeatedly on the uneven ground. The train was slowing and finally came to a stop before the semaphore, where the locomotive snorted and puffed impatiently. A brakeman's lamp bobbed alongside the freight cars. Anxiously they tracked his progress.

Then the semaphore changed to green. Too soon! The train started to move, slowly at first. Giving it their all, the three stragglers stumbled after it. It could be hours until the next train stopped. The icy air burned their throats and lungs. They willed their wasted muscles on, but the train was gathering speed and began pulling away. Milan lunged forward and grabbed onto the second-to-last car. Hoisting himself aboard, he reached back toward Radek and Pepa, who were desperately trying to grab hold of the side of the car, falling back as they ran with outstretched arms.

"Come on! I've got you!"

Hanging on to the metal rungs that went up the side of the car, he seized Pepa by the arm and dragged him aboard, feet kicking and scrambling for traction. Then he grasped Radek's hand and, with Pepa's help, hauled him onto the ledge. It had been a close call, but they were all aboard. Now the train was picking up speed and the cold wind was whipping their hair and thin, rain-drenched shirts, punishing their emaciated bodies.

Their frozen fingers could scarcely grip the cold metal sides as they scrambled up, clumsily feeling for the rungs with their numbed feet. Drained of strength, they fell over the rim onto a full load of potatoes. The brakeman was a mere two cars ahead of them, his booth protruding above the rims of all the open freight cars. From that vantage point he had a good view of the whole length of the train. They flattened themselves down on the potatoes and stared at the booth, afraid the man had seen them. When nothing happened, they started digging into the frozen potatoes with their bare hands. It was a Sisyphean task: the cold potatoes kept rolling back. In no time they had lost all feeling in their fingers and couldn't even move their wrists. They started pushing potatoes aside with their feet.

When the train arrived at the next railway station the three Czechs were still completely exposed. Almost all the larger railway stations in Europe had a glassed-in signal tower extending over the tracks. This station had such a tower—and it was occupied. The whole staging area was brightly illuminated. They lay motionless against the side of the car, buried their faces and hands in potatoes, and prayed that no one would spot them. As the train slowly trundled under the tower they waited, with a sinking sense of inevitability, to be picked up at the station. But the train didn't stop. Nor did it stop at several other stations up the line. The appearance of each one triggered a frantic burst of digging from the Czechs.

Then the potato transport arrived in a larger station and came to a halt. The three were still only half-buried in potatoes. Once again the whole facility was illuminated by bright lights glowing through the drizzle. Silently Pepa cursed the lights. Then the reshuffling of the railroad cars began. Back and forth rolled the train, directly under the switch tower. Three men were leaning out its open windows, watching. Three times Radek, Milan, and

Pepa passed under the tower, expecting to hear the alarm at any moment. When the reshuffling was finished, a few railcars had been added and the train chuffed out of the station. It seemed impossible—almost miraculous—that nobody had seen them.

As the train picked up speed, the icy wind whipped all feeling out of Pepa's body. Now he could hardly move his limbs. His teeth even stopped chattering.

"I bet this is how the concentration camp inmates felt when the Nazis moved them out of Auschwitz in the winter of '44," Radek yelled over the noise of the train.

"Can't you think of something more uplifting?" Pepa shouted.

The train squealed to a stop in yet another station, a few cars were added, and it was shunted into a siding between a tall building and what appeared to be a warehouse. People walked around, talking. The waiting seemed endless. Gradually the noise subsided and a slight jerk startled them.

Milan looked over the edge of their car: "The engine's disengaging! It's pulling away!"

The others cursed. Time passed. There was no sign of the engine's return.

"It looks like we're stuck here!" whispered Pepa. "Let's get off."

Radek and Milan nodded. But when they looked down they saw a sentry in a black uniform pacing around the train.

The minutes crawled by. The guard patrolled.

Suddenly a passenger train roared by, heading north. The friends stared after it longingly, envying the nameless people in the lit windows who were sitting inside warm cars, going to Berlin. They would arrive at their destination within half an hour. Pepa didn't know if he and his companions would ever arrive. Longingly he watched the red taillight of the last car disappear in the distance.

All of a sudden he felt a slight jolt. Risking a look above the rim of the car, to the front of the train, Pepa sighed with relief. They had an engine once more. After a while it lurched forward, and they were off again, chugging out of the station.

The signs at the next station said "Zeiblitz." When their train squealed to a halt, the sound of many voices drifted up from the platform below. A lot of people seemed to be moving about. Cautiously, the fugitives peered over the edge of their potato car. On the track next to theirs stood a halted train: several passenger cars and a long line of flat cars loaded with trucks and jeeps. Uniformed soldiers carrying StG44 submachine guns milled about on the platform just feet away from where they lay. Others stood about on the flat cars or sat in the cabs of vehicles. The officers had pistols. Quickly the Czechs ducked down again and pressed their bodies flat.

"Jesus, Mary and Joseph!" Milan whispered. "It's a troop transport!"

From the troops' conversation, Pepa gathered that these men were demobilizing from the manhunt. The Czechs lay motionless in their potatoes, the Vopos walking around just a few feet away from them, while the brakeman passed by at a leisurely pace, tapping the wheels to check for cracks.

"This is taking forever," Radek said under his breath. "I bet they're planning to park the train here." The clock on the platform read 2:30 AM. They had been stopped next to the troop train for hours.

"They've got to move us soon," replied Pepa, hopefully.

"I've got cramps. I have to take a crap!" Milan complained.

"Hold it!" Radek suggested.

"No. I can't."

Milan looked as if he really was in misery.

"All right, then. Let's go for it!"

They would get off here and continue on foot. They waited until some of the troops disappeared behind the trucks on the flat cars and then Milan rolled over the side of the car, while Radek and Pepa lay low, eyes on the guards on the other side of the train. They heard a dull thud as Milan hit the ground. None of the guards appeared to have noticed. A fraction of a second later, Radek and Pepa went over the side. They landed beside Milan almost simultaneously. Milan was already squatting with his pants down.

"Hey, chief. Get those pants down before you hit the ground?" Pepa teased.

Milan made a face.

The three of them were in the deep shadow cast by the train, but they could see no way to get across the brightly illuminated rail yard.

"It's at least a hundred yards to the fence," said Pepa.

"Those Vopos can see the whole yard!" Radek remarked. "This is a nonstarter."

"Let's just get back on," said Milan. "They're bound to bring the engine back sometime!"

"The farmer said that all the potatoes go to Berlin," Pepa reminded them. That comforted them a little.

They climbed back aboard to continue their wait.

Eventually, a locomotive shunted to the back of the train, and voices and footsteps traveled back and forth alongside. Suddenly, several cars, including theirs, lurched backward. The train started moving. Back, back it went, the way they had come.

Pepa looked at his friends in alarm.

"Please God, not again," Milan groaned.

But Pepa had to believe that the potatoes were going to Berlin. "Don't worry, the potatoes are going to Berlin!" he said with conviction.

Slowly the train continued chugging away from the station. It turned off the main track and picked up speed, the locomotive spewing steam into the cold night air. It was now going too fast for the Czechs to risk jumping off. After a while, they passed through a gate into a large, dark compound and came to a stop. Workmen disengaged the engine. When it had chugged away, the place was wrapped in silence. Peering over the edge of the car, they saw they were in another wide-open space, covered with a branching network of gray railroad spurs and dully gleaming tracks. Several buildings loomed behind the tracks. And a perimeter fence. The place appeared to be a distillery of some kind, shut down for the night.

They jumped to the ground. Stepping over the tracks at a leisurely pace, they tried to look like laborers as they headed toward the fence. Pepa pulled up the lowest strand of barbed wire for Milan. Just as he ducked under it the wire slipped out of Pepa's hand and tore Milan's pants.

Milan was furious. "You jerk, how could you do that! Now I won't have a decent suit to put on after we get to West Berlin."

They marched north between the railroad and the highway. Milan was still upset about his ruined suit. It was near sunrise on 1 November, and a cold gray dawn was creeping up from the horizon. Lights started coming on behind thick curtains. In one house an alarm clock shrilled just as they walked by. They started checking doors on barns and service buildings. But in this suburban residential area such hideaways were few and far between, and all were locked.

Finally, just as they were beginning to get really worried, they found a house with a little detached barn and a hayloft upstairs. They climbed up and moved the ladder back to its original position. The hayloft, which had an icy brick floor, was almost empty, with barely enough straw to cover them when they lay down. They were trembling with cold and sleep was impossible.

Not long afterward, they heard the door in the house close. A man's voice called "Tschüss" (Bye). Footsteps moved off and died away. After the man's departure, the house fell silent again and the lights in the windows went out. All day long Pepa shivered in the drafty loft, counting the minutes until evening when they could continue their journey.

At last, when they were sure that the people in the house had settled down for the night, they opened the door and clumsily clambered down the ladder, achy and stiff from lying on the cold brick floor all day. Pepa's feet had developed large and painful blisters and Radek had lost all feeling in some of his toes. Light spilled out around the edges of the drawn curtains and they could hear the sounds of a cozy family supper: cutlery clinking against plates and quiet conversation. For the three Czechs this would be another hungry night. Like fleeting ghosts, they faded into the darkness.

Chapter 31

THE RING AROUND BERLIN

"Zossen," the sign announced. The name told them nothing. "You think we're near Berlin?" Milan asked hopefully as they marched past.

"Hell if I know," Pepa shrugged.

"These look like suburbs anyway—no barns," Radek remarked. "The houses are close together."

"We should clear off the road," Milan commented worriedly. There were plenty of pedestrians about.

"How're we going to do that?" Radek said. "This place is all villas and garden fences." They were all tired and in no mood to climb fences.

"We'll be okay—there aren't any streetlights," Pepa said reassuringly.

They walked on in silence, pedestrians passing them in both directions as the merciful darkness hid their tattered forms. The next obstacle was a bridge and here they stopped, stuck.

"Just our luck! This bridge has the only streetlight in the whole damn district!" Milan fretted in a low voice.

"Well, we've got to cross it if we're going to keep heading north," Radek said.

"What about those two?" Milan countered, pointing at a boy and girl who were standing on the bridge with their motorcycle, kissing passionately. The lovers had eyes only for each other and no other pedestrians were about for the moment. There would be no better opportunity.

"Let's go!" Radek said in a low voice. The couple didn't heed the three scruffy figures hurrying across the bridge behind their backs.

Another road sign materialized out of the darkness. "Berlin 35 km,"* it read. So this wasn't the city yet. They pressed on with all possible speed.

"Where are all the Vopos hiding?" Pepa finally commented. They hadn't seen any sign of troops in miles.

"I had no idea you were so sentimental, chief!"

"Well, doesn't it seem strange to you?"

Just then a car passed. Several hundred yards ahead its red brake lights lit up and it came to a stop. Blue lights bobbed around the car.

"Are those really lights up there or am I seeing things?" Pepa whispered.

"Nope, you're not—and it doesn't look good."

They kept going, at a slightly slower pace. More cars approached the lights ahead and all of them halted. They heard voices. It was a police road-block, no question about it. Quickly the Czechs left the road, cutting across a meadow. The railroad tracks had to pass under the Berliner Ring somewhere up ahead.

Exhausted and footsore, they took a break next to some woods. The terrain ahead sloped down to the railroad track. Beyond it loomed a big factory, brightly lit with rows of lights. Short passenger trains sped by in both directions at brief intervals. Commuter trains, Pepa figured.

After descending to the track they trudged along the small service path beside it and soon entered a black mass of woods. A slope appeared ahead of them in the darkness, towering above the track like a perpendicular earthen wall. Coming closer, they saw that it was an overpass.

"Hey guys, you think this is the Berliner Ring?"

"I don't know. Could be, though."

"Well, I'll go check it out!" Pepa volunteered.

Radek and Milan continued slowly under the bridge as he laboriously climbed up the steep embankment. At the top he found himself on the edge of a four-lane highway that stretched in both directions, quiet and empty.

Radek and Milan were underneath the bridge span, marveling at its vastness.

"This is enormous!" Radek exclaimed.

"I never saw anything like it before," Milan said, awed. "I'll bet this is the Berliner Ring."

---

*Approximately twenty-two miles

"Yeah, it's got to be. Or maybe one of the autobahns going to it."

They emerged on the far side of the underpass and noticed a small wooden shack off to the right, in the black shadow of the tall trees.

"What do you think that shed's for?" asked Milan.

"Maybe one of those road works department deals. Like we saw back on the other roads."

"Naaah. This one's in lousy shape. It could—"

A soft noise surprised them. Something stirred and a black apparition got up from the ground.

"Wer da?" (Who's there?) a man's voice demanded.

"Wir!" (We are!) answered Radek, without missing a beat or breaking stride. He pulled the pistol from his pocket and pointed it at the man.

"Who?" the voice asked again. The man shone a strong flashlight right into Radek's eyes. "Hands up!"

Radek, blinded by the light, kept right on walking. He squeezed the trigger, but nothing happened. Grabbing the pistol with both hands, he used all the strength he could muster, but the blasted spring had disengaged again! There was only one way out—he had to bluff, keep moving forward, keep pointing his useless weapon.

"What are you saying? Hands up? *You* put your hands up!" Radek thundered.

He expected the man to fire at any moment. Instead, he dropped his flashlight and fell to his knees.

"Please don't shoot! Don't shoot me!" he begged, and began crying.

It was a Vopo, clad in a black rain poncho. Milan and Radek pounced on the man and jerked him to his feet. Milan seized his left hand and Radek groped for his right hand and the weapon under the voluminous poncho.

At that point Pepa reappeared. "Nobody's up there," he announced. "It's the autobahn."

"Well, we've got one over here," Milan replied.

"Let's chloroform him! Tie him up!"

The man shook with fear as Radek reached into his pocket for the rope and the chloroform.

Hurried steps echoed loudly from the bridge and two figures appeared at the railing.

"Was ist los?" (What's the matter?) one of them shouted down.

The prisoner didn't make a sound. A fraction of a second later, a deafening explosion erupted in their midst and Milan felt a powerful blow to

his left side. He let go of the Vopo and ran toward the woods. The two men
on the bridge fired a flare. Radek and Pepa released the Vopo and raced
away, hard on Milan's heels. The flare climbed up, up and exploded, illuminating the whole area in a burst of stark white light. Behind them, the
Vopo was firing his pistol and yelling like a madman, "Here they are! Here
they are!"

Within a few seconds men and machines were pouring out onto the
bridge from hiding places along the edge of the autobahn. Voices shouted.
Car engines revved. Staccato bursts of submachine-gun fire ripped into the
night and exploding flares threw their phosphorescent light deep into the
woods. The fugitives ran, driven on by an explosion of adrenaline, tripping
over creepers and roots as they rushed headlong into the dark.

"Anyone hit?" Pepa yelled.

"I think they got me," gasped Milan between breaths.

The news shook Pepa and Radek, but they kept running, albeit more
slowly, matching their pace to Milan's. Behind them, all hell was breaking
loose. Several hundred feet into the woods and out of the immediate danger
area they halted.

"Where?" Radek asked. Milan's chest was heaving, sucking in air.

"Here, in my stomach."

Milan grabbed Radek's hand and put it on his wound. Radek's thumb
slid in easily, all the way up to the second joint. When he pulled his finger
out again it glistened black with blood.

"Can you go on?" Radek ventured.

"Yes," Milan replied with a firm voice. "The wound is numb. I don't
feel anything."

Flares were exploding along the entire length of the Berliner Ring.
Truck engines growled and dozens of pairs of vehicle headlights were on the
move, visible through the trees. Radek and Pepa took off again, running by
Milan's side on the dirt service path parallel to the railroad track. Minutes
later, they heard a gurgling noise from Milan's stomach. Every time he took
a step, there was that sickening, gurgling sound. Blood was beginning to collect in his abdomen.

"You're lucky that you were on a diet!" Radek teased.

"Stomach wounds are never too bad if the stomach is empty," Pepa
said with authority. "You'll be fine, you'll see!" Radek and Pepa urged their
wounded buddy on.

"I don't feel too bad," said Milan.

But all of them knew that it was a question of minutes before shock set in.

Another train rushed past them, then came to a stop at the next station. Milan was beginning to slow down.

"I don't think I can go on. Leave me here, guys." And then he added, "I knew it was my turn this time."

"Come on, chief!" Pepa urged him.

"No, I can't go on. I'll just hide in those greenhouses."

On the other side of the tracks stood row upon row of large, low greenhouses.

"Nonsense!" scoffed Pepa. "That's the first place the Vopos will look." He knew that Milan would be dead before the Vopos even found him. "You can't quit here—we're almost in Berlin!"

So Radek and Pepa started to goad him on, calling him a chicken and an idiot if he wouldn't at least try to hack those last few miles. Then another train roared by and came to a halt about six hundred yards ahead. Radek and Pepa grabbed Milan and tried to drag him along to catch up with the train, but they were beyond exhaustion themselves. They urged him on, teasing and cajoling him. Milan felt a big knot building up in his stomach, jumping up and down inside him with every step he took. He was nauseated and weak.

Through the trees they saw columns of trucks and other military vehicles pouring north on both sides, rushing to cut them off. White illuminating flares and occasional red and green signal flares exploded in profusion, behind them, to their left and to their right. The convoys were outpacing them, that much was clear as the friends observed the advancing procession of headlights and the steady northward march of the exploding flares. Just like that terrible night when they'd lost Vasek! Radek and Pepa kept up a stream of encouragement to Milan.

"Keep going, buddy! Another few steps!"

"At least to the next station!"

"You can do it, chief. Don't quit now!"

A railroad station materialized in the darkness ahead. It was a simple affair, consisting of a raised embankment on one side of the track and a sign that read "Dahlewitz." Two people stood on the embankment, awaiting the next train. The friends cautiously crept closer inside a concrete-lined service ditch, taking care not to step on the cable wires and signal pulleys.

Another northbound commuter train roared past them and into the station, brakes squealing as it pulled to a stop. The last car, its red taillight glowing, halted about ten yards ahead of the huddled Czechs.

"Get underneath the train and lie on the brake bars!" Radek hissed.

"I can't bend over!" Milan protested.

Doors slammed. A few people got off the train and the two people on the platform got on. A whistle shrilled, the diesel engine began revving up: the train was departing. They had to decide—fast. This was their last chance to slip the jaws of the trap that was once again slamming shut on them.

Quickly the three friends jumped across the signal wires and made a mad dash toward the last car. Pepa and Milan clambered onto the bumpers while Radek crawled underneath the car, folding his body into the cramped space between the two wheels. He lay almost doubled over on the brake rods, his head next to one of the wheels and his feet touching the other. His elbows almost grazed the railroad ties below. In spite of the discomfort, he thought it was a pretty good hiding place.

"Get down here, you guys!" he urged Milan and Pepa.

"Get out of there, you idiot!" Pepa called back. "You're going to get hit by a flying rock!"

Pepa and Milan stayed put on the bumpers, Pepa straddling the left bumper and supporting Milan's sagging body on the right bumper with one hand.

Soon the train lurched forward and pulled away from the station, quickly gathering speed. This diesel-powered commuter train traveled much faster than the poky freight train they had been on before, and the friends were elated by the high speed at which they were moving. All around, as far as they could see, flares of all colors were blossoming in the sky. A few hundred yards past the station, the train clattered across a road. The crossing guards were down and a long convoy of military trucks and other vehicles were waiting, engines running.

"Did you see that?" screamed Pepa over the wind. "We just snuck out before they slammed the lid on us!"

Milan nodded. "God, that was close!"

Their spirits soared as the train roared northward, carrying them toward Berlin and safety.

"We won that last round, buddy!" exulted Pepa. "How are you holding up, Milan?"

"Everything's okay. The wound's crusting up."

Underneath the train, Radek clung to the brake rods. The railroad ties zipped by just a fraction of an inch below his knees and elbows. It was dizzying to look at. The slightest movement could knock him right off the brake rods and under the rushing wheels. Every time the brakes tightened or loosened a little, the rods came together and spread, and he had to redouble his effort to stay in equilibrium. The wheels roared and thundered by his feet and head. It was deafening and he couldn't hear a word of what Milan and Pepa were saying on the bumpers.

The train stopped briefly at the next station, pausing a minute at the most before rolling on. From his vantage point at the rear of the train, Pepa could see that the truck convoys in the distance were moving rapidly, easily keeping abreast of the moving train. The train roared through the next station, which was dark, without stopping. He leaned out into the rushing wind to get a good look up ahead. The icy wind hit his face full blast, rushing in his ears and whipping through his hair. They were approaching another brightly lit railroad station, the platform crowded with people. The sign on the station building read "Mahlow." The brakes screeched and the train began slowing down.

"Let's hope he doesn't stop too far down the platform," Pepa shouted in Milan's ear. Then he peered around the corner again and in that instant any remaining euphoria vanished. The platform was crawling with Russian troops and Vopos. Though he and Milan were sitting in the dark wake of the train, they were still clearly visible to anyone who took a closer look.

"They're waiting for us already!" he yelled to Milan.

The brakes released momentarily and the train coasted toward the platform. Volkspolizei and Soviet soldiers stood shoulder to shoulder, armed with submachine guns and pistols, and as the last car coasted past them, they started running after the train. So far none of them had noticed the two figures sitting motionlessly on the rear bumpers in the dark. Pepa leaned back as far as he could, trying to disappear into the darkness behind the last car. As the train squealed to a halt, doors on the right-hand side of the train, where there was no platform, banged open. Local residents were taking a shortcut home.

Chapter 32

HOME STRETCH FIASCO

"Jump down!" hollered Pepa. He and Milan scrambled off the bumpers and set off at a quick walk, away from the train and the lighted platform, stepping over the tracks as they went.

"Should we run?" Pepa asked.

"Better not," Milan replied.

Suddenly a Vopo jumped off the platform and began trailing them. "Where are you going?" he called out.

"Home!" Milan answered in German.

Pepa and Milan continued walking casually, trying to look as if they were commuters heading home. The Vopo yelled, "Halt!" Pepa and Milan broke into a run, acutely aware that the railroad yard was a wide-open space with no cover. More policemen and Russian soldiers were jumping off the platform and running after them.

"Stehen bleiben! Hände hoch! Stehen bleiben, oder wir schießen!" (Stop! Hands up! Stop, or we shoot!)

Pepa and Milan didn't stop. A submachine gun stuttered, then another, then they heard the pop-pop-pop of rifles and pistols and bullets were whistling around them. Fifty yards ahead, some people who had stripped down to their shirts were unloading potatoes from two freight cars into a Studebaker truck. Behind the truck stood a fence and some low-slung military barracks.

"You can do it, keep going!" Pepa urged his wounded friend.

They ran along the fence, toward the freight cars.

Suddenly Milan gasped, "I think I got hit again."

"Where?"

"In my finger. Christ!"

"Look, it's nothing. It doesn't count. Just keep going!"

"Shit, that sucker hurts bad."

"Hey, chief, come on, just keep going. You're doing great!" Pepa kept up a steady stream of encouragement. They were drawing near the Studebaker when Pepa got a better look at the men shoveling potatoes.

"Holy shit!" he gasped. They were Russian soldiers.

Incredibly, the soldiers kept shoveling, completely ignoring the two tattered figures rushing pell-mell toward them with the shooting Vopos and Red Army soldiers in hot pursuit.

With another jolt, Pepa realized that there was a man standing at the gate they were about to pass. A Russian sentry! He wore a calf-length overcoat and full uniform and stood frozen at attention, holding his submachine gun across his chest. To Pepa's total amazement, the Russian kept staring straight ahead as they ran by six feet in front of him, the troops close behind.

Milan was slowing down markedly.

"Jump over the fence!" Pepa hollered.

Pepa gave Milan a leg up over the chain link fence and then clambered over after him. They dropped down inside the Soviet military compound. The Russians next to the truck looked at them impassively and kept shoveling potatoes at their leisurely pace. As the two Czechs disappeared behind the vine-covered fence, the shooting died off. They jogged past two or three wooden buildings and came to a fence on the other side of the compound. Pepa pushed and pulled Milan over it, and they found themselves in a neighborhood of single-family homes.

As they ran along a blacktop road, Pepa slowed his pace to match Milan's. Close to the next intersection they heard the rumbling of innumerable truck engines. A hundred yards down the road a long line of headlights was approaching and soldiers were jumping out of the moving trucks.

A bell began clanging and the crossing guards descended, bringing the convoy to a halt at the railroad tracks. Troops piled out and milled about, trying to force the barrier up. The seconds ticked by. Pepa and Milan waited tensely in the shadows. At Mahlow station the shooting had finally stopped, but flares were going up as far back as the Berliner Ring.

A whistle wailed and the train thundered by in a rush of wind, blacking out the headlights of the waiting convoy with its bulk. Pepa and Milan hurried across the road. To their right, a second line of headlights had appeared, driving north.

The crossing guards clanged up. Engines revved and the convoy rumbled across the railroad tracks, troops jumping out at regular intervals. In a matter of moments, Mahlow station would be boxed in.

"So they got Radek!" Milan said. Both of them felt hollow inside.

Clutching his stomach, Milan dropped from a jog into a walk.

"I can't run anymore," he gasped.

"Does it hurt?" asked Pepa.

"No, no. It's the blood in my stomach. I can't run anymore. I feel dizzy. My vision is blurring."

Milan was staggering and the heavy pistol was clearly too much for him. Pepa took Milan's gun and stuck it in his other pocket.

"How far do you think it is to Berlin?" Milan was panting.

"I don't know. But it can't be more than two miles. You've got to keep going, chief!"

They continued at a walk, stopping every few steps when it looked like Milan couldn't go on. To their right, convoy after convoy rumbled past them on the northbound highway. Illumination and signal flares exploded at short intervals all along it, to their left and to the rear. Pepa peered ahead for signs of activity. In front of them lay an obstinate, opaque darkness. He couldn't even see the glow of the city lights in the sky ahead, and this seriously alarmed him. They were about to be cut off, and there was no trace of Berlin anywhere.

After a while a pine wood appeared on their right. In the ragged phosphorescent glare of the flares, Pepa started. A tall shadow was crawling across the bushes—was that a Vopo behind the tree? In a flash, Pepa dropped to the ground. He whipped up his gun and took aim. No—it was only a shadow. Relaxing, he glanced back and saw Milan lying on the ground, too. Painfully they got to their feet and moved on.

They were slowly moving across a wide open field.

"I can't go on," Milan croaked.

Encouraging speeches were useless now, Pepa realized. He could hardly walk himself, let alone run, but nevertheless he grabbed Milan around the waist and slung his arm over his shoulder. Slowly he staggered northward, half-dragging his friend. Again a descending flare nearby sent weird shadows flickering across the bushes. Another human silhouette? Pepa let go of Milan and hit the ground. For a tense minute Pepa waited, finger on his trigger. No—another false alarm. He picked himself up and pulled Milan, who had collapsed, to his feet. He slung Milan's arm over his shoulders once more and struggled onward, gasping for breath. Milan was groaning now, and mostly incoherent. Pepa saw another stalking Vopo silhouette and once again hit the ground with Milan. He dimly realized that he was beginning to hallucinate. With an immense effort he picked himself and Milan up again.

Blood was roaring in Pepa's ears, and they were moving slowly—much too slowly. Through the haze of his exhaustion, he saw lights up ahead that could have been from houses. Next thing he knew, he almost ran into a fence. It was over nine feet high, constructed entirely of barbed wire. A sign was fixed to a pole about six feet above the ground. Pepa tried to read it but, although it was directly in front of him, the letters remained an obstinate blur. From the ditch where he lay prostrate, Milan gasped, "Are we in the American sector yet?"

"I don't know, I can't read it."

Pepa climbed partway up the fence, almost pressing his face against the sign before he could make out what it said. His sight was so weak that even then he had the greatest difficulty. "You . . . are . . . entering . . . the . . . American . . . sector . . . of . . . Berlin!" he spelled out in Russian. The same message was repeated in English, French, and German. A short distance behind the fence was a big white sign with black and red lettering. Pepa was unable to read it: it floated in a fog. He climbed up on the fence and tried to wriggle through it, without success. Then he got off the fence. With a struggle, he pulled up the lower edge of the wire mesh and pushed Milan through the opening, crawling in after him.

"Stay here," he instructed Milan. "I'm going to find out where we are."

Milan nodded weakly. He wasn't about to go anywhere under his own power.

Pepa refused to believe that they had already reached the American sector. It had been too easy! The fence was unguarded, and all those convoys were clearly rushing toward some bottleneck farther north. His first thought was that this fence was yet another Communist ruse—a false border to catch the unwary, like the phony fences the Czech Communists had put up in several places along their border. People trying to escape the country came upon them and, when they got to the other side, thought they were in East Germany. Abandoning all caution, they were caught when they came to the real thing. Pepa was determined not to fall into such a trap.

Leaving Milan in the deep ditch right behind the fence, he went ahead to recon. Just yards away he came upon a well-lighted street, but it was completely deserted. He went back, picked up Milan and half-dragged him to the other side of the street. Milan collapsed under a tree.

"I can't go on," he groaned. His breath was rasping and he lay prostrate, unable to move. Pepa hurried off alone, anxious to find somebody who would help him carry his wounded buddy. Coming to an apartment building surrounded by a chain link fence, he saw a big panel full of doorbells by the door. He pressed one after another, willing somebody to answer. Nobody did. Then he pressed the last one, which belonged to an apartment on the top floor. A light was still on up there and after a while the window opened and somebody leaned out.

"Who is there?" said a man's voice.

"Which sector is this?" Pepa shouted.

"Western!"

"Come down, please, and help me with my buddy who is wounded," Pepa begged. "Show me where the police station is!"

The window slammed shut. Pepa rang the bell again and again but got no further response. People were afraid. It was night. This was the sector border, and these were dangerous times.

Pepa finally gave up and walked on down the empty street. He was feeling increasingly desperate. Milan, his best buddy and the only other survivor of their disastrous escape, was bleeding to death in the ditch. He encountered a man in a green military overcoat.

Drawing his gun, Pepa demanded, "Which sector am I in?"

The man looked at the gun and then at Pepa.

"You're in the Western sector," he replied carefully.

"Are you sure?" Pepa insisted. "Show me to the MP station!" he commanded. "I will shoot you if this is not the American sector."

"I'll show you how to get to the police station but I won't go there with you because I have a hard time walking," said the man. "I was a soldier in the war and was wounded in the leg." Pepa saw that he was indeed limping. The man added, "Also, you can see for yourself that you're in West Berlin because the streets are well lit and in good condition."

"You're going to show me where the police station is, whether you like it or not. Lead me there!" Pepa told him firmly, keeping his gun pointed at him. Pepa marched him back to the ditch were Milan lay and picked up his friend, who was moaning incoherently. The two of them struggled after the veteran, who was limping ahead of them, Milan leaning heavily on Pepa's shoulder.

Finally they came to the police station. A flight of three steps led up to the glass entrance door.

"Ring the bell!" Pepa ordered, "And beware—I know what the West Berlin police look like." Pepa had in fact seen a picture of a West Berlin policeman in a Czech newspaper some time ago. "If a Vopo comes out that door, I'll let you have it immediately!"

"I'm telling you, this is the Western sector. You can trust me!" the veteran zealously assured Pepa. He rang the bell. Pepa waited tensely, his finger on the trigger.

An officer in shirtsleeves opened the door. There were three other policemen inside, two in shirtsleeves and one in full uniform. To Pepa's immense relief, he wore the grayish-green uniform and cap of the West Berlin force. To the veteran's immense relief, Pepa put down his gun.

"We are the guys from Czechoslovakia," Pepa announced. "We've just come from East Germany. You must have heard about us—all the shooting tonight was because of us." All the other policemen rushed to the door. The three men from inside the station carried Milan indoors and laid him on the bench while the limping veteran, who was now feeling very important, made his report. The first policeman took down his statement and address and finally sent him on his way.

"Ambulance—Schnell!" Pepa said, pointing at Milan's stomach. "Bitte CIC rufen!" The Germans understood and hurriedly made some phone calls. Then Pepa pulled Milan's gun out of his pocket and handed it to one of the policemen. As the other officers crowded around and began inspecting it, he pulled out his own weapon. Seeing Pepa with the gun in his hand, they froze in shock. Pepa smiled to defuse the situation. When he turned over the weapon, along with his and Milan's documents, the policemen relaxed.

Milan still had three prints of his graduation picture in his pocket—pictures made from the same negative as the Most Wanted poster photo that had been so widely distributed in East Germany. The policemen recognized it immediately. Thrilled and full of questions, they began pressing their own lunch sandwiches on the two fugitives. One of them even ran off to fetch a meal from the pub, but the two friends could eat nothing. Milan's gut was full of blood and Pepa wasn't able to swallow a bite. Through it all, he felt slightly numb, still unable to fully grasp that he had actually made it to West Berlin and was alive.

After a seeming eternity an ambulance arrived. As the paramedics eased Milan onto the stretcher, Pepa hovered close by. It was time to say good-bye.

"Hey, chief," Pepa told Milan, "I'm going to come check up on you in the hospital. They'll patch you up; you'll be good as new! You'll see!"

A last look at Milan's pale, drawn face, and Pepa was alone. As they waited for the CIC to arrive, Pepa asked the policemen to find out if his brother had made it to Berlin. They obligingly placed telephone calls, Pepa watching, hoping with all his might that their search would turn up his brother. Finally the policemen turned to him. Regretfully they shook their heads; Radek was nowhere to be found. Radek, it seemed, hadn't made it.

Fifteen minutes later, two CIC men pulled up in a black Opel Kapitän. "Was hier los?" they asked in broken German. The policemen turned over Pepa's and Milan's weapons as Pepa tried to explain, in fractured English and German, who he was. The CIC men at first refused to believe that a couple of dirty, undernourished kids were responsible for the massive troop mobilization in East Germany. When Pepa told them that Milan was in the hospital, the CIC men asked where he had been taken. It turned out that nobody knew. Aghast, the CIC men began making rapid calls. The hospital, someone explained to Pepa, could easily be in East Berlin—in the Soviet sector!

Milan's fate still unknown, Pepa took his leave from the enthusiastic West German policemen. As his new friends stood at the door of the precinct waving him off, the black Opel pulled away from the curb with Pepa and the two CIC men inside. The Americans radioed headquarters to report Pepa's arrival. A short while later, headquarters radioed back that another refugee had just arrived at an MP station. Though the pronunciation was very distorted, Pepa thought he recognized the name "Masin." He couldn't believe his ears.

"It can't be possible!" Pepa cried.

"Yes," the CIC men assured him, "he just got off the commuter train."

"Where is he?" Pepa asked, daring to hope again. "Are we going there? I have to see him!"

The CIC men radioed back to request the name of the refugee camp. They set out toward it, Pepa burning with impatience.

As the CIC car drove through the complex, Pepa marveled at the vast size of this displaced persons camp and the modern-looking, well-equipped dormitory buildings. Finally the driver located the building where the new arrival was said to be staying. Pepa jumped out of the car, full of anticipation.

Accompanied by the two CIC men, Pepa walked into the dormitory building and eagerly scanned the hall. There stood a rail-thin figure in tattered rags and mismatched shoes, coated with mud. Radek! Pepa felt a surge of joy as he approached his brother. Their eyes met and their gaunt, bewhiskered faces cracked smiles. Their family had never been demonstrative; the brothers simply clasped hands. No one watching this low-key reunion could have guessed that each, as far as the other was concerned, had just returned from the dead.

"What happened to you guys?" Radek said. "I was sure you were goners, both of you."

"We just had a hell of a good luck," Pepa replied.

It was 2 November. Their odyssey was over, after thirty-one harrowing days. Two of their number had fallen into the hands of the enemy, and one was still unaccounted for.

The man in charge of intake assigned the brothers to a room with two vacant bunks. The CIC men took their leave, and Pepa and Radek set out to find their quarters.

"So how the hell did you get here?" Pepa asked, unable to contain his curiosity.

"Remember when you guys jumped off the train?" Radek said. "I heard a voice shouting 'Halt!' Then pandemonium broke out.

"There was a burst of gunfire and loud shouting. I reached for my weapon. I'd almost worked my hand into my pocket when I noticed somebody squatting at the end of the car and peering into the darkness underneath. It was a Russian soldier, and he was pointing his submachine gun straight at me. I froze. I stared back, and didn't even dare blink. I was completely motionless, watching the Russian guy's every movement and expression. *I'm finished if he discovers me,* I thought to myself. *Any moment now he'll shout for the others.* It seemed like time stopped. Then the Russian straightened and remained standing behind the car. Did he miss me? Or had he seen me and decided to say nothing? I don't know.

"The gunfire behind the train stopped and the soldiers came back. They were talking excitedly. 'Zwei Stücke,' (two of them) one said. 'There's another one somewhere out there.' Now Russians and Vopos were all over the train, searching it inside and out. But because the Russian trooper stood behind my car, nobody else bent down to search underneath it. After about fifteen minutes the troops started getting out of the train. There was an announcement. Something like 'Der Zug fährt ab. Bitte zurück bleiben!' (The train is departing. Please stand back!)

"Then the train began rolling, so I tightened my grip on the brake bars. We pulled away from the brightly lit platform. I couldn't believe that I'd almost made it, but the whole damn operation had turned into a total disaster. You. Milan. Vasek. Zbynek. All gone. That's all I could think of.

"The train made a few more stops and each time I checked the names of the train stations. The last thing I wanted was to pass through the Western sector and end up back in East Germany!* But the signs gave no indication. So then I decided to get off the train at the next stop, no matter what. When the train halted, I dropped to the ground and made myself as flat as possible. Then the train pulled away. When the last car rushed over me, I looked up right into the face of a guy staring directly at me out the back window of the train. You should've seen the look on his face!

"The station platform was empty. I got up off the track and ran toward the chain link fence opposite. I climbed over it and fell down on the other side, straight into a patch of thistles and weeds.

"I rolled and ran down the slope toward a wide asphalt road. The area looked like it had been wiped out by Allied bombing during the war. After the war, the Germans built a bunch of rickety cottages and shanties with little gardens, fences, streets, and so on. It was pretty dark. I ran across the street, jumped over the fence into the nearest garden, and continued climbing over fences as fast as I could to put distance between myself and the railroad station.

"I had to find out where I was. So I went up to one of those little houses and knocked on the door. A dog started barking like mad inside, but otherwise nothing happened. I looked in through the window. I saw the dog. Then some guy yelled at the dog to stop, and I noticed a fat guy in a long, white nightshirt getting out of bed opposite the window. The nightshirt hung on him like a tent and he looked like a fat white ghost with his legs sticking out under the nightshirt. He stood in the middle of the room.

"'Who are you?' he asked.

"'Is this the Western or Eastern sector?' I asked. He didn't answer.

"I knocked on the door again. 'Come outside!' I called.

---

*During this period, Berlin was not yet physically divided. Commuter trains from the surrounding country to the east still traveled to the western half of the city. People living in West Berlin worked in East Berlin, and vice versa. The final sealing of the sector border didn't occur until the construction of the Berlin Wall on 13 August 1961.

"'Get lost or I'll call the police!'

"There were no telephone cables going to this house, so I knew he was lying. Then I saw a large pot on the windowsill, probably left outside to keep it chilled. It was one-third full of goose tripe. I scarfed down the entire lot while the ghost glared at me. He was mad as hell. Since he wouldn't come out and I couldn't easily get in, I decided to move on.

"After climbing over a few more fences I came to a gate that someone was opening at that very moment. I stepped into the shadows and watched a short, very drunk old guy fumbling with the catch. I couldn't see his face in the darkness. When he was inside and about to close the gate, I stepped out with my gun.

"'Hands up!' I said. He put up his hands.

"'Wha's going on?' he said, slurring his words.

"I said I'd just come from Czechoslovakia and wanted to get to the nearest MP station immediately. I asked him if this was the Western Sector. The old guy said yes. He was sobering up quickly.

"'Lead me—now!' I ordered.

"He protested, but I grabbed him by the shoulder and firmly turned him around, pressing the muzzle of the gun to his ribs. 'Walk now and take me to the nearest MP station,' I told him. 'And just so we're clear on this, if you pull any stunts, my first bullet is for you and the last one is for me.'

"The man was drunk, but he could see the logic of my argument. He went ahead, leading me through the narrow, dark streets. Soon we came to a broad street lined with lamps. There were some shops, decorated with bright neon signs and advertising. He tried to initiate a conversation, but I didn't answer. We walked for a long time, saying nothing. Finally the old guy complained that the MP station was too far away and that we couldn't get there on foot. 'We should take a cab,' he said.

"'All right, get one,' I told him. When a big, black American limousine approached, the man stepped into the street to hail it. It pulled up to the curb. I motioned the guy inside first and got in right behind him. I closed the door and pointed the gun at the cab driver.

"'I've just come from Czechoslovakia,' I said. 'Take us to the nearest MP station immediately. I told this man already, if you go anyplace else or a Vopo shows up here, my first bullet is for you and the last one is for me!'

"The taxi driver said nothing and pulled into traffic. I was watching the driver, the old guy and the streets outside all at the same time. I had no doubt this was the Western Sector—the traffic was still busy despite the late hour, the shop windows were full of goods, and there were colorful neon signs everywhere. Still, I didn't drop my guard.

"After a long drive the cab pulled up to the curb. I got out in front of a gate with large buildings on both sides and behind it. A little red and white striped guard shack stood just inside. There was a bored-looking guard in front of it. He had a white helmet and overcoat on, with a carbine on his shoulder. My first look at the shape of the soldier's helmet and his gear and I knew: an American GI!

"I walked up to him. 'I am from Czechoslovakia,' I said in my best English. 'We just came through East Germany, and I need to speak to the CIC.'

"The American stared at me. He didn't understand.

"I tried again. 'I come from Czechoslovakia, I need to speak to the CIC. I went through East Germany.'

"Again, the guard looked at me and shook his head. He finally called out to somebody behind the fence. A guy wearing a long black overcoat and black *Gebrigsjäger* cap ran out—obviously a German. I tried again, this time in German. Suddenly this man had a look of recognition in his eyes and he babbled something to the guard. He was totally excited. Now the guard was becoming excited, too.

"The German pointed at my Parabellum. 'Was ist mit der Waffe? Bitte geben Sie die her,' (What's with the gun? Hand it over, please). I gave my gun to the guard.

"The interpreter and the guard stepped back and called out to someone behind the fence. After a few moments a group of soldiers came out. I didn't understand a word those guys were saying. It wasn't anything like the English we learned at school. At any rate, the soldiers turned and marched me into the compound. We were quite a procession—me surrounded by all the GIs, and the old guy and the cabbie tagging along in the rear. The cabbie was loudly insisting on his fare, and the old man, who'd sobered up, was demanding a ride home.

"They put me on a chair in the red-and-white guardhouse and all the GIs crowded around. Word must have gotten around quickly, because in no time flat, all of the duty personnel had piled into the guard shack to have a look at me. I pointed at my wrist and asked the time. Someone said it was a few minutes after midnight.

"One GI brought a carton of milk and several sandwiches. I pulled my spare magazines out of one pocket and the bottle with the chloroform and the rope out of the other, and explained what they were for in sign language. The GIs looked over my stuff and the sergeant told me they'd called the CIC.

"I was in a total daze. I couldn't believe I'd made it, but the whole time I was thinking about you guys, and that you hadn't. I was sure you were done for."

When Pepa and Radek opened the door to their assigned room, they got a nasty shock. It was occupied by a Vopo lieutenant and three Vopo troopers, still in their black uniforms. Pepa and Radek stood in the doorway, unshaven and unwashed, in their filthy clothes, Radek still wearing his mismatched shoes. The Vopos fell silent and turned to stare at the new arrivals. They recognized the brothers. The Masins stared back in equal astonishment. Hours ago, these six men had been opponents in the largest mobilization in the European theater since the Second World War. Now they stood face-to-face in a simple dormitory in a West Berlin displaced persons camp.

Then the Vopos started gabbing excitedly in German, welcoming them in, crowding around to shake Pepa's and Radek's hands, each trying to outdo the other. As it turned out, the whole camp was crawling with uniformed Volkspolizei.* Word that the Masin brothers had arrived spread among the Vopo defectors like wildfire. More and more men in black uniforms crowded into the little dorm room, eager to see Pepa and Radek.

In no time, the Vopo defectors were volunteering interesting details about the manhunt and everyone was laughing at the bizarre irony of the situation. On the other side of the fence they had been hunting Pepa and Radek as outlaws, and here in the camp all of them were meeting on the friendliest of terms. When they discovered that the brothers had had no food for days, the Volkspolizei defectors generously offered what they had.

They told Pepa and Radek that more than twenty-four thousand troops had been deployed in the hunt, half of them Russian forces. Pepa was stunned.

---

*In the month of October 1953, 537 Vopos defected to West Berlin, including 44 officers. This was a new monthly record. In January through September 1953, a total of 3435 had defected, or an average of 381 per month. (AP, 2 November, as quoted in *Philadelphia Inquirer*, 3 November 1953, 6.)

The defectors also confirmed that Communist troops had shot one of their own, a major, when they repelled the breakthrough attempt at the road where Radek lost his shoe. Pepa and Radek asked the Vopos about their feelings toward the brothers, in light of the fact that they had shot five of their comrades. No hard feelings at all, the Vopos assured them; they would have done the same thing themselves had they been in the fugitives' shoes. Anyway, since all the dead and wounded happened to be ardent Communists, Pepa and Radek had fortunately managed to shoot the right ones.

The Vopo lieutenant was the most articulate of the group. He said that his unit was normally stationed far from the border but had been pulled into the Luckau area to participate in the manhunt. When the hunt moved close to Berlin, he had seized the moment and taken off. He had waited a long time for the opportunity. He also explained that the East German mobilization had been quite disorganized. The brothers questioned him about Vasek. Yes, he knew that Vasek had been captured, not far from the village of Waldow; in fact, not far from the place they had left him that ill-fated night. Vasek was being interrogated. According to the lieutenant, he was being held in the Cottbus prison.*

The brothers had just traversed more than two hundred miles—on foot—and had been freezing and starving for a month, but then and there they decided they would go in again and rescue their friend.

---

*This was incorrect information.

Chapter 33

BERLIN SAFE HOUSE

As it turned out, the brothers' stay at the camp was of short duration. Before the canteen opened for breakfast, Pepa and Radek were called to the police station attached to the camp. Two CIC men had come for them and quickly whisked them away, telling them that people up and down the chain of command were getting chewed out because the two of them had been put in an open DP camp with all those Vopos.

Pepa and Radek were a little apprehensive. The CIC men were both young, in their early to midtwenties, and they would have been happier to see older people. After a little while, the two Czechs warmed up, though they continued to be extremely conscious of security.*

Political kidnappings and assassinations were routine in Berlin, and the two brothers topped the most-wanted list in both Czechoslovakia and East Germany. The CIC men impressed upon Radek and Pepa that they would be taken to an anonymous safe house, and were not to go outdoors under any circumstances. After several frantic hours of searching, the CIC had managed to track down Milan, who had fortunately been taken to a hospital in the Western sector. The CIC wasted no time in getting him transferred to a U.S. military hospital with a round-the-clock guard. One MP was in his room at all times, and another was just outside the door in the corridor.

When Pepa and Radek arrived at the well-appointed villa that was to be their accommodation for the duration of their stay in Berlin, the CIC men ordered a big plate of French fries and a huge steak for each of them, with

---

*One of the CIC men was Leonard Jankowski, a twenty-five-year-old American of Polish descent, who spoke Polish, Russian, and German.

plenty of trimmings. Halfway through the meal, their minders remembered that rich food should be off limits after such a long fast, but before they could take it all away again, Radek and Pepa had wolfed everything down.

Happily sated, they were escorted to the showers. There was shampoo. There was soap, and, to their wondering eyes, the luxury of unlimited running hot water. Then Pepa looked in the mirror and saw his face. The figure staring back at him from the mirror was unrecognizable. A month's growth of beard covered hollowed cheeks, and his eyes had sunk deep into their sockets. His hair was matted with filth. Radek was staring in the mirror too.

"Hey, chief," he suddenly guffawed. "Your head looks like a big onion stuck on that scrawny neck of yours."

"Yours is no better," Pepa shot back.

They turned away from the mirrors and began stripping off their ragged clothing. Only then did they realize how emaciated they were. Their spines, their hip bones, and their ribs were all sticking out. During the month-long ordeal, their bodies had been consuming themselves to stay alive. They were gaunt skeletons reminiscent of the concentration camp inmates they had seen eight years before.

Pepa and Radek laughed, tension washing away as they luxuriated in the unlimited supply of hot water. The month's worth of dust and dirt was so deeply ingrained in the pores of their skin, it proved impossible to wash off in one go. Each of them was given an old American military uniform that had been dyed black and a pair of military boots. They were enormously proud of these outfits because, wearing them, they felt that they were already part of the powerful U.S. Army.

Their old clothing stunk so awfully from stale perspiration and the ammonium their wasting bodies had excreted that they had to dispose of everything. Their mementos, their father's photograph and watch, had been lost or traded for food and money. And now the last of the lot, General Masin's hunting shirt, was being consigned to the trash, torn and beyond the power of any cleaning establishment. The brothers were unsentimental. They parted with these things without a backward glance, all their energy firmly focused on their mission: to destroy the Communist juggernaut in the East.

Fortunately Pepa and Radek didn't suffer any ill effects from their first feast. But afterward their handlers made sure they went easy on the food intake. Physically the two survivors felt okay, except that Radek had a mild case of frostbite on his feet. The tips of his toes had no feeling in them, and it turned out he also had a mild case of trench foot. The numbness would take several weeks to disappear.

The debriefing started as soon they had cleaned up. Pepa and Radek followed an aide into a big room where five Americans stood and introduced themselves, giving just their first names. The CIC men followed the brothers' story on a big map while taking copious notes. The Americans showed them a pile of newspaper clippings from both the Communist and Western press, confirming what the Vopos had said the previous night about the twenty-four-thousand-man mobilization. Only then did the brothers fully appreciate what an upheaval their flight had caused. The CIC men explained that reports reaching the West were confused and, until their arrival, the CIC had had no idea what was really going on in the Soviet zone. The one thing the CIC knew for sure was that the Communists had concentrated a tremendous number of troops around the town of Cottbus, completely sealing off the area.

The brothers and their friends had left home with a grand total of fifty-two rounds of ammunition. During their flight they had fired fifteen rounds, half of them unaimed to scare off pursuing troops, and had nevertheless averaged three rounds fired per killed or wounded enemy. They were proud of their tally, which would have been an excellent one for any professional soldier.

"Can we do anything for you?" the CIC men asked at the close of the briefing.

"Yes, as a matter of fact, you can." Pepa and Radek were young and believed that the CIC was omnipotent. In their minds each CIC man, as a representative of the U.S. government, had at his disposal the nearly unlimited power and resources of the American superpower. "We need to go back in and rescue Vasek and Zbynek," the brothers explained. "All we'll need are weapons and some intel. We know Vasek's in the prison in Cottbus. If you tell us where the prison is, and where in the prison he is, we'll take care of the rest."

The CIC men couldn't believe their ears. "You want to do what? You just got out and you want to go back in!"

"Sure! They'll never expect us to break in. They've only got one-way traffic over there. Everyone wants to go the other way—out."

As religious listeners of the VOA, Pepa and Radek knew that the Americans were extremely well-informed. It wouldn't have surprised them in the least if the Americans had produced a complete map of the layout of the prison where Vasek was being held.

The CIC men conversed among themselves and told the brothers they would get back to them. For the moment, then, the question was deferred. The same evening, Pepa and Radek gave their one and only press conference. About fifteen newspapermen and a man from Radio Free Europe attended. The two brothers gave an abbreviated account of their flight, with one of the CIC officials acting as an interpreter. The press conference lasted all of five minutes, after which Pepa and Radek, eager to minimize the publicity about their exploits, broke it off, but not before inserting some deliberately misleading information to protect their helpers in East Germany and their friends in Czechoslovakia from reprisal by the Communist authorities. After the press conference was over, they asked the RFE man to air the coded messages to let all the people who had helped them along the way know they had made it out safely.

The night of 2 November, the brothers went to bed in complete safety and with full stomachs for the first time in a month.

Chapter 34

RED REVENGE

When the report came over the West Berlin-based RIAS radio service, it caused a sensation in the Grunert home in Waldow, the second family in whose barn the Czechs had stayed. Marta Grunert, the young wife, was working outdoors when the news came. "They made it! They made it!" someone shouted from the living room, where the radio was tuned to the forbidden RIAS setting. Relief flooded over her—all three young men had reached their goal. It also meant that she, her courageous husband Werner, his parents, and the baby were beyond the long-armed reach of the secret police. Her family's dangerous secret had escaped West with the fugitives. The days of palm-sweating anxiety were over.

The family kept its secret for decades afterward, passing on the story of their part in those fateful October days and of their father's extraordinary and selfless courage to their children, who, in turn, kept and nurtured the family secret. At the local pub, the Luckau War was a topic of recurring interest. In whose barn did those Czechs stay? There were wild conjectures, and different families were put forward as candidates, but Werner Grunert and his father only listened and kept their secret to themselves. Had the family's identity ever become known, the Communist regime would have exacted a terrible revenge. The family knew that their actions in October 1953 could have meant death or life sentence in the slave labor camps. Yet they firmly believed they had done the right thing. "Delivering them up to their certain death," Marta Grunert recalled, "that is something we never could have squared with our conscience. Neither I, nor my husband, nor our parents. We never would have done that."

The Czech language service of Radio Free Europe broadcast word of the trio's arrival in Berlin on 3 November at 7:00 PM. The records of the Czech language service for those early years are sketchy, and it is not possible to reconstruct what, if anything, was broadcast about the turmoil in East Germany during the second half of October. Zdena Masinova knew her sons were leaving, although they never breathed a word to her about their exact plans. She did not expect them to; their silence was for her own safety. When an opportunity offered itself, they would surely send word.

Perhaps, after 16 October, there were reports on RFE and VOA about the upheavals and mobilization in East Germany, tens of thousands of troops sealing off the countryside and Ukranian or Polish partisan armies fighting their way through to Berlin. Zdena Masinova may have heard these reports and wondered if, by some mischance, her sons had been delayed, and whether their passage to Berlin would put them in the path of this massive clash of armies—their individual fates inadvertently caught up in this larger drama of the Cold War.

When word finally came on 3 November, it must have been a shock and a relief at the same time. The extraordinary troop mobilization had been for her boys! Now they were safe. Perhaps none of this came as a surprise. After all, they were the sons of their father.

The other members of the underground group found out, each in his own way. Some heard the news on RFE, others heard from friends. The Masins and Milan had made it, Zbynek and Vasek had not. After the small band had left on their journey West, the remnants of the group lay dormant. The guns, ammunition, and explosives were stashed underground in watertight containers. The war chest was in the hands of Zbynek Rousar, the group's treasurer. Borek shuttled among the group members, keeping an eye on them and waiting for his nephews' first communication. In October he visited Lidka Svedova, Vasek's wife, and gave her the first monthly living stipend of one thousand crowns.

When the news came of Zbynek and Vasek's capture, Borek knew that nobody was safe. He contacted Rousar and Egon Plech and they planned to make a run for Berlin while they still could. But as the days got shorter and the nights got colder, they waited. Rousar was a former diplomat. Perhaps he shied away from the rough exertion of a two-hundred-mile odyssey to Berlin and potential clashes with armed forces. Plech had walked up to the line and backed away once before. He didn't have it in him. But what about Uncle Borek?

As Borek moved among the group members, from the Svedas' house in Pivin (where he handed over a second thousand-crown stipend in November) to Podebrady and back to his doorman's job in Karlovy Vary, making plans that were not acted upon, the StB's agents were trailing him. For twenty-one days after the Masins' arrival in Berlin, nothing happened. Borek held down his post as doorman at the Hotel Pupp. Vladimir Hradec continued his chemistry studies in Prague. Plech continued in his job at the textile mill. Rousar showed up dutifully at his bricklaying job. Zdena Masinova, ill with the cancer that would later kill her, and perhaps anticipating the impending blow, checked into a hospital.

Zbynek and Vasek's capture in East Germany turned out to be a godsend for the Czechoslovak Communist authorities. It was the single strand, the loose thread that would progressively unravel a tissue of mysteries they had been unable to penetrate. The Volkspolizei put Zbynek in the interrogation room less than two hours after his capture; Vasek, delirious and weak from loss of blood, was quickly patched up and sent into interrogation a mere five hours after his capture. A marathon twelve-hour interrogation followed. Six more hours' interrogation followed five hours' downtime.

Both Zbynek and Vasek tried to save themselves and protect the people who had helped them. They trotted out the agreed-upon script: those who were caught would blame those who had gone free for everything. Their only goal in heading West was to better themselves economically. They had no political or military objectives.[1] But as the East German interrogators applied the tried-and-true NKVD* methods, their two Czech captives began to crack in a matter of days. Details in their respective stories began to conflict. The interrogators played one off against the other, covering the same ground over and over and pouncing on any discrepancies. They had all the time in the world. By November, beatings, brainwashing, and twenty-four-hour marathon interrogations had taken their toll. The captives started naming names.

For those who remained behind in Czechoslovakia, the trap sprang shut on 25 November 1953. In the space of forty-eight hours, the StB swooped

---

*NKVD, the Soviet secret police, renamed KGB after World War II. The NKVD broke prisoners using intense interrogation that went on for several days and nights. They used physical means of persuasion and threats to arrest and execute members of the prisoner's family to elicit confessions.

in on all the remaining group members, their friends, and their families—with the exception of Zdena Masinova, who was still in the hospital—and arrested them.

Vladimir Hradec was picked up off the street as he walked to the stadium, carrying his saxophone. Out of nowhere, two men appeared at his elbows, grabbed him between them and pulled him into a car.

"What do you have in your case?" they barked. "Machine guns or a saxophone?"

"A saxophone, naturally," Vladimir replied in shock. Five minutes later they blindfolded him. That was the last he saw of the outside world for the next twelve years.

Now that the Czechoslovak Communist authorities had everyone under lock and key, they extracted confessions through beatings, brainwashing, and blackmail. People began to tell everything they knew, and unfortunately not all the group members had operated on the need-to-know basis practiced by Pepa and Radek. Vasek in particular had shared his exploits with his family in damaging detail and had told much to others as well. Under pressure, friends and loved ones turned against each other in the hope of saving themselves. Ultimately, twenty-one individuals were indicted, and the "enemy activity" of one hundred twenty-seven other people was uncovered.[2]

To their chagrin, the Czechoslovak authorities found they had only minor players in their custody. The core members of the group had eluded them. While they fought to have Vasek and Zbynek extradited from East Germany and the two Masin brothers and Milan from the United States, they put plans for a dramatic show trial on hold.

The situation was diplomatically delicate and the authorities expended considerable effort in mapping out their strategy. They ultimately settled on a two-pronged approach. The extradition requests to the GDR for Vasek and Zbynek highlighted the group's anticommunist motivation. But the Czechoslovak authorities knew that the U.S. would never extradite members of the anticommunist underground to stand trial for acts of resistance. So they claimed that these three were common criminals.

This decision put the Czechoslovak Communists on the horns of another dilemma. "It is very implausible to accuse the ring leaders of only robbery and murder," one official pointed out, "while accusing the others also of treason [and] sabotage." He recommended splitting the trial in two—one trial for Vasek, Zbynek, and the minor players who had stayed in Czechoslovakia, and a second trial for the Masin brothers and Milan.[3]

But the U.S. authorities saw through the subterfuge and rejected three successive Czechoslovak extradition requests.* "In the light of information available to the Department of State," the United States admonished the Czechoslovak government, "it seems clear that the acts which are the real, as distinct from the alleged, basis of the charges against the three young men . . . assumed . . . the character of political offenses."[4]

Initially the Czechoslovak authorities were just as unsuccessful with the East Germans. For months, both regimes claimed first dibs to this propaganda prize, and the East Germans had the advantage of physical possession.

On 3 March 1954, the East Germans set plans in motion for a show trial of their own. The chief prosecutor's office of the GDR filed the government's case against Vasek and Zbynek with East Germany's High Court. The charges included "malicious boycott agitation against democratic installations and organizations. Malicious murder agitation against democratic politicians as well as fascist and militaristic propaganda," quitting the country, armed robbery, and killing and wounding members of the German People's Police. The remainder of the indictment was a lengthy, disjointed diatribe on the evils of the imperialist states, specifically the United States. The United States stood accused along with the two Czech youths.

Two weeks later, on 18 March 1954, the Czechoslovak Communists' lobbying finally produced a success. The East German Stasi formally advised its Czechoslovak counterpart that it intended to try the accused "in short order." However, if Czechoslovakia promised to sentence the prisoners to death, East Germany would extradite them.[†] The Czechoslovak Communists apparently gave the necessary assurances, because on 12 May representatives of its state security apparatus arrived in Berlin and took custody of the two prisoners.[5]

The Czechoslovak Communists kept their end of the bargain. On 13 December 1954, the Politburo decreed that Zbynek Janata and Vasek Sveda would receive death sentences in the coming trial.[6] The Politburo of the Central Committee of the Czechslovak Communist Party was the country's highest authority on all legislative, executive, judicial, administrative, political, and economic matters. It had absolute power. The fact that it took up

---

*These were submitted on 1 September 1954, 17 February 1955, and 29 March 1956.

[†]Endres/Bönnen papers. The Czechoslovak reply to this letter is not in the East German archive, and the Czechoslovak records on the case are still in the state prosecutor's office. It is government policy that all inactive legal files be retired to the archives from the state prosecutor's office after thirty years or destroyed. The files in question are now more than fifty years old.

the matter of *Masin et al.* a total of five times from December 1953 through December 1955 shows the importance the Communist leadership attached to the matter. The men of the Politburo had the final say on every aspect of the case: they approved the list of the accused, defined their crimes, determined the sentences, discussed the extradition strategy, and, after the trial, ruled on the requests for clemency. As in all the other major political trials of the period, letters by the bagful were orchestrated demanding the ultimate punishment for the accused.[7]

The trial of *Ctibor Novak et al.*, for Borek was now being styled as the group's leader, finally burst upon the national scene on 25 January 1955. In the preceding months, government prosecutors had carefully scripted the testimony to meet the regime's political objectives. The hapless prisoners had spent two months memorizing their parts under the direction of their interrogators. Since the death sentences for Zbynek and Vasek were a foregone conclusion, the trial was strictly theater: to justify the verdicts, to demonstrate the correctness of Communist ideology and the villainy of its opponents, and to teach its enemies that all resistance would be annihilated.[8] The prosecutor and judge were ready to play their parts. The defense attorney was ready to play his, which was to point out the crimes of his clients and remind the judge that lenience was not in the interest of the proletariat.

For four days Pepa's sister, young Nenda Masinova, and her grandmother, Emma, sat in this sea of hostile faces and watched as the accused were paraded before the court. Borek fought doggedly until the end, sidestepping the prosecution's thrusts and parrying them with denials. He firmly maintained his ignorance and his innocence and refused to admit to anything unless forced to do so by overwhelming evidence and testimony that the inquisitors had managed to wring out of other captives who yielded to the pressure.

Vasek and Zbynek were clearly broken men. According to the trial protocol, they admitted to all of the antiregime activities they had engaged in, plus a few others they had had no part in. At the end, each spoke briefly. Each acknowledged intending to destroy the socialist people's democracy; each apologized for his crimes and stated that he regretted having committed them.

In a different life, Vasek Sveda had written to his betrothed: "At the moment they read about Col. Masin, I was proud that this man was the uncle of the girl I love . . . I would like to be such a person myself." He had tried, but in the hours of greatest duress he had fallen short. The moments in court when he recanted his ideals and his principles must have been truly bitter ones for him. Or perhaps, having undergone months of torture and progressive erosion of his principles, those bitter moments had come and gone long ago, and he had become numb to it all, past the point of caring.

The sentences came down hard and fast: Borek, Vasek, and Zbynek were sentenced to death; Rousar life in prison; Vladimir Hradec, twenty-two years; Vasek's two brothers twenty years each. Vasek's wife Lidka and Vladimir's mother and father were each sentenced to eighteen years. Egon Plech and Horacek got seventeen years. Vladimir's brother Jiri and Jaroslav Cukr, the driver of the car at Kank, got sixteen years. Vasek's old father and another man got fifteen years. Bozena Cukrova, Jaroslav's wife, got four years for not reporting her husband.

When the accused were given a chance to say their final words to the court, Borek spat out a single word at the Communist judges and their syco-phants in the galley: "Murderers!"

In the end, the sentencing on 29 January 1955 hadn't gone quite as planned. Chief Prosecutor Ales had allowed himself a flight of unscripted initiative: instead of life in prison for Borek Novak, he requested and the court granted a death sentence.*

As they waited for death in lonely isolation, Zbynek, Vasek, and Borek were allowed no visitors. The doomed men were kept in solitary confine-ment on the third floor of Pankrac prison, in a special section for death row prisoners. The cells were stripped to the bone—no bed, no mattress, no blanket, just a single light bulb that was on day and night.

Vasek and Borek were each given prison paper to write a last letter to their loved ones. Each man produced a poignant, rambling, and in places

---

*This rather remarkable document gives some startling insights into the working of the Communist legal system in general and the Novák trial in particular. Aleš writes: "I was informed about the sentencing instructions by means of the Chief Prosecutor's order, with respect to which a note in the diary was made on 30 December 1954. This order includes the instruction that the Chief Prosecutor would request the death penalty for two of the accused, Janata and Václav Sveda, during the trial hearings. . . . Comrade Dr. Novák [head of the Senate-no relative to Borek Novák] . . . had received identical instructions. . . . During the trial hearings, most particularly during the detailed investigation of the accused Novák and his manner before the Court, I became convinced that the danger of his crimes, which were sub-stantially higher than recorded in the indictment. . . . The fact that the outcome of the trial is at variance with the instructions with respect to the death penalty is the responsibility of and can only be explained by the head of the Senate" (OZZ-I 120/54/2, 84). Aleš was trying to pass the buck for the unscripted death sentence to Comrade Dr. Novák.

incoherent message that spoke of his love for his family. Back in Pivin, Vasek's small children wrote their father in an unsteady hand. His wife, his father, and his mother sent him simple words of love and support. None of these letters were ever delivered. The correspondence disappeared into files somewhere in the bowels of the Ministry of the Interior and was consigned to oblivion.*

Again and again, Borek's old mother made the arduous journey from Jeseník to Pankrac prison, only to be refused permission to see her son. Meanwhile, Borek's jailers told him that his mother and his estranged wife were coming to see him one last time. On the day of the promised visit, in a gesture of gratuitous cruelty, the jailers told him the visit had been cancelled—his wife and mother didn't want to see him after all.† What was more, the jailers told Vasek and Borek, their families had disavowed them. One can only imagine the doomed men's bitter grief.

The fate of Zbynek Janata is perhaps the most tragic of all. When he was arrested, his stepmother, who had always favored her children over those of her husband's first marriage, harangued her husband into looking after his own interests: his career as school superintendent, her career as teacher, their children's future. It was the wise, prudent thing to do. The family turned away from Zbynek and ran for cover, collectively disavowing him. Nobody wrote to him. Nobody tried to visit him. Nobody attended his trial. Zbynek Janata faced death truly abandoned by his family.

Janata senior did make one last, not entirely disinterested, gesture on behalf of his son: He petitioned the president to grant Zbynek clemency. Mr. Sveda wrote requesting clemency for Vasek, and Emma Novakova for her son Borek. Zbynek, Vasek, and Borek each wrote on his own behalf. It was the last recourse. The Politburo duly met to consider these petitions and rejected them.

The clock was ticking now. None of the men knew when he was going to die. Their jailers, meanwhile, allowed themselves some more sadistic fun at their captives' expense. For several nights running, the prison guards rousted the

---

*Vašek's children received their father's letter in 1995, forty years after their father's sentencing and five years after the Velvet Revolution. His wife and parents didn't live to see it. Emma Novak also died before her son's letter saw the light of day; it was received by his niece, Zdenka Mašínová Jr., in 1995.

†This is related in a letter from Borek to his mother, now in the papers of Zdena Mašínová.

men from their sleep, telling each to prepare himself to die—then announcing an hour later that the execution had been postponed.

2 May 1955. Vasek was first. He was told to put on a pair of blacked-
out welders' goggles. Then his hands were tied. Blind and helpless, he was
marched out of his cell and down the hall. Doors were unlocked and clanged
shut behind him. He was put on a table and invisible hands applied straps
and restraints. A hydraulic mechanism whirred into action. The table began
to move, two halves splitting apart, until his head was torn from his body
by a hydraulic winch.[9] Vaclav Sveda was dead at 5:35 PM.

Borek Novak was the next to walk down the hall. At 5:45 PM he, too,
was dead.

Zbynek Janata came last. At 6:07 PM it was all over. Their bodies were
buried in anonymous mass graves.

The policemen arrested Zdena Masinova in her hospital bed. They transferred her to the Pankrac prison hospital and shortly thereafter pronounced
her healthy enough to stand trial. But preparations for the massive show
trial were too far advanced for her to be included, so she was tried separately. Once again, her daughter Nenda and her mother Emma sat in the
spectator's galley, surrounded by jeering representatives of the fighting
proletariat. The Central Committee of the Communist Party had already
decided that her sentence would be twenty-five years' imprisonment. The
charge: "[S]he is the mother of the Masins and . . . she approved and covered for their activities."[10] The judges rubber-stamped the verdict and the
spectators loudly shouted their approval.

Emma Novakova was seventy-seven years old when she saw her daughter Zdena sentenced. She had watched her son sentenced to death just a few
months before. The substantial property and investments she and her husband
had built up from nothing during a lifetime of hard work had been confiscated by the Communists. She had been reduced to working as a dishwasher
in a hotel. But Emma, too, was a fighter. She wasn't about to give up.

When she was allowed a rare visit with her daughter, at the capricious
whim of the jailers, Emma saw that there was something seriously wrong.
Forced to sleep on bare concrete floors with insufficient clothes, no mattress,
and no blankets, Zdena was deathly ill. Again and again Emma wrote to her
daughter's jailers, urgently requesting that her daughter be allowed to see a
doctor, that she be released because of illness. The requests were denied.

"[Zdena Masinova's] release is not recommended because of her attitude," wrote the prison warden, and because she "expresses hate for today's social order. She . . . doesn't recognize her guilt, has no interest in reeducation. . . . She is a hardened enemy of the social order."[11] Zdena, the prison warden went on, was fulfilling just 25 percent of her assigned work quota and "was not interested in increasing her professional qualifications."

She was not fulfilling her quota because she was dying. Zdena Masinova, wife of a hero of the World War II resistance, accomplished pianist, the first woman to graduate from Charles University in Prague with a degree in civil engineering, perished in prison on 14 June 1956, of cancer of the colon. She was left to suffer on the bare concrete floor of her jail cell, without a mattress or blankets or even sufficient clothing to protect her from the wrenching cold, and she was buried in an unmarked mass grave.

Chapter 35

TO LIBERATE CZECHOSLOVAKIA

Meanwhile, Pepa and Radek were gearing up for the decisive clash between Communism and the democracies of the West. Now it seemed as though they would begin making real progress. Within thirty-six hours of stumbling into Berlin they were booked on a special U.S. military flight for Frankfurt, West Germany. Normally refugees faced a minimum six-week wait to snare one of the hotly contested seats on a plane out of Berlin, but Pepa and Radek were spirited out of the city as quickly as possible. The risk of kidnapping was too great in spy-riddled Berlin, with its daily shooting incidents at the sector border and periodic high-profile kidnappings. The CIC was not about to lose the valuable properties that had fortuitously fallen into its hands.

In their last hours in Berlin, Pepa and Radek continued pressing their CIC contacts for word on their plan to rescue Vasek, but the answer was still no answer. Their other request, to see Milan once more, was granted. The brothers' CIC handlers had the last day in Berlin planned out: a sightseeing tour of the city in the morning and a visit to the hospital in the afternoon.

Radek and Pepa found Milan well guarded. Five German policemen patrolled the area around the building, a German plainclothesman sat in front of the door to Milan's room, and an armed CIC guard was inside with him twenty-four hours a day. Milan lay in bed with a white sheet pulled up all the way to his chin. He had been operated on immediately after his arrival. The doctors refused to believe that he had run ten miles with a bullet in his gut. Pepa and Radek gently told him that they were leaving that night.

They assured him that the CIC chief had given his word that he would follow as soon as his condition permitted.

Radek and Pepa had a bad feeling about this flight, which would take them
over the GDR, but the CIC men assured them that if worse came to worse
they were registered under false names. The brothers ate their first banana
split at the airport, and found it unimaginably delicious. When the departure time came, they boarded the plane, accompanied by two men in civilian clothes. There were also about ten other Americans wearing civilian
clothing. The plane roared down the runway and lifted off into a stormy
night sky, navigation lights flashing. Pepa's stomach tightened into knots.
Soon the lights of Berlin disappeared in the darkness behind them and the
black expanse of Communist East Germany sprawled below. The weather,
already poor, took a turn for the worse. As rain whipped the fuselage and
high winds buffeted them, the pilots struggled to hold the shuddering plane
at low altitude. Increasingly worried, Pepa and Radek quizzed those who
accompanied them about the procedure for emergency landings. They spent
the next couple of hours in a state of high tension, listening to the sounds of
the engines and watching for the first sign of trouble, and were immensely
relieved when the flight touched down at Rhein/Main Air Base without any
unscheduled stops.

Two new CIC agents met them with a Chevrolet automobile, which
they had pulled up right to the airplane. The Americans signed to take custody of them, then led the brothers to the car. As they passed through the
gate of the airbase, the CIC men instructed Radek and Pepa to lie down
on the floor and put blankets over them so that the gate guard wouldn't
notice them in the car. After inspecting the ID documents of the CIC men,
the guard waved the car through. Near the end of their journey Radek and
Pepa learned they were going to stay in Erlangen, a small university town
near Nürnberg.

In Erlangen, the brothers were put up in another safe house, a large,
well-appointed villa. Pepa and Radek were disoriented and unsure what
to think about the whole experience. On the one hand, they were the only
inhabitants of this villa, with a staff that consisted of a German cook and
two American guards, CIC enlisted men. On the other hand, they were
being given food fit for dogs and pigs. When the attending colonel showed
up and asked if everything was okay, Pepa and Radek complained bitterly.
They were deeply insulted. The puzzled colonel, buttonholing the cook in

the kitchen, asked what on earth she had served his two charges. The flustered cook explained she had done everything according to instructions. The two guardsmen shrugged and said that the spareribs and corn on the cob had been just fine. In Czechoslovakia at that time, though, spareribs were considered nothing but bones, fit only for dogs, and corn on the cob was reserved for pigs—unfit for human consumption.

The intensive schedule of debriefings continued. For six weeks the brothers described all the military installations they had observed in East Germany, the troop movements they witnessed, and all the information about strategic assets and military installations that they had memorized before leaving Czechoslovakia. They were asked to take a polygraph test. Apparently it was a success, because the next day the colonel in charge attended their debriefing and asked them whether they would be willing to return to Czechoslovakia to establish espionage contacts with friends who might still be in the military or whose knowledge could be of some use to the Allies. Radek and Pepa asked for a couple days to think over the offer. The CIC officers offered money, weapons, and men as further incentives.

Privately the brothers deliberated the viability of the suggestion and returned with an answer: a conditional yes. They wouldn't reenter the country on foot. Entry had to be a plane drop-off, and the brothers requested total control of the drop-off and the entire subsequent operation. No one—neither the CIC nor, for that matter, the pilot—would have advance knowledge of the drop-off location. Pepa and Radek had met too many CIC agents in Communist prisons who had walked across the border only to be met by Communist authorities, their plans systematically compromised. As dedicated as they were to the cause, the brothers were not suicidal. In their experience, the CIC leaked secrets like a sieve. In the end, the CIC wouldn't agree to the conditions.

For the same reason, they continued to guard Frantisek Vanek's secret carefully. Vanek was their father's friend, the officer who had helped the brothers spirit the Russian POW out of Podebrady in World War II and, since the February putsch, had been ready to help topple the Communist regime. They had to be sure they were talking to the top man before divulging it. Too much was at stake for Vanek and his men to be jeopardized by some low-level leak.

Several weeks into the interrogation, they concluded that the CIC colonel was the highest-ranking officer they would have contact with. They told him that Vanek was ready, waiting for the Americans' signal, and that his group could field fourteen thousand men. The colonel asked diversionary questions, but repeatedly returned to the topic. Over the next few days they were asked repeatedly to elaborate. Other officers appeared. Notes were taken. There was a flurry of activity in the safe house.

Pepa and Radek continued to ask their CIC contacts about the plan to rescue Vasek. The CIC men never actually refused. Instead, they deferred the question to death. Pepa and Radek were getting increasingly anxious about their friend. Puzzled and frustrated, they couldn't believe that the CIC wouldn't support their effort to go back and save Vasek.

The CIC handlers told their two charges that the Soviet, East German, and Czechoslovak authorities were pulling out all the stops to get them back. The CIC was sure that the Communists wouldn't hesitate to abduct them, if they could. Consequently, life in the safe house remained cloistered. Whenever the brothers wanted to go out for a walk, they were assigned a vehicle with a driver who took them away from the safe house, together with their guard. To break up the routine, the officers who conducted the debriefings sometimes took them out to the military movie theater, military clubs, or post exchanges. On weekends, top brass who wanted to enjoy the company of the Most Wanted could sign for them and take them to Berchtesgaden or some other place, and a dizzying succession of colonels and generals queued up for the privilege. The two Czechs, with their polite demeanor and immaculate continental manners, were the celebrities of the moment.

As for Milan, he was flown out to a military hospital in Frankfurt as soon as his condition permitted, on 7 November, where he was registered under a false name. Besides his nurses and doctors, no one had access to him. Soon thereafter, he joined the Masins at the safe house in Erlangen.

By then Radek and Pepa had been introduced to a Mrs. Matheson, who was in charge of the American Rescue Committee. She had very good contacts with the heads of the military governments in the occupied zones of West Germany, and arranged the Czechs' participation at various events and functions. Solicitous of her two charges, she came up with a bewildering plethora of opportunities: book deals and magazine articles on their great escape, even Hollywood movies. She wanted to put them in touch with future senator Pat Moynihan, who was a journalist at the time. Pepa and Radek appreciated her efforts, but their relatives were hostages of the Communist authorities in Czechoslovakia, and they were still hopeful that their loved ones and friends might escape the full brunt of the regime's fury. A low profile was the best protection.

Philanthropic organizations offered them scholarships to Ivy League schools or any other U.S. university of their choice. They turned them down without hesitation. The Czechs had not come as economic refugees looking to better their own circumstances. Their goal was unchanged: they were freedom fighters, and they wanted to join the U.S. military to liberate their country.

Pepa, eager to fulfill his dream of becoming a pilot, asked to join the Air Force, but his request was turned down. The only branch of the service open to foreign-born nationals was the Army, under the provisions of the Lodge Act.* So that was where Radek, Pepa and Milan went, impatient to begin their training.

In December 1953, the three young fighters embarked on the last leg of their great odyssey, crossing the Atlantic on the military troopship USS *General Butler*. When the *Butler* dropped anchor in New York, Pat Moynihan was the first civilian on board. He rushed up to the captain's bridge to meet them and urged the Czechs to consider the book project.

After basic training at Fort Dix, Pepa, Radek, and Milan elected to join the U.S. Army Special Forces, formed the previous year. At that time the Special Forces were heavily populated with East European exiles who hoped to fight a war of liberation to free their countries, like their older brothers and fathers who had fought in the British and French armies in World War II.

Even among these dedicated fighters, the Masins were something special. Not only had they taken on more than a division's worth of East German and Soviet troops, they had prevailed. They were put on the elite Special Forces demonstration team and singled out for introduction to visiting dignitaries. They were scheduled to meet President Eisenhower.† They trained hard for the imminent war. When other soldiers left the base for a weekend of partying, Radek and Pepa stayed behind, doing endurance runs, practicing marksmanship and timed assembly and disassembly of weapons in the dark. And all the time they waited for the coming conflict.

---

*The Lodge bill, passed by Congress in June 1950 (Public Law 587), provided for military recruitment of East European émigrés to fight against the Soviet Union in the event of war in the European theater. Subsequently, the scope of the enterprise was substantially reduced. Eastern Europeans recruited under the Lodge Act entered the Special Forces, where they were trained to work behind enemy lines as drop teams that would organize, train, and lead partisan resistance and sabotage of Soviet supply lines in Eastern Europe. (Prados, John, *Presidents' Secret Wars: CIA and Pentagon Covert Operations from World War II through Iranscam*, New York: Quill/Morrow, 1986, 89, 222-23, 235.)

†The meeting didn't take place; Eisenhower suffered a heart attack a few days beforehand and was indisposed.

In 1954 and again in 1956 men in civilian clothes arrived on base and questioned the two brothers about their contacts in Czechoslovakia and in particular about Vanek. Both times the visitors left, clearly interested and impressed. Nothing more happened. Because in Czechoslovakia Zdena Masinova and Borek Novak alone knew about Vanek, the secret remained safe. Vanek's group was never implicated in the spreading wave of forced confessions, accusations, and incriminations of the other group members. But neither did he get the word he desperately awaited from the Americans.

After the Korean War ended in a draw between the Communists and the western democracies, Milan, Pepa, and Radek remained confident that the U.S. would take the initiative to liberate Eastern Europe. Then in June of 1956 workers in Poznan, Poland, struck. The protests were savagely beaten down by the military, leaving several workers dead. The United States did nothing. Four months later, on 23 October, students and workers took to the streets of Budapest, Hungary. The uprising in Hungary electrified the world. Here was a broad-based popular revolt by a satellite people against their Communist oppressors. With Eisenhower's tough anticommunist talk during the election campaign and the stated U.S. policy of rolling back Communism, surely the moment had come for the West to act and free the East bloc.

Radek, Pepa, and Milan waited in tense anticipation for word that Special Forces would be airlifted in to help the rebels. But when Soviet tanks rolled into the country, the United States again did nothing. The days passed, and Hungarian calls for help on rebel-held radio stations became progressively more anguished and desperate. By 14 November the Soviets had crushed the resistance, unopposed by the West.

As in May 1953, when workers rose up in Plzen, Czechoslovakia; in June 1953, when East Germans revolted; and in June 1956 when the workers of Poznan rebelled, the American response was to provide "sympathy and asylum, but no arms."* More than thirty thousand Hungarians died and at least three hundred thousand fled across the borders. U.S. government policy

---

*CIA duty officer's instructions from Washington to the Berlin base as the Berlin Revolt erupted in June, 1953, as quoted in Gross, *Operation Rollback*, 215. Kracauer and Berkman, *Satellite Mentality Political Attitudes and Propaganda Susceptibilities of Non-Communists in Hungary, Poland and Czechoslovakia*, 124-5.

makers subsequently acknowledged that the Hungarian uprising was largely a result of the inflammatory broadcasts of VOA and RFE.

The Hungarians, like the Germans, Czechs, and Poles before them, had revolted in the expectation that the American government and its Western European allies would come to their aid, but Eisenhower administration policy papers show that the administration never seriously considered giving them help. Forced to face the horrific consequences of its policy of inciting rebellions it had no intention of supporting, the Eisenhower administration's response was a tactical retreat: it toned down the rhetoric on the VOA and RFE broadcasts.

Pepa, Radek, and Milan were bitterly disillusioned. Obviously the Western allies had no intention of putting their money where their mouths were. All hope of the Soviet demise was dashed.

The winter of 1956 was a time of agonizing soul-searching for the three Czechs. Saddened and embittered, they concluded that the West lacked the political will to free the captive nations of the East bloc. They wanted desperately to return to their families in Czechoslovakia. But they faced the terrible reality that they would never see them again.*

The three Czechs decided that there was no point in continued service with the U.S. military. Over the pleas of their superior officers, Pepa and Radek abandoned their applications to Officer Candidate School. With two years to go until their discharges, all three applied for overseas postings. Pepa and Radek were reassigned to Europe, and Milan went to Korea.

Other blows followed in quick succession. In 1957, after four years of uncertainty, Pepa and Radek began a correspondence with their sister by carefully coded proxy letters. They learned of the show trials, the sentences, and the executions. The tragic news compounded their disillusionment. They and their loved ones had paid a huge personal price for the belief that the United States was serious about its promises on Voice of America.

---

*This sense of abandonment at the realization that the West wouldn't act was shared by those behind the Iron Curtain. Nenda recalled, "After East Germany [1953] I thought that liberation would be possible." Her husband Rudolf Martin: "The situation was such that we thought there would be another war." Nenda: "But after Hungary, it was finished. That was a terrible, terrible moment for us. There was no hope anymore. None!"

Though Pepa felt personally betrayed, he remained a firm believer in American ideals, a patriot in the true sense of the word. But he was also a pragmatist. He lived in the present and planned for the future, putting the past behind him when it was clear all recourses had been exhausted and he could do nothing more about it.

EPILOGUE

"The criminals . . . had outside help," concluded Colonel Auersperg in the official Trapo after-action summary.[1] How else could they have continued their flight after Waldow and smashed through the cordon at the Berlin Ring?

After the East German authorities called off Operation Uckro on 4 November, the search for a scapegoat began in earnest. On 18 November, the top brass of the East German armed forces convened in a specially called conference to take stock of Operation Uckro. Head of the Armed Forces Karl Maron presided. In its analysis of Operation Uckro, the leadership tacitly acknowledged that the population remained hostile and restive.* It also acknowledged that problems observed during the June uprising with respect to training, equipment quality, and readiness and logistics had not yet been corrected.[2]

In October, however, the officer corps had had to contend with a new problem. Troops, green recruits as well as veterans, were terrified of the Czechs—the term "fear psychosis" was used repeatedly—and their ability to kill men at long range with single shots marked them, in the troops' eyes, as near-supermen. The fact that they escaped repeatedly even when surrounded and vastly outnumbered made their fearsome reputation grow to the point that troops would not move forward without armored personnel carriers supporting them. Although the Masin brothers and their friends

---

*BArch, MdI, DO 1/11/777, 000019. VP Kommandeur Schneider's report was typical of the evasive circumlocutions: "The connection with the population is an important question. In spite of the many measures like the creation of the ABV positions and the voluntary helpers, we have not yet achieved the connection to the workers that is required by the present times. We got virtually no leads."

were not alone in carrying arms to ensure their passage to Berlin,* they were virtually alone in daring to oppose the armed forces of the regime in a face-to-face, point-blank confrontation. In the June uprising, there is no documented case of protestors firing on troops—only the reverse.

In analyzing the June 1953 revolt, the Party had believed its own propaganda line: foreign agents and saboteurs had goaded the misguided masses to revolt. So when in October 1953 five armed foreigners engaged in a gun battle with Volkspolizei in a provincial train station, four short months after the near-foundering of the Communist regime in East Germany, it responded to the textbook nightmare: foreign elements controlled by the Western intelligence services instigating an uprising. The entire chain of command, up to the Head of the Armed Forces Karl Maron and Minister of Interior Stoph, was alerted.

Whereas the Volkspolizei had been caught napping in June, in October its response was a mind-boggling overreaction. Determined not to repeat past mistakes, the authorities threw everything they had at the first sign of trouble. The goal was, first, to stamp out the foreign provocateurs before they fomented unrest among the local population, and second, to repair the extremely blemished reputation of the armed forces by neutralizing the threat.

Though the Volkspolizei had a clear picture of its opponents by 11 October—one group of five young Czechs hell-bent on getting to Berlin—the leadership carried on as if it were facing another major existential threat. Even when all the wanted men were pinned down in a tiny area measuring some fifty-five hundred square feet on the night of 16 October, the actions in other parts of the country did not abate. They had taken on a life of their own.

Ultimately, the campaign was a humiliating failure for the East German security apparatus. Three of the five Czechs—including the group's leaders—made it to the West. The military leadership engaged in an orgy of finger-pointing during the 18 November conference. Training, political officers, supply officers, and unit leaders all came in for blame. Major General Dombrowsky, head of the Criminal Police, criticized Lieutenant General Seifert for deploying military-style perimeters, though his own order of 10 October had actually launched that method of operation. Seifert in turn blamed Helmut Strempel for letting the wanted men escape from Uckro train station.[3]

---

*It was common knowledge that attempting to leave one's country was akin to treason and carried high penalties: years in forced labor camps and the uncertainty of surviving the ordeal.

Head of the Armed Forces Karl Maron singled out Colonel Karl Mellmann,[4] Seifert's subordinate, for censure and sharply scolded those who claimed that the tactic of setting and searching perimeters was responsible for the fiasco. He pointed out that "our decisive failing is not tactical"; indeed, the tactic had worked flawlessly in the past, and "we pinned the bandits down . . . for about three weeks." In this case, the East German armed forces were simply outmatched: "this group of criminals was in my opinion absolutely an exceptionally daring group with good marksmen. . . . That the dead were finished off with a single shot, and furthermore pistol shots, shows that they must have been good shots."[5] The Czechs had simply been mentally tougher, better trained, and more determined than the Volkspolizei.

At the conclusion of the 18 November after-action review, the only thing that everyone could agree upon was that the troops needed more training. When the minutes of the after-action review were written up and filed away, the incident was allowed to recede into oblivion. The *Geschichte der Deutschen Volkspolizei* (History of the German People's Police), the official history of the East German People's Police published in 1979 by GDR Minister of Interior Friederich Dickel, makes no mention of one of the largest mobilizations of the East German armed forces in its entire history.

While the East German Communist authorities shrouded their humiliation in a conspiracy of silence, the Czechoslovak Communist authorities took the opposite tack. They had nothing to be ashamed of: after all, their army had not been humiliated by five men with pistols, and they had rounded up a satisfactory number of "class enemies" as scapegoats. Nevertheless, the escape of the group's leaders rankled for decades. In various books, articles and films, the anticommunist resistance, personified by the Masin group, was portrayed as a collection of bloodthirsty, drunken hooligans and casual murderers in the service of the Western imperialists.*

---

*In 1965, *Voják*, the official Czech armed forces magazine, ran a four-issue series on the Mašín brothers' resistance activities. State publishing houses published three books about the activities of the Mašín group: R. Jánský, *Tady Bespečnost* (Prague: Naše Vojsko, 1966); R. J. Suling, *Životy Pro Život* (Prague: Naše Vojsko, 1976); and Frantisek Vrbecky, *Mrtví Nemluví* (Prague: Naše Vojsko, 1985). State television dramatized one of the group's raids in a segment of *The 30 Cases of Major Zeman*, a cops-and-robbers show, in which the detective hero took on the Communist Party's enemies in historical sequence, from Nazi-era collaborators to a banned rock group modeled on Plastic People of the Universe, whose members were jailed by the Communists in the 1970s. (Green, Peter S., "'Major Zeman' leads Czechs to Question their Past," *International Herald Tribune*, 10 January 1999.)

Once he was out of the Army, Dad returned to live in Germany and marry my mother, a West German citizen. He was then the only one of the three survivors living in Europe, in the West German city of Cologne. In the spring of 1961, an FBI agent requested a meeting with him near the Cologne cathedral. He brought disconcerting news. "Watch your back," he said. Apparently a Soviet-bloc agent had just defected, turning himself in to the American authorities. His mission had been to assassinate my father. The FBI man's recommendation: "It's not safe here for you. We don't know how many other agents they've put on you. Go back to the States immediately."

My father demurred. He had just brought his new bride home to a little walk-up apartment and started a business, investing all of his money in it. He wasn't frightened, and he refused to turn his back on the new life he was building. He assured the FBI man that he could look out for himself. The FBI man continued to insist in the most urgent terms that he leave Germany, giving him a telephone number at the Bonn embassy to call if he observed anything suspicious, and another contact number for the Amt für Verfaßungsschutz, the German central intelligence agency, headquartered in Cologne.[6]

My father didn't notice anything suspicious. After a while he relaxed, dismissing the flubbed assassination as a one-shot attempt. But he was wrong: behind the scenes the StB had several case officers working diligently to capture or kill him.

The full scope of the effort became apparent after 1989, when some of the secret StB archives were opened. My aunt Nenda spent many days perusing the archives in Pardubice. She learned that she and her grandmother Emma had been the objects of an extensive espionage campaign that had kept dozens of agents busy for decades. There were bugs planted in their apartment, and every conversation had been recorded and transcribed. It didn't end there, though. My aunt knew she was under police surveillance, but she was shaken to find that people she had considered close friends, trusted confidantes, had been in the service of the StB for years, and that they had reported everything, from the most intimate to the most banal conversations.

The evidence in the files convinced her that the only reason the StB even let her go free in 1954, instead of sentencing her with the others, was to set her up as unwitting bait to snare her two brothers. The StB hoped the brothers would soon return to Czechoslovakia. When it became clear that my father and Radek wouldn't return, the StB decided to go after them.

The first documented attempt began in 1957 as a collaboration between the East German and Czechoslovak secret services.* On 11 June 1958 Czechoslovak Communist Interior Minister Barak signed off on Operation Brothers, whose objective was to assassinate or kidnap Radek and Dad.[7]

The StB began by recruiting longtime friends of the family. One was Oskar Cerny, a medical doctor who had been acquainted with my aunt Zdena since 1956. His StB cover name was Tomas. In late 1960 Tomas told my aunt that he was planning a trip to West Germany to visit relatives and suggested that he might use the opportunity to look up her brother. Zdena, thrilled, wrote the necessary introductory letter to my father. When Tomas met Dad on 2 May 1961, he brought photographs and greetings from Zdena and grandmother Emma. The meeting was cordial; my father received him with all the courtesy and hospitality due to a good friend of his sister. My mother, however, had her suspicions.

When he returned to the CSSR on 12 June 1961, Tomas filed an agent report packed with meticulous detail. He described my parents' car, the furniture in their apartment, and everything he found out about their business and personal affairs, their habits, and where and how they lived.

The next meeting between Tomas and his quarry took place in January 1962, in Vienna. His mother accompanied him this time. A file entry noted that a second agent, code-named Leo, was to travel there separately to spy on Tomas.

On 17 October 1963, Tomas's StB handler, Captain Tuma, was done gathering information. He submitted an abduction plan to his superior at the Second Department of Interior Ministry for approval and the following month Tomas was instructed to arrange a meeting between Nenda and Dad in Vienna. An entry in the project file dated 19 December 1963, stated laconically, "Should complications arise, Zdena Masinova should be isolated from public life. Eliminated." For reasons not recorded in the file the plan was not authorized.

---

*Only fragments of the original Masin files remain today in the former East German archives, but what remains shows that the Stasi was maintaining an active file on Joseph Masin as late as 1982. In a letter dated July 1, 1957, to East German Deputy Minister of State Security Lieutenant General Erich Mielke (later a member of the Central Committee and Minister of State Security) Lieutenant Colonel Dr. Karel Komárek advised that "a meeting took place in May of 1957, where representatives of the East German security apparatus advised their Czech counterparts that it might be possible to seize the two brothers in West Berlin and abduct them to the East German sector" (Berlin, 13.7.1957. BstU 00013).

In 1964, Tomas traveled to West Germany once again, this time to the town of Oettingen. He wrote a postcard to my father on 10 May inviting him to a meeting. Dad skipped the meeting, in spite of Tomas's dangled inducement that he was carrying photos and letters from his sister. Dad told Tomas later that he had had business to take care of in London. Dad didn't see the point in traveling so far and running up costs to see someone he had no particular desire to see.[8]

Subsequently, Captain Tuma put another agent on the case. Josef Jina, a former classmate and close friend of my father, was the son of a factory owner. He had taken over Kikina's band when the latter was sentenced to extensive jail time in 1955, and had continued with it ever since. Jina was assigned the cover name Jindra.

Though Jindra and Dad had been close buddies during high school, it had been more than thirteen years since their last contact. The StB was puzzling out the knotty problem of how Jindra could plausibly get ahold of Dad's address and contact him. Their solution was to publish it. The magazine *Vojak* ("Soldier") obligingly ran a sensationalized and defamatory article on 4 June 1966, which reported in outraged tones that the wife of the famous terrorist Josef Masin had visited her in-laws in Czechoslovakia. At the close, they printed her mother's full address in Germany. Jindra's story was that his band would be touring in the West and, having fortuitously discovered his long-lost friend Pepa's address in the magazine, he decided to look him up. Figuring it was a plant, my father didn't bother answering the letter.

The StB already had another agent lined up should Jindra fail. "Jana," in real life Edith Plech, was the sister of Egon Plech, who himself had been recruited by the StB. In fall 1966 Jana was primed for contacting Pepa in West Germany. Her first assignment was to scout the lay of the land in Cologne and effect preparations for another abduction. Jana dutifully filed contact reports after each meeting until she and her family emigrated to West Germany in 1968.[9]

After the string of delays and bungled kidnapping attempts, the Communist government finally gave up, it seems. Nevertheless, they continued the relentless surveillance and harassment of my aunt Nenda and my great-grandmother for decades.

Emma died in 1977, at almost one hundred years old. She never saw her grandsons, Pepa and Radek, again. By 1989, my aunt Nenda was the only immediate family member left alive.

My father's faithful nanny, Manya, prayed until the end that God might grant her one more chance to see her beloved little boys, particularly Pepa. My mother, sister, and I visited her in 1984 and 1986, in the little Moravian village of Novosedly where she lived alone after the untimely deaths of her husband and stepson. Both times, Manya showed us her carefully tended garden and treated us to a lovingly prepared banquet featuring all of Pepa's favorite foods. "Pepa asked me to make him my special stuffed quail and tvarohové kolace* when he came back," she said in a quavering voice. "I'm making them for you now." It must have taken her days, if not weeks, to obtain all the special ingredients in Czechoslovakia's shortage-plagued command economy. Tears ran down her wrinkled cheeks as she fingered my sister's curly ash-blonde hair, marveling at her resemblance to our grandfather in his youth. My father waited for us across the border in Vienna, less than one hundred miles away. Manya died in 1988 without ever seeing her two boys again.

In 1989 geopolitical forces outside the Czechoslovaks' control once again dictated their future. As the Soviet Union fell behind in the arms race and its leadership was forced to make difficult choices in the allocation of its stretched resources, Soviet President Mikhail Gorbachev informed the client regimes in Eastern Europe that they were on their own. Deprived of Soviet support and confronted with increasingly strident public demands for civil liberties, the majority of them collapsed quickly and bloodlessly. In Czechoslovakia, on 10 December 1989, over a hundred thousand demonstrators thronged the streets of Prague and Bratislava to observe the Day of Human Rights. The Communist regime saw the writing on the wall.

Five days later Marian Calfa, the then-head of the Communist government, requested a private meeting with Vaclav Havel, the candidate for presidency put forward by the citizens' groups Civic Forum and Public Against Violence. The one-hour meeting between the two men took place in Calfa's offices. No minutes exist. On 29 December, the Communist-era parliament convened in Prague to elect a new president. As usual, there was a single candidate and he was elected unanimously—without one dissenting vote.[10] Vaclav Havel, playwright, former Communist fellow-traveler and erstwhile dissident, was now president.

In December 1989 I was just out of college, living and working in Germany. I phoned my father as pictures of joyous demonstrators in the streets of Prague flickered on the TV screen. I was surprised by his reaction.

---

*Small, round pastries, filled with a crème-fraîche-like filling

"That son of a bitch," he fumed.

"Why?" I asked. "What's the matter? He was a dissident, he opposed the government."

"You don't know what you're talking about!" Havel, it turned out, had been a schoolmate of my father's. This was something else I had never known, another surprising glimpse into Dad's past. Havel was a few years younger and their social lives rarely intersected. But my father did recall vividly that, after the 1948 coup, Havel was one of the first in the school to sport the trademark blue shirt with the SCM logo.* "His whole life, Havel went along. He chose the path of least resistance. He's got no spine."

"But he spent time in jail!" I countered. "He suffered, too."

"Caviar and massages. Yeah, sure he suffered! He never did anything that put him in serious jeopardy," Dad scoffed. "He carefully watched which way the wind was blowing and never pushed beyond what was safe. He never fought to overthrow the regime. He stood in corners and recited poetry." To my father, the man of action, writing plays with a subversive subtext was playing at dissidence, just another form of inaction. "Even when they put him in jail things never got really tough for him—that was after Helsinki!"†

In spite of my father's gloomy misgivings, developments in Czechoslovakia seemed to augur well. The Czechs prided themselves on the bloodlessness of their 1989 Velvet Revolution and their playwright-president. They were euphoric at the promise of a new beginning. A few valiant anticommunists campaigned for elected office to battle the entrenched cadres and bureaucracy. A new Office for Documentation and Investigation of Criminal Actions of the Communist Party (UDV) was established and staffed with ex-political prisoners.

In 1993 Parliament passed a law[11] condemning the communist regime as "illegitimate" and the Communist Party as "criminal." Another law opened the way to legal rehabilitation of victims of the Communist terror.[12] The so-called Lustration Law,[13] which established a process for vetting candidates to high-ranking civil service jobs and army positions, was

---

*SCM—Svaz Česke Mládeze (Organization of Czech Youth), the Communist youth organization

†The 1975 Helsinki Accords granted the Soviets economic benefits and Western recognition of the Soviet "sphere of influence" in Eastern Europe in exchange for Soviet promises to uphold human rights.

supposed to exclude StB collaborators and high party functionaries from such positions for five years. Meanwhile the Office of Protocol had its hands full stage-managing the visits of Western leaders, who eagerly queued up to share a few sound bites on the nightly news with the mediagenic Czech president and to bask in his reflected glory. Havel's credentials as a world-renowned dissident, a humanist, and a man of principle went unquestioned by the Western media. On TV, the whole world could see that all was well in the Czech Republic.

Indeed, the Czech Republic was one of the star pupils of the postcommunist class.* Only the Czech Republic, Poland, and East Germany boasted laws of lustration.[14] But unlike East Germany, which had grafted itself onto West Germany, jettisoning its Communist-era law, political institutions, judiciary, senior bureaucracy, and senior military hierarchy, Czechoslovakia had no "West Czechoslovakia" with a working democratic tradition to graft onto. Like it or not, the Czechs had to muddle along for themselves. Numerous movers and shakers from the old regime continued to cling to power. They had skeletons in their closets and secrets to protect.

Everyone had expected the ex-Communists to fight lustration. As it turned out, many of the ex-dissidents were just as opposed. On 2 April 1990, four short months after the Velvet Revolution, Czech Minister of the Interior Richard Sacher, JUDr., issued a remarkable decree. All documents referring to the president, the cabinet, and members of Parliament and the leadership of the socialist political party were ordered removed from the operational archives and stored "in metal containers which are to be sealed." The alleged reason? "To secure the stability of the political development."[15] Curious citizens could be forgiven for wondering why it was necessary to exempt the president, his cabinet, and Parliament from the sharp beam of inquiry, to which every other citizen in the nation was subjected.

As the months rolled by, few former Communists were charged with crimes, and even fewer were sentenced. Between 1989 and 2003 only three Communist officials saw the inside of a prison for crimes committed under the former regime: one, briefly, for planning violent measures to stop the Velvet Revolution, and two for actions taken around the time of the Prague

---

*Czechoslovakia split into the separate states of the Czech Republic and the Slovak Republic effective January 1993.

Spring.* Not one for crimes related to the putsch or the massive Stalinist terror. Anticommunists were furious.

The victims of Communism had hoped to see justice done in court. It was not to be. The judges thumping their gavels on the rostrum were the same individuals who had once authorized politically inspired murders and sentenced their hapless victims to decades in prisons and the infamous Communist mental institutions. The legal standard they applied to Communist-era crimes was Communist-era law. If the prison guards and secret police had acted according to the law as it existed at the time they arrested, beat, and shot their victims, they were untouchable.

Dr. Milan Hulik was one of the new government's committed reformers in the early 1990s. By the time I spoke to him in September 2002, he had retired from public office, thoroughly disgusted at the Havel government's unwillingness to clean up the Communist skeletons still hiding in the nation's closets. He told me, "After the Velvet Revolution Vaclav Havel changed. . . . The sole ministry where people with a heavy Communist past were removed was the former security service, the StB, renamed SIB. Efforts to remove the entrenched Communists all failed. There was no support from the top."

Hulik reported directly to Prosecutor General Setina. In 1993, Setina sent him on a trip to Germany to research German methods of neutralizing entrenched Communist power structures by means of legal and institutional reform and systematic forced retirement of legacy personnel in high-ranking military and civilian posts. Hulik came back armed with data, reports, and research to be translated from German into Czech. The project was put on ice when Setina was forced from office that year. It was never revived.

That same year Hulik was summoned to lunch by Vaclav Havel. He took the opportunity of presenting his findings from Germany to the president and pointing out the total inaction in the Czech Republic with respect to cleansing itself from its Communist past. Havel said nothing during the whole disquisition. Hulik noticed that he fiddled with his cigarettes and

---

*Czechoslovak Communist Party leader Alexander Dubček introduced limited political reforms in Czechoslovakia in 1968, which he referred to as "socialism with a human face." This was not an attempt to overthrow the Communist regime, as in Hungary in 1956, but simply to modify it. The so-called Prague Spring ended when Warsaw Pact troops invaded on the night of 20–21 August 1968.

cigarette lighter and wouldn't make eye contact. After the meeting he heard nothing more from Havel and there was no change in policy.

Hulik's next and final meeting with Havel was three years later, at a private reception. Hulik confronted Havel, stating that nothing had been done with respect to the problem of Communists in power and pointing out that Havel had not supported reform. Havel was evasive, and finally answered, "We must look to the future and not the past."

The establishment elites were looking to the future. They had already moved to secure their position in the new order. Managers of the people's enterprises scooped up the factories they ran at fire-sale prices. Provincial apparatchiks hurriedly acquired the houses they inhabited in sweetheart deals at laughably low prices. In light of these flagrant abuses, the terms *privatization* and *free market* struck the public, which was not privy to these cozy deals, as a mockery.

As the promise of the Velvet Revolution soured, the case of *Novak et al.* came up for review at the UDV, the Office for Documentation and Investigation of Criminal Actions of the Communist Party, which had been set up ostensibly to obtain justice for the victims of Communism. The UDV's standard operating procedure called for stripping the political window-dressing from the charges and looking at what was left. In this way the UDV rehabilitated thousands of farmers, professional people, and small businessmen who had been sentenced to prison and labor camp simply because they were designated class enemies.

Zdena Masinova Sr. was fully rehabilitated under Law No. 119/1990, but Vasek Sveda, Borek Novak, and Zbynek Janata had engaged in "active" as opposed to "passive" resistance. Unlike virtually all of the rest of the UDV's "clientele," they were not victims. They had fought armed terror with weapons. And so when the UDV reviewed their cases, it simply applied its standard operating procedure, stripping the politics from the charges and looking at what was left. Under the UDV procedure, high treason, sabotage, and weapons possession became robbery, theft of state property, and attempted murder. The death sentences were posthumously commuted to fifteen years' imprisonment. It was a bitter day for my father—these men had fought to free their country from totalitarian dictatorship and paid the ultimate price, and the postcommunist government adjudged them to be nothing more than common criminals.

Meanwhile, charges against the Masin brothers and Milan Paumer had never been brought because the trio had received political asylum in the United States. But the groundwork for the case to be brought against them, named *Masin et al.* after it was split from the case against *Novak et al.*, still lay in the state prosecutor's office—still actionable. A number of the pro-reform newspapers began to question the status of the case of the Masin brothers and their resistance group. After every article, letters to the editor poured in. The case quickly became a flashpoint of controversy that sharply illuminated the fissures in the nation's body politic. Heroes, murderers. Patriots, gangsters. Conscience of the nation, bloodthirsty pariahs. All of these terms were applied to my father, my uncle, and their associates.

The UDV came up with a solution to make the problem go away without rocking the political boat. It ruled that *Masin et al.* wouldn't go to trial because some of the contemplated charges were no longer actionable under the new law and the others fell under the statute of limitations, which had run out in 1975. On 28 August 1995, the case was shelved by the district prosecutor's office at Prague (the Mestske Statní Zastupitelství, or MSZ).

Predictably, the decision infuriated both the proponents of continuity and the reformers. Instead of subsiding after the UDV's decision, the public debate crescendoed in a blizzard of feature articles, op-ed pieces, letters to the editor, and TV talk shows. Pundits, politicians, religious leaders, and ordinary citizens from all walks of life weighed in on the case.

It was a proxy battle. The Masin group had been the only group to conduct an extended campaign of armed resistance against the Czechoslovak Communist regime in the forty-one years of its existence. Where you stood on the case of the Masin brothers pretty much told the story of where you stood on the question of Communist guilt and the government policy of continuity. Those who advocated legal continuity with the past took the position that the Masins had not only violated the law, they had violated the sanctity of human life. They were murderers, pure and simple.

On the other side of the political chasm stood the reformers and the organizations representing former political prisoners. They took the position that it was the Communist regime and Communist Party that were guilty of unspeakable crimes against humanity. The Masins, they avowed, had courageously fought a vicious totalitarian regime, and the new post-communist government was letting the real guilty parties get away with thousands of counts of murder.

Forty high-profile members of Czech political, religious, and cultural life signed a petition that was formally submitted to the Ministry of Justice on 29 June 1995: "We regard criminal prosecution against them [the Masins] as morally impermissible and also as an act which is not legal. With weapon in hand, the Masin brothers fought against the Communist regime, which according to the law is a criminal and illegitimate regime that is reprehensible and [of which the law says] that every fight against it is worthy of honor." *

While this petition was being shuffled from one desk in the Ministry of Justice to the next, the city council of the little town of Sadska, in Bohemia, voted the Masin brothers honorary citizens. Polite answers were sent to the petitioners that their requests had been received and would be duly considered when the time was right. It turned out that Havel reciprocated my father's disdain, and, off the record, said that he was ashamed to be the schoolmate of men of violence like my father and uncle. His office took no action on the petitions.

The Czech Boy Scouts filed a petition on 16 February 1998, asking the Parliament of the Czech Republic to award the Order of T. G. Masaryk[†] to the two Masin brothers and their mother. The city council of Sadska also filed requests on two occasions. Of the three nominees only Zdena Masinova Sr., who was not actively involved in her sons' struggle, was ultimately decorated, posthumously on 28 October 1998, for her resistance to Communism.

There is a striking paradox at the heart of the debate about the *Causa Masin*, as it is known in the Czech Republic. The national consensus today is that armed resistance against the Nazi regime was moral and necessary, but many Czechs feel ambivalent about armed resistance against the Communists. On one hand, Josef Masin Sr. is canonized as a national hero for his armed fight against Nazi oppression. On the other, his sons, who used many of the same methods in their fight against the equally ruthless Communists, are the subjects of a political debate on morality.

---

*The petition was signed by author Jan Beneš, publicist Vladimír Just, Archabbot Anastaz Opásek, and parliamentary representatives for the ODS Party Ivan Mašek and Viktor Dobal, among others.

†The Tomas Garrigue Masaryk Order is awarded by the Czech president to persons "who have made eminent contributions to the furtherance of democracy, humanity and human rights."

General Masin's organization planted two thousand bombs in Reich factories, staged assassination attempts on Himmler, and exploded bombs in the Ministry of Aviation and the Reich Police Directorate. There is no doubt that civilians were injured and killed in actions conducted by the Three Kings directly or as a result of intelligence they furnished to the Western allies. But Czechs concur that even civilian casualties, though regrettable, were acceptable and justified in the struggle against the Nazi dictatorship. In fact, General Masin was posthumously awarded a number of medals and promotions for his resistance activities, most recently the Milan Ratislav Stefanik Order, second class, in 1992. His sons' resistance activities resulted in a mere six deaths: three were armed East German troops, two were armed Czech policemen, and one was an armed Czech militiaman who pulled his weapon on my father, who was unarmed at the time.

Dr. Pavel Rychetsky, at the time Minister of Justice, argued, "A fight against it [totalitarianism] is okay, but nobody may die as a result."* The view that resistance fighters could kill Nazis but not Communists is disingenuous in view of the fact that the Communists were busy liquidating entire segments of the population. They destroyed tens of thousands of lives, executing innocent civilians in what were essentially political murders, and killing many others through abuse and torture.

The reasons for this remarkable bipolar thinking are complex and deeply rooted. It is not that the Communists in the 1950s were somehow practicing a kinder, gentler form of totalitarianism than the Nazis in the 1940s. They were not. It is not that they murdered fewer people. They did not. Instead of race genocide, the Communists practiced class genocide. In the Stalinist-Leninist Soviet Union and its client states all over the world, millions more were murdered than under Hitler's Nazi regime. In the *Black Book of Communism,* the authors speak of over 100 million worldwide victims of Communism, versus 25 million victims of Nazism.[16]

However, the nature of the West's conflict with Communism evolved differently from its conflict with Nazism. In the 1950s, both Americans and Europeans believed that a third world war in the European theater was a real and imminent danger. After the Hungarian Uprising of 1956, the threat of war receded. It was clear to everyone on both sides of the Iron Curtain

*Television program "Aréna," broadcast 29 August 1995. Pavel Rychetský was a member of the Communist Party from 1966-69, Deputy Prime Minister from 1990-92, and is today Chief Justice of the Constitutional Court of the Czech Republic.

that the Americans wouldn't intervene on behalf of the captive peoples in Eastern Europe. By 1975 the Helsinki Accords set the stage for an ongoing dialogue. Détente and rapprochement were the buzzwords of the era.

The Communist regimes themselves also evolved over time. Younger generations who came of age in the 1970s and 1980s have no recollection of the Stalinist terror of the 1950s. It was not talked about in most homes and it was not taught in the schools. The experience of the East bloc baby boomers encompassed the years of détente and the Helsinki accords. The Communist Party of their day was effete and complacent, led by a group of geriatric apparatchiks. It was inefficient, perhaps; corrupt, certainly, but not all that bad, if you could put up with the petty indignities, a low standard of living, and the lack of civil liberties.

Opposing the regime could still get you locked up, but in the 1970s a prison sentence was not an implied death sentence, as it often was in the 1950s. Thanks to his high profile in the West, Vaclav Havel was able to study English and obtain books and current newspapers in prison. He could watch television, obtain massages for lumbago, and receive dental and medical attention, as well as frequent visits and letters from friends and family.*

Perhaps, as some have argued, the forty-one-year-old habit of cohabitation and ethical compromise had left everybody who stayed in the country at least a little bit guilty of collaboration. As Milena Kolarova points out, "The majority of us are not heroes . . . and for this reason I believe that it is impossible to compare the lives of the majority of the people who have found a way to accommodate themselves with the lives of the minority of people who did not accommodate themselves."[17]

Why does Czechoslovakia's inaction with respect to the country's Communist past matter? Isn't it better to just let bygones be bygones, and look to the future? The problem is that the past continues to inform the present, and the future as well. The issues at stake are really much larger than a fight about a handful of Communist-era death sentences and findings

---

*See his descriptions of prison life in Havel, Václav, *Letters to Olga*, New York: Henry Holt & Co., 1989, Letters 4, 5, 7, 14, 17, 20, 29, 49, 53, 61, 86, 87, 99, 114, 126. This experience stands in stark contrast to those of Milada Horáková and Heliodor Píka, and to those of Ctibor Novák, Zbyněk Janata, and Václav Svěda, who were not allowed to see their families even once between their arrest and their execution, who received no mail from their families, and whose last letters were not delivered to their families for the entire duration of the Communist regime. Also compare the case of Zdena Mašín, who was left to die of cancer on a freezing concrete floor.

of criminality made in absentia and without due process fifty years ago. The bitter conflict about the Masin case is merely one small symptom of a much larger ill. The promised reforms of the early years are petering out in political compromises and corruption at the highest levels.

The same Communist-era laws that legalized state-sponsored property theft, murder, torture, and blackmail continue on the books today. The same judges continue judging.* The same bureaucrats who benefited from the graft-ridden, corrupt command economy under Communism continue today in their positions of power: in the ministries, in the largest national enterprises, and in the provincial government offices. Instead of a clean break with the past, continuity was and is the name of the game.

The lesson to those paying attention was simple: collaboration pays. Those who had not joined the Party, who had struggled against the regime and lost their homes, their businesses, their livelihoods, and sometimes many years of their lives, were the big losers. Integrity, hard work, and personal responsibility counted for nothing.

Sadly, the case of Czechoslovakia is not unique. Communists continue in power in Hungary, in Poland, in Russia, in Belorussia, in Romania, and in Serbia. These "reformed" Communists make up the present-day business and political elites across the former Soviet Bloc. They are unrepentant of their crimes. As one observer has pointed out, the police do not need to catch all the criminals all of the time for most people to submit to public order, but they need to catch a significant proportion. Nothing encourages lawlessness more than the sight of villains getting away with it, living off their spoils, and laughing in the public's face.[18]

By contrast, the Nazi Reich was totally annihilated and its leaders were held publicly accountable for their crimes. In 1945 West Germany lay prostrate and received a new, democratic constitution and new laws from its occupiers. This constitution still continues in force today. A number of high-ranking Nazi officials were brought to justice in widely publicized trials, and the National Socialist party was banned. As a result, National Socialism as an ideology was thoroughly discredited. Whereas in the former West Germany neo-Nazis are ostracized, existing as pariahs on the political and social margins, in Eastern Europe it is quite acceptable and respectable to be a Communist.

And therein lies the crux of the problem. If the Czech Republic and other countries of the former Soviet Bloc fail to come to grips with their

---

*President Havel signed a bill into law giving life tenure to all Communist-era judges.

totalitarian pasts, the old elites will keep their hold on power. They will become more confident and act with greater impunity to smother the nascent stirrings of a free press, eliminate their political opponents, and prevent the development of the rule of law and an independent, apolitical judical system. The epochal defeat of Communism, which seemed to usher in a new era of freedom and democracy just a few years ago, is threatening to become a hollow promise.

In September 2002, I was invited to attend a commemorative ceremony for my grandfather in the Czech Republic. It was the sixtieth anniversary of his execution by the Nazis, and the little village of Losany, his birthplace, was pulling out all the stops to mark the occasion. In front of the ancestral farm stands a grove of birch trees Josef planted upon his return from Russia. They are now more than eighty years old, bearing witness to one man's odyssey through the vast Siberian birch forests and clear around the world in the quest for his people's freedom.

As I stood under the birch trees and watched the speakers and the audience who had come to honor my grandfather, I was deeply moved to see that he is revered and respected to the present day for his principled stand against totalitarian dictatorship. My aunt was one of the speakers at the ceremony. She quoted her father's testament and his mandate to his children: "I do not wish for you to live as slaves in the future, rather, you should live as liberated and free citizens. Do not forget that the first obligation of every conscious Czech is to defend the freedom of the nation. You too must in future proceed in this way."

She told the audience: "Our fight is not over. Much remains to be done." Milan Paumer and I laid a wreath at his memorial—I represented my uncle and father, who didn't attend. They still refuse to set foot in the country, as a matter of principle, "until they fix the laws and see to it that justice is done," as my father says.

Afterwards I wanted to see the archival records on my father and my uncle. Documentary filmmaker Martin Vadas and I made several trips to various archives, only to find that the relevant papers seemed to have disappeared. Archivists were still afraid. Quite a few were prepared to help, but some of them didn't want to talk on the telephone from their offices. And this was the twelfth year after the celebrated Velvet Revolution! We chased strangely elusive documents throughout the bureaucracy. It appeared they were in the president's office, then in one of Prague's other archives, and then again—an educated guess by Martin Vadas—that they were in the state prosecutor's office. And that is where we finally found them—some of them, at least. Key documents were still unaccountably missing.

I also wanted to see the letter that had started it all: the Pankrac Testament, the letter that my grandfather had written on toilet paper before he was executed. My arrival in Prague coincided with the largest flood in recorded history. Old-town Prague had been inundated. A few years earlier my aunt had given my grandfather's personal effects to the national archives for safe-keeping. They were stored in the archive building in Karlín. To my horror I learned that Karlín was the hardest-hit area of the city. In the chaos of the rising floodwaters, volunteers and archivists working around the clock had hauled materials from the lower stories to those that would hopefully lie above the water line. When the floodwaters finally receded, they left behind tons of mud and sodden papers, and nobody knew what was saved and what had perished.

The Karlín archives were closed for the duration of my visit. I left Prague in mid-September, not having seen my grandfather's letter. To this day, no one knows whether the Pankrac Testament survived or perished, swallowed up by the surging brown flood waters of the Vltava River.

APPENDIX 1

OATH FOR MEMBERS OF THE CZECHOSLOVAK PEOPLE'S MILITIA

I, a member of the People's Militia, swear to always sacrifice myself and loyally service the Communist Party of Czechoslovakia, the working class, and my socialist homeland, and the strengthening of the international connection with the Soviet Union and other socialist nations. I will with full responsibility and consciousness raise my political and battle preparedness and consciously fulfill all orders of the party organs and orders of my leadership and all tasks arising from membership with the People's Militia. I am prepared to defend, with weapon in hand, the interests of the Party, the revolutionary gains of the working class, and the socialist state, above all against internal and external enemies. In case of need [I] will not question the need to sacrifice my own life in their defense. This I swear.

OATH FOR SNB POLICEMEN

I, a member of the Corps of National Security, ceremoniously swear loyalty to my socialist homeland, the Czechoslovak Socialist Republic, to the proletariat, and to the working people who are lead by the Czechoslovak Communist Party. I swear to be an honest, brave, and disciplined member of the Corps of National Security, that I will unshakably defend the social institutions, the lawful rights of the citizens, and the public order. I shall improve my own political convictions on the basis of Marxism-Leninism and the level of my own general and specific education and my own purity. I will attentively guard the State's and Service's secrets. I will always resolutely fight the enemies of my socialist homeland, the enemies of the Soviet Socialist Republic, and of other allied Socialist states. I will guard the friendship and reinforce cooperation with the people of the Soviet Socialist Republic and other allied Socialist states, and the fighting alliance with their armed security organs. I shall stake all my powers and abilities on this and am prepared to stake my life in the ongoing combat for the interests of the Czechoslovak Socialist Republic and accomplishment of its international obligations in the fight for Peace and Communism. This I swear.

APPENDIX 2

GUIDE TO CZECH DIACRITICS AND PRONUNCIATION
(words shown in order of first appearance)

In This Book	Czech	Pronunciation
PROLOGUE		
Radek	Radek	**Rah**-deck
Pepa	Pepa	**Peh**-pah
Milan	Milan	**Mee**-lahn
Vasek	Vašek	**Vah**-shek
Zbynek	Zbyněk	**Zbih**-niek
Josef Balaban	Josef Balabán	Yo-sef **Bah**-lah-baahn
Vaclav Moravek	Václav Morávek	**Vah**-tslav **Moh**-rah-veck
CHAPTER 1		
Frantisek Masin	František Mašín	**Frahn**-tishek **Mah**-sheen
Kolin	Kolín	**Ko**-leen
Marie Masinova	Marie Mašínová	**Mah**-rie-eh **Mah**-shee-nova
Vladimir	Vladimír	Vlah-**dee**-meer
Mrazek	Mrázek	**Mrah**-zek
Pejsa	Pejša	**Pey**-shah
Tomas Masaryk	Tomáš Masaryk	**Toh**-mawsh **Mah**-sah-reek
Vojta Holecek	Vojta Holeček	**Voy**-tyah **Hol**-echek
Losany	Lošany	**Loh**-shah-nee
Zdena Novakova	Zdena Nováková	**Zdeh**-nah Noh-**vah**-kovah
Ctirad	Ctirad	**Tsti**-rahd
CHAPTER 2		
Jugovic	Jugovič	**You**-govich
Benes	Beneš	**Ben**-esh
Jan Syrovy	Jan Syrový	**Jahn See**-ro-vee
Ptak	Pták	**Ptahk`**
Ruzyne	Ruzyně	**Roo**-shin-yeh
Hacha	Hácha	**Hah**-ha
Sara	Šára	**Shaah**-rah
Skoda	Škoda	**Shkoh**-dah
Tri Kralove	Tři Králové	Tree **Krah**-loh-veh

In This Book	Czech	Pronunciation
CHAPTER 3		
Dolni Liboc	Dolní Liboc	**Dol**-nee **Lih**-bots
Palat	Palát	**Pah**-laht
Plzen	Plzeň	Pl-**zeh**-n
Semtin	Semtín	**Sem**-teen
Rehak	Řehák	**Reh**-hawk
Ctibor Novak	Ctibor Novák	**Tstee**-bor **Noh**-vahk
Likar	Líkař	**Lee**-car
V Boj	V Boj	V **Boy**
Manya	Maňa	**Mah**-nya
Perstejn	Perštejn	**Per**-shtain
Polibte mi prdel	Polibte mi prdel	Poh-**lib**-te mee **Pr**-del
Podebrady	Poděbrady	**Poh**-dee-eh-brah-dee
Radousku	Radoušku	**Rah**-dough-shkoo
Pankrac	Pankrác	**Pahn**-krahts
CHAPTER 4		
Vanek	Vaněk	**Vah**-niek
Milos	Miloš	**Mee**-losh
Vrnatova	Vrňatová	Vr-**nyah**-toh-vah
Vojtech	Vojtěch	**Voy**-tyehk
Pepicku	Pepičku	**Peh**-peech-koo
Nenuska	Nenuška	**Neh**-noo-shkah
Kadlec	Kadlec	**Kahd**-lets
Feshak	Fešák	**Fesh**-ahk
CHAPTER 5		
Tlapak	Tlapák	**Tlah**-pahk
Zdenek	Zdeněk	**Zdeh**-nyeck
Milada Horakova	Milada Horáková	**Mee**-lah-dah **Hor**-ah-ko-vah
Pribram	Příbram	**Pree**-brahm
Jachymov	Jáchymov	**Jah**-hee-mov
CHAPTER 7		
Chlumec nad Cidlinou	Chlumec nad Cidlinou	**Hloo**-mets nahd **Tsid**-lih-noh-oo
Sulc	Šulc	**Shults**
Jesenik	Jeseník	**Yeh**-seh-neek
Celakovice	Čelakovice	Che-**lah**-koh-vih-tse
Ceskoslovenska	Československá	**Ches**-kos-loh-ven-skah
Automobilova	Automobilová	A-**oo**-toh-moh-bee-loh-vah
Doprava	Doprava	**Doh**-prah-vah
CSAD	ČSAD	**Cheh**-sahd
Bezucha	Bezucha	**Beh**-zoo-ha
CHAPTER 8		
Bartolomejska	Bartolomějská	**Bar**-toh-loh-**may**-skah
Mirek	Mirek	**Mee**-reck

In This Book	Czech	Pronunciation
CHAPTER 9		
Marianska	Mariánská	**Mah**-ree-ahn-skah
CHAPTER 10		
Slansky	Slánský	**Slahn**-skee
Sveda	Švéda	**Shvey**-dah
Cineves	Činěves	**Chee**-nye-ves
Caslav	Čáslav	**Chah**-slahv
Hedvikov	Hedvíkov	**Hed**-vee-kov
Zleby	Žleby	**Zhleb**-ee
Rosicky	Rošický	**Roh**-shit-skee
Koci	Kočí	**Koh**-chee
Ludmila Minarikova	Ludmila Minařiková	**Loo**-dmee-la Min-**ah**-rikovah
Rousar	Roušar	**Row**-shahr
Cierne	Čierné	**Chee**-ehr-neh
Kank	Kaňk	**Kah**-nyk
Morice	Mořice	**Moh**-rih-tseh
Blazek	Blažek	**Blah**-zhek
Pivin	Pivín	**Pih**-veen
CHAPTER 34		
Horacek	Horáček	**Hor**-ah-check
Bozena Cukrova	Božena Cukrová	**Boh**-zhe-na **Tsu**-krova
Ales	Aleš	**Ah**-lesh
EPILOGUE		
Barak	Barák	Bah-**rawk**
Cerny	Černý	**Tsher**-nee
Tuma	Tůma	**Too**-mah
Jina	Jína	**Yee**-nah
Vojak	Voják	**Voh**-yahk
tvarohove kolace	tvarohové koláče	**tvah**-roh-hoveh koh-**lah**-tsheh
Calfa	Čalfa	**Tshal**-fah
SCM	SČM	Es-Tsheh-Em
UDV	ÚDV	**Oo**-Deh-Veh
Hulik	Hulík	**Hoo**-leek
Setina	Šetina	**Sheh**-tee-na
Mestske Statni	Městské Státni	**Meeyest**-neh **Stah**-tnee
Zastupitelstvi	Zastupitelství	**Zah**-stu-pee-**tel**-stvee
Sadska	Sadská	**Sahd**-skah
Stefanik	Štefánik	**Shteh**-fah-neek
Rychetsky	Rychetský	**Ree**-het-skee
Kolarova	Kolářová	**Koh**-lah-rov-ah

ABBREVIATIONS

BArch—Bundesarchiv (German national archives)
BStU—Bundesbeauftragte für die Unterlagen des Staatssicherheits Dienst (Gauck Behörde)
CFE—Crusade for Freedom
CIC—Counter Intelligence Corps
CO—Commanding Officer
ČSAD—Československá Automobilova Doprava (the state-owned trucking company)
GDR—Deutsche Demokratische Republik (German Democratic Republic)
HVDVP—Hauptverwaltung Deutsche Volkspolizei (Central Command of the People's Police/Armed Forces)
KVP—Kasernierte Volkspolizei, the East-German proto-army that was in existence from 1952 to 1956, when it was reorganized as the Volksarmee (People's Army)
MdI—Ministerium des Inneren (Ministry of the Interior)
NARA—U.S. National Archives and Records Administration, College Park
NCFE—National Committee for a Free Europe
NCO—Non-commissioned officer
ODS—Obcanská Demokratická Strana (Civic Democratic Party)
PTP—Pomocné Technické Prapory, the Czech army's penal batallions (labor batallions)
RAF—Royal Air Force
RIAS—Rundfunk Im Amerikanischen Sektor (Radio in the American Sector)
RFE—Radio Free Europe
SČM—Svaz Česke Mládeže (Organization of Czech Youth), the Communist youth organization
SfS—Staatssekretariat für Staatssicherheit, aka Stasi (State Secretariat for State Security)
SNB—Sbor Národní Bezpečnosti (National Security Service)
StB—Státní Bezpečnost (State Security)
StG—Sturmgewehr (assault rifle)

UDV—Ústav pro dokumentaci a vyšetřování zločinů komunismu (Office for Documentation and Investigation of Criminal Actions of the Communist Party)

UNRRA—United Nations Relief and Rehabilitation Agency

VOA—Voice of America

NOTES

CHAPTER 1

1 Jaroslav Procházka, *Sestupme ke kořenům* (Výboru, Lošany: Nákladem Mist. Nár., 1948), 44.
2 Procházka, *Sestupme ke kořenům*, 44. Mašínová is the feminine form of Masin.
3 Procházka, *Sestupme ke kořenům*, 45.
4 Procházka, *Sestupme ke kořenům*, 46.
5 Procházka, *Sestupme ke kořenům*, 46.
6 Procházka, *Sestupme ke kořenům*, 49.
7 Procházka, *Sestupme ke kořenům*, 50–51.
8 John Bradley, F. N., *The Czechoslovak Legion in Russia, 1914–1920* (New York: Columbia University Press, 1991), 55. East European monographs distributed by Columbia University Press.
9 Procházka, *Sestupme ke kořenům*, 53.
10 Procházka, *Sestupme ke kořenům*, 54. Mašín received a total of two St. George's Crosses of the 3rd degree and two of the 4th degree.
11 Bradley, *The Czechoslovak Legion in Russia, 1914–1920*, 70.
12 Procházka, *Sestupme ke kořenům*, 60–64.
13 Bradley, *The Czechoslovak Legion in Russia, 1914–1920*, 83–86, 103.
14 Procházka, *Sestupme ke kořenům*, 73.
15 Procházka, *Sestupme ke kořenům*, 68.
16 Procházka, *Sestupme ke kořenům*, 72.
17 Procházka, *Sestupme ke kořenům*, 68.
18 Procházka, *Sestupme ke kořenům*, 70–71.

CHAPTER 2

1 Leonard Mosley, *On Borrowed Time: How World War II Began* (New York: Random House, 1969), 22.
2 Mosley, *On Borrowed Time*, 22–23.
3 Keith Eubank, *Munich* (Norman, OK: University of Oklahoma Press, 1963), 100–101.
4 Mosley, *On Borrowed Time*, 29.

5   Mosley, *On Borrowed Time*, 47.
6   Donald Kagan, *On the Origins of War and the Preservation of Peace* (New York: Doubleday, 1995), 399.
7   Mosley, *On Borrowed Time*, 50.
8   Mosley, *On Borrowed Time*, 51.
9   Mosley, *On Borrowed Time*, 49.
10 Mosley, *On Borrowed Time*, 47.
11 Mosley, *On Borrowed Time*, 65.
12 Szulc, *Czechoslovakia since World War II*, 26.
13 Mosley, *On Borrowed Time*, 77.
14 Rudolf Ströbinger, *A-54, Spion mit Drei Gesichtern* (Munich: Paul List Verlag KG, 1966), 105.

CHAPTER 3

1   Procházka, *Sestupme ke kořenům*, 95.
2   Procházka, *Sestupme ke kořenům*, 99–100. The nationalist Sokol organization was a wellspring of resistance to the Nazis during the occupation.
3   Procházka, *Sestupme ke kořenům*, 103.
4   William Shirer, *Berlin Diary: The Journal of a Foreign Correspondent, 1934–1941* (Baltimore: The Johns Hopkins University Press, 2002), 462.
5   Procházka, *Sestupme ke kořenům*, 94.
6   Procházka, *Sestupme ke kořenům*, 107.
7   Němeček, *Mašínové*, 100.
8   Němeček, *Mašínové*, 100.
9   Procházka, *Sestupme ke kořenům*, 110.
10 Procházka, *Sestupme ke kořenům*, 110.
11 Ströbinger, *A-54, Spion mit Drei Gesichtern*, 195.
12 Ota Ramboušek, *Jenom ne strach* (Prague: Edice RR, 1990), 15.
13 Ramboušek, *Jenom ne strach*, 15.
14 Ramboušek, *Jenom ne strach*, 17.
15 Procházka, *Sestupme ke kořenům*, 95.
16 Ströbinger, *A-54, Spion mit Drei Gesichtern*, 194.
17 Ströbinger, *A-54, Spion mit Drei Gesichtern*, 196–98.
18 Procházka, *Sestupme ke kořenům*, 135.

CHAPTER 4

1   Táborský, *Between East and West*, 48. From the author's archive.
2   Procházka, *Sestupme ke kořenům*, 136.
3   Procházka, *Sestupme ke kořenům*, 139.
4   Procházka, *Sestupme ke kořenům*, 137–38.
5   Procházka, *Sestupme ke kořenům*, 138.
6   Ströbinger, *A-54, Spion mit Drei Gesichtern*, 232–33.
7   Procházka, *Sestupme ke kořenům*, 140.
8   Procházka, *Sestupme ke kořenům*, 141.

CHAPTER 5

1 Václav Kopecký, *30 let KSC (Thirty Years of the Communist Party of Czechoslovakia)* (Prague, 1951), 100; as quoted in Edward Taborsky, *Communism in Czechoslovakia, 1948–1960* (Princeton, New Jersey: Princeton University Press, 1961), 21.
2 Szulc, *Czechoslovakia since World War II*, 37.
3 Szulc, *Czechoslovakia since World War II*, 37.
4 Táborský, *Between East and West*, 27.
5 *The Czechoslovak Political Trials 1950–54; the Suppressed Report of the Dubček Government's Commission of Inquiry, 1968*, preface and postscript by Jiří Pelikán (Stanford, CA: Stanford University Press, 1971), 140.
6 C.j. 6497/010-1949, Směrnice pro využití TNP, signed 8 August 1949 by the Commander of State Security, Pokorny.
7 Stéphane Courtois and others, *The Black Book of Communism: Crimes, Terror, Repression* (Cambridge, MA: Harvard University Press, 1999), 413.
8 Recollection of Joseph Mašín, Ladislav Mencl, Vladimír Hradec.

CHAPTER 6

1 http://www.leipzig-award.org/englisch/990308b.htm.
2 Bennett Kovrig, *The Myth of Liberation* (Baltimore: The Johns Hopkins University Press, 1973), 148–49.
3 Kovrig, *The Myth of Liberation*, 93–94, 148–50.
4 Bennett Kovrig, *Of Walls and Bridges: The United States and Eastern Europe* (New York: New York University Press, 1991), 72.
5 U.S. General Accounting Office, *U.S. Government Monies Provided to Radio Free Europe and Radio Liberty*, report no. 173239, 25 May 1972, 79. Also http://www.rferl.org/50Years/history/rferl-history.html.
6 U.S. Congress, House, Committee on Foreign Affairs, The Mutual Security Program: Hearings, 82nd Congress, 1st session, 1951, 1106–9, as quoted in Kovrig, *The Myth of Liberation*, 102–3.
7 Public Law 164, sec. 101(a), as quoted in Kovrig, *The Myth of Liberation*, 103.
8 Peter Grose, *Operation Rollback: America's Secret War Behind the Iron Curtain* (New York: Houghton Mifflin Company, 2000), 213.
9 Kovrig, *The Myth of Liberation*, 140.
10 Grose, *Operation Rollback*, 174. The transcript of this 1952 hearing wasn't made public until 1980. See James D. Marchio, "Rhetoric and Reality: The Eisenhower Administration and Unrest in Eastern Europe, 1953-59" (dissertation), (Washington, D.C.: American University, 1990), 43, as quoted in *Operation Rollback*, 173–74. Marchio cites Congress, House, Committee on Foreign Affairs, *Selected Executive Session Hearings of the Committee, 1951–1956*, (Vol. XIV, Washington, D.C.: Government Publishing Office, 1980), 343.

CHAPTER 10

1 Council on Foreign Relations, Documents on American Foreign Relations, 1952, New York, 1953, 80–83, as quoted in Kovrig, *The Myth of Liberation*, 112–13.

CHAPTER 11

1 Torsten Dietrich, Der 17. *Juni 1953 in der DDR* (Berlin: Dietz Verlag Berlin GmbH, 1991), 33.
2 ZstAP, K-1, Nr. 9065, B1.199; Nr. 803, B1.47 ff as cited in *Brüche/Krisen/ Wendepunkte*, 105–108.
3 Dietrich, Der 17. *Juni 1953 in der DDR*, 159.
4 Torsten Dietrich, "Die Kasernierte Volkspolizei (1952–1956)," *Im Dienste der Partei*, 355.
5 SAPMO-BArch, NY 90/316, 128, Anlage zum Protokoll der Politbürositzung vom 29.7.1952; Lindenberger, "Die Deutsche Volkspolizei (1945–1990)," *Im Dienste der Partei*, 105.
6 Torsten Dietrich and Rüdiger Wenzke, *Die Getarnte Armee, Geschichte der Kasernierten Volkspolizei der DDR 1952–1956* (Berlin: Ch. Links Verlag, 2001), 180.

CHAPTER 14

1 Endres/Bönnen papers, BStU 50–51 "Ermittelungsbericht," 8 October 1953, BDVP Karl-Marx-Stadt, Abteilung K.

CHAPTER 16

1 BArch, MdI, DO 1/11/1435, 00055.
2 BArch, MdI, DO 1/11/1435, 00055-56.
3 Endres/Bönnen papers, "Interview of VP-candidate (name blacked out), Uckro, 10 October 1953, Beginning 9.34 hours, End 10.15 hours, Officer conducting inquiry: VPOK. Wonke."
4 Helmut Strempel, in an interview recorded in Ute Bönnen and Gerald Endres, *Der Luckauer Krieg* (2001), documentary film.
5 Endres/Bönnen papers, "Interview of VP-candidate, Uckro, 10 October 1953, Beginning 9.34 hours, End 10.15 hours, Officer conducting inquiry: VPOK Wonke."
6 Ewald Fitzek, in an interview recorded in Bönnen, *Der Luckauer Krieg*. The original term "scharfe Waffen" is translated as "live firearms."
7 HVDVP—Hauptverwaltung Deutsche Volkspolizei.
8 BArch, MdI, DO 1/11/777, 0026. The districts in question were Jüterbog, Luckenwalde, Zossen, and Königswusterhausen.
9 BArch, MdI, DO 1/11/777, 0027.
10 BArch, MdI, DO 1/11/777, 0029.
11 BArch, MdI, DO 1/11/777, 0034–35.

12 BArch, MdI, DO 1/11/777, 0035.
13 BArch, MdI, DO 1/11/777, 0033.
14 BArch, MdI, DO 1/11/777, 0033.
15 BArch, MdI, DO 1/11/1051, 1. The German term is Großfahndung Uckro.
16 BArch, MdI, DO 1/11/777, 00044.
17 BArch, MdI, DO 1/11/777, 0034–35.
18 BArch, MdI, DO 1/11/777, 0037.
19 BArch, MdI, DO 1/11/777, 00037–38.
20 BArch, MdI, DO 1/11/777, 00038. The Soviet colonel and general are not
    named.
21 BArch, MdI, DO 1/11/777, 0077. Also BstU, interrogation of Z. Janata dated
    27 November 1953 beginning of interrogation: 08.45 hours, end of interroga-
    tion: 09.40 hours.

CHAPTER 18

1 BArch, MdI, DO 1/11/777 00038.
2 BArch, MdI, DO 1/11/777 00047.
3 BArch, MdI, DO 1/11/777 00046.
4 Illig, Werner, in an interview recorded in Bönnen, *Der Luckauer Krieg*. By this
   time, both civilian and Volkspolizei eyewitnesses concur, significant numbers
   of Soviet forces were involved. The East German documentation, however,
   underreports the extent of the involvement: it makes only the barest, passing
   references to Soviet troops—four, in over three hundred pages of documents.
   Eyewitnesses claim friendly fire casualties occurred among Soviet troops, but
   the East German records mention none.
5 BArch, MdI, DO 1/111/777, 00048.
6 BArch, MdI, DO 1/11/777, 00050.
7 BArch, MdI, DO 1/11/777, 00063.
8 BArch, MdI, DO 1/11/777, 00064–65.
9 BArch, MdI, DO 1/11/777, 00081.
10 BArch, MdI, DO 1/11/777, 00051.
11 BArch, MdI, DO 1/11/777, 00051.
12 BArch, MdI, DO 1/11/777, 00061.
13 BArch, MdI, DO 1/11/777, 00048.
14 BArch, MdI, DO 1/11/777, 00063.
15 BArch, MdI, DO 1/11/777, 00063.
16 BArch, MdI, DO 1/11/777, 00066.
17 BArch, MdI, DO 1/11/777, 00068.
18 BArch, MdI, DO 1/11/777, 00069.
19 BArch, MdI, DO 1/11/777 00083.
20 BArch, MdI, DO 1/11/777, 00076.
21 BArch, MdI, DO 1/11/777, 00079.
22 BArch, MdI, DO 1/11/777 00085.

CHAPTER 20

1 Endres/Bönnen papers, BstU 000008, 000010, regarding the relative position.
2 Ramboušek, *Jenom ne strach*, 126.

CHAPTER 22

1 BArch, MdI, DO 1/11/777 00090.
2 BArch, MdI, DO 1/11/777 00105.
3 BArch, MdI, DO 1/11/777, 00107.
4 Endres/Bönnen papers, BstU 000008.
5 BArch, MdI, DO 1/11/1051, 00030–31.
6 BArch, MdI DO 1/11/777, 00129, BArch, MdI DO 1/11/777, 00106–00108.
7 BArch, MdI DO 1/11/777, 00108–00110.
8 BArch, MdI, DO 1/11/777, 00097.
9 BArch, MdI, DO 1/11/777, 00098.
10 BArch, MdI, DO 1/11/1435, 00051.

CHAPTER 24

1 BArch, MdI, DO 1/11/777, 00098-99. BArch, MdI, DO 1/11/1184, 210–12.
2 Regina & Walter Luehmann, in an interview recorded in Bönnen, *Der Luckauer Krieg*.
3 BArch, MdI, DO 1/11/1435, 00073.
4 BArch, MdI, DO 1/11/1435, 00070.
5 BArch, MdI, DO 1/11/1435, 00070.
6 BArch, MdI, DO 1/11/1051, 00015.
7 BArch, MdI, DO 1/11/777, 00134.
8 BArch, MdI, DO 1/11/777, 00142.
9 BArch, MdI, DO 1/11/777, 00099.
10 BArch, MdI, DO 1/11/777, 00110.
11 Anonymous eyewitness.
12 BArch, MdI, DO 1/11/777, 00111.
13 BArch, MdI, DO 1/11/777, 00112.

CHAPTER 26

1 BArch, MdI, DO 1/11/777, 00142. Interior Minister Stoph received a dispatch from Head of the Armed Forces Maron on 19 October. BArch, MdI, DO 1/11/777, 00115, 00136.
2 "Alle Fahnen auf halbmast," "Cottbus nimmt Abschied von den toten Helden," *Lausitzer Rundschau*, 20 October 1953, 1; "In heiliger Liebe zum Volke . . .", "Unsere Sache liegt in gute Händen!" *Lausitzer Rundschau*, 21 October 1953, 1. Hoffman was buried in Cottbus, Sunkel and Grummini were buried in their hometowns; the wake and funeral procession were held in Cottbus.
3 "Ewige Ehre und ewiger Ruhm unseren toten Helden!" posted proclamation by the Sekretariat, Bezirksleitung Cottbus der SED.

4 Ibid.

5 "Faschisten morden Volkspolizisten," *Berliner Zeitung*, 21 October 1953, 1; "Saboteure in die DDR eingeschleust," *Neue Zeitung*, 21 October 1953, 1; "Abschied von ermordeten Volkspolizisten," *Tägliche Rundschau*, 21 October 1953, 2.

6 Photo caption, *Lausitzer Rundschau*, 22 October 1953, 1.

7 BArch, MdI, DO 1/11/1051, 00037.

8 Ibid.

9 Götze, Andreas, "Po stopách Ctirada a Josefa Mašínových," *Lidové Noviny*, 9 August 1995, 12–13.

10 Wagner, Emil, in an interview recorded in Bönnen, *Der Luckauer Krieg*.

11 Fitzek, Ewald, in an interview recorded in Bönnen, *Der Luckauer Krieg*.

12 BArch, MdI, DO 1/11/777, 00155.

13 BArch, MdI, DO 1/11/1184, 401. No mention of the text or of the reappearance of the wreath.

14 Eyewitness testimony. No mention of the second appearance in the archival materials.

15 BArch, MdI, DO 1/11/777, 00156.

16 BArch, MdI, DO 1/11/777, 00156. Ostermann, Christian F., *Uprising in East Germany*, 1953, Central European University Press, Document No. 93 HICOG Report on the U.S. Food Aid Program for East Germany 17 September 1953, 376–89.

17 "Faschisten morden Volkspolizisten," *Berliner Zeitung*, 21 October 1953, 1; "Saboteure in die DDR eingeschleust," *Neue Zeitung*, 21 October 1953, 1; "Abschied von ermordeten Volkspolizisten," *Tägliche Rundschau*, 21 October 1953, 2.

18 BArch, MdI, DO 1/11/777, 00155.

19 BArch, MdI, DO 1/11/777, 00160.

20 Local eyewitness report.

21 BArch, MdI, DO 1/11/777, 00154.

22 BArch, MdI, DO 1/11/777, 00159.

CHAPTER 28

1 BArch, MdI, DO 1/11/777, 00155.

2 BArch, MdI, DO 1/11/777, 00164.

3 BArch, MdI, DO 1/11/777, 00165–66.

4 BArch, MdI, DO 1/11/777, 00169.

5 On 28 October. BArch, MdI, DO 1/11/777, 00180–81.

6 BArch, MdI, DO 1/11/11184, 0346.

7 "Widerstand in Potsdam und Cottbus," *Neue Zeitung*, Nr. 246, 21 October 1953, 1; "Volkspolizei-Razzia im Spreewald," *Süddeutsche Zeitung*, 27 October 1953, 2; "Groß-Razzien bei Berlin. Neue Zusammenstöße zwischen Volkspolizisten und Partisanengruppen," *Der Telegraf*, 25 October 1953, 1; "Steckbriefe gegen Partisanen," *Der Telegraf*, 27 October 1953, 1.

8   "Groß-Razzien bei Berlin. Neue Zusammenstöße zwischen Volkspolizisten und Partisanengruppen," *Der Telegraf*, 25 October 1953, 1.

9   "Widerstandskämpfer erschossen? Berichte von den Unruhen bei Cottbus," *FAZ*, 24 October 1953, 3.

10 Ibid.

11 Ibid.

12 "Underground fought by Reds in Germany," *Washington Post*, 29 October 1953, 4.

13 "3,000 Russian Troops Open Drive Against East Zone Partisans," *Boston Daily Globe*, 30 October 1953, 9.

14 Ibid.

15 "Volkspolizei-Razzia im Spreewald. Bewaffnete tschechische Flüchtlinge kämpfen um ihr Leben," *Süddeutsche Zeitung*, 27 October 1953, 2.

16 "Vo-po manöver im Spreewald," *Die Neue Zeitung*, Nr. 256, 1 November 1953, 2; "Bürgerkriegs-Manöver in der DDR," *Süddeutsche Zeitung*, Nr. 253, 2 November 1953, 2.

17 "Blutige Zusammenstöße im Bezirk Cottbus," *Die Neue Zeitung*, Nr. 248, 23 October 1953, 3; "Widerstandskämpfer Erschossen?" *Frankfurter Allgemeine Zeitung*, 24 October 1953, 3.

18 "Blutige Zusammenstöße im Bezirk Cottbus," *Die Neue Zeitung*, Nr. 248, 23 October 1953, 3.

19 "Underground Fought by Reds in Germany," *Washington Post*, 30 October 1953, 4.

20 "E. German Revolts Reported Becoming Armed Offensives," *Boston Daily Globe*, 28 October 1953, 36.

21 i.e.,"Blutige Zusammenstöße im Bezirk Cottbus," *Neue Zeitung*, 23 October 1953, No. 248, 3; "Vopo-Manöver im Spreewald," *Neue Zeitung*, 1 November, p 2; "Neue Zusammenstöße im Bezirk Cottbus," *Der Tagesspeigel*, 24 October 1953, 1; "Ein Todesurteil in Cottbus," *FAZ*, 4 November 1953, 3; "Red Resistance Wave in Reich kills 10 of foe; 5 partisans executed," *Philadelphia Inquirer*, 24 October 1953, 2; "8 Policemen, Party Leader Slain by East Zone Partisans," *Washington Post*, 25 October 1953, 3. Volkspolizei records, however, explicitly define the objective of the "Großfahndung Uckro" to be the apprehension of five Czechs. BArch, MdI, DO 1/11/705 00025.

22 "Vopo-Ueberfall auf Staaken," *Der Telegraf*, No. 248/8, 23 October 1953, 2.

23 NARA, 762B.00/10-2353.

24 NARA, 762B.00/10-2853.

25 NARA, 762B.00/10-2953.

26 NARA, 762B.00/10-2953.

CHAPTER 33

1   Interview with Leonard Jankowski, 30 July 2001.

CHAPTER 34

1   Endres/Bönnen papers.

2 Report of the Politburo of the Central Committee of the Communist Party of Czechoslovakia, 15 March 1954.

3 Cz archive SGPt 44/54 160/1954-ZO-TAJNE.

4 NARA, 211.4915-MASIN, CTIRAD AND JOSEF/3-2956.

5 Endres/Bönnen papers.

6 Minutes of Politburo meeting of 13 December 1954.

7 The minutes of 14 December 1953, 15 March 1954, 25 November 1954, 12 December 1954, and 22 December 1955 feature multipage treatises on the topic.

8 [Addendum to minutes of the Politburo meeting of 13 December 1954] "Report on the Court Case against Ctibor Novák and Co."

9 Hejl, Vilém, *Zpráva o organizovaném násilí*, Univerzum Praha, 1990, 230–31. This was standard procedure for executions in "strangulatio" after 1950.

10 Politburo protocol of 25 November 1954.

11 Zdena Mašínová archive excerpts.

EPILOGUE

1 Barch, MdI, DO 1/11/1435 00054.

2 BArch, MdI, DO 1/11/777 00001–00024.

3 BArch, MdI, DO 1/11/777 000021–22.

4 BArch, MdI, DO 1/11/777 00023–24.

5 BArch, MdI, DO 1/11/777 00023–24.

6 Interview with Joseph Masin, 22 April 2003.

7 Pacner, Karel, *Československo ve zvláštních službách*, 1945-61, Vol. 3, Themis, 2002, 624. Interior Minister Barak signed off on project "Bratři" on 11 June 1958.

8 Interview with Joseph Masin, 22 April 2003.

9 Mašín, Zdena, *Čtyři České Osudy*, (Prague: Paseka, 2001), 280–93.

10 For a detailed discussion see Suk, Jiří, "K prosazenî kandidatury Václava Havla na úřad prezidenta v prosinci 1989, Dokumenty a svědectví," *Soudobé Dějiny*, VI/2-3, Ústav pro Soudobé Dějiny Av Cr, 16.4.1993, 346-369.

11 Law no. 193/1993, "Law on the illegal communist regime and resistance against it."

12 Law no. 119/1990, "Law on court rehabilitation."

13 Law no. 451/1991 Sb., passed on 4 October 1991; in 1996 it was extended until 2000.

14 Anne Applebaum, "A Dearth of Feeling—An essay about the absence of memory of communist crimes," *The New Criterion*, October, 1996.

15 C.j.: OV-0017/x-03.

16 Courtois, *The Black Book of Communism: Crimes, Terror, Repression*, x-xi.

17 Milena Kolářová, member of parliament, ODS party, "Dokážeme se někdy vyrovnat s minulostí?" *Denní Telegraf*, 1995, 3.

18 Applebaum, "A Dearth of Feeling."

BIBLIOGRAPHY

PRIMARY SOURCES

U.S. Archives

National Archives and Records Administration, College Park, National Security
   Council Reports RG273.
Records of U.S. Department of State, Decimal Series, 1950-54, RG59.

German Archives

Bundesbeauftragte für die Unterlagen des Staatssicherheits Dienst (Gauck Behörde)
   Akte für Joseph Masin.
Deutsches Bundesarchiv, Ministerium des Inneren, Lichterfelde, Berlin, MdI,
   DO 1/11/70, DO 1/11/119, DO 1/11/120, DO 1/11/162, DO 1/11/705,
   DO 1/11/776, DO 1/11/777, DO 1/11/1051, DO 1/11/1184, DO 1/11/1185,
   DO 1/11/1435.
Endres/Bönnen papers—archival materials from the following archives with
   restricted access: Polizeihistorische Samlung Berlin, Polizeihistorische Samlung
   Sachsen Anhalt, Militärhistorisches Museum der Bundeswehr, Dresden.

Czech Republic Archives

Archiv Kancelář Presidenta Republiky T4532/54, T317/55, T318/55, T14/55,
   T1149/55.
Archiv Ministerstva Vnitra (AMV), Prague. H699, H700, H701, H713, H735,
   V239.
Archiv ministerstvo spravedlnosti O22-I.
Městské Státní Zastupitelství, District Prosecutor's Office, Prague, *Mašín a spol.*

Official Documents

"Ewige Ehre und ewiger Ruhm unseren toten Helden!" posted proclamation,
   Sekretariat, Bezirksleitung Cottbus der SED.
Czech Republic, law no. 198/1993, "Law on the illegal communist regime and
   resistance against it."

Czech Republic, Law no. 119/1990, "Law on court rehabilitation."
Czech Republic, Law no. 451/1991 Sb.

Personal Papers

This text cites the personal papers of Zdena Mašínová, Ray Masin, and Lidka Švédová.

SECONDARY SOURCES

Arlt, Kurt. "Sowjetische (Russische) Truppen in Deutschland (1945-1994)." *In Im Dienste der Partei: Handbuch der bewaffneten Organe der DDR*. Edited by Torsten Diedrich, Hans Ehlert, and Rüdiger Wenzke. Berlin: Christoph Links Verlag, 1998.

Bradley, John, F. N. *The Czechoslovak Legion in Russia, 1914-1920*. Eastern European monographs distributed by Columbia Universtiy Press. New York: Columbia University Press, 1991.

Courtois, Stéphane, Nicolas Werth, Jean-Louis Panné, Andrzej Paczkowski, Margolin Bartosek, and Jean-Louis Karel. *The Black Book of Communism: Crimes, Terror, Repression*. Cambridge, Mass.: Harvard University Press, 1999.

Dickel, Friedrich. *Geschichte der Deutschen Volkspolizei*. Berlin: Ministerium des Inneren, 1985.

Dietrich, Torsten. *Der 17. Juni 1953 in der DDR*. Berlin: Dietz Verlag Berlin GmbH, 1991.

———. "Die Kasernierte Volkspolizei (1952-1956)." *In Im Dienste der Partei: Handbuch der bewaffneten Organe der DDR*. Edited by Torsten Diedrich, Hans Ehlert, and Rüdiger Wenzke. Berlin: Christoph Links Verlag, 1998.

Dietrich, Torsten, and Rüdiger Wenzke, *Die Getarnte Armee, Geschichte der Kasernierten Volkspolizei der DDR 1952-1956*. Berlin: Christoph Links Verlag, 2001.

Eubank, Keith. *Munich*. Norman: University of Oklahoma Press, 1963.

Fricke, Karl Wilhelm. *Die DDR-Staatssicherheit. Entwickelung, Strukturen, Aktionsfelder*. Köln: Verlag Wissenschaft und Politik, 1982.

Goff, Kent J. "The Political Officer (Zampolit) in the Soviet Army." http://www.sovietarmy.com/documents/zampolit.html

Grose, Peter. *Operation Rollback: America's Secret War Behind the Iron Curtain*. New York: Houghton Mifflin Company, 2000.

Havel, Václav. *Letters to Olga*. New York: Henry Holt & Co., 1989.

Hejl, Vilém. *Zpráva o organizovaném násilí*. Prague: Univerzum Praha, 1990.

Holt, Robert T. *Radio Free Europe*. Minneapolis: University of Minnesota Press, 1958.

Jánský, R. *Tady Bespečnost*. Prague: Naše Vojsko, 1966.

Kagan, Donald. *On the Origins of War and the Preservation of Peace*. New York: Doubleday, 1995.

Keane, John. *Vaclav Havel: A Political Tragedy in Six Acts*. New York: Basic Books, 2000.

Kofsky, Frank. *Harry S. Truman and the War Scare of 1948: A Successful Campaign to Deceive the Nation*. New York: St. Martin's Press, 1993.

Kopecký, Václav. *30 Let KSC*. Prague: Naše Vojsko, 1951.

Kovrig, Bennett. *Of Walls and Bridges: The United States and Eastern Europe*. New York: New York University Press, 1991.

———. *The Myth of Liberation*. Baltimore: The Johns Hopkins University Press, 1973.

Kracauer, Siegfried, and Paul L. Berkman. *Satellite Mentality: Political Attitudes and Propaganda Susceptibilities of Non-Communists in Hungary, Poland and Czechoslovakia*. New York: Frederick A. Praeger, Publishers, 1956.

Lafore, Laurence. *The Long Fuse: An Interpretation of the Origins of World War I*. New York: J. B. Lippincott Company, 1971.

Lindenberger, Thomas. "Die Deutsche Volkspolizei (1945-1990)," *Im Dienste der Partei: Handbuch der bewaffneten Organe der DDR*. Edited by Torsten Diedrich, Hans Ehlert, and Rüdiger Wenzke. Berlin: Christoph Links Verlag, 1998.

Loebl, Eugen. *My Mind on Trial*. New York: Harcourt Brace Jovanovich, 1976.

London, Artur. *Ich gestehe—Der Prozeß um Rudolf Slansky*. Hamburg: Hoffmann und Campe, 1970.

MacDonald, Callum. *The Killing of SS Obergruppenführer Reinhard Heydrich*. New York: Collier Books, 1989.

Marchio, James David. *Rhetoric and Reality: The Eisenhower Administration and Unrest in Eastern Europe, 1953-1959*, dissertation. Washington D.C.: American University, 1990.

Mašínová, Zdena. *Čtyři České Osudy*. Prague: Paseka, 2001.

Michener, James. *The Bridge at Andau*. New York: Fawcett, 1957.

Mittmann, Wolfgang. *Fahndung Große Fälle der Volkspolizei*. Berlin: Verlag Das Neue Berlin, 1995.

Moravec, František. *Master of Spies: The Memoirs of General Frantisek Moravec*. New York: Doubleday, 1975.

Mosley, Leonard. *On Borrowed Time: How World War II Began*. New York: Random House, 1969.

Němeček, Jan. *Mašínove, zpráva o dvou generacích*. Prague: Torst, 1998.

Ostermann, Christian. *Uprising in East Germany*. New York: Central European University Press, 2001.

Pacner, Karel. *Československo ve zvláštních službách, 1945-61, Vol. 3*. Prague: Themis, 2002.

Pelikán, Jiři, preface and postscript. *The Czechoslovak Political Trials 1950-54; the Suppressed Report of the Dubček Government's Commission of Inquiry, 1968*. Stanford, Calif.: Stanford University Press, 1971.

Prados, John. *Presidents' Secret Wars: CIA and Pentagon Covert Operations from World War II through Iranscam*. New York: Quill/Morrow, 1986.

Procházka, Jaroslav. *Sestupme ke kořenům*. Nákladem Mist. Nár. Výboru, Lošany: privately published, 1948.

Procházka, Zdenek. *Kluci v Revoluci a jiné příběhy*. Victoria, Canada: Trafford Publishing, 2002.

Ramboušek, Ota. *Jenom ne strach*. Prague: Edice RR, 1990.

Remnick, David. *Lenin's Tomb: The Last Days of the Soviet Empire*. New York: Vintage Books, 1994.

Schulz, Dieter. "Die Agrarpolitik von 1952/53 und ihre Folgen." In *Brüche/Krisen/Wendepunkte, Neubefragung von DDR-Geschichte, Ruhe im Dorf?*. Berlin: Urania Verlag, 1990.

Schweizer, Peter. *Reagan's War*. New York: Doubleday, 2002.

———. *Victory*. New York: Atlantic Monthly Press, 1994.

Shirer, William. *Berlin Diary: The Journal of a Foreign Correspondent, 1934-1941*. Baltimore: The Johns Hopkins University Press, 2002.

Siegel, Heinz. *Volkspolizei, Staatssicherheit, Kampfgruppen—Leseheft für den Unterricht in Staatsbürgerkunde*. Berlin: Volk und Wissen, 1958.

Simpson, Christopher. *Blowback: America's Recruitment of Nazis, and its Disastrous Effect on our Domestic and Foreign Policy*. New York: Collier/Macmillan, 1988.

Smith, Howard K. *Last Train from Berlin*. London: Phoenix Press, 1942. Reprinted 2000.

Stránský, Jan. *East Wind Over Prague*. New York: Random House, 1951.

Ströbinger, Rudolf. *A-54, Spion mit Drei Gesichtern*. Munich: Paul List Verlag KG, 1966.

Suling, R. J. *Zivoty Pro Zivot*. Prague: Nase Vojsko, 1976.

Szulc, Tad. *Czechoslovakia since World War II*. New York: The Viking Press, 1971.

Táborský, Edward. *President Eduard Beneš: Between East and West, 1938-1948*. Hoover Institution Press, Stanford University, Stanford, California, 1981.

———. *Communism in Czechoslovakia 1948-1960*. Princeton, New Jersey: Princeton University Press, 1961.

Tatzkow, M. "Privatindustrie ohne Perspektive, Der Versuch zur Liquidierung der mittleren privaten Warenproduzenten," *Brüche/Krisen/Wendepunkte, Neubefragung von DDR-Geschichte*. Berlin: Urania Verlag, 1990.

Vrbecký, František. *Mrtví Nemluví*. Prague: Naše Vojsko, 1985.

Wheeler-Bennett, J.W. *Munich: Prologue to Tragedy*. New York: Macmillan, 1948.

Za svobodu a demokracii III, Třetí (protikomunistický) odboj. Universita Hradec Králové, Ústav filosofie a společenských věd, Hradec Králové 2002.

World Wide Web

http://www.cia.gov/csi/books/coldwaryrs/preface.html
http://www.kirjasto.sci.fi/karlmay.htm
http://www.leipzig-award.org/englisch/990308b.htm
http://www.rferl.org/50Years/history/rferl-history.html
http://www.brixmis.co.uk/contents.htm

Film & Television

Der Luckauer Krieg, documentary film by Ute Bönnen and Gerald Endres, 2001.
Aréna, debate, televised 29 August 1995 in Czech Republic.

Articles & Periodicals

Applebaum, Anne. "A Dearth of Feeling—An essay about the absence of memory of communist crimes." *The New Criterion*, October, 1996.

Brom, Prof. Dr. Ing. Libor. "Rezim Vaclava Havla je post-komunisticky podvod." *Nedelni Hlasatel*, 1 October 1995, 1.

Götze, Andreas. "Po stopách Ctirada a Josefa Mašínovych." *Lidové Noviny*, 9 August 1995, 12-13.

Green, Peter S. "'Major Zeman' leads Czechs to Question their Past." *International Herald Tribune*, 10 January 1999.

Kolářová, Milena. "Dokážeme se někdy vyrovnat s minulostí?" *Denní Telegraf*, 1995, 3.

Pfaff, William. "We Cultural Cold Warriors fought for Liberty." *International Herald Tribune*, 8 September 1999.

Suk, Jiří. "K prosazení kandidatury Václava Havla na úřad prezidenta v prosinci 1989, Dokumenty a svědectví." *Soudobé Dějiny*, VI/2-3, Ústav pro Soudobé Dějiny Av Cr, 16 April 1993.

Czechoslovak Periodical Publications

Rudé Pravo, 19 January 1955.
Voják, issues 17-20, 1956.

GDR Periodical Publications

Berliner Zeitung, 21 October–3 November 1953.
Die Volkspolizei. Vol. 6, Nos. 2nd issue 11/53 and 1st issue 12/53.
Lausitzer Rundschau, 20–22 October 1953.
Neue Zeit, 21 October–3 November 1953.
Tägliche Rundschau, 21 October–3 November 1953.
X3265 . . . Schweigt . . . (DDR Propaganda brochure, undated).

West German Periodical Publications

Berliner Nachtdepesche, 21 October–3 November 1953.
Der Kurier, 21 October–3 November 1953.
Der Telegraf, 21 October–3 November 1953.
Frankfurter Allgemeine Zeitung, 21 October–3 November 1953.
Neue Zeitung, 21 October–3 November 1953.
Süddeutsche Zeitung, 21 October–3 November 1953.

U.K. Periodical Publications

London Times, 29 October–4 November 1953.

U.S. Periodical Publications

Boston Daily Globe, 26 October–4 November 1953.

Chicago Daily Tribune, 26 October–4 November 1953.

New York Times, 21 October–4 November 1953, 21 March 1954.

Philadelphia Inquirier, 21 October–4 November 1953.

San Francisco Chronicle, 19 October–4 November 1953.

Stars and Stripes, 7 November 1953.

Time Magazine, 9 November 1953.

U.S. News & World Report, 10 July, 10 October 1953.

Washington Post, 21 October–4 November 1953.

INDEX

Page numbers followed by the letter n *indicate a footnote on that page.*

Abschnittsbevollmächtigte (ABV), 117, 179
air raid sirens, activation of, 223
Anhalt Railway Station, bombing of, 32
appeasement, by West, 20–28
aryanization, plans for Masin brothers, 42

Bachmach, Battle of, 15
Balaban, Josef: arrest of, 38; Gestapo's search for, 32–34; as one of Three Kings, 28; in resistance against Nazis, 5, 28–53
Bartolomejska prison: Masin, Ctirad (Radek) in, 84–92; Masin, Josef Vladimir (Pepa) in, 82, 84–92; Morse code in, 90–91; Novak, Ctibor (Borek) in, 82, 85, 89
Belorussia, inaction on Communist past, 339
Benes, Eduard: capitulation to Communist coup, 57–58; capitulation to Sudetenland annexation, 22–24; comparison with Masaryk, 27, 57; Dulles to, on American involvement, 45; government-in-exile, 28; Masin brothers decorated by, 52; resignation and exile of (1938), 24; resignation of (1948), 58

Benes, Jan, 336n
Berlin: airlift to, 63; Communist closing of, 63–64; martial law declared by Soviets, 116; targets of Czech resistance in, 31–32; Western sector: arrival of Masin, Ctirad (Radek) in, 297–98; arrival of Masin, Josef Vladimir and Paumer, Milan in, 292–96; Vopo incursion into, 260
Berliner Ring, 250, 258, 269, 283–88
Bezucha, Alois, 79–81, 86, 88
Black Barons, 59, 99, 108, 113
Black Book of Communism, 337
Bolsheviks: clashes with Czechoslovak Legion, 17; fear of Czechoslovak Legion, 17; peace treaty with Germans, 11–12, 15
Bonnet, George, 20
border crossing, of Masin brothers and associates, 126–37
Border Guards Act (1951), 78
Boston Daily Globe, 259
Boy Scouts: disbanded by Communists, 61; in post-war Podebrady, 48
Brandenburg/Görden prison, Sveda, Vaclav (Vasek) in, 233, 238
Brest-Litovsk, Treaty of, 15

Calfa, Marina, 330
Causa Masin, 336
Celakovice, raid on police station, 74–76, 88

Cerny, Oskar (code name "Tomas"), 328
Ceskoslovenska Automobilova Doprava (CSAD), 78–79
Chamberlain, Neville, 20, 22
Charles University, 60
Chlumec nad Cidlinou, raid on police station, 70–73, 88
Chomutov, in escape route, 122–23
collective farms, 99; guards posted on, 113; straw reserves destroyed, 110–14; Sveda's eviction from, 100–101
Communist Party, Czechoslovakian: Benes's capitulation to, 57–58; class war of, 58–59, 98; control seized by, 55–58; drafting of young men by, 59, 99; election victory of, 56; fall of regime, 330–31; Horakova's arrest and execution by, 58; Masin brothers' actions against, 67–83; military text of *(Kill or Be Killed)*, 57; nationalization policies of, 99; Novak, Ctibor's expulsion from, 101; Novak, Ctibor's membership in, 46; number of victims, 59; post-war support for, 45, 56–58; preparations for power grab, 56–57; resistance against, 59–60, 67–83, 97–114; retaliation against Masin family and associates, 306–15; sabotage against, 59–60, 108–14; Slansky group cast out by, 98–99; slave labor camps of, 59
Communist Party, East Germany, 115–17
Communist Party, European, rise of, 63
Communist Youth League, 61
commuter train, toward West Berlin, 283–91, 296–97
concentration camp survivors, 43–44
Cottbus district, alert and searches in, 197, 259
Counter Intelligence Corps (CIC), 61, 61n, 90; analysis of East German deployment, 261; contact and care of Czech escapees, 295, 302–5

Crusade for Freedom (CFE), 64
Cukr, Jaroslav, prison sentence for, 312
Cukrova, Bozena, prison sentence for, 312
Czechoslovakia, post-Communist: archival records on Masin brothers in, 340–41; attitude toward Masin brothers in, 7, 335–41; commemoration ceremony for Masin, Josef Frantisek, 340; Havel's election to presidency, 330; inaction on Communist past, 331–40; Lustration Law in, 331–32; Masin brothers' refusal to return to, 340; posthumous commutation of sentences for Janata, Novak, and Sveda in, 334; rehabilitation of Masinova, Zdena in, 334; review of *Masin et al.,* in, 335–36
Czechoslovakia, post-World War II: collapse of Communist rule in, 330–31; Communist coup in, 55–58; disappointment over U.S. failure to intervene, 321–23, 337–38; expectation of U.S. intervention, 2–3, 62–66, 77–78, 112–14, 121; extradition of escapees sought by, 309–10; reoccupation of Sudetenland, 48; resistance against Communists in, 59–60, 67–83, 97–114; retaliation against Masin family and associates, 306–15; Stalin's intentions for, 55; support for Communist Party, 45, 56–58; Velvet Revolution in, 330–34; Western view of, 55
Czechoslovakia, World War I, 8–19; independence sought for, 9, 17
Czechoslovakia, World War II: abandonment by West, 20–28; Allies movements toward, 43–45; American advance in halted, 45; annexation of Sudetenland, 20–24; concentration camp survivors in, 43–44; Germany's invasion of, 24–28; government-in-exile, 28; Jews in, 44; resistance in, 29–53; as inspiration to Masin

brothers, 3–5; Soviets' arrival and
welcome, 45; surrender to Germany,
27–28; Yalta agreement on, 45
Czechoslovak Legion, 9–18; in Battle
of Bachmach, 15; in Battle of Zborov,
10–11; Bolsheviks' clashes with, 17;
Bolsheviks' fear of, 17; commitment
to Czech independence, 9, 17; Czech
versus Czech confrontations of, 10;
escape from Russia, 11–12; evacuation from Russia, 11; in Kerensky
Offensive, 10–11; promotions within,
15–16; Trans-Siberian Railroad seized
by, 17
"Czech problem," 22

D-Day, 3–5
Dickel, Friederich, 326
displaced persons camp, in West Berlin:
Masin brothers in, 300–302; Vopo
defectors in, 300–301
Dobal, Viktor, 336n
Dombrowsky (East German head of
Criminal Investigations), 181–82, 325
Dubcek, Alexander, 333n
Dulles, Allen, 65–66
Dulles, John Foster, 45, 260–61

East Germany: advisory issued by, 259;
after-action review in, 324–26; air
raid sirens activated by, 223; border
crossing into, 126–37; citizen solidarity with Czechs, 247–50, 257; diversionary efforts on Czechs' behalf, 197;
early encounters with police, 148–49,
163; extradition of Janata and Sveda,
309–10; "fear psychosis" in, 324; gun
battle at Uckro, 168–87; identities
and descriptions of escapees issued
by, 192; kindness from citizens, 150–
52, 155–57, 200–202, 206, 262–70;
"Luckau War" in, 237–39; manhunt
in, 181–99; operational problems in,
238; propaganda by, 247–50; search

alerts issued in, 142, 178, 181; Soviet
military presence in, 153–54; Soviet
treatment of, 115; unrest and dissidence in, 115–17, 247–50; uprising in,
321–22; Western analysis of deployment in, 257–61
Eisenhower, Dwight, 113–14, 320–22
Elbe River crossing, 160–61
Elsterwerda, East Germany, train travel
to and from, 159–60, 165–67
Erlangen, West Germany, safe house in,
317–19
escape, of Czech band, 2–3, 118–301;
aid from baker and daughter, 150–
52; aid from innkeepers, 155–57;
American debriefing of Masin brothers, 304, 318; arrivals in American
sector of Berlin, 292–98; arrivals in
United States, 320; at Berliner Ring,
283–88; border crossing, 126–37;
capture of Janata, Zbynek, 184,
192–93, 267, 308; capture of Sveda,
Vaclav (Vasek), 233, 267, 308; car
heist attempt, 138–42; clothing for
barter, 164–65; codes and secrecy,
118–19; cold and snow endured, 135–
37, 234, 242, 303; commuter train
toward West Berlin, 286–91, 296–97;
contact with Americans planned,
121; dash from small woods, 216–21;
death sentence for Janata, Zbynek,
310, 312, 314; death sentence for
Sveda, Vaclav (Vasek), 310, 312,
314; decisions and commitment, 114;
departures from home, 119–20; early
encounters with police, 148–49, 163;
East German after-action review of,
324–26; Elbe River crossing, 160–61;
emergence and flight from Reichwalde
farm, 200–206; emergence from
woodpile, 251; engagement at edge of
woods, 208–21, 232; Erlangen safe
house, 317–19; extradition of Janata,
Zbynek, 309–10; extradition of Masin

brothers denied, 309–10; extradition
of Sveda, Vaclav (Vasek), 309–10;
flights to Frankfurt, 316–17; food
supply finished, 132; Grunert family as hostages/benefactors, 262–70;
gun battle at Uckro, 168–87; hiding in
"hay hotel," 251–56; hiding in woodpile, 1–2, 228–30, 235–43; hiding
on Reichwalde farm, 188–95, 200–
202; imprisonment of Sveda, Vaclav
(Vasek), 233, 238; interrogation of
Janata, Zbynek, 196–99, 234–35,
308; interrogation of Sveda, Vaclav
(Vasek), 233–35, 238, 308; journey
to border, 118–25; Mahlow station
trouble, 288–91; manhunt, 181–99;
maps and navigation, 118, 120–21,
130–31, 268; march through East
Germany, 137–65; money distributed
for, 125; most-wanted posters for,
249, 267–68; northern trek toward
Berlin, 271–81; official identifica-
tions and descriptions, 192; polygraph
tests for Masin brothers, 318; potato
transport train, 269, 276–80; press
conference of Masin brothers, 305;
pursuit from small woods, 222–28;
rescue of friends hoped for, 304, 316,
319; retaliation against family and
associates in Czechoslovakia, 306–15;
reunion of Masin brothers, 295–96;
safe house in Berlin, 302–5; search
alerts issued, 142, 178, 181; separate
group duties of Masin brothers, 122;
shooting of Paumer, Milan, 284–85,
289–90; shooting of Sveda, Vaclav
(Vasek), 208, 211–12; suicide pact
in, 210, 214, 219–21, 240; testimony
of Sveda, Vaclav (Vasek), 238; train
travel in (with tickets), 158–60, 165–
67; Vopos shot in, 209–10; weapons
carried in, 121
extradition: from Americans, denied,
for Masin brothers and Paumer,

309–10; from East Germany, of
Janata and Sveda, 309–10

factory militias, 56, 62
farms: collectivization of, 99; guards
posted on, 113; straw reserves
destroyed, 110–14; Sveda's eviction
from, 100–101
"fear psychosis," in East Germany, 324
Fibich, Karel, 16
Fierlinger, Zdenek, 56
Fitzek, Ewald, 180
Fleischer, Oskar, 33–34, 40–42
Forman, Milos, 47
France, in World War II: acceptance of
Czech annexation/invasion, 20, 28; in
Munich Agreement, 22
Frankfurt, West Germany, Masin broth-
ers' flight to, 316–17
Frankfurter Allgemeine Zeitung, 258

Germany: post-war (*See* East Germany;
West Germany); in World War I:
Czechoslovak Legion actions against,
10–19; peace treaty with Bolsheviks,
11–12, 15; peace treaty with Ukraine,
11–12; in World War II: annexation of
Sudetenland, 20–24; Czech resistance
to, 29–53; defeat of, 44–45; invasion
of Czechoslovakia, 24–28; invasion of
Poland, 28, 31
Geschichte der Deutschen Volkspolizei,
326
Gestapo: arrest of Balaban, 38; arrest
of Masin, Zdena, 41–42; arrest of
resistance members, 32–33; capture of
Masin, Josef Frantisek, 38–40; harassment of Masin family, 34–37, 41–42;
identities of Three Kings discovered
by, 32; infiltration of headquarters, 30
Goering, Hermann, 31
Gorbachev, Mikhail, 330
Gottwald, Klement, 56–58; death of,
107

Great Britain: post-World War II, analysis of deployment in East Germany,
259; in World War II: appeasement policy of, 20–28; in Munich
Agreement, 22
Grummini, Hermann, 179–80
Grunert, Marta, 306
Grunert, Werner, 306
Grunert family: as hostages/benefactors,
262–70; message promised for, 269–
70; news of escapees received by, 306
gun battle at Uckro, 168–87; Janata,
Zbynek's separation from group in,
174–75, 183–84; official East German
account of, 180; official East German
response to, 181–87

Hácha, Emil, 26, 26n
Hauptabteilung K (Criminal
Investigations Department), 181
Hauptabteilung S (Protective Police),
181
Havel, Frantisek, 24–26
Havel, Vaclav, 7, 47; conditions during
imprisonment, 331, 338; disparaging
comments by Masin, Josef Vladimir
(Pepa), 330–31; election to presidency,
330; inaction on Czechoslovakia's
Communist past, 333–34
"hay hotel," 251–56
Helsinki Accords, 331, 331n, 338
Himmler, Heinrich, attempted assassi-
nation of, 32
Hitler, Adolf, annexation of
Sudetenland, 20–24
Holecek, Vojta, 16
Holoubek, Albin, 25–26
Horakova, Milada, 58
Hotel Pupp, 101, 101n
Hradec, Jiri, prison sentence for, 312
Hradec, Vladimir (Kikina): arrest of,
309; arrest of family members, 61–
62; background of, 69; blacklisting
of, 60; chloroform obtained from, 70;

explosives acquired by, 108–9; mother's discovery of weapons cache,
83; personality of, 69; prison sentence for, 312; retaliation against, for
escape, 308–9
Hulik, Milan, 333
Hungary: demand for Czechoslovak
territory, 22; inaction on Communist
past, 339; uprising in, 321–22, 337

Iron Curtain, imposition of, 63–64
Italy, in Munich Agreement, 22

Jachymov uranium mine, 59; brutality in, 94; capture and treatment of
escapees, 94–95; comparison with
Soviet Gulag, 93; enslavement of
Masin, Ctirad (Radek) in, 92–96;
food rations in, 93–94; hypothermia
in, 94; intelligence sought by outside,
99; irradiation in, 94; plans to rescue
Masin, Ctirad (Radek) from, 101–2;
release of Masin, Ctirad (Radek)
from, 107
Janata, Zbynek: abandonment by family,
313; background of, 68–69; execution
of, 314; last letter to family, 312–13;
military training of, 67; in Pankrac
prison, 312–13; personality of, 68–69;
posthumous, post-Communist commutation of sentence, 334
Janata, Zbynek, in escape, 2, 118–84;
border crossing, 126–37; capture
of, 184, 192–93, 267, 308; car heist
attempt by, 138–42; chloroform controlled by, 122; code for, 118–19; cold
and snow endured by, 135–37; death
sentence for, 310, 312, 314; early
encounters with police, 148–49, 163;
Elbe River crossing, 160–61; extradition to Czechoslovakia, 309–10;
food supply finished, 132; gun battle
at Uckro, 168–87; injury of, 141–42,
145, 164; interrogation of, 196–99,

234–35, 308; journey to border, 118–
25; maps and navigation for, 118,
120–21, 130–31; march through East
Germany, 137–65; money distributed
for, 125; rescue of, Masin brothers'
hope for, 304; search alerts issued for,
142, 178, 181; separation from group,
174–75, 183–84; testimony of, 198–
99; train travel by, 158–60, 165–67;
weapon confiscated from, 140; weapon
demanded by, 138; weapon denied for,
114, 122; weapon fired by, 140
Janata, Zbynek, in post-war
Czechoslovakia: arrest by StB evaded,
81–83; associates' uncertainty
about, 114; as broken man, 311; in
Celakovice raid, 74–76; decision to
leave Czechoslovakia, 78; escape from
Czechoslovakia, first planned (1951),
77–83; explosives acquired by, 108–9;
in Kovolis robbery planning, 101,
103; resistance against Communists,
59–60, 67–83. See also Janata,
Zbynek, in escape
Jankowski, Leonard, 302n
Janotka, Alois, 16
Jehovah's Witnesses, enslavement in
uranium mines, 93–95
Jews, in Czechoslovakia, World War
II, 44
Jina, Josef (code name "Jindra"), 329
Just, Vladimir, 336n

Kadlec, Frantisek, 51
Kank silver mines, explosives stolen
from, 108–9
Karl-Marx-Stadt district, alert and
manhunt in, 197
Kasernierte Volkspolizei (KVP), 116–
17, 158; in manhunt, 181–87
Kennedy, Joseph P., 20
Kerensky Offensive, 10–11
Kersten, Charles J., 64–65
Kersten Amendment, 64–65

Kill or Be Killed, 57
King George College, 47–48,69
Koci, Frantisek, 102–7
Kolarova, Milena, 338
Kovolis payroll robbery, 101–7

labor details, 60–61
Lacroix, Victor de, 22
Lehmann, Martin, 232
Leipzig district, alert and manhunt in,
197
"Liberty Oath," 64
Likar, Josef, 31
Likar, Marie, 31
Lodge Act, 320, 320n
Luckau district, search and engage-
ments in, 196–99, 237–39
"Luckau War," 237–39
Lustration Law, 331–32
Lyon, Cecil, 260–61

Man, Felix, 31, 34
manhunt, in East Germany, 181–99
maps, for escape, 118, 120–21, 130–31,
268
Maron, Karl, 182, 198, 231, 324
Martin, Rudolf, 322n
Masaryk, Tomas, 10–11, 27, 57
Masek, Ivan, 336n
Masin, Barbara: archives search for
records on father and uncle, 340–41;
at commemoration ceremony for
grandfather, 340; father's stories told
to, 2–3; knowledge of grandfather's
exploits, 5; visit to D-Day site with
family, 3–5
Masin, Ctirad (Radek): archives records
on, 340–41; as assassination/kidnap-
ping target, 327–29; attitude toward,
in post-Communist Czechoslovakia,
7, 335–41; birth of, 19; commemoration ceremony for father, 340; concern for mother, 108; disillusionment
over U.S. failure to intervene, 321–22;

education of, 47–48, 60; father as
inspiration to, 49–50, 53; father's
fate acknowledged, 48–50; father's
last letter to, 49–50; father's last visit
to, 37–38; fortune-teller's prophecy
for, 211; German language skills of,
115; gun interests and ownership,
45–46, 48; Hodgkin's disease of, 3;
memories of, 7; military training of,
67; mother's death in prison, 315;
mother's farewell to, 120; personality of, 5; philanthropic offers for, 320;
post-Communist honors and awards
for, 336; protection of sister, 55;
refusal to return to post-Communist
Czechoslovakia, 340; rejection from
officers' academy, 60; sister used
as bait for, 327–29; social life in
Podebrady, 55–56; uncle's execution,
314; U.S. military aspirations of, 254;
U.S. military service of, 320
Masin, Ctirad (Radek), in escape, 2–3,
118–301; American debriefing of,
304, 318; arrival in American sector
of Berlin, 297–98; arrival in United
States, 320; at Berliner Ring, 283–88;
border crossing, 126–37; car heist
attempt by, 138–42; clothing for
barter, 164–65; codes and secrecy,
118–19; cold and snow endured by,
135–37, 234, 242, 303; on commuter
train toward West Berlin, 286–91,
296–97; contact with Americans
planned, 121; dash from small woods,
216–21; decision and commitment
of, 114; departure from home, 120;
in displaced persons camp, 300–301;
early encounters with police, 148–49,
163; Elbe River crossing, 160–61;
emergence and flight from Reichwalde
farm, 200–206; emergence from
woodpile, 251; engagement at edge
of woods, 208–21, 232; in Erlangen
safe house, 317–19; extradition to

Czechoslovakia denied by Americans,
309–10; flight to Frankfurt, 316–17;
food supply finished, 132; Grunert
family as hostages/benefactors of,
262–70; gun battle at Uckro, 168–87;
hiding in "hay hotel," 251–56; hiding
in woodpile, 1–2, 228–30, 235–43;
hiding on Reichwalde farm, 188–95,
200–202; journey to border, 118–25;
Mahlow station trouble, 288–91;
manhunt for, 181–99; maps and navigation, 118, 120–21, 130–31, 268;
march through East Germany, 137–
65; money distributed for, 125; most-
wanted posters for, 249, 267–68;
northern trek toward Berlin, 271–81;
official identification and description
of, 192; polygraph test of, 318; on
potato transport train, 269, 276–80;
press conference of, 305; pursued
from small woods, 222–28; rescue
of friends hoped for, 304, 316, 319;
retaliation against family and associates in Czechoslovakia, 306–15;
reunion with brother, 295–96; at safe
house in Berlin, 302–5; search alerts
issued for, 142, 178, 181; separate
group duties from brother, 122; shoe
shot off belt, 225; suicide pact of,
210, 214, 240; train travel by (with
tickets), 158–60, 165–67; Vopos shot
by, 209–10; weapon carried in, 121
Masin, Ctirad (Radek), in post-war
Czechoslovakia: amnesty for and
release of, 107; arrest by StB, 80–81;
in Bartolomejska prison, 84–92;
beatings and interrogation of, 84–
89; belief in U.S. intervention, 2–3,
63–66, 77–78; in Celakovice raid,
74–76, 88; cellmates of, 89–90; in
Chlumec raid, 70–73, 88; decision to
leave Czechoslovakia, 77–78; draft
feared by, 108; enslavement in uranium mines, 3, 92–96; escape from

Czechoslovakia, first planned (1951), 77–83; explosives acquired by, 108–9; information sought on, 99; in Pankrac prison, 91–92; plans for rescue of, 101–2; police suspicion/detention of, 62; reaction to Communist control, 58–62; in reoccupation of Sudetenland, 48; resistance against Communists, 59–60, 67–83, 97–114; sabotage against Communists, 59–60, 108–14; sabotage in uranium mine, 95–96; stash of explosives in mine, 96; straw reserves destroyed by, 110–14; trial of, 91–92; uprising anticipated by, 76–77; weapons smuggling/theft by, 69–76. *See also* Masin, Ctirad (Radek), in escape

Masin, Ctirad (Radek), in World War II: aid to concentration camp survivors, 43–44; aid to Jews, 44; aid to Russian POWs, 43; arrest of mother, 41–42; Gestapo harassment witnessed by, 34–36; Medal of Valor awarded, 52; Nazi aryanization plans for, 42; sabotage against Nazis, 43

Masin, Josef Frantisek: Austro-Hungarian army career of, 8–9; background of, 8; birth of children, 19; commemoration ceremony for, 340; courtship and marriage of, 18–19; death of, 52; dismissal from officers' academy, 8; education of, 8; as inspiration to sons, 3–5, 49–50, 53; last letter to children, 49–50; last visit to family, 37–38; last words of, 52, 52n; letters to wife on Sudetenland annexation, 21, 24; as national hero, 336–37, 340; news of fate reaches family, 48–50; in peacetime military, 18–19; Sveda's admiration of, 101

Masin, Josef Frantisek, in World War I, 8–19; baptism and Slavic name of, 9; in Battle of Bachmach, 15; in Battle of Zborov, 10–11; in Czechoslovak

Legion, 9–18; erroneous report of death, 9; in Kiev, 12–13; medals awarded, 9–11; promotions of, 15–16; relationship with subordinates, 16–17; return home, 17–19; as Russian POW, 9; stranding and escape of, 12–15; strengths of, 16

Masin, Josef Frantisek, in World War II: action urged against German invasion, 24–28; on Balaban's arrest, 38; beatings and interrogation of, 49–52; bomb designs of, 31; capture of, 38–40; confrontation with commanding officer, 26–27; disgrace and dismissal of, 27; disguises of, 30, 38; escape attempted by, 40; execution of, 52; Gestapo's search for, 32–34; granddaughter's knowledge of, 5; imprisonment of, 40, 49–52; infiltration of Gestapo headquarters, 30; network and collaborators of, 30; as one of Three Kings, 28; opposition to Sudetenland annexation, 21–24; rescue attempts planned for, 51; in resistance, 29–53; in resistance, associates of, 28–30; suicide attempts in prison, 52; weapons smuggling by, 30–31

Masin, Josef Vladimir (Pepa): archives records on, 340–41; as assassination/kidnapping target, 327–29; attitude toward, in post-Communist Czechoslovakia, 7, 335–41; aviation interests of, 6, 43, 320; belief in U.S. intervention, 2–3; birth of, 19; commemoration ceremony for father, 340; Czech agents' contact with, 328–29; disillusionment over U.S. failure to intervene, 321–23; disparaging comments on Havel, Vaclav, 330–31; education of, 47–48, 73; emergence and flight from Reichwalde farm, 200–206, 231–32; father as inspiration to, 49–50, 53, 305; father's fate acknowledged, 48–50; father's last letter to, 49–50; FBI warning to, 327; German language skills of, 115; gun interests and ownership, 45–46, 48; life as American, 5–7; life in West Germany, 6–7, 327; memories of, 7; military training of, 67; mother's death in prison, 315; mother's farewell to, 120; personality of, 5–6; philanthropic offers for, 320; polygraph test of, 318; post-Communist honors and awards for, 336; protection of sister, 55; refusal to return to post-Communist Czechoslovakia, 340; sister used as bait for, 327–29; social life in Podebrady, 55–56; uncle's execution, 314; U.S. military aspirations of, 254; U.S. military service of, 320; World War II resistance as inspiration for, 3–5

Masin, Josef Vladimir (Pepa), in escape, 2–3, 118–301; aid from baker and daughter, 150–52; American debriefing of, 304, 318; arrival in American sector of Berlin, 292–96; arrival in United States, 320; at Berliner Ring, 283–88; border crossing, 126–37; car heist attempt by, 138–42; clothing for barter, 164–65; codes and secrecy, 118–19; cold and snow endured by, 135–37, 234, 242; on commuter train toward West Berlin, 286–91; contact with Americans planned, 121; dash from small woods, 216–21; decision and commitment of, 114; in displaced persons camp, 300–301; early encounters with police, 148–49, 163; Elbe River crossing, 160–61; emergence from woodpile, 251; engagement at edge of woods, 208–21, 232; in Erlangen safe house, 317–19; extradition to Czechoslovakia denied by Americans, 309–10; flight to Frankfurt, 316–17; food supply finished, 132; Grunert family as hostages/benefactors of, 262–70; gun

battle at Uckro, 168–87; hiding in "hay hotel," 251–56; hiding in woodpile, 1–2, 228–30, 235–43; hiding on Reichwalde farm, 188–95, 200–202; home stretch for, 289–301; journey to border, 118–25; loss of coat and compass, 134–35; Mahlow station trouble, 288–91; manhunt for, 181–99; maps and navigation, 118, 120–21, 130–31, 268; march through East Germany, 137–65; money distributed for, 125; most-wanted posters for, 249, 267–68; northern trek toward Berlin, 271–81; official identification and description of, 192; on potato transport train, 269, 276–80; press conference of, 305; pursued from small woods, 222–28; rescue of friends hoped for, 301, 316, 319; retaliation against family and associates in Czechoslovakia, 306–15; reunion with brother, 295–96; at safe house in Berlin, 302–5; search alerts issued for, 142, 178, 181; separate group duties from brother, 122; suicide pact of, 210, 214, 240; train travel by (with tickets), 158–60, 165–67; weapon carried in, 121

Masin, Josef Vladimir (Pepa), in postwar Czechoslovakia: arrest by StB, 81–83; in Bartolomejska prison, 84–92; beatings and interrogation of, 85–87, 89; belief in U.S. intervention, 63–66, 77–78; cellmates of, 89–91; in Chlumec raid, 70–73; contact with Americans, failed attempt at, 99–100; decision to leave Czechoslovakia, 77–78; draft feared by, 99, 108; draft notice received by, 113; escape from Czechoslovakia, first planned (1951), 77–83; explosives acquired by, 108–9; father as class enemy, 73; information on imprisoned brother sought by, 99–100; killing by, 105; in Kovolis robbery, 101–7; logging truck driven by, 73; reaction to Communist control, 58–62; release from prison, 91; resistance against Communists, 59–60, 67–83, 97–114; sabotage against Communists, 59–60, 108–14; uprising anticipated by, 76–77; weapons smuggling/theft by, 69–76. *See also* Masin, Josef Vladimir (Pepa), in escape

Masin, Josef Vladimir (Pepa), in World War II: aid to concentration camp survivors, 43–44; aid to Jews, 44; aid to Russian POWs, 43; arrest of mother, 41–42; Gestapo harassment witnessed by, 34–36; Medal of Valor awarded, 52; Nazi aryanization plans for, 42; sabotage against Nazis, 43

Masin et al., post-Communist review of, 335–36

Masin family: Gestapo's harassment of, 34–37, 41–42; history of, 8. *See also specific family members*

Masinova, Zdena: appeals for husband's return, 46–47; arrest of, by Gestapo, 41–42; arrest of, post-escape, 314; birth of children, 19; clashes with mother, 47; courtship and marriage of, 18–19; death in prison, 315; disappearance of husband, 41; farewell to sons, 120; fortune-teller visit by, 211; Gestapo's harassment of, 34–37; heart ailment of, 42; hospitalization of, 308; imprisonment of, 314–15; letters from husband on Sudetenland annexation, 21, 24; Masin, Ctirad's concern for, 108; mother's petitions on behalf of, 314; nervous breakdown feigned by, 37; news of husband's fate, 48–50; news of sons' successful escape, 307; post-Communist rehabilitation of, 334; retaliation against, for escape, 307–15; return home from German imprisonment, 42; Studlar's reassurances to, 57–58; tacit acknowledgment of sons' plans, 80; Tomas Garrigue

Masaryk Order awarded to, 336; trial of, 314; uprising anticipated by, 76–77

Masinova, Zdena, Jr. (Nenda): arrest of mother, 41–42; as bait for brothers, 327–29; birth of, 19; brothers' protection of, 55; correspondence with brothers, 322; disabilities of, 19; disappointment over U.S. failure to intervene, 322n; father's fate acknowledged, 48–50; father's last letter to, 49–50; father's last visit to, 37–38; Gestapo harassment witnessed by, 34–36; speech at commemoration ceremony for father, 340; StB archives perused by, 327; surveillance of, 327–29; at trial of mother, 314; at trial of uncle, 311

Mellmann, Karl, 182, 198, 231, 326

Minarikova, Ludmila, 103–7

Moravec, Frantisek, 24

Moravek, Vaclav, 5; ambush of, 51–52; background of, 28–29; capture evaded by, 38–40; cigarette-lighting incident, 33–34; death of, 52; Gestapo's search for, 32–34; humor of, 30, 33–34; as one of Three Kings, 28; rescue attempts for Masin planned by, 51; in resistance against Nazis, 5, 28–53

most-wanted posters, 249, 267–68

Mount St. Katherine, escape route via, 118, 124–25

Moynihan, Patrick, 319–20

Mrázek, R., 10

Munich Agreement, 22–23

National Committee for Free Europe (NCFE), 64

nationalization, forced, in Czechoslovakia, 99

national police force, Czechoslovakia. *See* SNB

Neubauer, Maria (Manya), 35–36, 41–42, 47, 330

Neue Zeitung, 259, 261

newspapers: Czech, Communist control of, 61; Czech resistance, by Three Kings, 34; Western, analysis of East German deployment, 258–61

Newton, Basil, 22

NKVD methods, of interrogation, 308, 308n

Normandy, France, Masin family visit to, 3–5

Novak, Ctibor (Borek): arrest by StB, in first planned escape (1951), 81–83; assistance in first planned escape (1951), 79–80; in Bartolomejska prison, 82, 85, 89; bombings in Berlin, 31–32; Communist Party joined by, 46; execution of, 314; expulsion from Communist Party, 101; final words to court, 312; German imprisonment of, 32; interrogation of (1951), 89; mother's request for clemency, 313; in Pankrac prison, 312–13; posthumous, post-Communist commutation of sentence, 334; post-war reemergence of, 46; release from prison (1951), 91; retaliation against, for escape, 307–14; support for anti-Communist group, 101–2, 107, 307–8; trial of, 311–12

Novak, Ctibor et al. trial, 311–12, 334–35

Novak, Leopold, 18

Novakova, Emma: aryanization of grandsons opposed by, 42; clashes with daughter, 47; clemency request for son, 313; death of, 329; help to Masin family during World War II, 37, 42; petitions on daughter's behalf, 314; premarital advice of, 18–19; rules about table manners, 55; surveillance of, 327–29; at trial of daughter, 314; at trial of son, 311

Novakova, Zdena. See Masinova, Zdena

Office of Documentation and Investigation of Criminal Actions of the Communist Party (UDV), 331, 334–35

Opasek, Anastaz, 7, 336n

Palat, Josef, 30

Pankrac prison: Janata, Zbynek in, 312–13; Masin, Ctirad (Radek) in, 91–92; Masin, Josef Frantisek in, 40, 49–52; Novak, Ctibor (Borek) in, 312–13; Sveda, Vaclav (Vasek) in, 312–13

Passer, Ivan, 47

Patton, George C., 45

Paumer, Milan: background of, 68; at commemoration ceremony for Masin, Josef Frantisek, 340; military training of, 67; personality of, 68; U.S. military aspirations of, 254; U.S. military service of, 320

Paumer, Milan, in escape, 2, 118–301; aid from innkeepers, 155–57; arrival in American sector of Berlin, 292–96; arrival in United States, 320; AWOL and departure, 119; at Berliner Ring, 283–88; border crossing, 126–37; car heist attempt by, 138–42; code for, 118–19; cold and snow endured by, 135–37, 234, 242; on commuter train toward West Berlin, 286–91; dash from small woods, 216–21; decision and commitment of, 114; early encounters with police, 148–49, 163; Elbe River crossing, 160–61; emergence and flight from Reichwalde farm, 200–206, 2321–232; emergence from woodpile, 251; engagement at edge of woods, 208–21, 232; in Erlangen safe house, 319; extradition to Czechoslovakia denied by Americans, 309–10; fall into hole, 129; flight to Frankfurt, 319; food supply finished, 132; Grunert family as hostages/benefactors of, 262–70;

gun battle at Uckro, 168–87; hiding in "hay hotel," 251–56; hiding in woodpile, 1–2, 228–30, 235–43; hiding on Reichwalde farm, 188–95, 200–202; home stretch for, 289–301; hospitalization in Berlin, 294–95, 302, 316–17; journey to border, 118–25; loss of weapon, 129; Mahlow station trouble, 288–91; manhunt for, 181–99; maps and navigation, 118, 120–21, 130–31, 268; march through East Germany, 137–65; money distributed for, 125; most-wanted posters for, 249, 267–68; northern trek toward Berlin, 271–81; official identification and description of, 192; on potato transport train, 269, 276–80; pursued from small woods, 222–28; retaliation against family and associates in Czechoslovakia, 306–15; at safe house in Berlin, 302–6; search alerts issued for, 142, 178, 181; shooting of, 284–85, 289–90; suicide pact of, 210, 214, 240; train travel by (with tickets), 158–60, 165–67; weapon carried in, 121

Paumer, Milan, in post-war Czechoslovakia: arrest by StB evaded, 81–83; in Celakovice raid, 74–76; in Chlumec raid, 70–73; decision to leave Czechoslovakia, 78; disappearance of relatives, 62; draft of, 103; escape from Czechoslovakia, first planned (1951), 77–83; in Kovolis robbery attempt, 101–2; resistance against Communists, 59–60, 67–83; weapons smuggling/theft by, 69–76. See also Paumer, Milan, in escape

Pejsa, O., 10

Peltán, Frantisek, 38–39

Phipps, Eric, 20

Pietschen's shepherd hut, 198

Plech, Edith (code name "Jana"), as StB agent, 329

Plech, Egon: arrest by StB evaded, 81–83; background of, 78; decision to leave Czechoslovakia, 78; disqualified from escape, 114; escape from Czechoslovakia, planned (1951), 77–83; faltering in mission, 99–100, 114; personality of, 78; prison sentence for, 312; retaliation against, for escape, 307–9, 312

Plzen Skoda works, intelligence gathering in, 31

Plzen strike (1953), 99

Podebrady: American bombers over, 42–43; Communist Party in, 60–62; martial law in, 56; Masin family eviction from, 101; Masin family move to, 37; post-war social life in, 55–56; theft of weapons from museum, 69–70; weapons and explosives buried near, 118–19; youth gun culture in, 45–46, 48

Poland: demand for Czechoslovak territory, 22; German invasion of, 28, 31; inaction on Communist past, 339; strikes and uprising in, 321–22

police. See StB (state security); Transportpolizei (railroad police); Volkspolizei (people's police)

police station raids: in Celakovice, 74–76, 88; in Chlumec, 70–73, 88

Pomocné Technické Prapory (PTP, Black Barons), 59, 99, 108, 113

potato bug scare, 61

potato transport train, Masin brothers' band travel via, 269, 276–80

Potsdam district, alert and manhunt in, 197

Prague: collapse of Communist regime, 330–31; Communist militia in, 55–57; protests against Sudetenland annexation, 22–23; uprising anticipated in, 76–77

press conference, by Masin brothers, 305

Pribram uranium mine, 59

Prochazka, Jaroslav, 16

Radio Free Europe (RFE), 64–66, 77–
78, 114; Czech broadcast of escape
success, 307; Masin brothers' press
conference on, 305; responsibility for
uprisings, 321–22
railroad(s): access in Riesa, 153–57;
commuter train toward West Berlin,
283–88, 296–97; Dahlewitz station,
286–87; gun battle at Uckro station,
168–87; Mahlow station, trouble at,
288–91; roundtrip from Riesa, 158–
60; trip from Elsterwerda, 165–67
railroad police: gun battle at Uckro,
178–87; search alert issued by, 178
Rehak, Frantisek, 31
Rehak, Vaclav (Feshak), 31, 51–52
Reich Luftfahrtsministerium (Aviation
Ministry), bombing of, 31–32
Reich Police Directorate, bombing of,
31–32
Reichwalde, East Germany: assistance
from widow and son, 200–202; farm
hiding place in, 188–95, 200–202,
231–32; interrogation of widow, 238;
manhunt around, 198
René. See Thümmel, Paul
resistance: against Communists, 59–60;
in World War II, 29–53 (See also Three
Kings)
Riesa, East Germany, 153–57
Romania, inaction on Communist past,
339
Rosicky, Josef, 102–7
Rousar, Zbynek: prison sentence for,
312; retaliation against, for escape,
307–9, 312; as treasurer for anti-
Communist group, 107
Rundfunk Im Amerikanischen Sektor
(RIAS), 116
Russia: clashes with Czechoslovak
Legion, 17; fear of Czechoslovak
Legion, 17; inaction on Communist

past, 339; peace treaty with Germans,
11–12, 15; recruitment of Czech
POWs, 9, 11. See also Soviet Union
Rychetsky, Pavel, 337

sabotage: in Masin brothers' actions
against Nazis, 43; in resistance against
Communists, 59–60, 108–14; in resis-
tance against Nazis, 31–32; in ura-
nium mine, 95–96
Sacher, Richard, 332
Sara, Vaclav, 26–27
Schnellkommandos, 117, 179, 181
Seifert, Willi, 182, 198, 231, 325–26
Serbia, inaction on Communist past, 339
Shawcross, Hartley, 27
Sippenhaftung, 101
Skokan, Karel, 102–7
Skolimovsky, Jerzy, 47
Slansky group, 98–99
slave labor camps, 59, 92–96
SNB, Communist control of, 56, 59, 62
snowfall, during escape, 136–37
Social Democratic Party, 56
Sokol sports league: disbanded
by Communists, 61; in post-war
Podebrady, 48
Soviet Union: arrival in Czechoslovakia,
45; collapse of, 330; forces in
manhunt, 197; intentions for
Czechoslovakia, 55; Iron Curtain
imposed by, 63–64; military presence
in East Germany, 153–54; NKVD
interrogation methods of, 308, 308n;
treatment of East Germany, 115; wel-
come from Czechs, 45
Sparta I and II (transmitters), 32
Stalin, Josef, intentions for
Czechoslovakia, 55; Iron Curtain
imposed by, 63–64
state security force, Czechoslovakia.
See StB
StB (state security): arrest of Masin,
Ctirad (Radek), 80–81; arrest of

Masin, Josef Vladimir (Pepa), 81–83;
arrest of Novak, Ctibor (Borek), 81–
83; Communist control of, 59, 62;
opening of archives, 327; raid during
first escape plans (1951), 81–83; retal-
iatory arrests by, after escape, 308–9
straw reserves, destruction of, 110–14
Strempel, Helmut, 179–80, 325
Studlar, Jan: on awarding of Medal
of Valor to Masin brothers, 52–53;
disappearance of, 58; on impending Communist coup, 57; release and
departure from Czechoslovakia, 58;
reunion with Masin family, 46
Süddeutsche Zeitung, 260
Sudetenland: Czech reoccupation of,
48; evacuation of, 22, 24; Germany's
seizure of, 20–24; Munich Agreement
on, 22–23
suicide attempts, in prison, by Masin,
Josef Frantisek, 52
suicide pact, among Czech escapees,
210, 214, 219–21, 240
Sulc, Eduard (taxi driver), 70–73
Sveda, Vaclav (Vasek): background of,
100–101; as broken man, 311–12;
execution of, 314; farewell letter to
wife, 119; father's request for clemency, 313; German imprisonment in
World War II, 177–78; German language spoken by, 115; ideals recanted
by, 311–12; last correspondence to,
denied or lost, 313; last letter to family, 312–13; Masin, Josef Frantisek
admired by, 101; in Pankrac prison,
312–13; personality of, 100; posthumous, post-Communist commutation
of sentence, 334
Sveda, Vaclav (Vasek), in escape, 2,
118–233; aid from baker and daughter, 150–52; aid from innkeepers,
155–57; border crossing, 126–37; in
Brandenburg/Görden prison, 233,
238; capture of, 233, 267, 308; car

heist attempt by, 138–42; code for,
118–19; cold and snow endured by,
135–37; dash from small woods,
attempt and assistance in, 216–21;
death sentence for, 310, 312, 314;
decision and commitment of, 114;
departure from home, 119; early
encounters with police, 148–49, 163;
Elbe River crossing, 160–61; emergence and flight from Reichwalde
farm, 200–206, 231–32; engagement
at edge of woods, 208–21, 232; extradition to Czechoslovakia, 309–10;
food supply finished, 132; goodbyes
to, 216, 220–21; gun battle at Uckro,
168–87; hiding on Reichwalde farm,
188–95, 200–202; interrogation of,
233–35, 238, 308; journey to border,
118–25; manhunt for, 181–99; maps
and navigation for, 118, 120–21, 130–
31; march through East Germany,
137–65; money distributed for, 125;
official identification and description
of, 192; plea to be left behind, 213,
215–16, 218–20; rescue of, Masin
brothers' hope for, 301, 304, 316,
319; search alerts issued for, 142, 178,
181; shooting of, 208, 211–12; suicide
pact of, 210, 214; non-compliance
with, 219–21; testimony of, 238; train
travel by, 158–60, 165–67; weapon
carried in, 121
Sveda, Vaclav (Vasek), in post-war
Czechoslovakia: as class enemy, 100;
explosives acquired by, 108–9; in
Kovolis robbery, 101–7; resistance
against Communists, 97–114; straw
reserves destroyed by, 110–14. *See
also* Sveda, Vaclav (Vasek), in escape
Svedova, Lidka: farewell letter from
husband, 119; prison sentence for,
312; stipend for, 307–8
Syrovy, Jan, 22, 24–25

Three Kings, 29–53; arrest/capture of, 38–40, 51–52; attempted assassination of Himmler, 32; bombings in Berlin, 31–32; in Czech resistance, 29–53; disguises of, 30, 38; formation of, 28; Gestapo headquarters infiltrated by, 30; Gestapo's discovery of identities of, 32; identities of, 29–30; intelligence operations of, 31–32, 38, 51–52; network and collaborators of, 30; sabotage campaign of, 31–32; secret transmitters of, 32; Thümmel, Paul (René) as informant for, 32, 38, 51; underground newspaper of, 34; underground railroad of, 30–31; weapons smuggling by, 30–31

Thümmel, Paul (René, Franta, Eva, A-54): arrest of, 51; as informant for Three Kings, 32, 38, 51

Tomas Garrigue Masaryk Order, 336, 336n

trains: access in Riesa, 153–57; commuter, toward West Berlin, 283–91, 296–97; Dahlewitz station, 286–87; gun battle at Uckro station, 168–87; potato transport, Masin brothers' band travel via, 269, 276–80; roundtrip from Riesa, 158–60; trip from Elsterwerda, 165–67

Transportpolizei (railroad police): after-action review of, 324–26; gun battle at Uckro, 178–87; in manhunt, 181, 250

Trans-Siberian Railroad: Czechs' seizure of, 17; as escape route for Czechoslovak Legion, 12

Treaty of Brest-Litovsk, 15

Tri Kralové, 28. See also Three Kings

Uckro, East Germany: gun battle at railroad station, 168–87; official East German account of, 180; security perimeter around, 181–87; train travel to, 166–67

UDV (Office of Documentation and Investigation of Criminal Actions of the Communist Party), 331, 334–35

Ukraine, World War I: Czechoslovak Legion action in, 10–17; peace treaty with Germans, 11–12

Ulbricht, Walter, 115–17

underground railroad, of Czech resistance, 30–31

United States, post-World War II: analysis of deployment in East Germany, 257–61; anti-Communist information campaign of, 64–66, 77–78, 114, 321–22; arrival of Masin brothers and Paumer in, 320; Berlin airlift of, 63; contact with and care of Czech escapees, 295, 302–5; Counter Intelligence Corps of, 61, 61n, 90, 295, 302–5; Czech expectation of intervention by, 2–3, 62–66, 77–78, 112–14, 121; extradition of Masin brothers and Paumer denied by, 309–10; failure to intervene in uprisings, 321–23, 337–38

United States, World War II: acceptance of Sudetenland annexation, 20–21; adherence to Yalta agreement, 45; advance in Czechoslovakia halted, 45; bombers over Czechoslovakia, 42–43

U.S. Army Special Forces, 320

uranium mines, 59; brutality in, 94; capture and treatment of escapees, 94–95; comparison with Soviet Gulag, 93; enslavement of Masin, Ctirad (Radek) in, 3, 92–96; food rations in, 93–94; forced labor in, 59; hypothermia in, 94; intelligence sought by outside, 99; irradiation in, 94; plans to rescue Masin, Ctirad (Radek) from, 101–2; release of Masin, Ctirad (Radek) from, 107

Vadas, Martin, 340–41

Vanek, Frantisek: concentration camp survivor aided by, 43–44; plan to join

American interventions, 121, 318–19,
321
V Boj (resistance newspaper), 34
Velvet Revolution, 330–34
Voice of America (VOA), 65, 77, 114;
Czech broadcast of escape success,
307; responsibility for uprisings,
321–22
Volkspolizei (people's police): after-
action review of, 324–26; at Berliner
Ring, 284–85; defectors to West
Berlin, 300–301, 300n; early encounters with, 148–49, 163; engagement
at edge of woods, 208–21, 232; gun
battle at Uckro, 168–87; honors and
funerals for, 247–48; incusion into
West Berlin, 260; interrogation of
Janata, Zbynek, 196–99, 308; interrogation of Reichwalde farm widow,
238; interrogation of Sveda, Vaclav
(Vasek), 238, 308; lack of cooperation
from citizens, 247–50; in "Luckau
War," 237–39; in manhunt, 181–87;
most-wanted posters of, 249, 267–68;
official history of, 326; relaxation of
security perimeter, 250; search alert
issued by, 142; Western analysis of
deployment, 257–61
von Dirksen, Herbert, 20

Waldow, East Germany: Grunert
family as hostages/benefactors in,
262–70; "hay hotel" in, 251–56; news
of escape received in, 306; search and
interrogations in, 238–39, 247–49,
257–58
weapons smuggling/theft: by Masin
brothers and anti-Communist group,
69–76; by Three Kings, 30–31
West Germany: analysis of deployment
in East Germany, 258–59; arrival of
Czech escapees in, 316–17, 319; life
of Masin, Josef Vladimir (Pepa) in,

6–7, 327; safe house in Erlangen,
317–19
Wilson, Horace, 20
woodpile, as hiding place, 1–2, 228–30,
235–43

Yalta agreement, 45

Zatopek, Emil, 266, 266n
Zborov, Battle of, 10–11

ABOUT THE AUTHOR

BARBARA MASIN, a resident of Santa Barbara, California, is the daughter of Joseph Masin, one of the five youths featured in this book. She is fluent in English, German, French, and Spanish, and conversant in Czech.

ABOUT THE AUTHOR

BARBARA MASIN, a resident of Santa Barbara, California, is the daughter of Joseph Masin, one of the five youths featured in this book. She is fluent in English, German, French, and Spanish, and conversant in Czech.

THE NAVAL INSTITUTE PRESS is the book-publishing arm of the U.S. Naval Institute, a private, nonprofit membership society for sea service professionals and others who share an interest in naval and maritime affairs. Established in 1873 at the U.S. Naval Academy in Annapolis, Maryland, where its offices remain today, the Naval Institute has members worldwide.

Members of the Naval Institute support the education programs of the society and receive the influential monthly magazine *Proceedings* and discounts on fine nautical prints and on ship and aircraft photos. They also have access to the transcripts of the Institute's Oral History Program and get discounted admission to any of the Institute-sponsored seminars offered around the country.

The Naval Institute also publishes *Naval History* magazine. This colorful bimonthly is filled with entertaining and thought-provoking articles, first-person reminiscences, and dramatic art and photography. Members receive a discount on *Naval History* subscriptions.

The Naval Institute's book-publishing program, begun in 1898 with basic guides to naval practices, has broadened its scope to include books of more general interest. Now the Naval Institute Press publishes about seventy titles each year, ranging from how-to books on boating and navigation to battle histories, biographies, ship and aircraft guides, and novels. Institute members receive significant discounts on the Press's more than eight hundred books in print.

Full-time students are eligible for special half-price membership rates. Life memberships are also available.

For a free catalog describing Naval Institute Press books currently available, and for further information about subscribing to *Naval History* magazine or about joining the U.S. Naval Institute, please write to:

Member Services
U.S. NAVAL INSTITUTE
291 Wood Road
Annapolis, MD 21402-5034
Telephone: (800) 233-8764
Fax: (410) 571-1705
Web address: *www.navalinstitute.org*